Crossing the Ether

For Joanne, Jemma and Zoë

Connected with County and landed estates,
We never cross cutlery over our plates,
We crawl to the City, perhaps Mincing Lane
And potter to luncheon, then crawl home again.
We're frightfully rugger and soccer,
We're painfully quick off the tee,
We pile all our togs in a locker,
Our sweaters have quite a low V;
We know the announcers and Greenwich pip-pips,
We simply adore the gale warnings to ships,
We never pour vinegar over our chips –
We're frightfully BBC.
The Western Brothers, record, 1935

"The BBC programmes on Sundays were pretty solemn things. In Germany they had 'strength through joy'; in the UK we had 'strength through misery'."

Norman Burton, Bury, Lancashire, correspondence, 1996

Crossing the Ether:

Pre-War Public Service Radio and Commercial Competition in the UK

Seán Street

British Library Cataloguing in Publication Data

CROSSING THE ETHER:
Pre-War Public Service Radio and Commercial Competition in the UK

1. – Seán Street

ISBN: 0 86196 668 6

Published by
John Libbey Publishing, Box 276, Eastleigh SO50 5YS, UK
e-mail: libbeyj@asianet.co.th; web site: www.johnlibbey.com
Orders: **Book Representation & Distribution Ltd**. info@bookreps.com
Distributed in North America by **Indiana University Press**, 601 North Morton St, Bloomington, IN 47404, USA. www.iupress.indiana.edu
Distributed in Australasia by **Elsevier Australia**, 30–52 Smidmore Street, Marrickville NSW 2204, Australia. www.elsevier.com.au
Distributed in Japan by **United Publishers Services Ltd,**
1-32-5 Higashi-shinagawa, Shinagawa-ku, Tokyo 140-0002, Japan. info@ups.co.jp

Printed in Malaysia by Vivar Printing Sdn Bhd, 48000 Rawang, Selangor

Contents

Personal Preface

Radio Days

O n 8 October 1973, at 6.00 a.m., Britain's first Independent Radio station, LBC, began broadcasting, to be followed eight days later by the second, Capital Radio. I was working for BBC Radio at the time, and remember the excitement of the moment; there was something glamorous about the concept of the arrival of land-based commercial radio, on-air advertising and a freeing of the air-waves. It was a glamour which quickly dissipated as the reality of the new medium, over-regulated and constrained, became evident. To my generation, growing up in the 1960s, the perceived sound of commercial radio, imported from the United States, was the "Pirate" model created by the offshore stations, Radios Caroline, London, Britain Radio, Radio England and the rest. These were after all, the revolutionaries who had forced the government and the BBC into the creation of Radio 1. Before that, in the 1950s, I recalled in my younger childhood listening to the distant voices from Radio Luxembourg: Dan Dare, The Ovaltineys, Horace Batchelor and his "Infra-Draw" pools method (Keynsham was probably the first British place name I learned to spell as a result of the presenter's enunciation of the address for listener correspondence).

Much later, when I was working as a producer in commercial radio, I began to realise that the path back to those days was much more complex than I had originally understood. My parents had spoken of a long-dead station called Radio Normandy, and the significance of the glowing names on the old utility radio which had inhabited our 1950s home started to tease me: Radio Lyons, Toulouse, EAQ Madrid and many more. The received wisdom had always been that pre-war radio in Britain had been landscaped by the BBC. Turning to books revealed some evidence but very little; there had been some activity, but it was always discussed as peripheral to Public Service Broadcasting. It was a meeting with the broadcaster Roy Plomley's actress daughter that led me to the realisation that the creator of one of the BBC's iconic radio traditions, *Desert Island Discs*, represented a generation of pre-war broadcasters for whom the BBC was anything but a monopoly. Meetings with Plomley and Bob Danvers-Walker, both of whom had been employed as presenters and producers by the International Broadcasting Company before the Second World War, opened the door on a fascinating hidden world; British commercial radio had a history after all.

1

Sadly, it was not until after the death of Plomley and Danvers-Walker, my first inspirers, that I determined to explore this world in depth and seek to measure its importance in the scheme of British Broadcasting history. This writing is the result of that exploration.

Seán Street
15 December 2005

Acknowledgements

Ⅰt is a pleasure to record my gratitude to the many who have supported and directed my research into commercial radio history. The late Leonard Miall offered insights as well as primary material such as the SHAEF document relating the story of the allied liberation of Radio Luxembourg, reproduced in Appendix F. Mike Read, always a good friend, has helped with sources at Radio Luxembourg, and Roger Bickerton, Founder and Co-ordinator of the Vintage Radio Programmes Collectors' Circle has also supplied many valuable leads towards a deeper understanding of the subject. In particular I would like to acknowledge his extremely useful interview with the late Stephen Williams. Other members of the V.R.P.C.C., notably the late Antony Askew, Raymond Welch-Bartram, Norman Morrison and Andrew Emmerson, have provided programme material, some of which is very rare, and extremely valuable within the context of the study. Several other people who inspired this investigation into a little-told aspect of British radio history have not lived to see it completed. Roy Plomley and Bob Danvers-Walker were at the initial root of the research, while Frank Gillard and Dr Desmond Hawkins gave generously of their time for interviews; within weeks of my final conversations with them, in 1998 and 1999, both were to die.

The Continental side of the story has been greatly helped by two people in particular. Pierre le Sève of the BBC's French Service shared relatives' knowledge and memories of Radio Normandy and offered further contacts for research, while François Lhote, Secretary of the France Radio Club, and Editor of the French edition of *Offshore Echoes* gave insights into the complex workings of French media regulation with reference to Les Postes Privés. During various trips to France to explore this further, many helpers have become friends, including Vincent Hazard, Vivienne Vermes, John Kliphan, Yan Rucar, Pierre-Don Giancarli and James Immanuel. I should also add a word of thanks to the librarians of the Pompidou Centre and Radio France Archives, Paris, who offered guidance in the search for Continental sources. Likewise Carinne Hecker, Curator of the Dutch Radio Museum in Hilversum was unstinting with help and advice; I am grateful to Dr Pim Slot, Dr. Huub Wijfjes and Hans Knot for early guidance in Holland, and to Dr Francisco Montes for generously sharing his research into the history of E.A.Q., Madrid. In the same respect I am grateful to Mieke Hooker and Alastair and Chus Azorin-Danson for lending me their translation skills in Dutch and Spanish respectively.

Jacqueline Cavanagh and the staff at the BBC Written Archives Centre at Caversham responded to my early quest with enthusiasm and helped locate relevant material which effectively demonstrated to me that there was indeed a major case to explore. Likewise the staff of the History of Advertising Trust, Norwich have been both helpful and interested in my research. My daughter Jemma, working in the Science and Society Picture Library at the Science Museum was able to offer me information regarding items and documents relating to radio held by the museum, and her colleague Chris Rowlin also helped generously. Staff at the British Library Sound Archive have directed me to many appropriate sources; my thanks to Alan Ward, Andy Linehan and Peter Copeland. Don James, Archivist of the J. Walter Thompson Company Ltd, shared remarkable material which illuminated the industry of radio advertising prior to the Second World War hugely, providing primary sources without which this study would have been infinitely poorer.

My interviewees and correspondents have been patient and helpful in their memories of 1930s radio. Billie Love, daughter of "Joe Murgatroyd and Poppet" allowed me access to her unique recordings of her parents broadcasting their daily Keep Fit programme on Radio Normandy in 1938. Others who must be acknowledged for their knowledge and recollection of pre-war commercial radio are Russ Barnes, John Black, A. Briand, Norman Burton, B.R. Curtis, Alan Davies, P.S. Elliott, Norman Foot, Peter Good, Ray Henville, H. Kaye, J. Land, Jeff Link, the late Philip Marsh, Ron Montague, David Morris, Richard Mayne, Harry Reddin, Myfanwy Thomas, Don Turner. Jill Carder, wife of the late George Carder, an IBC engineer was kind and generous in loaning pictures and written memorabilia, and Fred Redding, former curator of the Selfridges Archive, gave me access to company files and press cuttings relating to the history of radio, prior to the removal of the material to the History of Advertising Trust's Archives, Norwich.

I am grateful to my colleagues in the Bournemouth Media School, Bournemouth University for their support and encouragement, in particular to Dr Jan Johnson-Smith and Dr Hugh Chignell for giving the time to read and advise on the manuscript as it grew and developed. Also I would like to acknowledge with thanks the School's Subject Librarian, Matt Holland for help in locating texts, and for access to the Library's *Radio Times* collection. Professor John Ellis has supported and advised on the project with enthusiasm and encouragement; I owe him a great deal and am extremely grateful. My thanks also go to Professor Paddy Scannell of the University of Westminster for his support, to Professor David Gauntlett, Julia McCain, and to Bournemouth Media School's Research Committee which generously funded a sabbatical to enable me to pursue my work.

Members of today's radio industry have offered support and encouragement; in this respect I would particularly like to acknowledge Tim Blackmore, John Bradford, Paul Brown, Gillian Reynolds, Tony Stoller and John Whitney, all of whom share my love of radio and a desire for the development of it as a subject worthy of academic study to inform today's broadcasting world. Len Kelly of Kelly Books has often found texts for me when I would otherwise have found it extremely hard to locate them; my gratitude to him.

Most of all I would like to thank my wife Joanne for her patience over the period of this research. It is impossible to repay her.

Seán Street

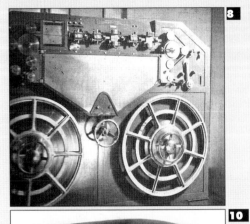

Introduction

The first Governors of this institution dedicated this Temple of the Arts and Muses under the first directorship of John Reith, Knight, Praying for Divine help that a good sowing may have a good harvest and that everything impure and hostile to Peace may be banished from this building, and that whatsoever things are sincere and beautiful and of good report and lovable, the people, inclining its ear to these things with a contentment of mind, may follow in the path of virtue and wisdom.[1]

Between 1930 and 1939, radio listening in Britain was a battlefield fought over on one hand by Public Service interests, represented by the British Broadcasting Corporation, and on the other by Continental-based commercial stations, transmitting populist sponsored English-language programmes. This book seeks to evaluate the importance of the tension between the two in terms of the cultural and technical evolution of British broadcasting. In so doing it interrogates the generally perceived view of the BBC as an unchallenged monopoly during the period, providing evidence that a number of crucial areas of broadcasting development in pre-war Britain resulted directly from the pressure of competition.

In order to do this it is necessary to examine a number of related areas. The extent of influence, both direct and indirect, from the United States is explored. The giant J. Walter Thompson advertising agency had been involved in American radio from the earliest days, and brought to its UK campaigns expertise and experience which proved of major importance in the making of sponsored programmes. The Organisation also developed its already sophisticated skills in product-consumer research on behalf of clients, into the field of radio audience research, an area not addressed by the BBC until 1936. Thus it is important to examine the nature of how such research was conducted, and how it changed the nature of programme scheduling, given population demographics of the time. This is contrasted with the extreme paternalistic moral stance taken by the BBC in its early years, particularly in respect of its Sunday policy, representing an attitude in which listener preferences played

---

1   Translation from the Latin of the Dedication inscription in the foyer of Broadcasting House, London, 1932.

no part. How this policy opened the door for highly developed and successful commercial competition forms an important part of the study. Through the use of primary source documentation held in the BBC's Written Archive at Caversham, Reading, we will see how the BBC responded internally to this growing threat to its autonomy, a threat only curtailed by the outbreak of the Second World War.

Out of necessity comes invention. The geographical constraints of the Continental stations, broadcasting programming made largely in Britain from distant transmission sites, required the development of durable recording techniques. The 1930s saw three main systems with which the BBC and the Commercial companies experimented. This technology will be examined, together with the reasons behind the adoption of particular types by the two competitors, relevant to the specific needs of both, thus demonstrating that competition fuelled progress.

Britain – almost uniquely – saw the development of land-based Commercial Television before Commercial Radio. We will explore evidence that the dynamic of pressure to establish the latter was in place from the earliest days of broadcasting – indeed, even before the creation of the BBC itself. While the high-point of pre-war competition was undoubtedly the mid to late 1930s, broadcasting of occasional English-language sponsored programming beamed at a British audience from Europe was taking place as early as 1919. It was this campaigning spirit which eventually burgeoned into the sophisticated and financially highly successful business ventures of the years prior to the outbreak of the Second World War. This study examines the issues this fact raised for the BBC and for its audience at the time, thus placing in historical context the subsequent development of the relationship between Public Service and Commercial Broadcasting in the United Kingdom. It utilises interview and archival analysis, as far as possible examining sources from key witnesses of the time, and written texts – published and unpublished – which have not thus far been presented as evidence of an industry much wider and diverse than has previously been claimed. This introductory chapter provides an over-view of the subject under discussion within the book, as perceived by writers considering the issues from the contrasting standpoints of pre and post-war perspectives.

Available texts

Texts which examine historically the era and issues under examination in this writing have placed agitation within Britain for commercial radio as something of a peripheral study, rather than as an integral part of British radio history, with implications beyond its time, and significance in the shaping of BBC policy. Writings which do seek to explore the historical relationship between early pioneers and the subsequent arrival of land-based commercial radio do so in a somewhat superficial way. Baron[2] gives a concise account of 1930s Commercial radio without investigating in any detail the response of – or effect on – the BBC at the time. His book is primarily concerned with the first two years of Independent Radio. The same criticism may be leveled at Skues,[3] who, in a narrative of 568 pages, devotes

2   Baron, Mike *Independent Radio, The Story of Independent Radio in the United Kingdom*, Lavenham,Terence Dalton Ltd, 1975.
3   Skues, Keith *Pop Went the Pirates, an Illustrated History of Pirate Radio*, Sheffield, Lambs Meadow Publications, 1994.

six of those pages to the pre-war pioneers and BBC policy. Even more academic
and specialized texts, such as Barnard examine the issue through secondary sources.
Indeed Barnard[4] states as a prelude to his summary of pre-war Commercial
broadcasting in Britain, " the history of the stations can be briefly sketched".

At the same time, unsurprisingly, works such as Black,[5] written in celebration of
the BBC's 50th anniversary in 1972, and published by the Corporation, can hardly
be expected to devote space to the discussion of a period when the monopoly was
first seriously challenged. Even the Local Radio Workshop's valuable *Capital, Local
Radio and Private Profit,* a text which takes latter-day British independent radio as
its theme, while offering many useful insights into the political machinations
leading to the 1972 Sound Broadcasting Act, has nothing to say about pre-war
developments in this area, despite a chapter entitled "The Origins of Commercial
Radio".[6]

Clearly there is an imbalance; the study of radio in the United Kingdom should
NOT be perceived as "A History of the BBC" up to the establishment of land-based
Independent Radio on 8 October 1973, yet the fact remains that, by and large, this
is the case. The present work rectifies this imbalance, highlighting as it does that
issues raised between 1930 and 1939 had long-term effects on BBC thinking and
public expectation, and sowed the seeds of regulated competitive broadcasting
which eventually emerged in Britain after World War II. In so doing I claim that
the erosion of the concept of the BBC's monopoly was actively under way long
before previous commentators have suggested. Further, it is possible to demonstrate that through necessity the commercial broadcasters contributed to – and
sometimes led – media debate into such areas as scheduling, audience measurement
and recording for radio, thus creating a partnership which advanced the overall
development of radio in this country. In this section I draw attention to relevant
works which explore in one form or another issues relating to the subject and period
under discussion. It will be noted that the texts divide into two kinds:

1.   Works written from approximately 1950 by modern commentators, survey-
      ing the years of continental commercial competition, attacking the BBC
      status quo within the context of a broader history. These in turn fall into two
      categories: scholarly texts such as those by Asa Briggs, Paddy Scannell and
      David Cardiff, and works by what might be described as "enthusiast writers"
      including ex DJs, followers of pirate radio and amateur historians. A number
      of works by the latter group of writers give superficial and often unreliable
      account of aspects of commercial radio history, and certainly neither of these
      categories has examined the area explored by this writing in a full and
      balanced way, both being limited in their historical research by the 1930s
      newspaper embargo on publicity for commercial English language stations

4   Barnard, Stephen *On the Radio, Music Radio in Britain,* Milton Keynes, Open University Press, 1989,
     p. 18.

5   Black, Peter *The Biggest Aspidistra in the World, A Personal Celebration of 50 Years of the BBC,*
     London, BBC, 1972.

6   Local Radio Workshop, Comedia Series, No. 15, *Capital, Local Radio and Private Profit,* London,
     Comedia Publishing Group/Local Radio Workshop, 1983.

from the Continent on one hand and a limited capacity for experienced academic research on the other.

2.   Books written by contemporary broadcasters and critics from 1922 onwards. These works, many of which are now rare and little known, are remarkable in both their quantity and the voluble nature of their discourse on the issue of commercial radio. It is clear from such texts that a matter which many modern writers have neglected to address in detail, was one of considerable significance at the time. While referring to such writings within this review, I shall also explore them in greater detail later in the dissertation as major witnesses to the controversies of the era.

Monopoly and public service

The decision in 1922 to create a monopoly broadcaster in the form of the British Broadcasting Company had far-reaching consequences bringing together as it did for the first time, a wide range of publics, with wide ranging and divergent tastes and interests, and seeking to cater to all of these through one comprehensive service. Scannell and Cardiff have said of this:

> On behalf of this public the broadcasters asserted a right of access to a wide range of political, cultural, sporting, religious, ceremonial and entertainment resources which, perforce, had hitherto been accessible only to small, self-selecting and more or less privileged publics. Particular publics were replaced by the *general* public constituted in and by the general nature of the mixed programme service and its general, unrestricted availability.[7]

Growing from this democratic broadcasting environment came the concept of a duty to the newly created "general" public, leading in turn to the concept of "public service". Briggs suggests that the first person to speak of public service in radio terms was the American David Sarnoff, the creator of the Radio Corporation of America (RCA) who anticipated the pronouncements of John Reith by arguing in 1922 that "broadcasting represents a job of entertaining, informing and educating the nation, and should therefore be distinctly regarded as a public service".[8] It was however Reith of the BBC who gave public service broadcasting an institutional form. McDonnell has distilled from Briggs, Reith's conception of public service in this context as having four facets:

> Firstly, it should be protected from purely commercial pressures; secondly, the whole nation should be served by the broadcasting service; thirdly, there should be unified control, that is, public service broadcasting should be organized as a monopoly; and finally, there should be high programme standards.[9]

Briggs himself, in his discussion of the third of these points, that of unity of control, cites Reith's 1924 book, *Broadcast Over Britain*, and demonstrates a shift from views

---

7   Scannell, Paddy and Cardiff, David *A Social History of British Broadcasting, 1922–1939, Serving the Nation*, Oxford, Blackwell, 1991, p. 15.

8   Briggs, Asa *The BBC, the First Fifty Years*, Oxford, Oxford University Press, 1985, p. 18.

9   McDonnell, James *Public Service Broadcasting, A Reader*, London, Routledge, 1991, p. 1. Briggs develops these points in the *History of Broadcasting in the United Kingdom, Vol.I, The Birth of Broadcasting 1896–1927*, Oxford, Oxford University Press, 1995, pp. 214–218.

as put forward to one of the earliest committees of enquiry into the development of British broadcasting: "Whereas the charge of 'monopoly' had been contested by the representatives of the BBC when they appeared before the Sykes Committee, Reith now openly and unashamedly admitted its existence".[10] It is worth turning to Reith's book itself at this point and quoting at some length:

> The objections to monopoly are numerous, and in many lines of activity, real and obvious. With the lack of competition slackness is often engendered, and from privileged positions there arises abuse. Doubts expressed on this score were on the surface to a great extent rational as there was some possibility of question as to whether one concern could really expand with the necessary facility and rapidity, and at the same time handle satisfactorily all the many diverse problems which would arise.

> I am quite sure that the fear of any unfortunate results of monopoly has been dispelled. I do not think there has been any evidence of complacency or slackness or indifference. On the other hand I believe it has been proved conclusively that in a concern where expansion is so rapid and the problems so unique, unity of control is essential.

> In this way, mistakes which might be fraught with far-reaching consequences to the service and to the community may be avoided or quickly rectified. Any development or improvement, wherever or however originated, is immediately put into effect for the benefit of the system as a whole. On grounds of efficiency and economy of working, the advantages of central control are obvious. The necessity for maintaining the general policy and high standards, and for ensuring that these are promulgated throughout the service, demands it.[11]

Cecil Lewis, writing after the first year of BBC operations, in one of the first books on British broadcasting, published in the same year as Reith's, gives an enthusiastic picture of the pioneering spirit of the time. Existing when the issue of monopoly was shrouded in the excitement of experiment and new experience, the book nevertheless tells us much about the paternalism of public service broadcasting as perceived by the BBC's founding fathers. Lewis was the Company's first Organizer of Programmes, and also played the part of one of the early radio "Uncles and Aunts" in programmes for children under the name, "Uncle Caractacus":

> What, then, is the general policy by which our programme organization is run? Broadly speaking, I think it is to keep on the upper side of public taste, and to cater for the majority, 75 per cent of the time, the remainder being definitely set aside for certain important minorities.

> What is meant by the "upper side" of public taste? Well, we strive, as far as possible, to avoid certain things, desirable or undesirable, according to the point of view, which are as readily and more fully obtained elsewhere. Such things, for instance, as sensational murder details, or unsavoury divorce cases.

> These things appeal strongly to the curiosity of certain types of people, and they can always be read in cold print. But reading, after all, is *a private thing*

---

10 Briggs 1, p. 216.
11 Reith, J.C.W. *Broadcast Over Britain*, London, Hodder & Stoughton, 1924, p. 70.

between the reader and the matter read. Many things, harmless-looking enough in print, sound very different read aloud ...

... Of course, we could probably increase the number of our subscribers in a few weeks by changing our policy on these things, but it would leave us open to attack from many quarters. If broadcasting is to be a permanent asset to our national life, it must at all costs avoid offence in any shape or form to the widely varying susceptibilities of the vast public which it serves.[12]

It is clear from Lewis's book that within a year of commencing broadcasting, aspects of its paternalism were irritating some listeners, music being one of the most vulnerable areas of broadcasting policy:

I think few listeners have studied our problem. They write to us and say, "Why don't you give us music like such-and-such a musical comedy? Something with punch in it." This music is, of course, a very small percentage of all the music written, and the fact of the matter is that this type of stuff has been played regularly at our concerts. When the orchestras have played it out, what can be done but repeat it *ad nauseam*?

Again, the fact that the average fox trot has a six-months' life, and the average musical comedy a year, shows that this music has nothing really satisfying in it. It is a drug, and when one drug fails to operate a new one must be prescribed.

In this way "Who tied the can to the old dog's tail?" lasts until "Sweet Hortense" comes along, and that, in turn, is forgotten when "Yes, we have no bananas!" arrives. That in its turn (which may Heaven send soon) will disappear to make room for another.[13]

Arthur Burrows, formerly of the Marconi Company, was by the year of publication of Lewis's book, the BBC's Assistant Controller and Director of Programmes. In 1924 his was another of the pioneering texts, and undoubtedly the most poetic in its sense of the wonder engendered by the almost supernatural nature of wireless. When he comes to the practical matter of programme policy however, Burrows identifies the same problem as Lewis regarding the cosmopolitan nature of the listening audience, while seemingly coming to a rather more flexible conclusion:

The provision of nightly entertainment for something approaching a million homes, ranging from the palace to the humblest cottage, is not a simple matter. Recognition has to be given to the fact that in a single stratum of society there is a large variety of tastes. Even in the average family will be found a wide divergence of interests, ranging from all that is light and flippant to those things which are learned and abstruse. It has also to be remembered that these preferences for light entertainment or for serious informative matter are not peculiar to any one section of the community; that the homes of many working-class men are rich in popular editions of serious publica-

---

12   Lewis, C.A. *Broadcasting from Within*, London, George Newnes, Ltd, 1924, pp. 48–49. Lewis, Deputy Organiser of Programmes to A.R. Burrows from 1922, later went on to work in Hollywood as a script writer.

13   Ibid., pp. 50–51.

tions, and that even amongst great musicians there are a number who find interest in jazz or trick music of a similar order.[14]

This is the Reithian view of an over-arching public service policy which seeks to encompass all tastes within a single service, providing through serendipity rather than schedule or streaming output, all things to all people. It is also a view, the natural conclusion of which is that the broadcaster must be the arbiter of what the listener should be given in terms of a broadcast "diet". It is, in sum, a view which the present writer acknowledges to have been abandoned subsequently by broadcasters. Further, it is my premise that commercial competition during the years 1930–1939 was the movement which began a shift towards branded programmes, targeting specific audiences which continues to refine itself in the 21st century. The implications for public service broadcasting in this pivotal period were considerable. Crisell is correct when he states Reith's understanding of the issue, that:

> ... if the listening public had a choice between continuous light programming and a mixture of serious and light programming it would gravitate towards the former, and his concept of public service broadcasting was therefore at risk from the moment the Corporation's monopoly was broken.[15]

The Sykes Committee on Broadcasting was set up by the government in 1923. Two and half years later the Postmaster General established a further review of wireless, to be chaired by the Earl of Crawford and Balcarres. The Crawford Committee, which presented its report in the summer of 1926, effectively set the form of the British Broadcasting Corporation as it was to exist for the next thirty years, and confirmed the notion of monopoly. Coase has noted a key shift in attitude regarding monopoly between the two committees, and points to its origin:

> To the Sykes Committee, the question of how broadcasting should be organized in Great Britain was an open one. It was something to be examined further. Yet only two and a half years later, in the report of the Crawford Committee on Broadcasting, we find that a monopolistic form of organization is accepted as being the desirable one for broadcasting in Great Britain. There can be little doubt that this crystallization of view was largely due to the influence of one man, Mr. J.C.W. Reith.[16]

He also notes the concerns of the Newspaper Proprietors' Association, representatives of which addressed the Crawford Committee; part of their submission contained the following statement: "It is in the national interest that newspapers should be safeguarded against unfair competition from a monopoly given by the State."[17] A subsequent chapter will consider American radio as an influence and model for much of the commercial developments in Britain. It is important to note that debates relating to cultural issues and the control of a broadcasting monolith

14 Burrows, A.R. *The Story of Broadcasting*, London, Cassell, 1924, p. 112. A year after publishing this book, Arthur Burrows was to become Secretary of the newly formed, International Broadcasting Union. He would go on to become one of the staunchest opponents of commercial competition.

15 Crisell, Andrew *An Introductory History of British Broadcasting*, London, Routledge, 1997, p. 48.

16 Coase, R.H. *British Broadcasting, A Study in Monopoly*, London, The London School of Economics/ Longmans, Green & Co., 1950, p. 46.

17 Ibid., p. 105. Coase is quoting from a memorandum submitted to the Crawford Committee by the Newspaper Proprietors' Association.

(in the case of the US controlled by Capitalist interests) were present in America during the 1920s and '30s. "America's public intellectuals – those thinkers who sought to reach an audience that was both broad and well-educated – generally took a critical view of broadcasting."[18]

> They feared the concentration of social power in the hands of the few who controlled the centralized medium … [and] attacked radio as a source of mass culture that undercut elite cultural standards and eroded personal creativity and uniqueness … Others, from what amounted to a more radical position, assailed radio for centralizing authority. Commentators such as journalist and poet James Rorty blamed the new broadcasting system for enhancing big business's power to control society at large. In the early decades of the century these thinkers feared that capitalism was overwhelming individual voices and democratic ideals; as a national medium run by a few business interests pushed the United States further along its path towards the rule of concentrated capital.[19]

Cleghorn Thomson, writing in 1937, questions whether there need be a major difference between Commercial and public service programming in Britain, "so long as the licence payers keep on increasing and paying their dues, so long as the advertisers continue to find radio-advertising commercially worth while."[20] This statement, together with Reith's words from the 1936 *Encyclopaedia Britannica* which Cleghorn Thomson uses to justify it, seems curiously to relate more to the over-regulated era of British Independent Local Radio between 1973 and 1990, than the radio battleground of the 1930s:

> Whether broadcasting is conducted as a public service as in Great Britain and several other countries, or also as a means of attracting commercial goodwill as in the United States of America and elsewhere, the results tend to become unexpectedly similar, and the material that is acceptable from the point of view of commercial goodwill differs only by fine shades from what is suitable from the point of view of the non-commercial broadcaster animated by a sense of his public mission.[21]

The concept that one "people" could be unified by one comprehensive and all embracing output, and that a public service which meant giving that audience what was considered best for it, rather than what it wanted, may be seen as naïve, or arrogant and cynical. The contention that the class of person in managerial positions within the BBC was largely divorced culturally from a high proportion of its potential audience is debated later in this writing.[22] Lacey implies doubt as to the motive behind a BBC policy which permitted:

18 Lenthall, Bruce "Public Intellectuals Decry Depression-era Radio, Mass culture and Modern America", in Hilmes, Michele and Loviglio, Jason (ed.) *Radio Reader*, London/New York, Routledge, 2002, p. 41.

19 Ibid., p. 42.

20 Cleghorn Thomson, D. *Radio is Changing Us*, London, Watts, 1937, p. 44.

21 Ibid., Cleghorn Thomson's quotation of Reith is unreferenced apart from the acknowledgement of the *Encyclopaedia Britannica*.

22 D.G. Bridson, recounts an amusing anecdote regarding his first meeting with Admiral Sir Charles Carpendale, at the time (1934) the BBC Controller of Administration, and shortly to become Deputy

Occasional instances when unemployed men were invited to speak directly about their experiences, such as the 1932 series *Men Talking* and *Time to Spare*, though this was the exception rather than the rule in a schedule dominated by the professional middle classes. But these programmes did represent, in part, a continuation of the prevailing trend to construct a sense of shared participation in national life by papering over the profound social and class divisions in Britain and ignoring the radicalization of politics which accompanied the current social and economic dislocation.[23]

This may be seen in the context of the wider climate of the time; in the financial crisis of 1931, the Labour Government collapsed and was replaced by a National Government, "which presented itself as the true expression of national consensus and the guarantor of democracy, standing foursquare with other great institutional representations of stability: the Monarchy, the Church, and the British Broadcasting Corporation".[24] Notwithstanding its deliberate policies to unify a number of societies into one, the present writer believes there was, underlying its perception of its audience, a profound ignorance of working-class culture within the BBC in the first fifteen years of its existence which was also present more generally within the middle class, and which in broadcasting terms manifested itself in either the ignoring or the patronising of that audience's tastes and requirements of a broadcasting service.

In reviewing texts written at the height of the 1930s battle between public service broadcasting and commercial opposition – or shortly after – one becomes aware of the voice of vested interest, prejudice and bias. The investigator is required to read these texts within their historical and cultural context, and to understand their dialectical nature. An example of such a work is P.P. Eckersley's 1942 book, *The Power Behind the Microphone*. Eckersley's career is summarised later in this book. His place, firstly as a radio pioneer, then as the BBC's first Chief Engineer and subsequently as a rival of Corporation interests and a developer of Relay Exchanges, is not untypical of many who became disenchanted with the Corporation, and whose writings must be viewed with the knowledge of that disenchantment. Thus, Eckersley, somewhat idealistically:

> If I were asked to say which is better, a purely State-run or purely commercially inspired broadcasting system, I would find it impossible to give a definite answer. I would say that monopoly broadcasting systems could afford to take a much wider view of their cultural responsibilities, but that

---

Director-General: "He was a small, lean man with thin grey hair and a somewhat desiccated look. Hardly an Admiral in the bluff Elizabethan tradition, he rather reminded me (when I saw it later) of Charles Laughton's Captain Bligh in *Mutiny on the Bounty*. Perhaps I reminded him of Fletcher Christian, for his face was about as bleak as the North Cape in February. He motioned me to a chair and began his examination. What school had I been to? *Which?* Then which University? *I hadn't???*" & c. (Bridson, D.G. *Prospero and Ariel, The Rise and Fall of Radio, A Personal Recollection*, London, Gollancz, 1971).

23   Lacey, Kate "Radio in the Great Depression, Promotional Culture, Public Service and Propaganda", in Hilmes and Loviglio, p. 29.

24   Jeffery, Tom "A Place in the Nation: The Lower Middle Class in England", in Koshar, Rudy (ed.) *Splintered Classes, Politics and the Lower Middle Classes in Interwar Europe*, New York, Holmes and Meier, 1990, p. 79.

they have a danger of being too dominated by government in the field of politics and sociology. I would say on the other hand that the freedom of any reputable individual to broadcast his views is a great recommendation for the commercial system. The justifications for advertisement broadcasting are exactly those used in support of the free Press … The Press has quite naturally done everything it could to put down commercial broadcasting, just as any commercial enterprise will always fight a rival interest. The Press will therefore always praise the BBC, however dull, but in recommending the Corporation's programmes because of their "cleanness" one might whisper: "Whose proprietor hasn't been using Persil yet?"[25]

Nevertheless, if there were vested interests at work within the commercial sector, Charles Siepmann suggests they were also present within the BBC. Writing in 1950, this ex-BBC émigré to the USA evaluated the BBC's claim to monopoly in the period under examination thus:

The general support accorded to the BBC in the British press undoubtedly derived in large part from the latter's fear of the competitive danger of advertising on the air. We in America know from practical experience that such fear is unwarranted. Nevertheless its existence has been one operative factor in influencing decision on the BBC's charter during the 23 years of its existence.[26]

Siepmann develops his point by adding that "while the BBC, the radio manufacturers and the press, each with their own interests in mind, bespoke one policy, the people bespoke another." César Saerchinger's anecdotally conversational journalistic account of European radio seen from an American viewpoint expands on the issue:

The British, having profited by the sad experience of pioneer America, had avoided the chaotic conditions which ensued after the early days of broadcasting in the United States. They had solved their problem in the British way, by putting their heads together and effecting a compromise. … The Corporation, licensed by the Government, would serve everybody – the public, by providing programmes; the manufacturers, by creating a demand for radio sets; and the Government, by providing an effective, unified instrument for nation-wide communication, especially in a national emergency – not to mention a handsome revenue.[27]

25   Eckersley, P.P. *The Power Behind the Microphone*, London, The Scientific Book Club, 1942, p. 150.

26   Siepmann, Charles A. *Radio, Television and Society*, New York, Oxford University Press, 1950, p. 144. Charles Siepmann, born in Bristol, joined the BBC in 1925, and served, successively , as Director of Adult Education, Director of Talks and Director of Programme Planning. In 1937 he left the Corporation, and was awarded a Rockefeller Foundation fellowship to study and report on educational broadcasting in the USA. From 1939 to 1942 he lectured at Harvard, and during the Second World War he worked with the US Office of War Information, ending as Deputy Director of the San Francisco office, concerned with short-wave propaganda to the Far East. In 1945 he served as consultant to the Federal Communications Commission. In 1946 he was appointed Professor of Education and Chairman of the Department of Communications in Education at New York University, and Director of its Film Library.

27   Saerchinger, César *Hello America! Radio Adventures in Europe*, Cambridge, Massachusetts, Houghton Mifflin, 1938, p. 16.

Reith

There is criticism of Reith and some of his attitudes and policies within the coming pages. It should be established therefore that I am not by any means blind to the greatness and achievement of the man. Miall has written from personal recollection that "at his best ... he was charming, effervescent and excellent company. At his worst he was morose and consumed by self-pity".[28] Reith's extraordinary dual personality[29] is explored by his two principal biographers. Boyle rightly points out that:

> He left a living monument in the BBC, yet believed in his obstinately childish fashion that his heirs had wantonly defaced it. He left everything too late, his own departures from public responsibilities included, even his reluctant departure from life itself. If any great man can ever be said to have atoned for his misdeeds on the elaborate rack he made of his own conscience, that man was surely John Reith.[30]

Stuart, in his fine biographical introduction to his edition of Reith's diaries reminds us that:

> The tragedy of his public life was not, as he often claimed, that he had failed in achievement, but rather, in the words of his great enemy, Winston Churchill, ... that "his personality and temperament were not equal to the profound and penetrating justice of his ideas".[31]

McIntyre adds to this:

> Certainly there are few who have been so grievously maimed by their own temperament; Stuart's words capture the man with precision. Beside them ... may be set those with which *The Times* concluded a leading article on the day after John Reith died: "The corporate personality of the BBC still gets, and will continue to get, a twitch on the thread from that angular Scots engineer, of unabashed earnestness and unbending strength."[32]

Siepmann has commented upon the autocracy of Reith, and the extraordinary fact

---

28   Miall, Leonard *Inside the BBC*, London, Weidenfeld & Nicolson, London, 1994, p. 3.

29   During research, the present writer came across a remarkable cutting from the Personal Columns of *The Times*, 15 May 1961 which was placed by a previous owner between the pages of a copy of *Broadcast Over Britain*. It repays quotation in full as an illustration of Reith's sometimes eccentric conduct: "LORD REITH SEEKS ADVICE – He has kept a diary, not a day missed, for over 50 years; it is in two parts: 12 volumes manuscript, 10 with letters, photographs, newspaper cuttings and such like. He is more and more minded to destroy it because: (1) he does not wish to put a burden on either of his children by leaving it to them; (2) he does not like to think of it lying in some library for a hundred years and then being scrapped (he would prefer to scrap it himself); (3) he does not want there to be such records of himself. Has anyone any kindly advice?" What kind of advice he expected – or received – is unknown. The tone of the words is that of a man who is pleading for an assurance that his place in history is secure. Also, in the pages of Reith's 1949 autobiography, *Into the Wind* (Hodder and Stoughton) was found a letter dated January 1950 to Sir Louis Sterling, one-time Head of EMI, in response to the latter's comments on the book. Reith writes: "Yes – it's all rather sad; and nothing to show for all the effort. What good? I should feel better if there were a sum of money in the bank; if I were starting over again I think that's what I'd go for."

30   Boyle, Andrew *Only the Wind Will Listen: Reith of the BBC*, London, Hutchinson, 1972, p. 351.

31   Stuart, Charles (ed.) *The Reith Diaries*, London, Collins, 1975, p. 70. Churchill's quotation, cited by Stuart was directed at the French General Michel.

32   McIntyre, Ian *The Expense of Glory, A Life of John Reith*, London, Harper Collins, 1993, p. 404.

that his personality was such a crucial element in the development of the BBC, when "monopoly alone could not have moulded British radio …"[33]

> Sir John Reith was so certain he was right that no research seemed necessary. Regardless of its actual effects, for him his policy stood self-justified. Secure in his personal conviction of what was right and wrong, he imposed upon a nation the imprint of his personality.[34]

Barnouw, in one of the best commentaries on early American broadcasting, cites concisely, the perceived essential differences between the BBC model of broadcasting and that of the US:

> That it had a responsibility to help shape public tastes and interests was implicit in the BBC point of view. It considered it a duty to look far beyond momentary public tastes. This meant, in Sir John's words, "an active faith that a supply of good things will create a demand for them, not waiting for the demand to express itself". It was the job of BBC personnel to know what was good … To the men of the BBC the chaos of American radio seemed an extraordinary phenomenon. Travellers regularly reported on its extreme commercialism. The eruption of competing networks, vying for public events as well as advertising dollars, created a bizarre picture, totally unlike the more orderly BBC.[35]

To turn to some contemporary accounts of Reith's personality is to discover a less sympathetic assessment than that of McIntyre and Stuart. Cleghorn Thomson, writing in 1937, and by that time a former member of the BBC, provides a summary of current images:

> There are some who conceive of Sir J.C.W. Reith as a Mussolinic dictator, ever hungry for power, who "sets all hearts in the state to what tune pleased his ear". Others imagine him a covenanting idealist, a Praise-God barebones dwelling on chill Olympic heights of motive, resolved to uplift the groundlings, "thus neglecting worldly ends, all dedicated to closeness and the bettering of my mind". A section of the public thinks of the Director-General as a veritable ogre of regimentation, fiercely paranoiac, secretly tapping telephones, listening at keyholes, breaking spirits and careers, banishing all save "yes men" from the immediate entourage of his trembling court. Yet Church dignitaries look upon him as a defender of the faith; the most eminent civil servant I know considers him the greatest public servant Britain has seen since the War. He is clearly the dominating force in a ship which is not yet a happy ship.[36]

33 Siepmann, p. 129.

34 Ibid., pp. 129–130. Siepmann goes on to make the startling (and undeveloped) statement, that "This blithe assumption of infallibility is partly responsible for depriving us of ten years of cultural history-making by broadcasting." (Ibid.)

35 Barnouw, Erik, *A Tower in Babel, A History of Broadcasting in the United States to 1933*, New York, Oxford University Press, 1966, pp. 247–248.

36 Cleghorn Thomson, pp. 63–64. David Cleghorn Thomson, like Reith a Scot, was a totally different personality, ebullient, charming, "probably homosexual" according to Desmond Hawkins, who knew him personally. His character, role in the BBC and relationship with Reith are discussed by Hawkins later in this writing. Further extracts from his writings will also be cited. It should be noted that within a year of the publication of *Radio is Changing Us* Reith had left the BBC.

Cleghorn Thomson's final assertion here – "a ship which is not *yet* a happy ship" – is significant because it implies that the BBC to this point never *had* been "a happy ship". This is borne out by Gorham, recalling the Savoy Hill days. Gorham had joined the BBC in 1926, and his writings portray him as a somewhat rebellious figure, who on principle refused to show undue deference to Reith, a point he illustrates with the example of telephone conversations with the Director General: "I would say 'Gorham here'. He would say "Gorham?" I would say "Yes", and (to my imagination at least) he would wait for the "Sir" like an actor waiting for the laugh."[37] Beyond the personal, Gorham shows that the attitudes to Reith as Director-General of the Corporation described by Cleghorn Thomson in the late 1930s were largely present among many staff more than ten years earlier, in the Company days at Savoy Hill:

> In some form or other he influenced everybody and everything there, and, to my mind, usually in the wrong direction. There was an air of fear, suspicion, and intrigue, with many of the staff trying to please the boss and fool him at the same time. I believe that during these years Reith was doing his best work in keeping the BBC independent, and we owed him more than we knew. But inside the office there was every desire to placate him and little desire to imitate him.[38]

He goes on to give us a startling picture of moral conditions at Savoy Hill, considerably at odds with Reith's own code, an environment in which, although "people dressed respectably ... they did not behave respectably".[39] Although Reith frowned on divorce, and many staff were made to leave the BBC for figuring in divorce proceedings or similar, the tone of many staff relationships at Savoy Hill – whether the General Manager was aware of them or not – were, according to Gorham, hardly in keeping with his views on appropriate conduct:

> I never knew an office where sex played so large a part, where so many people lived with their secretaries, where the hunters and the hunted were so conspicuous as they went about their sport. And ... it was not always the men who did not chase secretaries who were the most moral. But some of us always argued that Reith just did not understand about that.[40]

Sunday broadcasting

Coase highlights an issue which is central to my premise:

> The character of Mr. Reith's views and of his policy may best, I think be illustrated with reference to the place which religion occupied in broadcasting and to the problem of the Sunday programme ... Mr Reith's views on Sunday

---

37 Gorham, Maurice *Sound and Fury, Twenty One Years in the BBC*, London, Percival Marshall, 1948, p. 19. Gorham's career in the BBC included the Editorship of *Radio Times*, the BBC's wartime broadcasts to America, the Allied Expeditionary Forces Programme for the invasion troops, the Light Programme and the post-war Television Service.

38 Ibid., p. 20.

39 Ibid.

40 Ibid.

broadcasting give a comprehensive illustration of his fundamental attitude towards broadcasting standards.[41]

Coase proceeds to quote Reith's own writings, including evidence given to the Crawford Committee in support of this statement. The matter is discussed fully, later in the book, as is the complex personality of Reith himself. The BBC's attitude towards broadcasting on the Sabbath was the main factor which allowed Commercial competition to flourish. Almost all existing texts examining this period of broadcasting make reference to it in some way, and it is explored in further detail in later chapters of the present study. The observance of Sunday may be seen within the BBC's wider policy of the observance of the offices – sacred and otherwise – of the year. To the present time much programme policy within the BBC frequently revolves around the recognition or observance of an anniversary or otherwise significant date. Scannell and Cardiff have noted that:

> Nothing so well illustrates the noiseless manner in which the BBC became perhaps *the* central agent of the national culture as its calendrical role; the cyclical reproduction, year in year out, of an orderly and regular procession of festivities, rituals and celebrations – major and minor, civil and sacred – that marked the unfolding of the broadcast year.[42]

The idea of a shared calendar as a unifier of class, a common timetable that would be significant to all strata, was manifested on a weekly basis by Sunday observance. Strictly observed, the BBC Sunday grew from Reith's view that the Sabbath was for God:

> The programmes which are broadcast on Sunday are … framed with the day itself in mind … The Churches did not take the initiative … There was no undue pressure, nor indeed pressure of any kind, brought to bear upon us, as was once suggested. It was one of our earliest decisions that the power and resources of the [wireless] service would be available in this way, and an invitation was extended to the Churches to co-operate.[43]

Saturday was for a time almost as barren as Sunday. Briggs speaks of how long hours of dead air were slowly filled with programming: "It was not until the end of 1932 that 'continuous' broadcasting took place every Saturday from noon to midnight: a few months later, in September 1933, a 'silent period' between 6.15 p.m. and 8 p.m. on Sundays was filled in …"[44] Content, however, was as important, if not more so, than hours broadcast. Briggs, in *The BBC, the First Fifty Years* makes it clear that: "As early as 1932 … Reith had told his Control Board that he was willing to extend Sunday hours 'if it was likely to form a successful bargaining point with the exchanges'."[45] [Relay exchanges, see discussion below] It is important to examine the *type* of programme which was broadcast on Sundays – and the style of work which was omitted. Scannell and Cardiff write of: "the weekly observances

---

41   Cleghorn Thomson, pp. 47–48.

42   Scannell and Cardiff, p. 278.

43   Reith, *Broadcast Over Britain*, London, Hodder and Stoughton, 1924, pp. 196–197.

44   Briggs, Asa *The History of Broadcasting in the United Kingdom, Vol. II, The Golden Age of Wireless, 1927–1939*. Oxford, Oxford University Press, 1995, p. 26.

45   Briggs, *The First Fifty Years*, p. 130.

of the Sabbath through church services and a programme schedule markedly more austere than on other days ...".[46] Later chapters will illuminate this with examples. Wolfe conveys the idea that Reith was rather more flexible than his critics maintained. He points out that Reith's instruction to the Churches' Religious Advisory Committee on Broadcasting in January 1935 seemed quite liberal:

> Reith had always regarded Sunday as a day not only of religion, but of refreshment and rest. He wanted his staff to realize that Sunday policy "does not mean simply the exclusion of anything which is incompatible with the religious observances of the day – and at this rate, half of what we are doing already would go out – but a rather different intellectual standard".[47]

It was however in the nature of the interpretation of that "rather different intellectual standard" that the BBC proved itself out of touch with the popular mood and cultural demands of so many of its listeners. For Frederick A. Iremonger, its Religious Director, it simply meant that: "The programmes should be varied: a broader definition of plays and not only Shakespeare. More music of light opera type, he thought, would be the most drastic alteration. As for the rising popularity of the Wurlitzer organ, it was vulgar in the extreme!"[48] It is extraordinary that such a debate was continuing within the BBC as late as the middle of the decade. "Even the *Church Times*[49] spoke of giving at least some of the public some more of what it wants."[50] Moseley provides a strong link between the BBC's Sunday policy and the opportunities for competition:

> The Sponsored Programme, and later the Wired Wireless concerns banked upon the support of disgruntled British listeners and some business, operating from the Continent, proceeded to stop the gaps in the BBC's Sunday service with broadcasts arranged "through the courtesy" of so-and-so's pills or somebody else's face powder ... Then, certainly the BBC began to sit up and take notice, but by that time the opposition movement was too big and too firmly established in popular favour to be effectively countered.[51]

Commercial competition

It is significant that Boyle and McIntyre give little space in their biographies of Reith to the issue of commercial competition from his standpoint. Both devote approximately two pages to the issue as a brief discussion of the Ullswater Committee's hearing and findings. Boyle states in his summary of events that:

> demands for limited sponsoring appeared in the evidence submitted by Philco, one of the big radio manufacturers; an even stranger demand for a separate wavelength devoted exclusively to advertising came from the International Broadcasting Company. This stung Reith into retorting that the

46   Scannell and Cardiff, p. 279.

47   Wolfe, Kenneth M. *The Churches and the British Broadcasting Corporation, 1922–1956, The Politics of Broadcast Religion*, London, SCM Press,1984, pp. 68–69.

48   Ibid., p. 69.

49   *Church Times*, 9 August 1935. Wolfe states that "In 1933 the *Birmingham Post* had begun a campaign under the heading, 'Save Sunday from the Saxophone!' Letters continued for weeks".

50   Wolfe, p. 69.

51   Moseley, Sydney A. *Broadcasting in My Time*, London, Rich and Cowan, 1935, p. 163.

committee would be well advised to examine the firm's programme schedules. Such an examination might convince them that commercial competition
of the kind, whatever else it did, would certainly not "raise the standard".[52]

While both Boyle and McIntyre acknowledge that the success of the Continental
stations which this book examines in detail was due to the BBC's Sunday policy,
and that "Reith's somewhat austere and unalterable sabbatarian concepts had
continued to play into the hands of the IBC ..."[53], they do little to develop the
point, which is curious in that this area has been well documented, as illustrated
above. Indeed while Boyle states that "by the early thirties ... Radio Luxembourg
and Radio Normandie [sic] had begun to catch the ears of a disturbingly large part
of the BBC's audience on Sundays ...".[54] He ignores the fact that the greatest
successes of the Commercial stations were at that point still to come, producing by
1935/36 a crisis within the BBC which indirectly led to the creation of the
introduction of an audience measurement unit for the first time. On the other hand
Curran and Seaton's comment that "the BBC had been subject to competition from
foreign commercial stations since the 1930s. That it was the challenge of Radio
Luxembourg which had broken the dismal Reithian Sunday on the radio",[55] is
something of an over-simplification. I show in the next chapter, and in Part Four
of the book that the threat of commercial radio from the Continent pre-dates the
arrival of Radio Luxembourg by many years. Likewise Appendix A demonstrates
the number of stations transmitting sponsored programmes in addition to Radio
Luxembourg. It is perhaps hardly surprising that biographers of Reith and other
commentators should deal with the matter of commercial competition in so
desultory a fashion, given that Reith himself barely mentions it at all, either in his
published diaries, edited by Stuart, or in his autobiography.[56] An exception is his
account of the Ullswater Committee in *Into the Wind*, in which he refers to the
International Broadcasting Company's demand for recognition as "amusing" because "it was not a broadcasting organization at all ...".[57] There is also a sardonic
passage in *Into the Wind* which describes a visit made by Reith to the United States
during 1931, in which he describes a visit to a commercial radio station in Portland.
The picture he creates also gives us a sense of the dismissive disdain with which he
treated this type of radio generally:

> A programme about valvolene. The announcer read a dozen lines of puff,
> turned on an outsize record of a jazz band; in the middle of it the conductor
> of the band gave his opinion of valvolene. After the record the announcer
> had another dozen lines to say about valvolene; listeners were urged to note
> the same time next week for another jolly twenty valvolene minutes.[58]

52   Boyle, p. 271.
53   Ibid.
54   Ibid.
55   Curran, James and Seaton, Jean *Power Without Responsibility, The Press and Broadcasting in Britain*,
      London, Routledge, 1997, p. 165.
56   Reith, J.C.W. *Into the Wind*, London, Hodder & Stoughton, 1949.
57   Ibid., p. 228. Reith, although naming the IBC in the text, chooses not to dignify it with a place in the
      index of the book.
58   Ibid., p. 150.

Although the issue of BBC Sunday policy and its implications for the opening of competition is not discussed by Reith and only touched on by his biographers, Briggs is correct in his statement that at the fourth International Radio Telegraphic Conference held in Madrid in September 1932, "more important ... than most other matters was the development of commercial broadcasting in Europe".[59] He goes on to rehearse the rise of Radios Normandy and Luxembourg and other stations, and pinpoints the early experiments of Captain L.F. Plugge. March 1930 brought the creation of Plugge's IBC and "and the first concession to a French company, the Société Luxembourgeoise d'études Radiophoniques, for a wireless station of not less than 100 kilowatts in Luxembourg in September 1930".[60] Scannell and Cardiff, examining the nature of the commercial stations targeting of BBC audiences, identify clearly the BBC Sunday policy "guided by Reith's strict sabbatarianism" as the principle loophole through which Luxembourg and the others obtained their audiences:

> Through the week Luxembourg broadcast in English each evening, but in French, Italian and German during the day. On Sundays however, from eight in the morning until late at night, it provided a non-stop service of entertainment for a British audience. This was a brilliant thrust at the BBC ...[61]

Briggs confirms that by 1938, when an audience survey demonstrated that "over 1 million households, it was estimated, were listening to Luxembourg between 1 o'clock and 2 o'clock on Sunday afternoons"[62] the BBC and the Post Office were concerned enough – even in the shadow of war – to attempt to drive the commercial stations off the air through legislation. This event occurred at the World Telecommunications Conference in Cairo,[63] and was unsuccessful, even indirectly drawing into question the very issue of the future funding of the BBC.[64] Thus Briggs is illuminating on a number of political issues raised by the competition of the 1930s and the BBC's response to it. At the same time the complexities of the commercial station franchises, their operation and in particular the role of advertising agencies in the supply of programmes, is not dealt with. Elsewhere however Briggs acknowledges more fully the impact of the commercial stations on BBC Sunday policy, stating that in April 1938:

> It was recognized that there had to be a lightening of Sunday programmes, "without destroying the special nature of the day". The new policy was introduced, however, more as a response to foreign competition than as a change of heart.[65]

To compare Briggs' account of the growth of competition with that of Coase, written more than a decade before the first edition of Briggs' work, is to understand how much the latter owes to the former. In Coase's 1950 account , almost all the

59 Briggs II, p. 324.
60 Ibid., p. 326.
61 Scannell and Cardiff, p. 232.
62 Briggs, II. p. 337.
63 Ibid., pp. 339–340.
64 Ibid., pp. 340–341.
65 Briggs, *The First Fifty Years*, p. 129.

basic facts are present, and it is noteworthy how little has been added to this by subsequent commentators.[66]

Scannell and Cardiff also chronicle the development of BBC concern from the late 1920s as the threat from Continental radio grew.[67] Additionally, they create an atmospheric picture of the nature of sponsored programmes, including a direct quote from the theme tune of *The Andrews' Liver Salts Concert* on Radio Luxembourg, which "opened with a chorus of 'Merry Andrews' singing, to the tune of *See Me Dance the Polka*":

> We're the Merry Merry Andrews
> As fit as fit can be.
> And there's no reason why you
> Should not be as fit as we.
> So drink your Andrews in the morn
> And then you'll sing with glee,
> I'm a Merry Merry Andrew,
> As fit as fit can be.[68]

Also dealt with briefly by Scannell and Cardiff is the foundation and early development of BBC audience measurement under Robert Silvey.[69] The key achievement to come from this is rightly stated to be that "it enabled the structural framework of [BBC] broadcasting – the arrangement of programme output through the days of the week, through the seasons of the year – to be arranged on a rational basis".[70] Silvey himself, coming to the BBC in 1936 from the statistical department of the London Press Exchange, was well placed to bring the age of audience research to a Corporation which had, through its paternalistic application of the public service ethic, eschewed any such measurement. The London Press Exchange was:

> One of the larger British advertising agents and there it fell to me to write the report on a survey of listening to continental stations. The LPE needed to have this kind of information for its clients were being increasingly pressed by these stations to include radio advertising in their advertising appropriations.

Crisell points out that a major "challenge to Reith's broadcasting philosophy came mainly from within the BBC itself ... the demand for regular and systematic research into audience behaviour and tastes, about which virtually nothing was known other than through casual letters from listeners".

The fact that the BBC fought so hard, particularly during the latter part of the 1930s, to eradicate commercial competition is questioned and answered succinctly by Coase. Countering the argument that "since all owners of radio receiving sets in Britain had to take out a licence, and since a proportion of the licence fee went to the Corporation, it would have no objection to people listening to sponsored

66 See Coase, pp. 101–121 in his chapter, "Foreign Commercial Broadcasting".
67 Scannell and Cardiff, pp. 228–234.
68 Ibid., p. 296.
69 Ibid., notably on pp. 234–235 and 376–377.
70 Ibid., p. 376.

programmes, since the revenue of the Corporation would not suffer",[71] he goes on:

> So far as the Corporation was concerned this argument would appear to be beside the point. Those directing the policy of the Corporation were not interested by the profit motive. They were not interested in the material welfare of the Corporation; their interest was in the intellectual and ethical welfare of the listeners.[72]

In other words, "the purposes sought by the unified control of broadcasting have been infringed".[73] What it leaves unanswered is how such purposes could ever be fully protected, given the freedom of the individual to tune to foreign broadcasts, whether intended for British ears or not. Thomas, well suited to make the comparison between 1930s commercial radio and 1950s commercial television, places the issue of competition succinctly into historical context:

> It took five years for Radio Luxembourg to attract one-third of the BBC radio audience, with no publicity in the British press; whilst ITV, with a blare of nationwide publicity, took two years to win a quarter of the television viewers in its three central Britain areas.

Thomas thus concisely identifies – as none of the other writings on the subject can claim to – the issue which is at the heart of this present research.

Advertising

Given that little has been written about the structure and functionality of Continental commercial stations between 1930 and 1939, it is hardly surprising that the nature of radio advertising in Britain at this time should likewise be neglected. Nevett[74] briefly explores the known facts whilst adding little fresh information. Dyer is even more disappointing in that she does not even recognize radio as a part of the advertising equation during the 1930s, although she rightly identifies the anxiety-based advertising which played a major part in sponsored programmes:

> At a time of economic gloom and uncertainty, the pedlars of nerve tonics, vitamin pills and mouth-washes came into their own. And the nerve war gave advertisers plenty of scope for their talents of invention: readers were told of the dangers of contracting hitherto unknown conditions such as "halitosis", "summer sluggishness", "tell-tale tongue", "listlessness", "night starvation" and "body odour". The ads were often as lurid and exaggerated as the "quack" advertising of the eighteenth century and were filled with pseudo-scientific argument.[75]

As so often, one turns to the first-hand witnesses of the time. The appropriateness of product placement on pre-war commercial radio was instinctive noted by Roy

71 Coase, p. 117.
72 Ibid., pp. 117–118.
73 The Ullswater Committee report, quoted in Coase, p. 117.
74 Nevett, T.R. *Advertising in Britain, A History*, London/Norwich, Heinemann/The History of Advertising Trust, 1982, pp. 157–158.
75 Dyer, Gillian *Advertising as Communication*, London, Routledge, 1982, p. 46.

Plomley, in 1930 a young actor, but later to be a key broadcaster for the IBC and subsequently the BBC:

> I was listening to a commercial radio station ... Among the advertisers on Radio Normandy, among the laxatives and packet soups and soaps and gravy mixes, a firm was selling pianos, and pianos struck me as expensive items to be vended to a mass and mainly C-class audience.[76]

Turner[77] gives few insights into British Commercial radio's use of advertising during the 1930s, although he provides an entertaining, although unreferenced, insight into the American model:

> The layman, glancing through text-books on American radio advertising, cannot but marvel at the lengths to which programme research and inquiry into consumers' habits are carried. He will find, for instance, charts showing what percentage of housewives in the Eastern Time Zone are engaged in ironing, washing-up, tending children or performing toilet at any time between 8 a.m. and 5 p.m.; or diagrams "showing recall by New York women of advertising for gelatine desserts in various media in 1947"; also figures proving that mystery stories are more popular than serials in big cities, with the moral:

> Consider how much more effective the mystery story would be for decaffeinated coffee (a big city product), and how much more efficient the serial would be for baking powder (a small town product).[78]

Commercial radio as developed in the United States is appropriate for discussion within the context of the subject of this study, and receives a chapter devoted to its evolution. G.H. Douglas states that the coming of the first great American network, the National Broadcasting Company, in 1926, "was a powerful impetus to the advertising agencies, who now saw rich sugarplums dancing before them".[79] The fact that one announcement, broadcast on a national station or network of stations, was capable of reaching millions of people in the comfort of their own homes at a single reading was clearly enormously attractive to manufacturers. As the realization of this became clear to agencies and broadcasters, Turner points to the almost obsessive nature of US product-based audience research. Of the many books to proliferate on the subject in America during the first years of the 1930s, one of the more considered was by Arnold, quoted here because, written as it was in 1931, it represents the thinking which crossed the Atlantic at the time the British commercial stations were launching in earnest:

> Broadcast advertising is no longer an experiment. Broadcasting is an established advertising medium. Over two hundred national advertisers used the networks of the National Broadcasting Company alone in 1929. This new

76 Plomley, Roy *Days Seemed Longer, Early Years of a Broadcaster*, London, Eyre Methuen, 1980, p. 104.

77 Turner, E.S. *The Shocking History of Advertising*, London, Michael Joseph Ltd, 1952, p. 282.

78 Ibid., p. 282.

79 Douglas, George H. *The Early Days of Broadcasting*, Jefferson, North Carolina, McFarland & Company, Inc.,1987, p. 89.

medium now has back of it [sic.] enough years of actual record to prove its profitable acceptance by the general public.[80]

The negative results of advertising on American radio are cited by Smulyan in terms which are easily recognizable in the commercial radio modeled on it and shaped by US-founded companies operating in Britain in the 1930s, such as the J. Walter Thompson Organisation:

> Commercialised radio, funded by the sale of time to advertisers, proved rigid in form and less responsive to its audience. Advertisers soon dominated radio and, because of the long-held uncertainty about listener response, ... advertisers' impressions of what listeners liked actually controlled the programming. Advertising forced radio to appeal to mass, rather than specialized (even if quite large) audiences. Advertisers believed they knew the pattern that over-the-air commercials should take. To accommodate the advertisements properly, the format of radio programmes became inflexible.[81]

Susan Douglas links this advertiser-led radio programming to the inevitable quest for information about audience, mocked by Turner. In so doing she points to the fact that audience measurement, so long resisted by the BBC, and introduced to Britain by the Continental stations and their feeder-agencies, had its origins in non-commercial considerations within early American radio:

> As people's voices became disembodied and were sent out over the airwaves, the growing questions about how the "invisible audience" reacted to these emanations stemmed from curiosity, vanity, and a fear of embarrassment or rejection. But by the late 1920s, when advertisers began sponsoring more shows, these became not only metaphysical questions but also economic ones. Curiosity about who was listening turned into calculations about how much these listeners were worth.

> Beginning in the 1920s, and escalating to a fevered hysteria today, the corporate obsession with the tastes and preferences of the broadcast audience has produced a nationwide, technologically instantaneous network of audience surveillance. This is a system most Americans do not encounter directly on a daily basis. Indirectly, however, it shapes the entire media environment in which we live.[82]

Turner's tone is surely ironic when, turning to the issue of advertising in British radio he says:

> There are some who believe that only the intransigence of Mr. J.C.W. (now Lord) Reith kept the advertiser at bay in those early days at Savoy Hill. Others prefer to think that it was the innate decency and good sense of the British public that prevented the profanation of a new cultural medium.[83]

---

80 Arnold, Frank A. *Broadcast Advertising, The Fourth Dimension*, New York, John Wiley and Sons, 1931, pp. 68–69. Arnold's credentials as list on the title page are "Lecturer on Broadcast Advertising at the College of the City of New York, Director of Development of the National Broadcasting Company, Inc., and formerly Secretary of the Frank Seaman Advertising Agency".

81 Smulyan, Susan *Selling Radio, The Commercialisation of American Broadcasting, 1920–1934*, Washington D.C., Smithsonian Institution Press, 1994, p. 9.

82 Douglas, Susan J. *Listening In, Radio and the American Imagination from Amos 'n' Andy and Edward R. Murrow to Wolfman Jack and Howard Stern*, New York, Times Books, 1999, p. 124.

Notwithstanding, accusations had been leveled against the BBC by its opponents that it had infringed the regulations under which it had been awarded its charter. Moseley, for example:

> Grossly and unblushingly the BBC constantly advertises the records manufactured by certain companies, giving the name and make and number of each record before it is played, and again afterwards. It is true that this is done no less blatantly on the Continent, but there they make no secret of monetary contact between the advertiser and the radio interests.[84]

Stone, writing in 1933, had voiced the same issue:

> I am all for the judicious broadcasting of gramophone records. It has been proved that it not only entertains listeners better than a great many expensively prepared programmes, but that it helps the gramophone industry to sell its goods to the public. There is nothing artificial or unhealthy about it. The BBC is allowed to advertise the records, and it does and cannot very well help doing so. On the other hand it is not allowed to take money for this purpose. But ... I cannot see why the BBC should be expected to pay my fee for arranging and presenting the records. In this matter I ought to be an accredited announcer for the recording companies and paid by them – handsomely.[85]

Stone has been called "The world's first 'disc jockey'".[86] Scannell and Cardiff mention that in September 1934 Admiral Charles Carpendale, Reith's Second in Command told the Post Office that "we are now warning artists unofficially that it is not in their interests to broadcast from Luxembourg ..."[87]

> The BBC expected a flood of protest when Stone was taken off the air, and were surprised to receive only ten letters in the week his programme was cancelled. One reason for the apparent indifference might have been that he was preferred in his new show. A letter to *Radio Pictorial* declared: "One misses him from Daventry, but already one hears in his voice from Luxembourg a nuance of greater freedom. Those hampering and petty restrictions at the BBC must have been very difficult to cope with."[88]

Roger Eckersley, who became Organiser of Programmes in 1925, and was the brother of the BBC's first chief engineer, Peter Eckersley, defended the issue of apparent advertising, whilst admitting that it was a complex matter, open to interpretation:

> It is difficult to say what constitutes advertising by Radio and what does not. After all, if we take a band from an hotel – and publicise it in the *Radio Times*

---

83 Ibid., p. 283.

84 Moseley, p. 86.

85 Stone, Christopher *Christopher Stone Speaking*, London, Elkin, Mathews & Marrot Ltd, 1933, pp. 144–155. At the time of writing his book, Stone was working both for the BBC and Radio Luxembourg, where he was indeed "paid handsomely" by companies for playing music by their artists on record.

86 Scannell and Cardiff, p. 230.

87 Head, Martin *The Beginning of Radio Luxembourg 1930–1939*, unpublished dissertation, Polytechnic of Central London, 1980, p. 19, quoted by Scannell & Cardiff, p. 230.

88 Ibid., pp. 230–231. Scannell and Cardiff extract the *Radio Pictorial* quotation from Head, p. 25.

and the daily press, the name of that hotel is blazoned in publicity up and down the length of the country. On the other hand we have consistently turned down programme hours suggested to us from time to time from some of the big stores. The subtle dividing line there is that hotels cater in their normal business for entertainment, while stores do not.[89]

It is hardly surprising that the "subtlety" of Eckersley's argument failed to satisfy the BBC's critics in this area.

Wireless relays

The development of commercial competition exploiting the BBC's Sunday policy was aided by the growth of Radio Relay stations which were "capable ... of providing better reception of foreign programmes than many low or even high-priced wireless receiving sets ... They were bound to be used, in a free market, for the rediffusion of foreign commercial programmes if these programmes genuinely made an appeal to large numbers of listeners".[90] The system, which operated by using telephone lines to disseminate radio programmes to subscribers, became extremely popular during the 1930s.

A major entrepreneurial figure in the relay movement was Peter Eckersley, a pioneer of the Marconi experiments at Writtle near Chelmsford. Eckersley was to become a major developer of the wired concept of radio transmission. His son, Myles, has left us a vivid picture of his controversial and charismatic father, in which he describes the idea of the system, perceived by Eckersley as early as January 1927, and developed out of 1925 experiments conducted by the wireless amateur, A.W. Maton of Hythe, near Southampton.[91] Eckersley had sought to persuade Reith to explore the idea within the BBC:

> Theoretically it is possible to transmit programmes over telephone lines or electric light power cable. Five or six programmes can be (theoretically) sent over one cable simultaneously. It seems a pity that we do not exploit this idea ... We should be the first to make use of the system. I doubt if the P.M.G. has any right to stop us or anyone else from entering into a contract with a particular electric light company. There is a large profit to be made from such an arrangement.[92]

In fact the Government through the Postmaster General, did object to the new Corporation becoming involved in a commercial operation, but saw no reason why the Post Office itself should not licence relay services to private companies.[93] The Labour government fell in 1931, and was replaced by a coalition, dominated by the Conservative party, which allowed the fledgling Wireless Exchange companies more freedom:

> They could have as many towns or areas as they wanted and could relay English language commercial radio programmes from Europe. Cable broad-

---

89   Eckersley, Roger *The BBC and All That*, London, Samson Low, Marston & Co. Ltd. 1946, p. 90.

90   Coase, p. 331.

91   Eckersley, Myles *Prospero's Wireless*, Romsey, Myles Books, 1997, p. 234.

92   Eckersley, Peter in a memo to John Reith, January 1927, quoted in Eckersley, Myles, p. 235.

93   Ibid., pp. 235–236.

casters were NOT allowed to originate their own programmes in this country, and were *advised* [my italics] to rely mainly on the material from the monopoly BBC. There was no compulsion to relay only BBC programmes but most relay companies varied their daily programmes, offering BBC programmes with the programmes from Radios Luxembourg and Normandy (especially on Sundays, when the BBC was in solemn mode).[94]

Coase explains further the appeal of wire broadcasting between the years 1930 and 1935:

1. The loudspeaker which was installed in a subscriber's home was simpler to operate than a receiving set. Furthermore, it was less likely to develop faults; or if it did there was the maintenance staff of the relay exchange to set it right.

2. The substitution of a small weekly payment for the larger sum required to pay for a receiving set was a convenience to some subscribers. None the less, the advantage which the relay exchange subscriber would have over the purchaser of a set on hire purchase terms would be small.

3. In areas such as ports in which there was considerable interference or in which, owing to natural features or the location of the transmitting station, reception was difficult on an ordinary receiving set, the subscriber to the relay exchange was able to hear the programmes very much more clearly. This was due both to the superior efficiency of the master set and to the special aerials which the relay exchange could erect.

4. The master set of the relay exchange was able to pick up programmes from foreign stations which it would difficult, or impossible, to receive on an ordinary set.[95]

The growth of Relay Exchange subscribers from 1927 to 1939 is tabled by Pegg[96]:

Date	Exchanges	Relay subscribers	Subscribers multiplied by persons per private family
September 1927	10	446	1,784
December 1928	23	2,430	9,720
December 1929	34	8,592	34,368
December 1930	86	21,677	86,708
December 1931	132	43,889	165,462
December 1932	194	82,690	311,741
December 1933	265	130,998	493,862
December 1934	318	192,707	726,505
December 1935	343	233,554	955,899
December 1936	333	250,978	958,736
December 1937	331	255,236	975,002
December 1938	325	256,294	979,043
December 1939	284	270,596	1,033,677

94   Ibid., p. 236.

95   Coase, p. 75.

96   Pegg, Mark *Broadcasting and Society, 1918–1939*, Beckenham, Croom Helm, 1983, p. 60.

Eckersley, writing in 1942, extended the idea of the potential of wired broadcasting to a vision of a system which is only at the start of the 21st century coming to fruition through the development of cable transmission:

> I have a dream about the future. I see the interior of a living-room. The wide windows are formed from double panes of glass, fixed and immovable. The conditioned air is fresh and warm ... Flush against the wall there is a translucent screen with numbered strips of lettering running across it ... These are the titles describing the many different "broadcasting" programmes which can be heard by just pressing the corresponding button ... Not a hint of background noise spoils the sound even though some of the performances take place half across Europe, the quality is so lovely that reproduction criticizes every detail of the playing and speaking ...

> Of course it is only as dream, but not so completely fantastic as some might imagine. It could all be done by using wires rather than wireless to distribute programmes. Let a cable, no thicker than a man's finger, be laid along the streets, outside the houses, and the main part of the installation is completed. The cable would only contain two or three conductors and tappings would be made on to these for branch feeders to bring the service into the houses. The branch ends in the houses would be connected to house receivers. The street cables would be taken to transmitters which would inject programmes into them.[97]

It is clear from the witnesses quoted above that there is a discrepancy between the passionate discourse and debate of the 1930s regarding the place of commercial broadcasting in Britain as a legitimate alternative to the public service model, and the subsequent consideration of the importance of the issues raised at the time. In the context of the various accounts discussed above, this historical enquiry seeks to provide a full and coherent exploration of commercial radio's impact both on audiences and on BBC policy before the Second World War. In doing so it tests the hypothesis that competition was of an order significant enough to have been a shaping force in the long-term development of broadcasting in Britain; specifically, that issues of audience measurement, scheduling and technology development were addressed as a result of commercial imperatives in addition to those of Public Service broadcasting. Beginning in anecdote and personal recollection based on conversations and correspondence with practitioners and listeners, the study examines documentary evidence to evaluate the veracity – or not – of claims made, frequently at some chronological distance from the times they recall. In this respect the author perceives his historical process in the creation of this work in terms similar to those described by E.H. Carr in his description of the historian's starting point:

> The historian starts with a provisional selection of facts and a provisional interpretation in the light of which that selection has been made – by others as well as by himself. As he works, both the interpretation and the selection and ordering of facts undergo subtle ... changes through the reciprocal action of one or the other ... [Thus History] is a continuous process of interaction

---

97   Eckersley, P.P. *The Power Behind the Microphone*, London, The Scientific Book Club, 1942, pp. 195–196.

between the historian and his facts, an unending dialogue between the present and the past.[98]

Elsewhere Carr comments that "The study of history is a study of causes";[99] this would seem to have an appropriateness in defining the present investigation, given that one of the main premises being tested herein is the reason for change in BBC policies in respect of its pre-war audience.

The primary research upon which the study is based has been developed through the following methods:

1. Correspondence from former listeners

Requests for recollections of listening in the 1930s were placed in a number of magazines and journals: *The Stage*, *Ariel* (the BBC staff journal), *Prospero* (the BBC journal for retired staff), *The Daily Telegraph*, *The Oldie*, *The Huddersfield Daily Examiner*, *The Star* (Sheffield), *The Liverpool Echo*, *The Lancashire Evening Telegraph*, *The Southern Daily Echo*, *The Evening Standard*, *Radio Bygones* and *The Vintage Programme Collectors' Circle Newsletter*. This produced 120 responses, of which a representative 10 per cent are quoted in Appendix C. While the material received was usually anecdotal and sometimes fallible in terms of memory, it did serve to illustrate a certain *zeitgeist* and cumulative sense of the cultural mood of the time. In addition a number of replies provided information of primary significance. For example, a reader of *The Stage*, Miss Billie Love, responded and provided information relating to her parents' work on Radio Normandy. The request in *Ariel* was fruitful in a number of ways; a response from Pierre Le Sève of the BBC World Service led to considerable family information relating to the running of Radio Normandy. Even more significant was a reply from Jacqueline Cavanagh, Director of the BBC Written Archive, Caversham, who was able to state that that the Archive contained a large number of files of material relating to the BBC's attitude to commercial competition in the 1930s. Furthermore, Ms Cavanagh was able to explain that much of this material had not been taken into account by previous historians.

2. Written archives

The Caversham Archive provided an underpinning of primary material, as did visits to the Selfridges Archive, prior to and after its absorption into the History of Advertising Trust's collection at Norwich. Visits to all three of these centres were necessary to establish corporate and industry thinking and responses, and demonstrated clearly that a sense of competition within British radio was a very real issue in the 1930s. In addition French libraries have been consulted, notably at the Pompidou Centre and the Archives of Radio France, in order to seek a Continental perspective. This proved particularly valuable in gaining a picture of individual stations, described in Appendix A.

---

98   Carr, E.H. *What is History?* Basingstoke, Palgrave, 2001 (reprint) p. 24.
99   Ibid., p. 81.

3. Interviews

Oral history work had always been seen as a key part of the research, and although in some cases time had proved the victor in this quest, the author has been fortunate to speak to a number of witnesses involved in the pre-war radio world; notable among these have been the late Frank Gillard, the late Desmond Hawkins and Leonard Miall. In addition, recordings from collectors of interviews with Stephen Williams, Roy Plomley and Bob Danvers-Walker have proved invaluable to the study. Regarding an understanding of contemporary technology, meetings with Peter Copeland, Conservation Manager at the British Library Sound Archive was necessary to clarify understanding of the relationship between content and technical issues.

In addition, some fieldwork has been undertaken. Visits to Fécamp (home of Radio Normandy), Paris (Poste Parisien) and Toulouse (Radio Toulouse) proved useful only to the extent that they demonstrated how comprehensively time has eradicated physical evidence and local human memory of the stations' existence.

For any historical researcher, within the "gathering" process of facts, information and evidence, not to mention the process of interpretation, there lies the danger of subjective and partial selection and emphases; that is to say, an agenda, albeit perhaps sometimes subconscious, that seeks to make convenient material fit a preconceived premise at the expense of evidence which proves a contrary viewpoint. In the present writer's case, it might be said that, given the anecdotal beginnings of the research, and the lack of any previous sustained examination of the subject, there could be a temptation either to select "friendly" facts and discard others, or to allow one discovery to simply initiate another, without a set plan of investigation.

Certainly, for every historian, the journey from the spring of an initial premise to the sea of a finished work is inevitably going to be one of discovery. That said, for this writer, that process was tempered by an awareness that the depth and importance of the commercial/Public Service broadcasting debate during the 1930s was one which required to be tested beyond the partiality of interested parties. Thus, just as IBC and JWT claims for rising audience figures are placed against BBC and Independent statistics, so the recorded interviews of commercial radio practitioners – Williams, Plomley and Danvers-Walker – have been balanced by BBC perspectives among primary and secondary sources, and tested against the commentaries of more recent independent historians such as Cardiff and Scannell, the statistical material found in the Caversham archive, and the numerical researches of Silvey and Pegg. Subjectivity of viewpoint has likewise been frequently observed and understood; it is clear for instance that a number of the ex-BBC personnel who wrote books criticizing the Corporation's policy during the years 1930–39 – for example, Eckersley, Cleghorn Thompson and Gorham – left the BBC under controversial and often acrimonious circumstances. Such factors require to be taken into account when evaluating the reliability of their roles as witnesses. At the same time, as a number of the American accounts state, the BBC had its own interests too. It is here that the study's variety of research sources has been most useful. Through a balance of oral history interviewing, analysis of textual sources, (including recordings of actual programmes) and field research such as visits to the British Library Sound Archive's recording conservation department and Continental station locations, a comparative and complementary picture has emerged which demonstrates to the satisfaction of this writer an underlying historical context in which the various witnesses' accounts may be examined and a trustworthy conclusion arrived at.

In short, the response to the material as it came to light has been cautious, evaluative in the context of other accounts, contemporary and otherwise, finally arriving at a critical conclusion where the sum of the parts – allowing for the partiality of subjective witnesses – can be seen to be undeniably greater than the whole. It is also important to remember that while this study focuses on one aspect of broadcasting between 1920 and 1939, this was by no means the only area of debate at the time. The BBC, the United Kingdom and the World were moving through complex times, and the issue of a broadcasting monopoly and the nature of Public Service radio were only two of many issues preoccupying those in policy-making decisions relating to the media of the time.

The structure of the writing itself is based on the concept that in order to test the hypothesis that competition between commercial and Public Service forces was a significant part of pre-war British broadcasting, the central exploration of the period (Part 3, "Competition and Response") has to be placed within the context of early developments in radio, and the subsequent social and cultural debates prevalent at the time of the expansion of broadcasting, both nationally in Britain and internationally, particularly within the USA. (Part 1, "Climate"). Part 2, "Production Issues" demonstrates how practical matters emanating from both commercial and Public Service imperatives shaped the sound and structure of 1930s radio. The technological issues relating to the recording and transportation of programme material was shown by research to have been of concern both to commercial and BBC interests, and a chapter documents this. Likewise primary evidence from BBC files and the J. Walter Thompson Archive requires a supporting chapter of evaluation which demonstrates the importance of radio advertising in the development of audience measurement in Britain. These areas of the writing provide practical "building blocks" upon which corporate policy and the evolution of new styles and attitudes to broadcasting are discussed in Part 4.

The decision to write Part 3, "Competition and Response" chronologically was based upon the fact that research showed an evolving and flexible situation, in which corporate thinking and response changed according to developments in technology, audience measurement and the circumstances of commercial competition. Thus, for example, BBC thinking regarding attacks on its monopoly differed considerably in 1928 and 1939, and it is therefore necessary for a study such as this to reflect how changing contemporary issues governed this thinking.

Although the main era under discussion is pre-war, it is considered necessary to develop the story beyond this time to encompass reasons for the demise of the 1930s form of Continent-based commercial radio, and the evolution of post-war Independent Radio. Thus, "The Fall and Rise of Post-War Commercial Radio", examines the temporary disappearance of French commercial radio as a supporting factor for the British entrepreneurs, the survival of Radio Luxembourg and the emergence of the 1960s pirate stations. The subsequent social and political pressure debates leading to the creation of Independent Local Radio require to be explained in order to demonstrate the wider context, and the long-term continuity in which this fuller picture of British radio history can be understood.

It will be noted that the work concludes with an extensive series of appendices; it is necessary to explain here the reasons for their range and extent. While the material contained therein is crucial to the study, its inclusion as appendices rather than within the main body of the text is based on several related factors, which may be summarized thus: the material represents discreet aspects of relevant research which the author wishes to draw specifically to the attention of the reader, as complementary yet self-contained source work. It is the author's intention to persuade the reader to focus attention on this material, while not "holding up" the narrative contained within the main body of the work. It is also felt that to extend the content of the main narrative further would be make the work unacceptably unwieldy.

Thus, through newly discovered evidence, primary sources and a re-evaluating of texts, many of which have not been taken into account in previous media histories of the time, *Crossing the Ether* seeks to reveal, explain and revalue an important part of broadcasting history, and in so doing to demonstrate that the evolution of British radio owes more to a competitive partnership between Public Service and commercial enterprise than has previously been acknowledged.

PART I
Climate

Chapter one

The Historical Context

I
It was all rather fun ... [100]

n order to reach the point where a full examination of a concerted pre-war attack on monopoly Public Service Broadcasting in Britain is possible, it is necessary to understand the process by which early radio evolved. We will therefore examine here the context in which this occurred. In so doing, we begin with an event which typifies the fraught relationship between sponsored entertainment and what was seen by some as a higher and more worthy purpose for the new medium.

Pre-History

On 15 June 1920, the Australian Prima Donna, Dame Nellie Melba, gave a thirty minute recital by wireless from the Marconi Company's Chelmsford works. It was the first broadcast by a professional performer, and it was sponsored by the *Daily Mail*.[101] Lord Northcliffe paid Melba £1,000 for the recital, and the next day his newspaper reported that: "The singer's glorious voice was clearly heard in Paris and Berlin and at The Hague, and messages from listeners-in in all parts of England record the success of this unique and wonderful concert."[102] Briggs rightly claims that "the Melba broadcast was a turning point in the public response to radio. It caught people's imagination."[103] Nevertheless although it was the highest profile of the Marconi Company's experiments, it was not the first. In January 1920, a 6 kW transmitter was erected at Chelmsford, and a month later a 15 kW aerial. Using this and some local musicians, the Marconi Company broadcast a short concert which received 214 reports from wireless amateurs and ships' radio operators, the greatest range being 1,450 miles.[104]

---

100   Peter Eckersley, quoted in Wander, Tim, *2MT Writtle, The Birth of British Broadcasting*, Stowmarket, Cappella, 1988, p. 69.

101   Ibid., p. 21.

102   *Daily Mail* 16 June 1920, quoted in Leslie Baily *Leslie Baily's BBC Scrapbooks, Volume 2: 1918–1939*, London, George Allen & Unwin, 1968, p. 78.

103   Briggs, Asa *The History of Broadcasting in the United Kingdom, Volume 1, The Birth of Broadcasting 1896–1927*, Oxford, Oxford University Press, 1995, p. 43.

104   Baker, W.J. *A History of the Marconi Company*, London, Methuen, 1970, pp. 184–185.

39

The success of this and the Melba recital, led to an enthusiastic exploration of the medium through the latter months of 1920. Baker states that:

> Demonstrations of the broadcasting of news items from the Chelmsford station to newspaper offices in Sheffield, Preston, Newcastle and Belfast, and also to Norwegian, Danish and Swedish Journals, were given during July and August ...[105]

On the other side of the Atlantic, on 2 November a newly established East Pittsburgh radio station owned by the Westinghouse Electric and Manufacturing Company, began broadcasting by reporting election returns in the Presidential race between Warren G. Harding and James M. Cox. In the United States this moment is traditionally seen as the birth of public radio.[106]

Even at this point a divergence in regulation was becoming apparent; the Pennsylvania broadcast had come under no form of control from a governing authority, while the Chelmsford transmissions were only possible through the approval of the British Postmaster-General, and was only granted for experimental purposes. The Melba broadcast had demonstrated that content, more than the wonder of technology, was what captured the imagination in the long term, and this was an element quickly seized on – without bureaucratic hindrance – by the early American broadcasters.[107]

It is important however to understand that the claim for the first *scheduled* radio broadcast lies neither with Britain nor the United States but with Holland. On 6 November 1919 from 8.00 p.m. – 11.00 p.m. a concert was broadcast from The Hague, organized by two Dutch pioneers, Hanso Henricus Schotanus and Steringa Idzerda. The programme was entitled "Soiree Musicale", and its claim as the first "real" radio broadcast in the world rests on the fact that the time, frequency and content was announced in advance of the broadcast in the press.[108] Idzerda, Dutch by birth, had been a student in Berlin, and had conducted radio experiments as early as 1913. At the start of the First World War he established the only radio manufactory in Holland, a company entitled "Wireless", and in 1915 the Dutch government invited him to develop a Direction Seeker Receiver, designed to pick up radio signals and determine their direction. This device proved so successful that German Zeppelin bombers stayed largely outside of Dutch airspace.[109] The electrical firm Philips was attracted to Idzerda's experiments, and during 1918 was a partner with Wireless in the development of wireless valves, enabling a dramatic improvement in transmission.[110]

The success of the first Soiree Musicale concert led to subsequent broadcasts, and Idzerda created a station identity – Telefonie-Station PCGG – under the banner of which the programmes could be received. From the start it became clear that an

105 Ibid., p. 185.
106 Douglas, p. 1.
107 Baker, p. 187. I explore the beginnings of American popular radio in my chapter "The American Way", see below.
108 *Steringa Idzerda*, pamphlet published by the Dutch Museum of Broadcasting, Hilversum, Holland, 1979, p. 1.
109 Ibid.
110 Ibid.

audience beyond the boundaries of Holland, with radio equipment they were keen to utilize, were tuning in, the largest audience being in Britain. Idzerda received gifts of records, cakes and even money from British listeners in grateful response to his broadcasts, and developed the habit of responding to English audiences in their own language during his programmes.[111]

Visitors from Britain came to The Hague to join the audience for the concerts, and Idzerda was able to finance his Soirees increasingly with money from Dutch and English benefactors. *The Daily Mail*, as we have seen, very much aware of the potential of this new medium in publicity terms, sponsored a series of Sunday Concerts which it advertised in its pages to English listeners. The circumstances behind this sponsorship might be seen as a microcosm of the subsequent development of continental-based programming supported by British advertising. On 23 November 1920 the Postmaster General informed the House of Commons that broadcasting of concerts from Chelmsford was to be suspended.[112] There was – in spite of growing public interest in radio as an entertainment medium – a sense that radio transmissions should not be used for other than official or military purposes. The wording used by the Postmaster General on this occasion is significant. He speaks of "interference with legitimate" services, on this occasion these being specifically the effect of Croydon aerodrome's newly installed air traffic control system.[113] Two significant consequences arose from the cancellation of the Chelmsford licence: firstly, public pressure grew for the continuation and development of entertainment broadcasting, which in turn ultimately resulted in the creation of the legendary Writtle station (see below). Secondly the *Daily Mail* looked elsewhere for popular radio to sponsor, taking out a year long contract with PCGG in the Hague.[114]

The success of these broadcasts, as far as the author of the Dutch Museum of Broadcasting's pamphlet is concerned, was partly instrumental in the establishment of the BBC.[115] Although it would be wrong to make such a claim as the exclusive origins of systematic British broadcasting, it is clear that the Dutch broadcasts played a major part in the development of public demand for a service. On 24 April 1922, just under six months before the first transmission of the British Broadcasting Company, the *London Illustrated News* carried a picture of a family in their sitting room, gathered around a receiving set while the father figure tuned in a signal. The caption was "This is how an English family listens to the Dutch concerts".[116]

After the creation of the BBC, the *Daily Mail*'s involvement with sponsorship of the Dutch broadcasts continued until 1924. By this time, under agreement with Northcliffe's organization, the broadcasts were in English. This provoked criticism from Dutch listeners, who wanted PCGG to broadcast programmes in their own language, and in November of that year, due to a change in regulation that

111   Ibid., p. 4.
112   Wander, p. 33.
113   Ibid.
114   Ibid., p. 154.
115   *Steringa Idzerda*, p. 6.
116   *Illustrated London News*, 24 April 1922, reproduced in *Steringa Idzerda*, p. 7.

prohibited foreign sponsorship, the transmission ceased. In 1926, they returned in a limited "pirate" form, this time sponsored by Kolster-Brandes (KB) radios.[117]

2MT Writtle

Subsequent to the suspension of the Marconi Company's Chelmsford broadcasts by the Post Office in November 1920, pressure grew on the government to provide listening material for the increasing number of Wireless clubs around Britain. In March 1921 the Wireless Society of London held a conference of 63 such societies with the intention of exploring "the possibility of regular telephone transmission from a high-power station to include all matters of interest to amateurs and to be on different wavelengths for calibration purposes".[118]

Pressure from this conference, in the press, and the clear success of PCGG gained a small amount of progress when on 15 August the Post Office granted the Marconi Company permission to broadcast half an hour of wireless telegraphy calibration signals from Chelmsford per week, stating that, while "the authorities concerned see no objection to the proposals so far as wireless telegraphy is concerned ... they are unable to agree to the inclusion of wireless telephony in the arrangement".[119] Williams has underlined the discrepancy between commercial and political interests in the birth of radio:

> Questions of the security and integrity of the nation-state were implicitly and at times explicitly raised, but were complicated by the fact that the political authorities were thinking primarily of wireless telephony while the manufacturers were looking forward to broadcasting.[120]

On 29 December 1921 the Societies presented a further request to the Right Hon. F.G. Kellaway, MP, the Postmaster General in the shape of a signed petition representing more than 3,300 wireless amateurs. The petition included a statement stressing the importance of radio as an educational medium of scientific significance to the general public, "and to keep them interested it is necessary to make the occupation interesting and even entertaining; hence the need for wireless telephonic speech and even music".[121] The statement ended:

> That the French authorities recognize the force of these considerations is evidenced by the transmission of speech and music that have already commenced under Government auspices from the Eiffel Tower. It is understood that it is intended to make these a regular feature like the time signals and meterological reports and it will be lamentable if England, where Wireless Telegraphy originated and whose Greenwich time is the time of the world, but who sends out no wireless time signals, should again fall behind other countries by reason of failure to move with events.[122]

117 Ibid., p. 10. See also Baron, p. 12.
118 Agenda item, London Wireless Conference, Mar 1921, quoted in Wander, p. 35.
119 Quoted in Wander, p. 35.
120 Williams, Raymond *Television: Technology and Cultural Form*, London, Fontana, 1974, p. 32.
121 Joint letter from the Wireless Societies of Great Britain, to the Postmaster General, 29 December 1921, reproduced in Wander pp. 149–150.
122 Ibid.

In less than a month, the pressure produced a positive response from the Post Office; on 13 January 1922, at the Third Annual Conference of Affiliated Radio Societies, Kellaway announced the authorisation of a 15 minute programme of music and speech to be included with the weekly calibration transmission.[123] Thus – almost overnight – the true birth of British broadcasting was achieved; from 14 February 1922 for eleven months, until 17 January 1923 a young team of Marconi engineers based in a hut at the village of Writtle, two miles from Chelmsford, provided the first scheduled broadcasting service in the country.[124] It is noteworthy that in order to establish regular entertainment on radio in the first place, pressure had to be exerted on official British government departments at a time when elsewhere around the world, including the USA and France, the idea of the medium as the disseminator of speech and music was widely accepted.

It is also significant that the main figure to emerge from Writtle's broadcasts was himself an anti-establishment figure in the form of Captain Peter Pendleton Eckersley. His character at once made him a popular favourite with listeners as British radio's first personality, and gained him suspicion from those in authority, in particular the Marconi Company's Head of Publicity, Arthur Burrows[125] (see below). Under its call sign, 2MT, the Writtle transmissions contained gramophone records, and occasionally "live" recitals, including on 2 February 1923, in the station's last days, the famous Danish tenor, Lauritz Melchior.[126] Other highlights included the first drama performed on radio: the charismatic Eckersley directed an extract from *Cyrano de Bergerac*, taking the title role himself. The broadcasts were full of a combination of technical jargon and schoolboy rhymes:

Hey diddle podrode
Two grids in one quadrode
The outer one forming the plate.
The electrons got muddled with so many grids
But the final mu value was eight.[127]

One of the most famous broadcasts remains one of the very first; Eckersley's summoning of listeners across the ether in February 1922:

Hello CQ, Hello CQ
This is Two Emma Toc, Two-oo Emma Toc.
Hello CQ this is Two Emma Toc,
Two-oo Emma Toc Wr-r-r-rittle calling.

---

123 Ibid., p. 36.

124 Ibid., p. 55.

125 Eckersley, Myles p. 46. Myles Eckersley here refers to his father as "part amateur comedian and actor, and part chattering professional technician". This author owes a debt of gratitude to Myles Eckersley for his support, for the valuable conversations about the early days of broadcasting, and for his generous donation of a number of rare recordings of his father delivering talks to various Wireless Societies during the 1950s and 1960s. P.P. Eckersley is one of the most fascinating and controversial figures in broadcasting history.

126 Wander, pp. 78–79. Melchior caused consternation when he sang with too much volume for the Writtle equipment to sustain, believing that the louder he sang, the further his voice would carry on the airwaves. (Wander, p. 79) The subsequent technical problems gave rise to a phrase which was to remain in Radio Engineers' vocabulary for some years – "Melchior breakdown" (Wander, 79–80).

127 Eckersley, Myles p. 49.

Is it all right Ash?
Kirke is it all right? You're sure?
What, what do you say?
Oh it's blasting, Hello CQ, CQ it's blasting, do you want a blast;
I blast the whole lot of it.[128]

One of Eckersley's most notable confrontations with authority, and one which in some ways acts as a metaphor for his place in the history of broadcasting, is recounted by his son Myles:

> ... Peter burst into the hut [during a broadcast], grabbed the mike and said he was sorry he was late and added: "There was fog on the line ... of course there wasn't really; if the porter even breathes on the line at Stratford, the London and North Eastern railway trains run late for the next fortnight".

> That innocent statement brought him an immediate rebuke from Head Office. A furious railway company director had rung up to complain ... Peter was made to realize, forcibly, that in the serious-minded Britain of 1922 there was more to broadcasting than lighthearted banter.[129]

The British Broadcasting Company

The BBC – as the British Broadcasting Company – was formed on 18 October 1922. Daily broadcasts began on 14 November from 2LO in Marconi House, the Strand. It was registered on 15 December, but did not receive its Post Office licence until 18 January 1923.[130] Under the Chairmanship of Lord Gainford, the Company's first board of directors represented the electrical firms from which the Company was constructed: Marconi's Wireless Telegraph Co. Ltd, Metropolitan-Vickers Electrical Export Co. Ltd, The Radio Communication Company Ltd, The Hotpoint Electrical Appliance Co. Ltd, The General Electric Company Ltd and The Western Electric Company Ltd. A number of these companies had already been involved with radio experiments; alongside Marconi's 2LO, Western Electric had opened another London station, 2WP as well as 5IT in Birmingham, and Metropolitan Vickers began broadcasting in Manchester on 2ZY – all in early 1922.[131] The Company that brought the interests of the electrical manufacturers together was launched with a share issue of 99,993 Cumulative Ordinary Shares of £1 each, and the prospectus stated:

> The holders of the Cumulative Ordinary Shares are entitled to receive out of the profits of the Company a fixed Cumulative Dividend at the rate of seven and a half per cent per annum on the capital for the time being paid up or credited as paid up thereon but are not entitled to any further or other participation in profits.[132]

Thus the BBC was at its beginnings a commercial company, and it remained so

128 Quoted in Wander, pp. 71–72. "CQ" was the radio code for "everybody" – the audience. "Kirke was
     H.L. Kirke, one of the Writtle team, and "Ash" Noel Ashbridge, who ultimately succeeded Eckersley
     as the BBC's chief Engineer in 1929.
129 Eckersley, Myles, p. 50.
130 Briggs vol 1, p. 112.
131 Crisell, Andrew An Introductory History of Broadcasting, London, Routledge, 1997, p. 13.
132 BBC Prospectus, 1922, in Briggs Vol. 1, p. 115.

until receiving its charter in 1927. The involvement of commercial interests enabled the fledgling organisation to house itself temporarily, prior to finding its first real home in Savoy Hill. The General Electric Company, one of the partners in the new enterprise, opened its London Head Office in a new building on London's Kingsway in 1921. The BBC's first office was here – in two rooms in which were housed the entire staff of the BBC.[133] When broadcasting began it was from the London premises of another of the constituent owner-companies, Marconi's, who had operated 2LO during the summer of 1922 from Marconi House, The Strand, and it was from here that the first BBC transmissions took place in November 1922.[134] On 19 March 1923 Reith and his 31 staff moved to its first permanent base, 2 Savoy Hill,[135] within the building of the Institution of Electrical Engineers, built in 1889 and with frontage which overlooked the Thames Embankment just west of Waterloo Bridge. The policy of the Institution of Electrical Engineers was "to make space available for letting to 'allied' companies or organizations with electrical interests. The BBC was an obvious candidate as it was, in 1923, largely financed by major electrical companies intent on selling wireless receivers".[136]

Other BBC stations opened around the country in quick succession; on 15 November 1922 both the Birmingham and Manchester stations – 5IT and 2ZY began transmissions, on 24 December Newcastle (5NO) went on air, on February 13 Cardiff (5WA) opened and on 6 March Glasgow (5SC) started broadcasting, followed on 17 October by Bournemouth (6BM) and finally on 24 October 1924, Belfast (2BE).[137]

A Wireless Receiving Licence which had been introduced for experimental listeners previously, the so-called "Wireless Amateurs", was transferred to ordinary listeners on 1 November 1922, the cost being ten shillings per annum.[138] The purchase of receiving licences provides a vivid picture of the enthusiasm with which the new medium was taken up and is valuable at this point to consider over the period covered by this dissertation. In the first five weeks after 1 November 1922 35,777 licences were sold. By the turn of the decade sales were increasing at the rate of one million per year, with 3,411,910 sold in 1930 and 5,263,017 in 1932.[139] 1936 saw the distribution of licences to 65 per cent of households in Britain, that is to say 7,955,944 sold out of an estimated number of 12,259,885 households, representing a total population (utilizing figures from the 1931 census) of 46,189,445.[140] Three years later, at the end of the decade, 8,893,582 licences were sold.[141] Given that a central premise of this book is that BBC paternalism and

133 Hennessey, Brian *Savoy Hill, The Early Years of British Broadcasting*, Romford, Ian Henry Publications, 1996, p. 7.
134 Ibid., p. 8.
135 Ibid., p. 14.
136 Ibid., pp. 13–14.
137 BBC Reference Library, Broadcasting House, *Outstanding BBC Dates*, unpublished fact sheet, 1954, pp. 1–5.
138 Pegg, p. 40.
139 Ibid., p. 7.
140 *BBC Annual, 1937*, London, BBC, p. 59.
141 Pegg, p. 7.

sabbatarianism alienated much of the licence-paying audience during this period, allowing the development of populist commercial competition in breach of its monopoly, it is important to note that of the last figure quoted, half was made up of people earning between £2.50 and £4.00 per week, with another 2,000,000 earning considerably less than this.[142] Unlike the theatre or the concert hall, radio was an invasive medium, and as Hobsbawm has said:

> Its capacity for speaking simultaneously to untold millions, each of whom felt addressed as an individual, made it an inconceivably powerful tool of mass information and, as both rulers and salesmen immediately recognized, for propaganda and advertisement.[143]

As has been already stated, the British Broadcasting Company was commercial in the sense that one reason for its creation was the impetus from electrical manufacturers to capitalize on the growing demand for radio receivers and therefore programmes to RECEIVE on those sets. In addition the issue of direct sponsorship was raised in both the Wireless Broadcasting Licence of 1923[144] and The Sykes Committee Report of 1923[145], the first major official documents on British Broadcasting. An obscurity in clause 4 of the original licence relating to the prohibition of advertising was rewritten by the Sykes Committee after a witness to the Committee, Lord Riddell questioned the legality of a concert broadcast by the BBC and "sponsored" by Harrods.[146] F.J. Brown, Secretary to the Post Office defended the broadcast stating in an oral reply to Riddell that it would be unfortunate if the Postmaster-General had refused to allow the BBC "to accept a concert of a character markedly superior to that which they could themselves provide out of their present comparatively limited resources, merely because the giver announced in the newspapers beforehand that he was giving this concert".[147] Thus a significant change to legislation was put in place by the Sykes Committee whereby Clause 4 of the original licence, which forbade advertising, was modified in Clause 2 of the Sykes Report "so that it forbade direct advertising while specifically allowing the BBC to broadcast sponsored programmes and commercial information approved for broadcasting by the Postmaster-General".[148] Under the agreement set out by the Sykes Committee a certain amount of sponsored programming was broadcast by the BBC during 1925 and 1926. Eight such programmes during 1925, included sponsorship by *The Evening Standard*, *The News of the World*, *The Daily Herald*, *The Weekly Dispatch* and *Titbits*. *The Daily Graphic* sponsored one concert in 1925 and another (the only one that year) in 1926.[149] By this time the

142   Briggs, p. 254.
143   Hobsbawm, Eric *The Age of Extremes*, London, Michael Joseph, 1994, p. 196.
144   Cd. 1822 (1923), Wireless Broadcasting Licence by the Postmaster-General to the British Broadcasting Company Limited.
145   Cd. 1951, (1923), Broadcasting Committee Report. The Sykes Committee Report was published on 1 October 1923.
146   Briggs II, p. 172.
147   F.J. Brown in oral evidence of Lord Riddell to the Sykes Committee, 29 May 1923, quoted in Briggs Vol. 1, p. 172.
148   Briggs, p. 172.
149   Ibid.

Crawford Committee had published its report which paved the way for the Company to move towards becoming a Corporation, and sponsorship of programmes ceased.[150] It was the Crawford Committee which finally set the seal on a system of broadcasting which would differ radically from that of America, stating that "the United States system of uncontrolled transmission is unsuited to this country".[151] The first *BBC Handbook*, published in 1928 contained a statement which encapsulated the newly founded Corporation's attitude to its audience:

> In sum, experience has evolved a practical working rule, "Give the public something slightly better than it now thinks it likes". One has to be in the business itself to realize all the implications that are involved in this terse formula.[152]

The General Strike

It may be seen that the birth of English language broadcasting into Britain – both domestically and from outside the United Kingdom – was driven strongly by commercial imperatives of one kind or another. Set against this was a sense within the BBC which grew as it moved towards and beyond its first charter of 1927, of an almost divine responsibility towards the moral well-being of its audience. It was this increasing paternalism which alienated working class listeners and prepared the way for the commercial assault on the Corporation's monopoly from 1930 onwards. A pivotal moment in this shift was the (then) Company's performance during the General Strike of May 1926. The BBC as Giddings has said, considered its approach to the Strike to have been correct, as did Baldwin's government after the event. However,

> This may well be a difficult impression to hold in the light of the fact that the Prime Minister had access to the microphone (and had BBC help in drafting his broadcast speeches) but the leader of the Opposition, Ramsay MacDonald, was not allowed to broadcast. Nor were the trade-union leaders given access to radio broadcasting, and even the Archbishop of Canterbury, who wished to broadcast a message of reconciliation, was denied access to the airwaves. The government's was the sole voice to be heard during the crisis.[153]

In the *Radio Times* Ellen Wilkinson, Labour MP for Middlesborough voiced the following complaint:

> The attitude of the BBC during the Strike caused pain and indignation to many subscribers. I travelled by car over two thousand miles during the Strike and addressed very many meetings. Everywhere the complaints were bitter that a national service subscribed to by every class should have given only one side of the dispute. Personally I feel like asking the Postmaster General for my licence fee back.[154]

---

150   Cd. 2599, *Report of The Broadcasting Committee, 1925*, published 1926, para 4., p. 5.

151   Ibid.

152   *BBC Handbook, 1928*, London, BBC, p. 71.

153   Giddings, Robert "John Reith and the Rise of Radio", from *Literature and Culture in Modern Britain, Volume 1, 1900–1929* ed. Bloom, Clive, London, Longman, 1993, p. 160.

In fact Reith found himself walking a political tightrope between maintaining complete independence and being directly commandeered by the Government as advocated by Winston Churchill. He was forced to take decisions which, if proved wrong, would strengthen the lobby for outright political control of the BBC. It was for this reason that, as Scannell and Cardiff state "against his own better judgement, he refused the requests from the Archbishop of Canterbury and from Ramsay MacDonald ... to be allowed to broadcast",[155] thus being seen by advocates of take-over as moving someway towards meeting their demands. The position of the new Corporation in relation to the Government remained a difficult one, and as Curran and Seaton have pointed out, "the General Strike initiated a pattern that was to recur throughout the 1930s: the BBC was forced to pass off government intervention as its own decision".[156] Reith, in a letter to Prime Minister Baldwin on 13 May 1926, had justified his actions then in these terms: "Assuming the BBC is for the people and that the Government is for the people, it follows that the BBC must be for the Government in this crisis too."[157] Projecting forward from this statement to future crisis, Scannell and Cardiff have commented:

> Munich was the first major crisis (Suez was another) which put to the test that syllogism as a definitive precedent for the role of the BBC in a national crisis. In this case the BBC came to see that the government, in spite of own claims, was manifestly not acting in the national interest. Having grasped that nettle, the BBC saw its final responsibility as resting with and to the audience, not the state.[158]

The BBC's position in relation to the problem of the years immediately after the General Strike may be summed up in its attitude to the projected radio play, Reginald Berkeley's *Machines*, which carries the distinction of being the first banned play for radio. Berkeley had negotiated for a radio play which explored the danger of mankind becoming dominated by machinery and technology in the Spring of 1927 with the BBC's Director of Drama, R.E. Jeffrey.[159] Jeffrey was a strong-minded man with specific and dogmatic ideas about what radio drama could and could not do.[160] On 4 March 1927 Jeffrey had sent a letter to Berkeley stating that

---

154   *The Radio Times*, 28 May 1926, p. 16.

155   Scannell and Cardiff, p. 32.

156   Curran and Seaton, p. 121. Curran and Seaton cite the case of Government intervention in the matter of Harry Pollitt, a communist, a talk by whom the BBC had proposed to broadcast in 1935. When the BBC questioned the protest, "the Postmaster General wrote to Reith pointing out that as the Corporation licence was due for renewal, it would be wiser to comply with government demands".

157   John Reith to Baldwin, 13 May 1926, quoted in Reith, *Into the Wind, Hodder & Stoughton*, London, 1949, p. 108. Much pressure was coming from Churchill, Chancellor of the Exchequer, to "suppress news of successful stoppages ..." (ibid., p. 109). Reith's account is fascinating, and demonstrates the clear disagreement between Prime Minister and Chancellor, conveying a real sense of the anguish behind some of the decisions made.

158   Scannell, Paddy and Cardiff, David "Serving the Nation: Public Service Broadcasting Before the War", in *Popular Culture Past and Present*, ed. Waites, Bernard et al, Croom Helm, Beckenham, 1982, p. 177.

159   Beck, Alan *The Invisible Play, BBC Radio Drama 1922–1928*, Canterbury, Sound Journal CD Book, 2000, 8.4.3.

160   See Briggs vol. 1, pp. 256–257. Jeffrey had been Station director at the Glasgow station, 5SC, moving to Aberdeen (2DB) before transferring as Drama Director to Savoy Hill in 1924 (Briggs vol. 1, p. 192).

"controversial matter was to be excluded".[161] The script arrived at the BBC – by this time a Corporation – in October 1927, and immediately Jeffrey was alarmed by the content. It was clear that the play was a political comment on the Government's handling of the General Strike, with stereotyped characters painting a strongly left-wing case, and a central character, firmly rooted in the working class, pitted against Conservative despots. Writing to Berkeley in an undated letter quoted by Beck, accompanying the returned script, Jeffrey rejects the play with the words "The subject of the play is far too controversial for purposes of broadcasting."[162] He goes on:

> Much of the context of this play could be extracted and used with great force against us as being of a propaganda nature ... The hero, if I may call him such, is drawn as almost the sanest man in the piece, which is another argument against our using it. The character of Colonel Willoughby, the Conservative, is of the conventional type which again does not help matters from our point of view.[163]

Reith's own view of the BBC's role during and immediately after the Strike was one of satisfaction, and pointed the way forward. In a letter written in May 1926 to Sir Evelyn Murray, Secretary of the Post Office, he said:

> The recent Emergency proved conclusively, if proof were required, how important a factor Broadcasting can be in the life of the community ... We are anxious to take a lead in ordinary times, as we were through force of circumstances bound to take in the Emergency ...[164]

The change brought about by the establishment of the BBC's Charter saw it transformed from "company" to "institution" committed to carrying out functions cooperative with the will of Parliament and – as with the General Strike – sharing, often under sufferance, the idea of what was to be the "national interest".[165] As Scannell and Cardiff have further commented:

> The limits to this collaboration were set by the broadcasters' sense of responsibility to their audience and a realization, hard won in the light of

161   Beck, 8.4.3.

162   Ibid., 8.4.5.

163   Ibid.

164   Letter, Reith to Murray, 27 May 1926, BBC Written Archives, Caversham, WAC R34/317/1, also quoted in Scannell and Cardiff, p. 34. Scannell and Cardiff go on to cite Murray's significant reply, also held in the same file, that "the existing policy of avoiding the broadcasting of controversial matter should be maintained during the remaining period of the Company's licence" (Scannell and Cardiff, p. 34).

165   Middlemas, Keith *Politics in Industrial Society*, London, Andre Deutsch, 1980 : "The phrase 'governing institution' is to be understood as a description of a body which assumes functions devolved on it by government, shares some or all of the assumptions about national interests held by government, and accepts aims similar to those laid down by government; with the fundamental qualification that this form of association is not compulsory, but voluntary to the extent that it takes place within general limits derived, negatively, from the evidence of what the institution's constituent members will or will not accept. Prevailing economic and social circumstances, like the conditions which led to the shop stewards' movement in the First World War, or to the employers' volte-face on state intervention in the late 1920s, rather than theoretical considerations of where collaboration conflicted with their natural or primordial interests, governed the speed with which institutions succumbed to government's desires", p. 373.

experience by 1939, that in the last resort their task was to serve the interests of the people not the government of the day.[166]

Ironically just such a view had been expressed by Cecil Lewis, Organiser of Programmes under Arthur Burrows in the British Broadcasting Company. In 1924, he writes of:

> the fundamental necessity that this force should remain the independent servant of the people, willing to accept everything in fair debate, but non-political, non-governmental and non-sectarian in control, and that it should be in some adequate manner insured against the possibility of being bribed, or bullied into partisan view on any question whatsoever.[167]

The Sacred Cause

The early days of British broadcasting provide a fascinating study of human character in its chief protagonists. One of the most ebullient of these – as we have seen – was Peter Eckersley, who, during broadcasts from the Marconi Writtle station combined experiment with entertainment, and at the very start his original personality, and his ability for mimicry, defined the medium as one with the potential for immense popular appeal. He delighted early listeners with his humour, and his parody of a popular Tosti ballad at the close of test transmissions:

> Dearest, the concert's ended, sad wails the heterodyne,
> You must switch off your valves, I must soon switch off mine.
> Write back and say you've heard me, your "hook-up", and
> where and how.
> Quick! For the engine's failing, good-bye, you old low-brow![168]

Eckersley became the BBC's first Chief Engineer, but was sacked by Reith in 1929 after a divorce scandal. That apart, the two personalities were diametrically opposed in terms of their image of the new medium. As Eckersley's son, Myles, has stated in his biography of his father,

> Eckersley and Reith were quite different in manner and outlook. Reith was a flinty Aberdonian, aware of sin in himself and in others … with a view of broadcasting which, in Peter's opinion, was too cautious and limited. In Peter there was some inconsistency and a tendency to argue for argument's sake; a born broadcaster, a sceptic and an agnostic, … Eckersley was to fundamentally disagree with Reith about the aim of the BBC.[169]

As we shall see, Eckersley was to become a powerful supporter and developer of Continent-based commercial radio in competition with the BBC, as well as an advocate of Radio Relay broadcasting which would consolidate the damage caused to the BBC monopoly by these major competitors during the 1930s. Significantly

166   Scannell and Cardiff, p. 39.
167   Lewis, C.A. *Broadcasting from Within*, London, Newnes, 1924, p. 177.
168   Baily, Leslie *Leslie Baily's BBC Scrapbooks, volume 1, 1918–1939*, London, George Allen and Unwin, 1968, p. 76.
169   Eckersley, Myles, p. 66.

he was later to write in his book, *The Power Behind the Microphone*, "Britain is … a free country, but freedom is doled out in limited quantities".[170] Elsewhere he states:

> The attitude of the BBC has always been wholly political. If it is conscious of the artistic point of view it abhors it. There is, it is true, an attempt, not always successful, to avoid the more obvious forms of vulgarity, but this has little value when there is so little appreciation of the difference between good and bad taste.[171]

In the closing pages of this most prophetic book, Eckersley looks back from 1941 to the radio war of the 1930s, whilst at the same time predicting a system of broadcasting which must have seemed almost impossibly remote at the time, yet which have nevertheless come to pass:

> I do not think for a moment that commercial broadcasting should replace the BBC, I do suggest it would most usefully accompany it … My idea is that we should go on using foreign stations for advertising programmes until the wires offer us enough channels to introduce the commercial in parallel with the BBC service.[172]

It is interesting to note that a number of the leading figures in the foundation of the BBC wrote memoirs within a very short time of the launch of the service, and these texts form an important source of witness to the *zeitgeist* of the era, and the thinking that informed the policy of broadcasters. In addition to Lewis, Arthur Burrows, the first Director of Programmes and later the first secretary of the International Broadcasting Union[173] wrote *The Story of Broadcasting*,[174] published in 1924, the same year Hodder and Stoughton published Reith's *Broadcast Over Britain*[175]. There is a sense in all three of these works of aspiration as much as achievement. Burrows speaks of the future as being an "uncharted sea":

> Broadcasting today … is really only in the position of the prehistoric fisherman who put out a few hundred yards from shore in his frail coracle or dug-out. He could see the greater ocean, but its extent was hidden by a horizon set by the fisherman's limited knowledge of materials and their uses.[176]

There is also a sense pervading these early texts of the loftiness, even the divinity of this aspiration. Burrows' book ends with the following postscript:

> In a letter written by Edward Pease, the "Father of Railways", in 1857 (a year before his death), there is the following:
>
> > "I only did what every well-wisher to his friends and his country ought to do. It seems to me that Divine Providence has condescended largely to bless our designs and efforts for the good of the world, and we have great cause to thank Him for the benefit He has enabled us to confer on humanity".

---

170   Eckersley, p. 51.

171   Ibid., p. 55.

172   Ibid., p. 248.

173   Briggs vol. 1, p. 34.

174   Burrows, A.R. *The Story of Broadcasting*, London, Cassell, 1924.

175   Reith, J.C.W. *Broadcast Over Britain*, London, Hodder and Stoughton, 1924.

176   Burrows, p. 177.

What finer ideal could be placed before those who are privileged at this moment to be serving the nation on the staff of the BBC?[177]

Reith is even more reverential:

It is well that we should be conscious of the relativity of all things, and remember that complete dissolution of the manifested universe would quickly follow on any suspension of the functionings of the universal ether. We should also be aware of the feebleness and errors of our own perceptions and intelligence, and from this awareness, turn to the contemplation of the Omnipotence holding all things together by the word of power, in Whom, as in the ether, we live and move and have our being.[178]

The idea of a divine cause, and of being guardians of an almost magical and sacred power, was to inform the famous Latin inscription in the entrance hall of Broadcasting House, quoted at the start of the previous chapter. The concept also partly explains the growing righteous indignation with which the BBC sought to defend its monopoly against populist programming from the Continental stations during the late 1920s and early 1930s. Broadcasting House at its opening in 1932 was a consecrated "Temple"[179], and that temple was not to be violated. Williams has discussed the nature of public service broadcasting in the context of British society, and identifies the fact that the BBC was a producer of programmes rather than simply a "transmitter of broadcasting".[180] Reith was later to pour scorn on the commercial operators for not being programme *makers* but merely advertising agencies (see below). The complete control over both technology and content implied by the BBC monopoly and its confirmation by Charter in 1927 was informed by the fact that "the definition of broadcasting as a public service … had … been specialized, by its early controllers, to a positive programming policy".[181] Williams also identifies a key element in what he calls "the British solution" to broadcasting as being the fact that:

A dominant version of the national culture had already been established, in an unusually compact ruling-class, so that public service could be effectively understood and administered as service according to the values of an existing public definition, with an effective paternalist definition of both service and responsibility.[182]

Later in this book we will examine the issue of the BBC's Sunday broadcasting policy, and the opportunities this provided for commercial competition. There is further evidence of the lofty image the BBC conceived for itself in its relation to its

---

177 Ibid., p. 183.

178 Reith *Broadcast Over Britain*, p. 224.

179 Inscription in Broadcasting House Entrance Hall. See head of introductory chapter for full translation.

180 Williams, p. 33.

181 Ibid.

182 Ibid. Williams contrasts the British model with the American, where "… the finance for production … was drawn from advertising, in its two forms of insertion and sponsorship. More clearly than anywhere else, because all countervailing factors were less strong, the American institutions realised the pure forms of a simple applied technology. The manufacturing institutions, both directly from the sale of sets and indirectly in the supply of advertising money, determined the shape of broadcasting institutions. Thus the broadcasting public was effectively, from the beginning, the competitive broadcasting market." (pp. 34–35)

audience in terms of the nature of its programming relating to the monarchy. Curran and Seaton state of the 1930s that "during a decade of hunger marches and 'red united fighting fronts' the BBC regarded a succession of royal broadcasts as the triumph of outside broadcasts and actuality reporting."[183] Crisell qualifies this criticism as not being straightforward insensitivity:

> Though the 1930s were a period of economic slump and severe unemployment, the Corporation held the artless if well-meant belief that it could bring greater solace to working people by giving them a glimpse of the lives of their king and queen than by holding a mirror to their own.[184]

Escapism in the popular arts and media played a role in public entertainment. Away from the polarized images of regal pomp and social deprivation, radio offered the possibility of a third option, that of pure uncompromising populist entertainment specifically aimed at the part of society that would most appreciate it. BBC policy was here at its most vulnerable, particularly in respect of its Sunday programming, and the gap in its popular understanding was to be ruthlessly exposed by a determined group of entrepreneurs, under the example of one man.

Captain Leonard Plugge

Central in the commercial challenge to the BBC was the character of Captain Leonard F. Plugge, who in 1930 founded The International Broadcasting Company in premises at 11 Hallam Street, London W1, immediately adjacent to the still unfinished Broadcasting House. Plugge was one of the most remarkable personalities in British broadcasting, a man who went on to become a millionaire through radio, and about whom legends grew up. In 1939 the – by this time – hugely profitable IBC published a promotional booklet, in which Plugge's first attempt at commercial broadcasting was explained:

> One evening in 1925 a few listeners trying to "get" a foreign station on their primitive receiving sets picked up the Eiffel tower station from Paris and heard what proved to be the first commercial broadcast to Great Britain – a fashion talk sponsored by Selfridges. Three of them actually took the trouble to write and say so![185]

As has already been stated, the first sponsored concert had in fact already been broadcast from Idzerda's Dutch station by this time; however the importance of Plugge's first experiment was that it was to develop into an on-going industry which would spawn rivals and imitators throughout the subsequent fifteen years, only to be halted by the outbreak of the Second World War. Leonard Plugge features strongly throughout this story, as the true founding father of British commercial radio. Plugge's central precept was to sell air-time to British advertisers on Continental stations from whom he in turn had purchased transmission time during periods when the stations were not broadcasting in their native language. He carried out many experimental broadcasts across Europe, but by far the most

183 Curran and Seaton, 1991, p. 145.

184 Crisell, p. 39.

185 Promotional Booklet, *This is the IBC*, London, IBC, London, 1939, p. 3.

successful of these was the partnership he established with Radio Normandie, renaming the station in an English image as Radio Normandy. This in turn prompted competition from the rival Wireless Publicity Ltd, which firm ultimately developed Radio Luxembourg, the station which finally eclipsed the IBC stations in terms of financial and audience success, and which was to be the only station to survive World War II. Programming requirements from the Continental stations prompted the establishment of recording studios at the London headquarters of a number of Advertising agencies, notably the London Press Exchange, the J. Walter Thompson Organization and the IBC's own programme wing, the Universal Programmes Corporation. These developments will be examined in depth in the chapters, "Radio for Sale" and "Recording Strategies for Radio Before World War II" (see below).

Plugge chose to pronounce his name as "Plooje", from Dutch ancestry, until he stood (successfully) as prospective Conservative candidate for the Chatham constituency of Rochester in Kent at the 1935 General Election, when, using Free Radio as his ticket, he punned his name on handbills with the slogan "Plugge in for Chatham".[186] In a radio programme broadcast in January 2000, his son Frank spoke of his father as a man of many talents, an inventor of radio telephones for cars, as a scientific researcher for the RAF and an engineer for the London Underground, who broke pickets to drive trains during the General Strike.[187] By the end of the 1930s the IBC had moved into impressive new premises at 37 Portland Place, and Plugge possessed a yacht at Cannes and a villa overlooking Hyde Park.[188] Plomley states that Plugge also claimed to be the first person to own a car radio.[189] In the mid 1920s he developed a profitable business by obtaining publishing rights in Britain for continental stations' programme schedules (rights which were gladly given for publicity purposes) and then reselling the details to the British press, at that time anxious to satisfy the public curiosity for overseas listening. His profits were high, and "probably his biggest customer was the BBC, which published a weekly magazine called *World Radio*".[190] Plugge's first foray into broadcasting after the Eiffel Tower experiment of 1925 came in 1929, with series of half hour programmes sponsored by Vox records which were broadcast from

---

186   BBC Written Archives, Caversham, R34/959.

187   Plugge, Frank, interviewed for radio programme, *The First Pirate*, BBC Radio 4, 14 January, 2000, producer, King, Brian. The French Government was later to award Plugge with the Order of the Chevalier de Légion d'Honneur. Plugge complained that he was at the lowest level of the order (Frank Plugge).

188   Ibid.

189   Plomley, Roy, p. 122 Plomley also locates the house as being "a four-storied stone mansion in Hamilton Place, with a floodlit terrace overlooking Hyde Park. A household staff of fifteen ministered to him and his family, as well as looking after the dining-room with its fountains and its walls of pale Carrara marble, the library, which was a Florentine room decorated in Renaissance style, the private cinema which seated fifty and – surely the most remarkable room in the house – the master's bathroom, which featured a Dictaphone, a radio, four telephone lines and a television. His yacht, the "Lenny Ann", which was registered at Cannes, was reputed to have gold-plated taps"(Plomley, p. 126). Frank Plugge disputes the gold-plated taps (Radio 4, January 2000). The Hyde Park House was used during the 1960s as the main location for the Mick Jagger/James Fox film, *Performance* (BBC Radio 4 Feature).

190   Ibid.

Radio Toulouse. According to Plomley "those programmes produced the extraordinary number of 1,500 letters each week."[191]

That Plugge was an unusual personality is evident to anyone who examines not only his life and work but his relationships with others. For his son Frank he was not an easy father:

> He wasn't really like a father, because he was never around. We lived in separate houses so if he wanted to bring some friends round he would arrive and introduce his family as if we were on parade, and we would be expected to come down and sit and meet his friends, and then he'd go off and we wouldn't see him again for three weeks. I remember my sister Gail saying to me when she was about 5 or 6, "I wish we had a real Daddy".[192]

Leonard Plugge died in 1980 in California at the age of 92.[193] After the war, and the demise of his personal radio interests, the IBC continued to make programmes for Radio Luxembourg as an independent production house, and also to act as a recording studio, run by George Clouston, the musician, and Eric Robinson, well known during the 1950s and 1960s as a television conductor under the title "IBC Sound Recording Studios Ltd".[194] Complete continuity in the story of British Commercial Radio was assured when, on 8 October 1973, the first land-based Independent Local Radio Station opened, London Broadcasting Company, with the IBC owning 13.3 per cent of its shares.[195]

While the development of Plugge's 1930s radio empire is a motif throughout this story, it is important to continually remind ourselves that commercial competition would not have achieved the success it did without the BBC's steadfast adherence to its Sunday broadcasting policy, a policy directly emanating from John Reith's strict Sabbatarian principles, which alienated a large number of working class listeners during the 1930s. It was the direct confrontation between these two elements, the BBC's lofty pursuance of a public service ideal, and the spirit of the entrepreneur as personified by Captain Leonard F. Plugge, which was to inform the conflict within the media during the decade prior to the Second World War. Change in the BBC has frequently come as a result of exterior pressure, be it from competition or from the international climate of the time. In the 1930s this pressure created a real crisis in the BBC's concept of itself as a monopoly Public Service Broadcaster, a crisis which was resolved in the short term by the coming of the War, only to re-emerge in the latter half of the twentieth century.

191   Ibid., p. 123.
192   Plugge, Frank BBC Radio 4. Gail Plugge later joined a black revolutionary group, and was ultimately murdered by its leader, Malcolm X.
193   Ibid.
194   Skues, p. 4. See also Baron, pp. 21 & 81.
195   Baron, p. 21.

Chapter two

Culture at a Crisis[196]: Broadcasting and British Society in the 1920s and 1930s

Oh yes, all down the backs, there'd be poles everywhere. They'd use clothes props and brooms and things like that – nail 'em together. As long as it was high up you'd get a better sound, d'you see?[197]

Introduction

In 1937 G.D.H. and M.I. Cole, in *The Condition of Britain* drew a comparison with Britain as Disraeli had seen it in 1845 in his novel, *Sybil*, which he had subtitled "The Two Nations": "There were, he said, two nations in England, confronting each other for the most part with mutual disapproval and lack of understanding, and incapable of living together on terms of common humanity".[198] For Disraeli the two nations were rich and poor, the eradication of which divisions the Coles were to question in their book:

> Is the British people still divided by the same irreconcilable antagonisms as confronted the Chartists in 1836, or has modern "progress" succeeded if not in obliterating the sharp distinction between the two sections of the people, at any rate in so softening antagonism that the old indictment no longer rings true?[199]

---

196   The title of this chapter derives from Leavis, F.R. *Mass Civilisation and Minority Culture*, London, The Minority Press, 1930, p. 3.

197   Oral history interview, Warrington, conducted by Moores, Shaun and quoted in " 'The Box on the Dresser': memories of early radio and everyday life", in *Media Culture and Society* Volume 10, No. 1, January 1988, p. 29.

198   Cole, G.D.H. and M.I. *The Condition of Britain*, London, Gollancz, 1937, p. 25.

199   Ibid.

The social climate of the United Kingdom during the 1930s was indeed still a climate of divisions; this chapter explores the social *zeitgeist* of the period, and examines the impact of the times' social turbulence on the public's demands of the media. The issues of class and notions of culture were thrown into relief with the advent of radio as never before; for the first time here was a medium capable of reaching the whole population at a single moment. In its first era, broadcasting sought not to target specific audiences within the population, but to aim at one audience as a public service. It was with the Crawford Report of 1925, recommending as it did the replacement of the British Broadcasting Company with a new authority "in view of the broader considerations now beginning to emerge"[200] that the issue of audience expectation was officially confronted. The Committee, which suggested the title, "British Broadcasting Commission" for the new authority, made it clear that the issue of divergence of taste was not an easy one to satisfy: "Classical music depresses one sector of listeners; the Jazz band exasperates a second; and a third desires greater immunity from each".[201] The listener, the Committee felt, "must not be pressed to assimilate too much of what he calls 'highbrow' broadcast, and the Commissioners would not be wise in transmitting more educational matter than licencees are prepared to accept".[202] On the other hand it concluded from the evidence placed before it that listeners could be educated to welcome improved standards "unconsciously at first, but with growing appreciation amongst those who will instinctively learn to desire better performances".[203] The Report goes on:

> Special wave-lengths or alternative services may provide an escape from the programme dilemma, but we trust they will never be used to cater for groups of listeners, however large, who press for trite and commonplace performances.[204]

Radio brought with it for the first time the possibility of a democratisation of language and ideas. Scannell and Cardiff have spoken of "a renewed emphasis on the 'apostolic' and 'missionary' task of humanizing the masses whose contempt for culture and enlightenment pointed to a morbid condition of the body politic".[205]

> Radio, in an organized social form, seemed to be one significant and unprecedented means of helping to shape a more unified and egalitarian society.[206] Through radio a sense of the nation as a knowable community might be restored by putting people in touch with the ceremonies and symbols of a corporate national life.[207]

Reith's BBC established both National and Regional stations, thus enabling the

---

200   *Report of the Broadcasting Committee, 1925*, Cmd. 2599, para. 4, p. 5.

201   Ibid., para. 14, p. 12.

202   Ibid.

203   Ibid.

204   Ibid.

205   Scannell, Paddy and Cardiff, David *A Social History of British Broadcasting*, Oxford, Blackwell, 1991, p. 12.

206   For a different interpretation of this see Lacey, Kate as quoted in Chapter 1 "Radio in the Great Depression, Promotional Culture, Public Service and Propaganda" in Hilmes, Michele and Loviglio, Jason (ed.) *Radio Reader*, New York, Routledge, 2002.

207   Scannell and Cardiff, p. 13.

population to share in programming broadcast to everyone, whilst retaining the choice of their own localised material; in other words two transmitted senses of community – national and regional. Both services were eclectic, providing a wide range of material in all genres.[208] Thus, "particular publics were replaced by the *general* public constituted in and by the general nature of the mixed programme service and its general, unrestricted availability".[209]

Inherent within this democratisation was the problem of a service that could never be all things to all people – just as Crawford had stated. Drama was a clear case in point. Ian Rodger has pointed out that the social status of "straight" theatre at the time of radio's birth – and indeed long before it, in the works of, for example, Farquar and Molière – was such that an audience could be assumed to be from a certain social class[210]:

> It had indeed often been a comic device in the theatre to depict certain social types in the sure knowledge that such people were not likely to form a part of the audience. In other plays, where the comedy served a didactic purpose, a social type well known to the audience is portrayed for their instruction and amusement but once again the joke was very private.[211]

Such private jokes could not have a place in the new medium. At the same time there existed a social divide in the very theatre the British public consumed: straight and classical on one hand and music hall and variety on the other. As Peter Bailey suggests, music hall contained its sense of parody too, although he argues that there was self-mockery here as well as parody of types and groups outside of the perceived audience:

> The bulk of the music hall crowd were working-class, but as an audience they constituted a different and more volatile collectivity, dissolving and recomposing as members of other groups by nationality, age, gender and stratum as invoked in performance.[212]

These largely divergent worlds of entertainment represented the two poles between which the BBC/commercial radio battles of the 1930s were to be waged, with the Reithian Sunday policy as their principal incendiary.

The Victorian England out of which the first half of the 20th century grew had been solidly paternalist and imperialist with an almost undisturbed acceptance in the right of authority, and for many this thinking remained the yardstick. Seaman has commented:

> In matters of manners and morals, the years between the wars saw a running battle ... between those who claimed to stand for what they deemed to be

---

208 Ibid., p. 14.

209 Ibid.

210 Rodger, Ian *Radio Drama*, London, MacMillan, 1982, p. 11.

211 Ibid. The genius of Oscar Wilde was that, in *The Importance of Being Ernest* and other of his plays, he could subvert this "club" and attack the British middle and upper classes before their eyes, using the guise of the Comedy of Manners. (Conversation between the author and Declan Kyberd, Professor of Anglo-Irish Literature, University College, Dublin, December 2000.)

212 Bailey, Peter "Making Sense of Music Hall" in *Music Hall, The Business of Pleasure* ed. Bailey, Peter, Milton Keynes, Open University Press, 1983, p. xvii.

traditional values, and those who emphasised adventurousness and novelty.[213]

The BBC, while representing the former of these sets of values, was by no means isolated, given the prevailing mood of the time. The social circumstances, although changing during the 1920s and the early 1930s, retained elements of attitudes towards public morality and thinking which were reflected rather than initiated within the ethics of broadcasting. In an interview with the present author, the late Desmond Hawkins, spoke shortly before his death of these circumstances:

> It wasn't just Reith by any manner of means. There was generally a very real puritan, sabbatarian culture. In the early 1930s I was a young man living in Wimbledon, and active within a group that was canvassing for the opening of cinemas on Sundays. When it eventually came it was very limited, not before Evensong, and a high percentage of the box office would go to charity. My generation was very rebellious about such things. You see, it's thought that Reith was a strange sort of one-off who had some strange ideas and no backing. That is not so.[214]

Class, Age and Geography

There is an underlying paradox which has to be confronted in any study of Britain in its inter-war years. We see, on one hand, "new levels of prosperity contrasted with conditions which had changed little since the Edwardian period and new industries grew alongside depression in the old staples".[215] Priestley's *English Journey* of 1934 showed him a land of:

> filling stations and factories that look like exhibition buildings, of giant cinemas and dance-halls and cafés, bungalows with tiny garages, cocktail bars, Woolworths, motor-coaches, wireless, hiking, factory girls looking like actresses, greyhound racing and dirt tracks, swimming pools, and everything given away for cigarette coupons.[216]

Social conditions were a major issue during the 1930s when increasing tension internationally and continuing hardship and unemployment amongst the working class created an appetite for escapism which could be met only in the field of entertainment. In 1937 there were 1,600,000 jobless in Britain and as late as December 1938 Oxford Street was blocked by unemployed men who lay down in

---

213   Seaman, L.C.B. *Life in Britain Between the Wars*, London, Batsford, 1970, p. 52.

214   Dr Desmond Hawkins was in his time a producer, a writer, Controller of the South West Region of the BBC, and founder of the Natural history Unit. In the interview with the present author, May 1998, Hawkins cites a specific example of the general sabbatarianism of the time: "My father took us to Torquay for a summer holiday in 1925, and on the Sunday, my brother and I thought we'd have a game of something or other; the croquet hoops were in the lawn, but we had difficulty finding the box with the mallets in. We then found it was padlocked, as it was Sunday, so we thought we'd play what in those days was called Ping-Pong. There was the table and there were the bats, but unfortunately there was no sign of a ball. Now we were there paying for a holiday, and these people were in the holiday business, but it wouldn't have been worth their while with many of their clients if they had allowed us to play croquet or Ping-Pong on a Sunday. You see that ethos to understand the opportunity the Commercials had given to them."

215   Stevenson, John *Social Conditions in Britain Between the Wars*, London, Penguin, 1977, p. 12.

216   Priestley, J.B. *English Journey*, London, William Heinemann, 1934, p. 401.

the road in front of Christmas shoppers chanting "We want work or bread".[217] On the other hand the 1930s was a period "of growing consumerism and leisure. Those in work, particularly the salaried middle class, benefited from the fact that, during the early 1930s, prices fell faster than wages, so real earnings rose."[218]

The social divide manifested itself in leisure activities. Stevenson and Day have both drawn attention to the class lines along which leisure was organised.[219] Middle and upper class interests tended to be such as motoring, tennis, cricket, golf and yachting, while the working class watched football ("still essentially a proletarian game"[220]), boxing and horse racing. Observing that there were some cross-overs in interest, at the same time Day points out:

> This does suggest that middle-class leisure activities were, on the whole, participatory, whereas working-class ones were more spectator-orientated. The popularity of gambling, particularly in horse-racing, greyhound-racing and the football pools, suggested an attitude of fatalistic acceptance, a trust in blind chance rather than in working-class power to change things politically.[221]

While middle-class audience pursuits included theatre, classical music, opera, ballet, the working-class frequented the pub, the dance hall and increasingly, the cinema.[222] This provided the imported spectacle of Busby Berkeley movies, blending kaleidoscopes of dancing girls in dreamlike patterns with social comment in such musical numbers as "My Forgotten Man" in *Gold Diggers of 1933*. For the poorer paid – or the unemployed – entertainment provided a relief from hardship and worry – at a price. For those who could afford it the gramophone became a prized family possession alongside the wireless. Radios were not cheap: quality sets retailed at between £10.00 and £24.00, although many people made their own, and the old "Crystal Sets" from the 1920s continued to give service.[223] Many of the American records played on wireless and gramophone traded in nostalgia for better times, whilst the artists of the British Music-Hall era continued to appear alongside cinema bills and in the remaining halls. One only has to study the work of Max Miller or Nellie Wallace to realise that the material could often be of questionable taste. Notwithstanding that, there was no doubt that their presence remained a major draw, particularly in the industrial areas up until the middle of the decade, after which as Stevenson says, "music-hall and variety theatre fought a steadily losing battle with the growth of cinemas, new cinemas being opened at a rate of three per week in 1939".[224]

The idea of a cinema as a place of performance was understood by its audience

217 Furth, Charles *Life Since 1900*, London, Batsford, 1956, p. 88.

218 Day, Gary "Culture, Criticism and Consumerism" in *Literature and Culture in Modern Britain, Volume Two, 1930–1955*, ed. Day, Gary London, Longman, 1997, p. 15.

219 Stevenson, pp. 44–45; Day, p. 15.

220 Stevenson, p. 45.

221 Day, p. 15.

222 Ibid.

223 Hill, Jonathan *Radio! Radio!*, Bampton, Sunrise Press, 1996, p. 98.

224 Stevenson, p. 44. Stevenson adds that "whatever the theoretical components of their 'poverty line', most families found the money to visit the cinema once or more each week" (ibid.).

during the 1930s as having grown out of "live" variety. The Art Deco picture palaces in themselves provided escape from reality, even before the entertainment began; they also generated their own class system as John Ellis has vividly explained:

> Audiences in large cinemas were segregated by price into sub-groups, with the balcony costing more than the stalls. Subdued by the monumental architecture, relaxed by the comforts and secure in the sense of being in the company of "your own type", members of the audience were then treated to live entertainment shows.[225]

As the cross-over continued between "live" variety and film, many of the artistes from music-hall found work in the new medium. A notable showcase for such talent came in 1934, with the Will Hay comedy, *Radio Parade of 1935*, the second in a series of *Radio Parade* films made by British International Pictures[226] which capitalised on the growing public status of radio as a mass medium. While the film depended on the BBC "for its very existence",[227] at the same time it satirised both Reith and the BBC unmercifully. Hay plays "Mr Garlon/Garland" (Wreath/Reith) an autocrat running the NBG (National Broadcasting Group/No Bloody Good) in an ivory towered, thinly disguised parody of Broadcasting House,[228] overseeing an organisation completely out of touch with popular public tastes and desires. At one point "Garland" is even shown as impersonating Hitler in a washroom mirror. The film was largely peopled by well known variety acts many of whom would have been known to the cinema-going audiences by their voices only, through the medium of radio[229]. These included a number of personalities whose music-hall based humour had already created problems with BBC policy. Among them were Clapham and Dwyer, a musical comedy act who had received a five month ban from BBC programmes for broadcasting a riddle which had actually provoked a public apology on 21 January 1935 during a BBC news bulletin:

> The BBC apologizes to listeners for the inclusion in the *Music Hall* programme, broadcast on Saturday night, of certain highly objectionable remarks, violating standards which have been firmly established by the practice of the BBC.[230]

The nature of the "highly objectionable remarks" may seem to us today to have been somewhat innocuous:

225   Ellis, John "British Cinema as Performance Art, *Brief Encounter* and *Radio Parade of 1935* and the circumstances of film exhibition", in *British Cinema, Past and Present* ed. Ashby, Justine and Higson, Andrew, London, Routledge, 2000, p. 97. By contrast Ellis cites an example of cinema-going in Rawnestall, Lancashire, where "the men were nearly all out of work. But somehow the families still managed to come to the cinema. One reason was the prizes for lucky tickets – tea, sugar, packets of bacon and all kinds of groceries." (Brown, Charles in *Picture Palace: A Social History of the Cinema*, Field, A., London, Gentry Press, 1974, p. 102, quoted in Ellis, p. 97.)

226   Low, Rachael *Film Making in 1930s Britain*, London, George Allen and Unwin, 1985, p. 123.

227   Ellis, p. 104.

228   Ibid., p. 103.

229   Ibid., p. 105.

230   Scannell and Cardiff, p. 227. The public apology is quoted in the BBC's response to a letter of complaint received from one Rev. E.E. Sibley (WAC,R34/283).

Question: What is the difference between a champagne cork and a baby? Answer: A champagne cork has the maker's name on its bottom.[231]

In truth BBC regulations were so full of provisos that it was hard for any variety act developed out of the broad humour of music-hall, and seeking to cater to its erstwhile audience to create anything but a bland middle-class humour of distinctly limited appeal. Scannell and Cardiff point to the fact that jokes were forbidden if they contained references to:

> politics and politicians, advertisements, drink and prohibition in the United States, clergymen, medical matters and human infirmities, Scotsmen and Welshmen, but not apparently, Irishmen. In 1931 it was reported that producers were trying to exclude "such worn-out topics for humour as sea-sickness, flat feet, cheese, kippers, bunions etc".[232]

---

231   Quoted in Scannell and Cardiff, p. 227. In 1933, the comedian Norman Long had recorded commercially a satire of BBC attitudes entitled "We Can't let you Broadcast That":

Now the BBC once wrote to me and said "Dear Norman Long,
We thought you'd like to face the mike with your piano, smile and song,
So will you bring your repertoire along for us to see,
To go over it with a pencil of the blue variety."

So I looked my list of songs up, to the studio I flew,
I said "Here's nice song called *Violets*", "Oh", they said "That's much too blue",
I said "Is *Robin Adair* alright?" They said "*Robin Add-Hair*, my hat,
Just think of the bald-headed men you'll upset, we can't let you broadcast that."

The song continues for a number of verses each with the same refrain and idea, that of BBC censorship:

So I looked my list of songs up, and found an army one,
There's something about a soldier, they said "That can't be done,
There's something about a soldier'would get over nice and pat
To a Sergeant's wife with fourteen kids, we can't let you broadcast that."...

So I looked my list of songs up, I was getting fed up to the roots,
I said "Here's a good song by Kipling, a military song called *Boots*."
They said "My dear good fellow, do you realise where you're at?
You're advertising a chemistry firm, we can't let you broadcast that."...

Concluding:

So I packed my list of songs up, I said "Hang it, I won't sing,
I can do some adagio dancing, or a spot of conjuring,
Trick cycling, walk the tight rope, I'm a darn good acrobat",
I'd love to tell you what they said – but I can't even record that.

(Norman Long, Recorded 16 September, 1933, Columbia Records, CA 13302, reissued 1989, Conifer Records, MCHD 163 as part of the compilation, *Radio Days*.)

232   Scannell & Cardiff, p. 226, quoting from *Radio Times*, 16 January 1931, p. 111. In 1943, when censorship of issues potentially helpful to an enemy were understandable, the BBC was still concerning itself with issues which seem absurdly trivial today. In an edition of the popular programme, *Workers' Playtime*, a performance was given by the violinist, Stanelli, the recording of which was the subject of the following memo; "I attach two scripts, *Workers' Playtime*, Midland Region, August 10 and September 3; in the first one Stanelli's 'turn' contains some doubtful matter.1. The chambermaid lines, which should not have been passed. 2. 'Hot water bottle': doubtful. 3. 'Eternal Triangle': out on

In 1929 Will Hay had said, when referring to "My friend Mike", that "You must be on your best behaviour in front of Mike. You must not say naughty words or anything the least bit lurid."[233] It was to become a public joke at the BBC's expense, jibing as it did at the Corporations' censorious nature.

The distrust held by the BBC of so many of its variety performers ran parallel to a hostility – particularly in the early years of broadcasting – from the artistes and their unions, notably the Variety Artistes' Federation and the Entertainment Protection Association. In 1923, with radio still young, the organisations had urged members not to cooperate with the BBC, fearing a number of issues, not least the cruel universality of a medium which consumed material at a fearsome rate; a comedian on "The Halls" could peddle his or her act for many months – even years – safe in the knowledge that his audience was receiving it for the first time. Radio ended that concept, but there were other issues:

> Comedians in particular faced formidable problems. They lost their live audience and got no direct response from the absent listeners. They could not rely on visual humour, and they worried that they would very quickly use up all their material, which was now subject to censorship on grounds of taste and vulgarity.[234]

The issue remained a major one until the late 1920s, and "there were few live broadcasts from variety theatres before 1928".[235] Such an omission did little to enfranchise working-class tastes within the social content of broadcasting, and the medium was inevitably biased towards middle and upper class taste as a result.

Dream England and the Sense of Community

The BBC's role at the time of the General Strike of 1926 was briefly discussed in the previous chapter. Curran and Seaton have noted that "one effect of the strike was to create a national audience for broadcasting" due to the absence of any other media at the time.[236] They also speak of "communal listening ... as people gathered in halls and outside shops to hear the news".[237] In this instance "communal listening" should not be equated with "community listening". The BBC as we have seen, placed itself with the government in terms of what it saw as the public good, and "obligingly kept both the Archbishop of Canterbury and the Leader of the Opposition (Ramsay MacDonald) off the air, and ... (even more obligingly) played

---

general policy grounds." Memo from Controller of Programmes to producer, *Workers' Playtime*, 14 September 1943 quoted in *What About the Workers*, BBC Radio 4, 21 August 2001, producer Jayne Gibson. The censorious nature of BBC programme policy, and the deeply paternalistic sense of responsibility it demonstrates was present after the war too. In 1948, the *BBC Variety Programmes Policy Guide*, issued by the Corporation "for writers and producers", was unequivocal: "There is an absolute ban upon the following:- Jokes about – Lavatories, Effeminacy in men, Immorality of any kind. Suggestive references to – Honeymoon couples, chambermaids, fig leaves, prostitution, ladies underwear, e.g. winter draws on, animal habits, e.g. rabbits, lodgers, commercial travellers." (BBC, 1948, Guidance booklet, p. 5, facsimile published 1997.)

233   Hay, Will *BBC Handbook*, 1929, pp. 185–186. Scannell and Cardiff (p. 226) also quote this.

234   Scannell & Cardiff, p. 226.

235   Ibid.

236   Curran, James and Seaton, Jean *Power Without Responsibility*, London, Routledge, 1997, p. 119.

237   Ibid.

Blake's *Jerusalem* on the heels of Baldwin's eventual announcement that the strike had collapsed".[238] Listeners will have been sharply divided by class as well as by their political views. The use of the Blake/Parry setting, with all its iconic significance was a conscious cultural reference to "Englishness". It was also an appeal to something anti-revolutionary in the British working-class psyche. Referring to the Strike, James Klugmann was to write:

> There was a tremendous overestimate of the political meaning of the economic crisis and of the reaction of the workers to the crisis. Every demonstration against poverty was interpreted as a symbol of the new revolutionary period, and therefore between 1928 and 1930 every action was interpreted as a revolutionary action needing a revolutionary tactic and strategy.[239]

Far from provoking an era of Left Wing revolutionary zeal, the immediate post-Strike short-lived economic improvement had a negative political effect on the Communist Party in Britain. In January 1927, membership of the Party was 12,500; in 1930–31, the figure had fallen to just 2,500, with a gradual recovery thereafter through the 1930s.[240] Statistics for unemployment between 1926 and 1930 demonstrate that a temporary fall in unemployment gave a false sense of recovery. It is useful to relate this to radio listening at the time[241]:

Year	Population	% insured persons	Unemployed listeners
1926	45,185,000	12.5	8,713,000
1927	45,394,000	9.6	9,581,000
1928	45,580,000	10.7	10,513,500
1929 (Wall Street Crash)	45,685,000	10.3	11,827,000
1930	45,878,000	15.8	13,648,000

Subsequently, between 1931 and 1932, when unemployment was at its worst (21.1 per cent and 21.9 per cent respectively),[242] the radio audience rose by more than 3,000,000 listeners, from 16,327,000 to 19,841,500,[243] the largest increase between 1922 and 1939. The social turmoil of the times was matched by intense media activity and reorganisation[244]:

238 Wright, Patrick *On Living in an Old Country*, London, Verso,1985, p. 105. See also Henry Fairlee, "The BBC" in Hugh Thomas, ed., *The Establishment*, 1959 who also recounts this incident.

239 Klugmann, James "The Crisis of the Thirties: A View from the Left", in *Culture and Crisis in Britain in the '30s*, ed. Clark, Jon, Heinnemann, Margot, Margolies, David and Snee, Carole, London, Lawrence and Wishart, 1979, p. 23. Klugmann joined the Communist party in 1933, while doing research at Cambridge. Later, from 1947 until his death in 1977, he worked full-time for the Communist Party of Britain, editing its theoretical monthly magazine, *Marxism Today* from 1962 until 1977.

240 Klugmann, pp. 23–24.

241 Unemployment figures from Baily, Leslie *Leslie Baily's BBC Scrapbooks, volume 2, 1918–1939*, London, George Allen and Unwin, 1968, p. 150. Licence statistics from Pegg, Mark *Broadcasting and Society 1918–1939*, Beckenham, Croom Helm, 1983, p. 7.

242 Baily, p. 150.

243 Pegg, p. 7.

244 Foster, Andy & Furst, Steve *Radio Comedy 1938–1968*, London, Virgin, 1996 pp. ix–x.

1926/27	The British Broadcasting Company becomes the British Broadcasting Corporation
1930	BBC National and Regional Programmes replace 2LO and other local stations
1931	Radio Normandy commences broadcasting English language programmes
1932	BBC Empire Service launched
1933	Radio Luxembourg commences broadcasting

The coming of commercial radio, based directly on the capitalist American system, and widely and quickly embraced by the working-class audience, was to accentuate the divisions in British society, while running counter to the Marxist viewpoint developed by a number of young intellectuals of the time. George Orwell, writing in 1939, was to identify another Englishness which he saw as being at odds with this idea, within the British working-class psyche in relation to the popular cinematic dramatisations of the work of Charles Dickens:

> The common man is still living in the mental world of Dickens, but nearly every modern intellectual has gone over to some other form of totalitarianism. From the Marxist or Fascist point of view, nearly all that Dickens stands for can be written off as "bourgeois morality". But in moral outlook no-one could be more bourgeois than the English working classes ... In his own age and ours he has been able to express in comic, simplified and therefore memorable form the native decency of the common man ... In a country like England, in spite of its class structure, there does exist a certain cultural unity ... Nearly everyone, whatever his actual conduct may be, responds emotionally to the idea of human brotherhood.[245]

This is not to deny a sense of a divided society, but merely a means of dealing with it from a working-class perspective. Orwell significantly mentions "humour", a quality so often cited as an example of a factor in the "Britain Triumphant" of 1945. Laughter as a communal weapon against an adversary was certainly present in Herbert Farjeon's parody in his popular review, *Nine Sharp*, of 1937, a year before John Reith's resignation, in which the actor George Benson impersonated him in a song adapted from – and sung to the tune of – the Admiral's song from *HMS Pinafore* by Gilbert and Sullivan:

> When I was a bairn, I lived up north
> In the land of the leal and the Firth of Forth.
> All through ma' youth in ma' ain countree
> I polished up ma' English verra carefullee.
> I polished up ma' English verra carefullee
> That I became the Ruler of the BBC!
>
> That nae man's morals should be lax nor loose,
> I decided when I built Broadcasting Hoose,
> So I summoned up ma' staff and said, 'Hoots mon, hoot,
> If I hear of ye canoodling, ye gang right oot!
> I sat upon canoodling sae successfullee –
> There's never been a babby at the BBC![246]

---

245   Orwell, George *Collected Essays, Journalism and Letters, volume 1*, p. 503, quoted in Richards, Jeffrey *Films and British National Identity*, Manchester, Manchester University Press, 1997, p. 339.

Radio listening as a group activity was initially an extension of public entertainment in the music-hall. Moores quotes an article from the *Warrington Guardian* in 1923 which illustrates this:

> An original and up-to-date novelty was introduced at a social evening held in the Parr Hall on Saturday. It was a wireless feature, which gave much pleasure to all, and especially those who had never "listened-in" before. It was very successful, concerts from Birmingham and Manchester being well heard.[247]

The movement of radio from a public entertainment to a private one, part of what Jacques Donzelot refers to as "the withdrawal to interior space",[248] was a significant one for many commentators, removing the family from being such a visible presence in working-class society. In 1939 the BBC commissioned Hilda Jennings and Winnifred Gill to conduct a survey into the effects of broadcasting in society. Their findings, derived from research carried out in a working-class district of east Bristol demonstrated what Moores has spoken of as indicating "radio as part of a general move away from the collective occupation of exterior space towards a family grouping which had withdrawn to interior space".[249]

> Until a comparatively recent period the street and the public house offered the main scope for recreation ... the whole family would stand at the street door or sit in armchairs on the pavement. When tension in a street ran high, quarrels easily arose and quickly spread. Witnesses told the survey worker that "There was a row every night in some streets ... Rival street gangs raided each other or even pursued victims into their own homes".[250]

Two years later B. Seebohm Rowntree was writing of a time in York, pre-radio, when a

> large proportion of young working people spent their evenings lounging about in the neighbourhood of their houses or promenading up and down certain streets in the city. The main street was so thronged with them that it was difficult to make one's way through ... On Saturday nights special policemen were drafted into the poorer districts of the city in order to deal with the fights and brawls.[251]

The concept of "The Mob" or "the Masses" as a threatening entity in its own right was strongly present in the work of a number of intellectuals towards the end of the nineteenth and start of the twentieth centuries, in which the phrases "highbrow" and "lowbrow"[252] were coined not only as terms of relative intelligence but of

246   Farjeon, Herbert *Nine Sharp*, 1937, reproduced in Snagge, John and Barsley, Michael *Those Vintage Years of Radio*, London, Pitman, 1972, p. 51.

247   *Warrington Guardian*, 10 March 1923, quoted in "The Box on the Dresser, Memories of early radio and everyday life", *Media Culture and Society* , Volume 10, No. 1, January 1988, p. 24.

248   Donzelot, Jacques *The Policing of Families*, London, Hutchinson, 1980, p. 93, also quoted in Moores, p. 24.

249   Moores, p. 25.

250   Jennings, Hilda and Gill,Winifred *Broadcasting in Everyday Life, A Survey of the Social Effects of the Coming of Broadcasting*, London, BBC, 1939, p. 21.

251   Rowntree, B. Seebohm *Poverty and Progress*, London, Longman, 1941, p. 468.

252   Carey, John *The Intellectuals and the Masses, Pride and Prejudice among the Literary Intelligensia, 1880–1939*, London, Faber, 1992, p. 10.

opposed social classes often storing acrimonious suspicions and fears of each other, a climate of distrust in which "the minority is made conscious, not merely of an uncongenial, but of a hostile environment".[253] The antidote to the idea of the potential anarchy of the mob, the image of which rose again in the General Strike, was to be found in an idealised dream of England which manifested itself strongly in the 1920s and 1930s. One may see it in Brian Cook's dust jackets for the Batsford series of countryside books of the time, and in the railway posters advertising idyllic painted locations utilising the tri-colour techniques of the Jean Berté printing process.[254] It was present too in literature, through the works of such as G.K. Chesterton, H.A.L. Fisher, and notably (in this context) in the writing of Stanley Baldwin himself. In the very year of the General Strike Baldwin published a book entitled *On England, and Other Addresses*, from which one passage deserves to be quoted at length, presenting as it does a manifesto for nostalgic values as a basis for patriotism:

> The sounds of England, the tinkle of the hammer on the anvil in the country smithy, the corncrake on a dewy morning, the sound of the scythe against whetstone, and the sight of a plough team coming over the brow of a hill, the sight that has been seen in England since England was a land, and may be seen long after the Empire has perished and every works in England has ceased to function, for centuries the one eternal sight in England. The wild anemones in the woods in April, the last load at night of hay being drawn down a lane as the twilight comes on, when you can scarcely distinguish the figures of the horses as they take it home to the farm, and above all, most subtle, most penetrating and most moving, the smell of wood smoke coming up in an autumn evening, or the smell of the scotch fires: that wood smoke that our ancestors, tens of thousands of years ago, must have caught in the air when they were coming home with the result of the day's forage when they were still nomads, and when they were still roaming the forests and the plains of the continent of Europe. These things strike down into the very depths of our nature, and touch chords that go back to the beginning of time and the human race, but they are chords that with every year of our life sound a deeper note in our innermost being.[255]

Wright has pointed out that the political use of "England" as an aspirational symbol:

> is one of the fundamental tendencies within the established public culture of the interwar years. If this is a time when an upper-class idealisation of "tramping" coexists uneasily with hunger marches, homelessness and unemployment, it is also the time of Baldwin's "England": a kind of Conservative government in aspic …[256]

---

253   Leavis, F.R. *Mass Civilisation and Minority Culture*, London, The Minority Press, 1930, p. 25.

254   Cook Batsford, Brian *The Britain of Brian Cook*, London, Batsford, 1987.

255   Baldwin, Stanley *On England, and Other Addresses*, London, Philip Allan, 1926, p. 7. The book is a collection of speeches and extracts from speeches by Baldwin made between 1923 and 1925. "England" was delivered on 6 May 1924, at the annual dinner of the Royal Society of St. George at the Hotel Cecil. Between April and October 1926, Baldwin's book went through 5 impressions.

256   Wright, pp. 104–105.

Musically it manifested itself in the music of Ralph Vaughan Williams, himself feeding off a tradition that belonged to the conscious collection of English folk song prior to World War One. The political and cultural exploitation of patriotism within the United Kingdom has so often employed the bucolic and rural rather than the industrial and urban for its effect, just as it has usually turned to an image of "England" rather than "Britain". It is as Jeffrey Richards has called it "the politics of nostalgia".[257]

Within a culture which finds it politically expedient to celebrate a traditional past as a main virtue, external contemporary influences – in this context, largely transatlantic in its spirit – sent a quite different message. It was something which inevitably appealed to the young.

A young person born in 1910, and therefore aged twenty in 1930, was born of Victorian parents. It is important to keep this in mind in order to understand the major divide between generations which affected social and media attitudes in the third decade of the twentieth century. Interviews conducted by Shaun Moores point to the replacement in some homes of social activity by an electronic compromising alternative provided by radio, perpetuating a Victorian and Edwardian memory-concept of the danger to the morals of the young in certain public places:

> And the thing I remember about the radio was listening to music. I used to love listening to the dance bands.
>
> [Question] Did you used to go out dancing much?
>
> Oh no, you see my father wouldn't let me. He was a policeman and he thought these dance halls were dens of iniquity, so there would've been trouble if I'd ever gone there ... but I used to listen to jazz on the radio at home. My father wouldn't let me go to the dance halls, but if it was on the radio at home, well that was different you see.[258]

As the nature and character of the dance-halls changed, so did the sense of escape. Wild, in his study of recreation in Rochdale, Lancashire up to 1940, notes that the *Rochdale Observer* carried an advertisement on page 1 of its issue dated 29 September 1934, for the "first permanent, purpose-built dance hall" in the town.[259] This was The Carlton, and carried the same kind of ambience as the new cinemas that were starting to open. (See below). "It was, from the start, a far more glamorous establishment than the Drill Hall or Ambulance Hall, which were both used regularly for dances."[260]

The coming of the new opulent halls were not in themselves sufficient to cater for the growing craze for dancing which Wild identifies in Rochdale as being "the thing for all between sixteen and twenty-five ... In Rochdale the dance venues and dance schools continued to cater for an expanding audience of mainly young people throughout the late 1920s and into the 1930s.[261] Such was the demand in the town

---

257   Richards, p. 351.

258   Moores, p. 25.

259   Wild, Paul "Recreation in Rochdale, 1900–40", in *Working class Culture, Studies in History and Theory*, ed. Clarke, John et al, London, Hutchinson, 1980, p. 149.

260   Ibid.

261   Ibid.

that the coming of the new halls did not satisfy the requirements for social space; Wild states that on one Saturday night in Rochdale in 1938, "there was a dance at the Ambulance Drill Hall (price 1s.3d.), the Dunlop Mill Companies Social Club held a dance (1s. 6d.) and at the fire station, "Johnny Rosen and his famous Broadcasting Band" played from 7.00 p.m. till midnight for 1s.6d."[262] In nearby Salford, another chronicler recalled:

> The great barn we patronised as apprentices held at least a thousand. Almost every evening except Friday (cleaning night at home) it was jammed with a mass of young men and women, class de-segregated for the first time. At 6d. per head (1s. on Saturdays) youth at every level of the manual working class, from the bound apprentices to the "scum of the slum", fox trotted through the new bliss in each other's arms.[263]

The huge enthusiasm amongst the young for dancing fed the emergent record and gramophone industry, which in turn was to significantly fuel the public appetite for popular music radio as home-centred entertainment grew: "Columbia records claimed to have sold over two million of their 'new process' records from their London factory in one month in 1928 ..."[264] Dance records of all descriptions "found their way into countless homes ... In a mood informed by some of the films being shown then, record and dance bands jostled to reveal the latest step or routine before an audience increasingly tuned to a world of novelty and the appearance of glamour".[265]

In some households even a second-hand experience was frowned on. One correspondent writing to the present author recalled an example of generational/cultural division within his own family in Derby:

> My father came from a family influenced by the Anglo-Catholic revival of the 1890s and Sundays during my childhood were restrained, and if the wireless was used, it was for BBC programmes only ... The neighbour played their set very loudly, and Radio Luxembourg was heard over a number of gardens during the summer months. I used to listen with envy to the latest dance tunes coming through the hedgerow.[266]

The BBC, notably through the programmes of Henry Hall and his BBC Dance Orchestra, addressed this musical need; however, given the scale of the requirement, and the tone of so much BBC speech radio, particularly in the early years of the 1930s, there was the opportunity to exploit the insatiable demand of the dance fans much further. To claim that there was a disenfranchisement of the music and dance-hungry working class youth of Britain would be an exaggeration, and it would certainly be wrong to say that the commercial operators set out consciously to engender a sense of community which the BBC had neglected. On the contrary, geographical "community" as far as the IBC was concerned went little further than

262   Ibid.

263   Roberts, Robert *The Classic Slum*, Manchester, Manchester University Press, 1971, p. 188. Roberts was writing of life up to the mid 1920s.

264   Wild, Op. cit, p. 149, quoting the *Rochdale Observer*, 18 January 1928, p. 2 (Advertisement).

265   Wild, Op. cit., p. 149.

266   Good, Peter, Derby, in a communication to the present author, August 1996, see Appendix B, Listeners.

a potential sales market. Radio Normandy's inability to reach all of Britain in its early years due to lack of transmitter-power was turned to a positive advantage in the company's publicity to potential advertisers, claiming as it did the station's policy, which was "to blanket the prosperous south".[267] The phrase highlighted the major geographical and economic division which was a central issue between the wars for Britain. At the same time, the unremitting lightness of the commercial stations fed a need consistently, while as Giddings has pointed out, the BBC created some strong and often controversial programming during the 1930s which, often to the discomfiture of the Government, gave an accurate picture of the crisis within the country at large, and thereby remained true to its own image of its public service duty.[268] While the BBC's attitude to more "popular" entertainment often misjudged the mood and appetite of its working-class audience, to call the Corporation – as Marwick does – a "tight-lipped, prissy, propagator of basic assumptions, mirror of myths, dominated by the upper-class"[269] is, while not wholly untrue, something of an over-simplification. There were programmes from the mid-1930s until the outbreak of war which directed themselves specifically at the unemployed,[270] many of these written and presented by some of the best writers and thinkers in the country, and frequently reproduced in *The Listener*.

In January 1933, the travel writer, S.P.B. Mais gave a moving opening to a series of eleven talks entitled "S.O.S.":

> Here is an S.O.S. message, probably the most urgent you will ever hear, and it vitally concerns you. You are called upon to create an entirely new order. The bottom has apparently fallen out of the old world in which everybody was subordinated to the day's work. We are now faced with a world in which one of the major problems is how best to occupy the day's enforced leisure. Some millions of our neighbours, without any preparation for it, have now got this leisure enforced upon them, and, not unnaturally, are unable to cope with it. They do not understand how it has come about any more than you or I ...[271]

In the same year the series, *Other People's Houses* included eye-witness accounts of slum-living in deprived areas,including the North West of England, Glasgow and parts of London. Giddings refers to these as "courageous programmes which made a novel contribution to social reporting; thus they were among the landmarks of sociological history".[272] While this is certainly true, an extract taken from a commentary by Howard Marshall, well known for his cricket coverage, on his visit to a slum dwelling in Gateshead, conveys a sense that these were programmes not so much FOR the working-class as educating the middle and upper-classes ABOUT them, (although none the worse in intention for that):

> The old grandfather was huddled by the fire, a very sick man, and the husband

267 Plomley, Roy *Days Seemed Longer*, London, Eyre Methuen, 1980, p. 124.
268 Giddings, Robert "Radio in Peace and War", in Day (ed.)pp. 132–162.
269 Marwick, Arthur *Class: Image and Reality in Britain, France and the USA Since 1930*, Manchester, Manchester University Press, 1980, p. 157.
270 Giddings in Day, p. 141.
271 Mais, S. P.B. *The Listener*, 25 January 1933, p. 118.
272 Giddings in Day, p. 142.

pointed to a lump of plaster a foot wide which had fallen from the ceiling onto the rickety bed. Bare boards with rat holes here and there, a wooden box or two, uncurtained windows with broken sash cords, permanently closed, a great patch of moisture where damp had soaked through several layers of wall paper by the baby's cot: this was the room I saw by the cheerless light of an unshaded gas mantle. And always it was the same story: no water, no conveniences ...[273]

Whoever the talk was aimed at it was a long way from the one-sided Government perspective the BBC (believing it to be in the "National Interest") had delivered during the National Strike although as we have seen in Chapter One, the conflict between Government and broadcaster as to what should and should not be broadcast, was all the more present as a result, and drew the Corporation into conflict, as with the Pollitt and Mosley talks cited previously. An indication as to what could happen in an unrecorded – although scrupulously scripted talk – occurred during a 1934 series entitled *Modern Industry and National Character*. In one programme Sir Herbert Austin, the motor magnate gave a talk in which he criticised the Trade Unions for not moving with the times. Giddings explains the aftermath:

In its fair-minded liberal way the Corporation had planned that this salvo was to be answered by a representative of the industrial working class – one William Ferrie. In the traditional manner his script had been written, submitted, approved, edited and rehearsed. But when the moment of the broadcast came, this courageous man said to the nation:

"Last week a big employer of labour, Sir Herbert Austin, gave a talk about the British working man, and I have been invited to say what I think about the British worker. I am a working man myself, but what I wanted to tell you has been so censored and altered and cut up by the BBC that I consider it impossible for me to give a talk without it being a travesty of the British working class. I therefore protest against the censorship of the BBC and will give the talk instead to the press."

Ferrie was then cut off.[274]

When the talk was published in its entirety one of the most significant and indicting statements in it as far as the BBC was concerned, was Ferrie's claim, in his introductory remarks, that "I also refused to drop my 'aitches' and to speak as they imagine a worker does".[275] Perhaps, after all, there was still some way to go to escape the shadow of 1926, but as the decade proceeded, there were genuine attempts by the BBC to address the issue of class, and Giddings cites a memo by Reith stating his hope that upper, middle and working-class representatives could meet in a studio without the danger of "getting 'left wing propaganda across'".[276] The result was a series entitled *Class: An Enquiry*, the first programme of which

273 Transcript taken from *The Listener*, 18 January 1933, p. 74.
274 Quoted in Marwick, pp. 159–160 and cited in Giddings, pp. 143–144.
275 Ferrie, William *The Banned Broadcast of William Ferrie*, London, Workers' Bookshop Ltd., 1934, quoted in Marwick, p. 160.
276 Giddings, in Day, p. 144,quoting Reith in a memo dated 5 May 1938 in the Talks Advisory Committee Minutes, WAC, Caversham.

included a discussion between an anthropologist (Tom Harrison) and a trade union leader (George Isaacs).[277]

By this time employment was rising fast, although the very fact that such a discussion should occur, pointed to the fact that, whatever the economic facts, the distrust ran deep between the classes, and culturally the country remained divided. That the BBC sought to deal with this issue is evident in the nature of much of its programming after 1936, when audience measurement began. Internally as externally there were major changes from mid to late decade, and Cardiff has pointed out that between 1936 and 1939, speech radio on the BBC became more "popular" in two ways:

> First there was a greater attempt to represent the opinions and experiences of "ordinary people" and in particular of working class people. Second, the format for radio talk became lighter; greater use was made of the round table discussion, of the miscellany of short talks in a magazine format and of interviewers, chairmen and presenters chosen for their qualities as broadcasters rather than for their expertise in a subject.[278]

He adds, "Reith's departure, early in 1938, appears to have facilitated the process of popularisation",[279] so that by 1940 the *BBC Year Book* could issue what for some might be construed as a veiled apology: "… rightly or wrongly, it was being urged a year or two ago that the BBC was aloof from its listening millions, offering programmes with a complacent air of 'Take it or leave it'."[280] The article continued, almost sheepishly, "the ice, if it ever existed, has rapidly melted. New and friendlier contacts have been established on the air."[281]

Many years prior to this however, the long running *In Town Tonight*, which began in 1933, the brainchild of the BBC's Variety Department, had made steps in a more populist direction by taking as its well-meaning although (consciously or unconsciously) patronising and class-ridden policy statement, "the simple, fascinating things that humble folk do, and the high points achieved by men and women of distinction".[282] Howard Marshall presented *At the Black Dog,* a series broadcast from a pub setting which Cardiff has suggested as "the original British chat show".[283]

It is clear that the BBC's approach to social issues in the ten years up to the outbreak of war grew consistently in its sophistication. Scannell has commented on this:

> In the early thirties the form and content of programmes had not been systematised and routinised, and neither had their producers. That process of adaptation was to become increasingly evident in London (less so in the

277 Giddings in Day, p. 144.

278 Cardiff, David "The Serious and the Popular: aspects of the evolution of style in the radio talk, 1928–1939" in Collins, Richard (ed.) *Media, Culture and Society, A Critical Reader,* London, Sage Publications, 1986, p. 233.

279 Op. cit., p. 234.

280 *BBC Year Book 1940,* London, BBC, p. 83.

281 Ibid.

282 Cannell, J.C. *In Town Tonight,* London, Harrap and Co., 1935, quoted by Cardiff op. cit. p. 234.

283 Cardiff, op. cit.

regions) after 1935 within the different politics (fascism and the threat of war) of the late thirties. Lessons had been learnt …[284]

The fracture that ran through the years between the two wars cut across every cultural and economic consideration, including religion. There was "a noticeable migration to Anglicanism and Romanism in the thirties by some intellectuals and towards an eclectic mysticism by others".[285] C.S. Lewis, T.S. Eliot, and Aldous Huxley were among many writers who sought to demonstrate through their work that the spiritual was an extension of the intelligence and therefore only open to a select few:[286] "Evelyn Waugh combined contempt for all who were not gentlemen with a staunch adherence to the Roman faith".[287] The ultimate expression of this school of thinking was the Oxford Group, which later renamed itself "Moral Rearmament", a confessional group aimed directly at the young and affluent, led by the American Frank Buchman:

> Bouncy, jolly, well dressed and always well connected, the Buchmanites disposed of all their critics by indicating that only sinners, atheists or crypto-Communists could possibly want to criticise them.[288]

Religion and mysticism as a divisive weapon used by certain intellectuals in the class war of the 1930s found fuel in the Bloomsbury writer Clive Bell's *Civilization*, published in 1928. Civilization, in Carey's reading of Bell, "depends … on the existence of a small group of people of exquisite sensibility, who know how to respond to works of art, and who also have a refined appreciation of sensory delights such as food and wine".[289] An understanding of high Christian ideals may be equated therefore with an appreciation of good wine and fine art – something belonging to the very few. Carey's conclusion from this is chilling, given what was awaiting society at the end of the 1930s:

> The "barbarian" in his "suburban slum" may notice that the elite scorn gross pleasures ("football, cinemas"), such as he wallows in, and this may entice him to sample refined artistic pleasure himself. A flaw in Bell's scheme is that the barbarian, even if he develops artistic tastes, will not be able to indulge them, as he will remain deprived of the leisure obligatory for civilized life. This is not a complication Bell pursues, but he seems to anticipate some discontent on the part of the slaves, for he stipulates that his civilization will need an efficient police force.[290]

Fascism and Communism were the extreme poles of a time which was a period of major advances and prosperity for some, but it was also a time "dominated by the dislocation of Britain's economic life which followed closely upon the First World War and the vulnerability of the industries that had once assured her dominance in

---

284 Scannell, "Broadcasting and the Politics of Unemployment 1930–1935" in Richard Collins et al., (eds.) op. cit., p. 226.

285 Seaman, L.C.B. *Life in Britain Between the Wars*, London, Batsford, 1970, p. 68.

286 Ibid.

287 Ibid.

288 Ibid.

289 Carey. p. 80.

290 Ibid, p. 81, quoting from Bell, *Civilization*, London, Chatto and Windus, 1928, pp. 204–206, 210, 218–219, 240, 243.

world markets. A short-lived boom after the cessation of hostilities was followed by a severe slump, felt most sharply in the very industries upon which Britain had most heavily depended up to the outbreak of the First World War."[291]

The vast majority of those industries was situated in the North and Midlands of Britain; it is therefore important to view the period in terms of various sets of circumstances as Mathias has said:

> So much depends upon whether the spot-light is turned upon Jarrow or on Slough; on Merthyr Tydfil or on Oxford; on Greenock and Birkenhead or on Coventry, Weston-super-Mare and the environs of London.[292]

When unemployment started to fall during the 1930s it was partly – and increasingly – due to the developing arms race as the threat of war became more apparent. From 21.1 per cent of the population in 1932, the figure had fallen to 9.1 per cent in 1939.[293] At the same time Britain's expenditure on armaments rose from £103 million per year in 1932 to £254.5 million in 1939.[294] It would not be long therefore before the ideal of "Dream England" would be used to create solidarity between a divided people against a common enemy.

The "American Dream" on the other hand was of a different order, and its manifestation in the early development of radio will be explored in the next chapter. I am suggesting here that, in general terms, the heritage dream of England was an upper-class escape, while the working-class sought its relief in popular culture – the cinema, the pub, sport and dance music. Seen from an American standpoint, the BBC's desire to impose cultural control through its programmes was anachronistic and inappropriate to the needs of its audience. Socially, financially and in terms of

---

291 Stevenson, pp. 12–13.

292 Mathias, P. *The First Industrial Nation*, London, Methuen, 1971, p. 431. The geography of
      class-consciousness is amusingly illustrated in the Stoke-born poet Charles Tomlinson's poem "Class"
      in which he recalls one of his early literary jobs between the wars:
      "Those midland *a*'s
      once cost me a job:
      diction defeated my best efforts –
      I was secretary at the time
      to the author of *The Craft of Fiction*.
      That title was full of class.
      You only had to open your mouth on it
      to show where you were born
      and where you belonged. I tried
      time and again I tried
      but I couldn't make it
      that top *A-ah*
      I should say –
      it sounded like gargling.
      I too visibly shredded his fineness:
      it was clear the job couldn't last
      and it didn't. Still, I'd always thought him an ass
      which he pronounced arse. There's no accounting for taste." Tomlinson, Charles *The Way in and
      Other Poems*, Oxford, Oxford University Press, 1974, reprinted in *Collected Poems*, Oxford, Oxford
      University Press, 1985, pp. 248–249.

293 Baily, p. 150.

294 Ibid., p. 152.

education, a set of privileged criteria stood between the BBC and its audience. Of this, Siepmann has said:

> Such "taste" is ... the result of a social milieu (and to some degree of a status of comparative economic well-being) in which the cultivation of such taste is native and traditional – in the home as well as in the schools and universities. Neither the home circumstances nor the family traditions nor the abbreviated education of the ordinary listener is conducive in any comparable sense to the development of culture in the sense in which the BBC conceives it.[295]

When the dire issues of unemployment began to recede, they were replaced by an age of anxiety in which the working class, increasingly and thankfully employed again in the arms race, sought comfort and relaxation on the one day of the week given to them for this purpose. It was here that the BBC, for all its intentions, was to be found wanting; the divided land in which Commercial radio manifested itself so powerfully during the 1930s was one in which issues of class, geography and generational differences exercised themselves in a climate of diverse and complex social requirements which ultimately – in recreational as opposed to cultural and intellectual terms – the BBC was unable to successfully interpret when matters were reduced to a central and basic essence – a day of rest at the end of a hard-worked – and hard-won – working week.

---

295   Siepmann, Charles A., *Radio, Television and Society*, New York, Oxford University Press, 1950, pp. 147–148. It is interesting that, although writing post-war, Siepmann identifies a number of the problems of BBC pre-war thinking as having survived the years of international conflict.

Chapter three

The American Way? Tension and Inspiration in Transatlantic Influence

"Introduce advertising, and we'll be selling jars of Cholera Balm and liver pads and Sagwa Resurrection Tonic made from healing herbs and elm bark and sacred buffalo tallow. But we won't be able to get out of town like the medicine show does."[296]

Hoover's Children – Reith's Offspring

In 1927, the US Radio Act provided the basis for the institutionalization of American commercial broadcasting in the very year the British Broadcasting Company became a chartered corporation. At precisely the same moment, the two countries thus established formal criteria which were to govern their subsequent development.

This chapter examines the emergence of radio in the United States, demonstrating how the commercial model which evolved there was of significant influence, directly and indirectly, in the development of British radio, both in terms of the emerging Continental output, and the determination of the regulators to ensure that such a model should be resisted within the State system of broadcasting. By so doing it will become clear that the tension between Public Service radio and commercial interests, while being at the heart of the issues in Britain, also represented a source of much debate on the other side of the Atlantic. Importantly it will become clear that the American idea of the Advertising Agency as both acquirer of client revenue and at the same time programme maker was one which was to inform broadcast strategy in British commercial broadcasting, and in turn influence the development of audience research within the United Kingdom.

Engelman has said that "Herbert Hoover is the representational figure in the early history of American broadcasting as Reith is for British broadcasting".[297] It was

---

296 Keillor, Garrison *Radio Romance*, London, Faber and Faber, 1993, p. 38.
297 Engelman, Ralph *Public Radio and Television in America, A Political History*, California, Sage, 1996, p. 39.

Hoover's belief in an enlightened business elite that led him to consider that the state's role in US broadcasting was to create a legislation limited to "ensuring an orderly marketplace".[298] It was as a consequence as Williams has suggested, "a classic kind of market-regulatory control, into which were asserted, always with difficulty and controversy, notions of non-market public interest".[299] This was in marked contrast to what he claims to be an English elite's "effective paternalistic definition of both service and responsibility"[300] which was central to defining the character of the BBC. Whether the establishment of these models was inevitable for either country is an issue we shall examine later in this chapter.

Parallel Beginnings, Divergent Development

In *Broadcast over Britain*, John Reith wrote in 1924 with considerable self-assurance of American radio that:

> with characteristic energy it had been developed wholesale, largely on a commercial basis, and without any method of control whatsoever. There is no co-ordination, no standard, no guiding policy; advertising, direct or indirect, is usually the sole means of revenue. I gather from many American visitors that they consider that the delay which took place before a service was begun in this country, is more than justified by the progress subsequently made.[301]

The birth of radio in the United States is usually claimed to be 2 November 1920, when a radio station in East Pittsburgh, Pennsylvania broadcast the Presidential election results relating to the race between Warren J. Harding and James M. Cox. The station, owned by the Westinghouse Electric and Manufacturing Company, carried the call sign KDKA.[302] Significantly, KDKA's broadcast represented what Barnouw has called "the transitional moment" in early American radio,[303] the determination of the Westinghouse Company to develop radio beyond the area of experimental technical applications it had so far demonstrated in the hands of a relatively few radio amateur enthusiasts into something of wider social and cultural importance. As has been stated by Douglas, "KDKA was started with the idea that it might encourage the sale, not of a few, but of thousands of receiving sets for homes within the receiving range of the station".[304]

It was precisely the same thinking which led to the creation of the British Broadcasting Company two years later. Indeed, also pre-empting the British model,

---

298   Ibid.

299   William, R. *Television: Technology and Cultural Form*, New York, Schocken, 1975, p. 35.

300   Ibid., p. 33.

301   Reith, J.C.W. *Broadcast Over Britain*, Hodder and Stoughton, 1924, London, p. 81.

302   This moment had been anticipated in 1916, when Lee de Forest had announced to the audience listening to his experimental broadcasts that Charles Evans Hughes had been elected President. (Erik Barnouw, *A Tower in Babel, A History of Broadcasting in the United States to 1933*, New York, Oxford University Press, 1966, p. 46.

303   Ibid., p. 70.

304   Douglas, George H. *The Early Days of Radio Broadcasting*, Jefferson, North Carolina, McFarland & Co. Inc,1987, p. 1.

within eight months of the Election results broadcast, Westinghouse was to become part of a powerful alliance of companies with similar interests, the other partners being General Electric, RCA and AT & T.[305] The original moving forces behind the station were Dr Frank Conrad of the Research Department at Westinghouse, and Harry P. Davis, its Vice President in Charge of Broadcasting. At its opening the directors of Station KDKA formerly set out a number of objectives:

> To work hand in hand with the press recognizing that only by published programs can the public fully appreciate the broadcasting service.
>
> To provide a type of program that will be of interest and benefit to the greatest number, touching the lives of young and old, men and women in various stages and conditions of life.
>
> To avoid monotony by introducing variety in music, speeches, etc.
>
> To have distinctive features so timed as to assure their going on at regular periods every evening, in other words as a railroad does by its timetable.
>
> To be continuous, that is to say, to operate every day of the year.[306]

In the early days of KDKA, Westinghouse was forced to "buy" an audience by issuing sets free of charge to employees and friends. "Thus it was that the first audience was drafted."[307] It was not a situation that lasted long, and very quickly the airwaves were seized on by entrepreneurs; subsequently the early development of American radio was chaotic:

> In 1921 anyone who had a little bit of money, a smidgeon of aptitude, and the time could have a radio station. He could operate on any frequency, any time he felt the urge, programming what his inner muse prompted.[308]

This anarchic situation was – to a certain extent – eased by the creation of the Federal Radio Commission, the main function of which was to prevent would-be station proprietors from invading other programmers' wavelengths. Within a year, forty stations were licenced by the commission. A year later this figure had risen to 550.[309]

Paying for Radio

There is some confusion as to the date of the first American radio commercial. Sweeney claims it to be 8 August 1922,[310] while Robertson suggests 28th August.[311] Berkman on the other hand states it as being "August 1923".[312] WEAF had begun broadcasting as WBAY on 25 July 1922, from offices at 24 Walker Street, New York, moving to sumptuous new studios at 195 Broadway on 10

305   Barnouw, p. 72.
306   Quoted in Arnold, Frank A. *Broadcast Advertising: The Fourth Dimension*, New York, John Wiley and Sons, Inc, 1931, p. 9.
307   Ibid.
308   Sweeney, Kevin B. "How Radio Advertising Developed", in *Advertising Age*, 7 December 1964, p. 166.
309   Ibid.
310   Ibid., p. 167.
311   Robertson, Patrick *The New Shell Book of Firsts*, London, Headline, 1994, p. 323.
312   Berkman, Dave "The Not Quite So Inevitable Origins of Commercial Broadcasting in America" in *Journal of Advertising History* Vol. 10, No.1, 1987 p. 39.

August 1923.[313] What all are agreed on is that it was a 10–15 minute talk on Station WEAF, New York, given, Robertson tells us, by a Mr Blackwell (Sweeney states "Stockwell") of the Queensboro Corporation selling space at Hawthorne Hill, a new co-operative apartment block at Jackson Heights, New Jersey.[314] The advertiser was later able to report that as a response to the broadcast, two apartments had been sold.[315] Within a year other advertisers on WEAF were Tidewater Oil, American Express, Macy's, Metropolitan Life, Colgate's and I. Miller Shoes.[316] Robertson states that:

> The station itself provided no programme material at all, but anyone could come in and give his or her message to the world, commercial or otherwise, or demonstrate his particular talents, for a set fee of so much a minute air time.[317]

This form of advertising was named by the station's owner, the American Telephone & Telegraph Company as "toll broadcasting".[318]

It is important to understand that AT & T's situation as a telephone network supplier was at this time a monopoly, and what it sought to achieve with radio was of a similar status. As Berkman has said, "It initially saw a radio station as nothing more than a giant telephone. Just as it rented telephones to any customer who wanted one, it would make its station available on the same 'Toll' or fee basis".[319] As response from potential advertisers came in after this initial experiment, it became clear to WEAF executives that durations of advertisers' announcements would have to be curtailed if listener patience was to be retained. To counter this, advertisers suggested sponsoring programmes with an occasional brief "identifying" message.[320]

With its power as a telephone operator, AT & T began in January 1923 to network programmes to stations in Schenectady (WGY, owned by the General Electric Company), KDKA, Pittsburgh and KYW, Chicago, both Westinghouse Stations.[321] This led in turn to the development of a rate card offering to distribute sponsored programmes along its wires to cities other than that of the home town of the advertiser, at an appropriate additional cost.[322] Thus was created the first commercial network in the world. AT & T's radio interests were subsequently sold

313   Arnold, p. 11.
314   There is disagreement on what the Queensboro Corporation paid for the space: Sweeney (p. 167 states $35, while Robertson, p. 323 mentions "500 dollars for five successive 'spots' ").
315   Lee de Forest however, could be said to have pre-empted all this in 1916. In a letter to Charles Scribner, Chief Engineer at the Western Electric Company, and dated 21 November 1916, and quoted in Barnouw, p. 46 he wrote, "My company has amplifiers to sell, and we have announced the fact several times on our nightly wireless concerts". The irony, as Barnouw points out, was that de Forest "would soon become ... a leading critic of the commercialisation of radio". (Ibid., p. 47)
316   Robertson, p. 323.
317   Ibid.
318   Ibid.
319   Berkman, p. 39.
320   Berkman p. 40.
321   Arnold, p. 11.
322   Berkman p. 40.

to the Radio Corporation of America (RCA), and in 1926 evolved into the National Broadcasting Company. At the creation of NBC, RCA's Owen D. Young published a statement. Given that on both sides of the Atlantic, radio was seeking to define itself at this time, it is instructive to examine certain paragraphs in Young's statement to the press:

> Any use of radio transmission which causes the public to feel that the quality of the programs is not the highest, that the use of radio is not the broadest and best use in the public interest, that it is used for political advantage or selfish power, will be detrimental to the public interest in radio, and therefore to the Radio Corporation of America ...
>
> ... The Radio Corporation of America is not in any sense seeking a monopoly of the air. That would be a liability rather than an asset. It is seeking, however, to provide machinery which will insure a national distribution of the highest quality ...
>
> ... In order that the National Broadcasting Company may be advised as to the best type of program, that discrimination may be avoided, that the public may be assured that the broadcasting is being done in the fairest and best way, always allowing for human frailties and human performance, it has created an Advisory Council, composed of twelve members, to be chosen as representatives of various shades of public opinion, which will from time to time give it the benefit of their judgment and suggestion ...[323]

NBC's first official broadcast, from the Waldorf Astoria, New York, took place on 15 November 1926, and featured the New York Symphony Orchestra and the operatic stars, Titta Ruffo and Mary Garden among others. It was heard by an estimated radio audience of more than 10,000,000 people.[324]

To BBC or not to BBC

In 1930, the vice president of CBS, Henry Bellows, visited Sir John Reith of the BBC in London, for a meeting to discuss a working relationship, whereby CBS could use BBC facilities where occasion required it. An American journalist traveling with the CBS group, César Saerchinger, wrote of the event, and later published his account.[325] Characteristically, Reith was unable to resist the opportunity of a passing jibe at the expense of his CBS visitors: "What I'd like to know", he reportedly said, "is how you Americans can successfully worship God and Mammon at the same time".[326]

There was a growing consciousness, originating in the earliest days of broadcasting within the USA, that radio was a medium to be handled responsibly. This was largely as a result of the fact that early lack of legislation had led to near anarchy in terms of wavelengths and content. It may also be seen as a self-conscious attempt

---

323 Quoted in Arnold, p. 15.

324 Ibid., p. 16.

325 Saerchinger, César, *Hello America! Radio Adventures in Europe*. Boston, Houghton Mifflin, 1938.

326 Ibid., p. 17. The incident and Saerchinger's account is also quoted in Barnouw, p. 248. Saerchinger refers in his book the Reith as "the autocrat of the BBC" and "the czar" (ibid., pp. 17–18).

to demonstrate such responsibility to a world that had already been made aware of the British approach to broadcasting by the Sykes Committee of 1923, which set out the terms from whose recommendations were created under Act of Parliament the British Broadcasting Corporation:

> Broadcasting holds social and political possibilities as great as any technical attainments of our generation … For these reasons we consider that the control of such a potential power over public opinion and the life of the nation ought to remain with the state, and that the operation of so important a national service ought not to become an unrestricted commercial monopoly.[327]

This in turn leads us to recall Reith's famous 1949 statement, cited with relish by more than one American media commentator, including Burton Paulu in his 1956 book on British Broadcasting:

> It was in fact, the combination of public service motive, sense of moral obligation, assured finance, and the brute force of monopoly which enabled the BBC to make of broadcasting what no other country in the world has made of it … [and] that made it possible for a policy of moral responsibility to be followed. If there is to be competition it will be of cheapness, not of monopoly.[328]

Indeed the Sykes Committee (of which Reith was himself a member) had been set up by the British Post Office as a direct response to the wavelength chaos of the early unregulated American experiment. The issue of advertising, and a defining of its place in broadcasting, was central to the Committee's deliberations on finance. Particularly interesting is the Committee's decision against advertising, while permitting certain forms of "sponsorship", that is to say such as concerts presented by organisations of commercial origins, with introductions containing short statements to that effect. It is therefore worth quoting from the document at some length:

> Most of the broadcasting services in the United States and Canada are provided mainly to advertise the operating organizations; and in some cases revenue is obtained by direct or indirect advertisements of other concerns. An example of direct advertising would be the broadcasting of a speech by a representative of a Motor Company extolling the virtues of his Company's cars. An example of indirect advertising would be an announcement before a broadcast that it was being given free through the generosity of a specified firm. We have received representations from the Press protesting against the use of broadcasting in this country for advertising purposes, mainly on the ground that it would seriously affect the interests of newspapers, which rely largely on advertising revenue. They also contend that, while broadcasting in this country remains of the nature of a quasi monopoly, it should not be allowed to compete with newspapers as an advertising medium. [This was to

---

327   Cd. 1951 (1923) Broadcasting Committee Report, [The Sykes Committee Report].
328   Cited in Paulu, Burton *British Broadcasting:Radio and Television in the United Kingdom*, Minneapolis, University of Minnesota Press, 1956, p. 31.

form the main part of the argument against Commercial Radio when the threat from the Continental stations became an issue during the 1930s.]

There appear to be three alternatives, viz.:

(a) that advertisements should be the main source of revenue of broadcasting;

(b) that they should be barred absolutely as at present; and

(c) that they should be accepted only to such an extent as may prove necessary to supplement the main sources of revenue and make ends meet.

We attach great importance to the maintenance of a high standard of broadcast programmes, with continuous efforts to secure improvement, and we think that advertisements on a large scale would tend to make the service unpopular, and thus to defeat its own ends. In newspaper advertising the small advertiser as well as the big gets his chance, but this would not be the case in broadcasting. The time which could be devoted to advertising would in any case be very limited, and, therefore, exceedingly valuable; and the operating authorities, who would want revenue, would naturally prefer the big advertiser who was ready to pay highly, with the result that only he would get a chance of advertising. This would be too high a privilege to give to a few big advertisers at the risk of lowering the general standard of broadcasting. *We consider, however, that there would be no objection to the operating concern being allowed to accept the gift of a concert and to broadcast a preliminary announcement giving the name of the donor; and also to broadcast the name of the publisher and the price of a song which is about to be broadcast.*[329] [My stress]

Public opinion within the USA also had a voice. Radio listening evolved in America as it did elsewhere through what may be seen as three distinct but overlapping stages,[330] led in the first instance – roughly between 1919 and 1924 – by young men of a technical disposition (as with computing and the Internet some sixty years later.) These were the DXers – radio amateurs whose aim was to establish contact with distant stations. For these individuals, the radio receiver was a piece of machinery – a technical device the presence of which in amongst living room furniture would be visually inappropriate. Concurrent with this, but developing out of it as a second stage, was music radio, which increased in popularity with the progressive replacement of headphones by loudspeakers as the principle means of listening.

The third stage, which could hardly have been predicted, and was precipitated by the remarkable success of one programme: *Amos 'n' Andy*, is discussed later in this chapter. Advertising on radio within this evolution in the United States was by no means as certain at the time as may appear in hindsight. There were many opponents to the idea, albeit always battling against a tide of necessity regarding how broadcasting was to be funded within a system that did not allow for the following of a British model of licence-fee support. Garrison Keillor's novel *Radio*

---

329   Broadcasting Committee Report (Cmd 1951, 1923) paras 40–41, p. 19.
330   Douglas, Susan J. *Listening In: Radio and the American Imagination*, New York, Times Books, 1999, pp. 57–58.

Romance gives us an entertaining and largely accurate picture of the dilemmas affecting small station owners:

> Radio was sacred, mysterious, and people talked about it in hushed tones ("Got WJZ in Newark and KDKA in Pittsburgh last night, clear as anything, and last week I got WSM in Nashville", you'd hear men murmur on the streetcar), and ministers preached on its enormous potential for good, its power to bridge great distances and reach great multitudes and promote mutual understanding and world peace. Newspapers printed editorials about "The Responsibility of Radio" and urged the new industry to follow a path of sober adherence to solemn duty. To use such a gift and a godsend to peddle soap – would people stand for it?[331]

Barnouw has shown by reference to trade magazines of the time that this view was by no means uncommon:

> Published reactions were lukewarm, and in some cases indignant. *Radio Dealer* condemned its "mercenary advertising purposes"; it expected "a man-sized vocal rebellion". *Printer's Ink* felt that use of radio as an advertising medium would prove "positively offensive to great numbers of people".[332]

Siepmann has commented on a growing acceptance of the place of advertising through the years in American radio, interestingly at odds with many of the recalled experiences and attitudes of British listeners to continental stations, (see Appendix C). Writing in 1950 he was to remark that "from early aversion, the public has veered around either to reluctant acceptance, or, as with millions, to positive enjoyment of advertising plugs".[333]

The idea of State involvement in terms of monopoly broadcasting and control was an issue which was much debated; in December 1922 the journal *Scientific American* sponsored a round-table discussion on how radio should be financed which was part of a school of thought which led to the very real possibility that a government supported and/or operated radio service was one way forward:

> Many feel it is the Government's duty to maintain several broadcasting stations scattered throughout the country and serving not only for the dissemination of news, Government reports, weather forecasts, agricultural prices and advice, and important announcements and messages by the nation's leaders, but also music, educational talks and so on. Thus the Government would bring about the monopolistic control of broadcasting.[334]

Herbert Hoover, and subsequently the Federal Radio Commission solved this issue

---

331   Keillor, Garrison, p. 37.

332   Barnouw, pp. 107–108.

333   Siepmann, Charles A *Radio, Television and Society*, New York, Oxford University Press, 1950, p. 40. Barnouw (pp. 157–158) cites some amusing concerns about early advertising broadcasts: "A 'discreet' talk on the teeth and their care, offered by a toothpaste company, was delayed while executives argued whether anything so personal as tooth-brushing should be mentioned on the air … .The executives yearned for profits but also for total respectability, and therefore kept devising rules. Prices were not to be mentioned. The color of a can or package was not to be mentioned. Store locations were a taboo subject. Samples were not to be offered. A vacuum cleaner company was not to use the line "sweep no more, my lady" because lovers of the song, *My Old Kentucky Home* might be offended.

334   "About the Radio Round-Table" in *Scientific American*, Vol. 127, No 1, July 1922, p. 9.

with an answer which was to lead to the creation of the American Public Radio and Television System, the "paradoxical ruling that commercial radio served the general public whereas noncommercial broadcasters represented special interests".[335]

David Sarnoff, an early pioneer of the American Marconi Company, who had subsequently moved to RCA, had suggested as early as 1922 an alternative means of funding radio, given its early origins in the USA – as in Britain – of being a means devised by radio set manufacturers of selling radios by the provision of desired content:

> Let us organise a separate and distinct company, to be known as the Public Service Broadcasting Company, or the American Radio Broadcasting Company, or some similar name ... Since the proposed company is to pay the cost of broadcasting as well as the costs of its own administrative operations, it is of course necessary to provide it with a source of income sufficient to defray all its expenses. As a means for providing such income, I tentatively suggest that the Radio Corporation pay over to the Broadcasting Company, two per cent of its gross radio sales, that the General Electric and Westinghouse Companies do likewise and that our proposed licencees be required to do the same.[336]

Sarnoff championed this idea for a number of years, but in the end it came to nothing.[337] Throughout the 1920s the issue of technical progress balancing (or not) with social dehumanization was exercising the minds of American thinkers, and the coming of radio created a very real focus for these deliberations, as did the popular ownership of the automobile and the coming of cinema – firstly in its silent form, and from 1927 with the added wonder of the spoken word – as popular entertainment. It was a time not dissimilar to the last decade of the twentieth century, when consumers were increasingly prompted to invest in new technology, whilst at the same time questioning the value of the content that technology was providing. As late as 1934, Jerome Kerwin, a professor of political science at the University of Chicago was citing the BBC as a partial model for a form of American radio to combat what he saw as its rampant commercialism and uncontrolled monopoly ineptly policed by the FRC:

> In order to secure the large audiences which the advertisers want and will pay for, it is necessary to stage the least elevating types of program during the best listening hours ... practically every program suggests a surrender to current standards of taste.[338]

---

335   Engleman, p. 39.

336   Sarnoff, David, letter, 17 June 1922, cited in Douglas, pp. 81–82.

337   Barnouw (p. 157) puts forward the following possible cause of its failure: "If it did not materialize in the form in which Sarnoff proposed it, one reason may have been that RCA and its manufacturing partners, GE and Westinghouse, were divided from the rest of the industry by a chasm of hostility. Virtually all other set manufacturers had been pilloried by the allies as patent-infringers, and were in turn assailing the allies as 'the trust'. Under the circumstances the co-operative plan outlined by Sarnoff seemed only a remote possibility."

338   Kerwin, Jerome *The Control of Radio*, Chicago, University of Chicago Press, 1934, pp. 20–24.

Advertising Agencies

By 1934 the commercial developments of the previous decade had entrenched themselves in the American broadcasting system to such a degree, and with such increasing sophistication, that there was no going back. In addition to the expansion in radio the 1920s had seen the country in the grip of a consumer revolution which brought with it an explosion in its national advertising industry, and the coming together of these two facts created an impetus which could not and would not be gainsaid:

> A profound social upheaval was underway in the 1920s ... Victorian standards of taste, personal conduct, and morality were disintegrating. The temper of the times favored radio's commercial trend. A dignified broadcasting service, reflecting the hushed atmosphere of a public library, would have been an anachronism. The advertising men, more conscious of the trend of the times than the network executives, took advantage of the jazzed-up tempo of the age. Almost before the broadcasters knew what had happened, the advertising agencies took over – and it was they who set the tone.[339]

The role of advertising agencies is crucial to this study. The fact that the major agencies developed radio interests to a high level of sophistication in the emerging commercial climate of American radio, against opposition from many broadcasters who saw the idea of sending commercials into the ether as being almost tantamount to sacrilege, given the almost miraculous nature of the medium, created a bank of knowledge and experience that was to prove vital in the European adventure of the 1930s. At the same time, within the United States, this expertise solved efficiently the problem of how radio was to be paid for. It also brought with it major implications for audience research. The idea of precision of audience targeting was an issue in advertising which developed surprisingly slowly. It was to gain its first real sense of focus at exactly the time the radio industry was offering potentially new fields to conquer:

> Until well into the new century, agents and advertisers bought literally billions of dollars of advertising space – worrying all the while – without a reliable idea of how many copies of the publications they were using actually were printed or reached customers.[340]

The growing determination of advertisers to be assured that the relevant members of the public were being made aware of their product, led them to place their confidence in the expertise of specialists in the field. By the 1920s advertising agencies had come from being little more than buyers of space to designers and makers of advertising copy, moving finally into the role of advisers. With regard to one of the most important agencies for this study, the J. Walter Thompson Organization, demonstrable evidence of this process being in place in Britain can be traced to 1923:

339   Head, Sydney *Broadcasting in America*, New York, Houghton Mifflin Co., 1956, p. 1924.

340   Starch, Daniel *Revised Study of Radio Broadcasting*, Division of Electricity, National Museum of American History, Smithsonian Institution, Washington DC, cited in Smulyan, Susan *Selling Radio – the Commercialization of American Broadcasting, 1920–1934*, Washington, Smithsonian Institution Press, 1994.

200 customers and 60 dealers from London and Glasgow were interviewed for Sun-Maid Raisins. Between then and 1930, another 10 surveys were carried out for this client alone. In November 1930, a JWT letter to Pond's refers to the "79,000 individual interviews with consumers and traders which this office has conducted during the past few years". And what is striking about the records of "investigation" is their frequency. On Kraft in the seven years between 1929 and 1935, there were 24 investigations (excluding product samplings) ranging from 1,250 housewives to 50.[341]

The idea that the agencies had the knowledge through such surveys to take the guess-work out of advertising, transferred itself to radio in the most practical of ways; if advertisers – and broadcasters – knew who was most likely to be listening at a given time, wastage, both of programme content and advertising revenue, could be kept to an absolute minimum. The next step for the agency was to take over the production of the programme-making process itself. In America JWT established a radio department in 1931, writing and producing programmes utilizing star names, and building the sponsor's message into the very fabric of the broadcast. The control was entirely in commercial hands. A JWT employee of the time, Carroll Carroll, quoted by Smulyan, states that:

> "Because everybody was ad-libbing his way through the air-waves", the J. Walter Thompson agency decided that "to get radio shows that would work as advertising" it would have to write and produce them.[342]

It is significant that these developments were happening in the United States only shortly before they would become possible in Britain, with the infrastructure of a (as yet unconnected) group of Continental radio stations taking shape which agency expertise would help mould into some sort of network in partnership with British radio entrepreneurs. It had been the coming of the US networks, NBC in 1926 and CBS in 1927, and the opportunities to broadcast – and sell – nationally rather than locally, that changed programming and advertising, and helped develop the long-term model for commercial broadcasting, as Siepmann has pointed out:

> Programme service ... tended toward the increasing subordination of locally originated programmes to national programmes conceived and executed by the networks and carried out by their affiliates. The character of advertising also changed and the national advertiser came to dominate the scene as the patron, or "sponsor", of programmes. This last development involved the mushroom growth of advertising agencies, which now function as middle-men between advertiser and broadcaster and have assumed a commanding position in the choice and production of programmes.[343]

In particular the Thompson organization had learned its craft through its American operations in terms of making shows for clients, "right from an opening like 'Heigh-ho, everybody, this is Rudy Vallee' through to such closings as Eddie

---

341 Treasure, Dr. J.A.P.Group Chairman, JWT Co. Ltd., *The History of British Advertising Agencies 1875 –1939*, Jubilee Lecture to Edinburgh University Commerce Graduates' Association, 1976, Edinburgh, Scottish Academic Press, 1977, p. 7.

342 Carroll, Carroll: *None of Your Business: Or My Life with J. Walter Thompson (Confessions of a Renegade Radio Writer)*, New York, Cowles Book company, 1970, p. ix, cited by Smulyan, p. 118.

343 Siepmann, p. 14.

Cantor singing, 'I love to spend this hour with you/As friend to friend I'm sorry it's through'.[344] The major connection between sponsorship and programming however came not through JWT in the first instance, but through the Lord and Thomas Agency in 1929, when the company persuaded one of its existing account holders, the makers of Pepsodent toothpaste, that they should sponsor a new form of radio – the situation comedy. The form had been developed locally in the Chicago area from 1926 by two white comedians, Freeman Gosden and Charles Gorrell who played a pair of black taxi drivers in a variety of comic storylines on their 15-minute shows. Lord and Thomas's suggestion that Pepsodent sponsored their show nationwide changed the course of commercial radio in the United States. *Amos 'n' Andy* began on the NBC Blue Network in 1929, and generated the concept of what Susan J. Douglas has called "story listening, in which people sat down at the same time each day or each week to listen to the same characters enact comedic or dramatic performances".[345] The show's remarkable hold on the American public was such that thousands bought radios just to listen to this one programme, and the sales of Pepsodent soared. It was this event, linked to the onset of the Depression, causing potential audiences to stay in rather than seek entertainment outside their homes, that cemented radio in the United States as a major entertainment – and selling – force. Until this point advertisers had not been sure that the audience was there; now, there could be no doubt what they were listening to, and what the effect on the sponsor's product had been as a result. By 1930 NBC was charging between \$3,350 and \$4,980 an hour at prime time on its two networks.[346]

This extraordinary phenomenon led directly to another which was to characterize the 1930s: the Radio Star. On both sides of the Atlantic the coming years were to be hard, and the idea that entertainment could be brought into the home – at the same time as the listener could search the ether for distant voices from the comfort of his or her armchair – cemented the glamour and wonder of radio. The fact too that mass production made radio sets relatively cheap (by 1933 nearly 75 per cent of radios sold in the US were low-price table models), ensured to the sponsors that their message WOULD be heard. This thinking crossed the Atlantic in the early part of the decade, and was noted by a young Press writer at JWT at Bush House Studios in London's Strand:

> We (my colleagues and I on the Press side) began to realize that the Radio Department had cornered the topical celebrities of the world of entertainment in a way which challenged the former supremacy of the movie stars. Hollywood, though still strongly influential, was now very remote, but the Radio Stars were being created as we sat in our armchairs at home, and their appeal was very personal and "real" to the UK audience.[347]

344   Ibid., p. x, cited in Smulyan, pp. 118–119.
345   Ibid.
346   Douglas, p. 204.
347   Soper, Sam, Press Production Controller, J. Walter Thompson, London *My Life at JWT*, unpublished memoir 1994, manuscript held in J. Walter Thompson Archive, History of Advertising Trust, Mss1994/cat.5.11.97.

87

Transatlantic Comparisons

American agencies and advertisers continued to observe the Continental developments with great interest through the 1930s, noting the similarities and differences demonstrated by audience research. In 1938 Hermann S. Hettinger, Assistant Professor of Marketing at Wharton School, University of Pennsylvania, and a former Director of Research for the National Association of Broadcasters, wrote *Practical Radio Advertising* in partnership with the President of the Neff-Rogow Agency, and a former Sales Manager for Radio Station WOR, New York, Walter J. Neff. Their book is aimed at the American market, but devotes a significant amount of space to exploring the commercial climate in Europe. Their analysis of British stations' content, seen from a US perspective, is illuminating. They note that more classical and semi-classical music seemed to appeal, with fewer sporting events, "since these are relatively undeveloped on the Continent".[348] They note also that popular drama seems to be on the increase, with "one of the most interesting dramatic programs for British listeners during the spring of 1937 being 'The Adventures of Fu Manchu',[349] popular in this country several years ago". Hettinger and Neff go on to observe that British audiences at the end of the decade seem to enjoy the creation of personalities more than their American counterparts:

> Many variety shows are presented. However they are presented in the Continental manner and emphasize the featured soloist much more than the American variety shows do. While most of the talent on European programs is local in origin, a number of American artists including Morton Downey, the Four Ink Spots, and others have won great popularity. British talent on leading European stations is of the caliber of Jessie Matthews and Jack Payne's Band.[350]

To compare schedules between a US company and one of the Continental stations is instructive, particularly in terms of durations and formats. The samples are taken from weekday output during the year 1935. At this time the BBC National Programme did not open until 10.15 a.m., when it broadcast the Daily Service followed by the weather for farmers. Accordingly stations such as Radio Normandy targeted the audience BEFORE the BBC went on air, that is to say transmitting from 8.00 a.m. to 10.15 a.m. exactly, and then closing down until the afternoon. For the purposes of comparison, two hours of afternoon output have been sampled from WEAF (Tuesday, 28 May 1935) Radio Normandy (Friday, 13 December 1935) and the BBC National Programme (Thursday, 11 April 1935):

WEAF[351]
3.30 p.m.   *Ma Perkins* (Serial)
3.45 p.m.   *Dreams Come True* (Serial)
4.00 p.m.   *Women's Review*

---

348 Hettinger, Hermann S. and Neff, Walter J. *Practical Radio Advertising*, New York, Prentice-Hall, 1938, p. 259.

349 Ibid. *Dr. Fu Manchu* by Rohmer, Sax was broadcast on Radio Luxembourg in the strong position of 7.00 p.m. on Sunday evenings. It was sponsored by Milk of Magnesia. The British version of the show starred Frank Cochrane as Fu Manchu, with a strong supporting cast, including a young Mervyn Johns who played "other characters".

350 Ibid., p. 260.

351 *New York Times*, 26 May 1935.

4.30 p.m.   *Marie Deville* (songs)
4.45 p.m.   *Adventures of King Arthur Land* (children)
5.00 p.m.   *Ross Graham* (Baritone)
5.15 p.m.   *Pan American Musicale*

Radio Normandy[352]
3.30 p.m.   *Edith Lorand and her Viennese Orchestra*
3.45 p.m.   *The Rendezvous* (Light Classical music)
4.00 p.m.   *Tea Time with Debroy Somers and Other Artists*
4.45 p.m.   *Children's Corner, with the Uncles*
5.00 p.m.   *Dance Music* (Records)
5.15 p.m.   *Popular Melodies* (Records)

BBC National Programme[353]
3.30 p.m.   *Evensong from Westminster Abbey* (Commenced, 3.00 p.m.)
3.50 p.m.   *Classical Gramophone Records*
4.45 p.m.   *Organ Recital from Coventry Cathedral*
5.15 p.m.   *The BBC Dance Orchestra, Directed by Henry Hall* (until 6.00 p.m.)

A number of points become immediately apparent. Firstly, the durations of programming between the two commercial stations are very similar: mostly these are of a 15 minute span, contrasting sharply with BBC output where programme durations are longer, and less geared to regularity (WEAF and Normandy both choose start times either on the hour or at quarter/half hour timings, easing listener identification of programme change times).

Regarding content, the commercial stations are, as one would expect populist in approach, while the BBC only moves into this mode with Henry Hall's daily programme at 5.15 p.m. It is noticeable however that there is much more evidence of higher production values and considered scheduling on WEAF than on Radio Normandy. Clearly the American station has identified a female audience and has produced speech-based programming – soap operas, magazine programmes etc – to cater to that audience, whereas Normandy is largely content to follow the less expensive option of records. (The crucial difference however is that WEAF was being networked and was assured of a much wider geographical span of listeners than was Radio Normandy, in addition to being more open to competition.) By the end of the decade Normandy's afternoon output would become much more sophisticated, and, with agencies more strongly at the helm, with soaps and magazine features aimed exclusively at the housewife, including four daily serials: *Mr Keen, Tracer of Lost Persons, Young Widow Jones, Backstage Wife* and *Stella Dallas*, separated only by a fifteen minute *Home and Beauty* feature. At 5.00 p.m. *Crime Reporter*, starring Norman Shelley, continued the theme with a wider audience in mind.[354] The BBC on the other hand remained true to its Public Service principals: by the end of the decade it was devoting an hour of its weekday schedules to Schools broadcasting. This was followed by half an hour of light classical music on record, a programme by the BBC Variety Orchestra and a Symphony concert conducted by Sir Adrian Boult.[355]

352   *Radio Pictorial*, 13 December 1935.

353   *Radio Times*, 5 April 1935.

354   *Radio Pictorial*, 18 August 1939.

355   *Radio Times*, 4 September 1939.

It is therefore possible to show that British-produced commercial programming developed through the latter part of the 1930s with US radio as a clear model, and learned in this time to be increasingly responsive to audience requirements. It was however a response adjusted to the tastes and requirements of a British audience; the formats fitted both audience and advertiser, while the content retained differences symptomatic of local cultural/national idiosyncracies. The lessons learned by programmers and advertisers were absorbed; that agencies could demonstrate their power and audience research in support of the clients' requirements as a proven fact was explored by a number of other major London-based agencies:

> This attitude of research and information, although derided at first, clearly established itself fairly quickly in other agencies. Looking through trade advertisements by agencies in 1934, one finds Samson Clark & co. putting "market investigation" first among their services, and claiming "No Samson Clark advertising campaign is commenced until the market facts and figures have been studied under a magnifying glass".[356]

Other agencies adopting a similar "selling" stance to clients included the London Press Exchange. In a 1932 letter to *The Times* the following assurance is sent:

> As you are no doubt aware, this agency during the past few years has paid particular attention to the scientific and factual side of Advertising, and in consequence we have enjoyed a considerable measure of success in our operations.[357]

Radio in Economic Depression

The American lesson had been learned the hard way; during the 1920/22 US Depression, many things had been explored which were later to help smooth the way during the difficult '30s. In April 1927, Roland S. Vaile of Harvard College had published a paper on *The Use of Advertising During Depression*. In his study, concentrating on magazine advertising, Vaile had taken three groups: those who did not advertise in the relevant period, those who increased their advertising, and those who decreased their advertising. His findings showed that:

> The sales of the non-advertising firms were 20 per cent lower in 1921 than in 1920. In contrast the slump was only 12 per cent for the firms which increased their magazine advertising, while it was 26 per cent for the firms which decreased their advertising expenditures.[358]

In his survey he also explored the effects of advertising within the three groups on specific goods genres: personal items, clothing, house furnishings, automobile equipment, automobiles, groceries and building materials. The results of his investigations were as follows (100 = 100 per cent as a norm, therefore any subsequent deviation represents a percentage change):[359]

---

356 Treasure, p. 8.
357 Letter: E. Ward Burton, London Press Exchange, to W Lints Smith, *The Times* 1 February 1932 (History of Advertising Trust Archive, LPE Archive, Box 1).
358 Vaile, Roland S, "The Use of Advertising During Depression" in *Harvard Business Review*, April 1927, reprinted in *Journal of Advertising History*, No. 4, February 1981.
359 Ibid., p. 21.

	1920	1921	1922
Personal items			
Increased advertising	100	116	129
No advertising	100	100	100
Decreased advertising	100	91	99
Clothing			
Increased advertising	100	118	117
No advertising	100	100	100
Decreased advertising	100	90	70
House furnishings			
Increased advertising	100	118	125
No advertising	100	100	100
Decreased advertising	100	102	102
Automobile equipment			
Increased advertising	100	115	112
No advertising	100	100	100
Decreased advertising	100	107	93
Automobiles			
Increased advertising	100	80	109
No advertising	100	100	100
Decreased advertising	100	77	98
Groceries			
Increased advertising	100	102	96
No advertising	100	100	100
Decreased advertising	100	90	87
Building materials			
Increased advertising	100	108	103
No advertising	100	100	100
Decreased advertising	100	104	105

There were valuable issues here for product advertising in Britain during the 1930s. Vaile's conclusions were equally useful:

> Increased magazine advertising during depression generally resulted in an increase in sales relative to the sales of competitors who did not make such increases.

> Reduction in advertising during depression generally resulted in a greater falling off of sales than occurred with firms that did no consumer advertising.

> Different classes of commodities respond in different degree to changes in advertising.[360]

Another conclusion could have been drawn from Vaile's figures: that if a company did not indulge in any advertising, their sales were not affected in either direction. To state this however would have run counter to the doctrine of the developing advertising agencies. With a ready-made "book" of clients and statistics, the agencies were also in a position – given the expanding world of client choice offered

---

360 Ibid.

by radio – to study issues of class in terms of potential advertising outlets. In some cases these were self-selecting. The correspondence at the History of Advertising Trust's archive between the London Press Exchange and *The Times* contains this revealing comment, in which, among potential advertisers, Reckitts Bath Cubes, Meltonian shoe polish, Radiac Shirts and Startrite Shoes are "not regarded as suitable for *The Times*".[361] Interestingly all these products were subsequently successfully advertised on both Radio Normandy and Radio Luxembourg. The sophistication of research in Britain was to be eloquently demonstrated by 1938 in William Crawford's book, *The People's Food*, an exhaustive study of the eating habits of the British population. The work is an enlightening examination of diet, but the purpose behind it was by no means completely altruistic; Crawford's of Holborn was a major advertising agency, and Sir William – with his co-author, K. Broadley – was clear in his introduction as to the reasons for his research:

> With the rise in the standard of living which is continuously taking place and the accompanying improvement which that rise is bringing in our national diet a vast new market is coming into being for the food producer and food manufacturer ... Its development will bring in its train increased turnover for large and small shopkeepers alike, better health for the nation, increased prosperity for British agriculture. Who is better than the advertising practitioner to explore this market; to direct the attention of this new public to the health-giving foods; to assist producers and manufacturers to plan ahead and avoid wasted effort? Planned marketing and advertising will be the spear-head in this new development.[362]

Potential for Expansion

The fact that major American agencies were developing transatlantic interests is demonstrated by the increasing attention given to the British and European markets in journals and books during the late 1930s in the United States. Numerous such works came from American publishers at the time, among them *Radio as an Advertising Medium*, by Warren B. Dygert, Assistant Professor of Marketing at New York University, and Secretary and Account Executive of the FJ Low Advertising Agency, who claimed in 1939:

> It has often been pointed out that the British Broadcasting Corporation has not succeeded in keeping broadcast advertising off the air waves of British [sic], but merely off the British broadcasting stations. A recent survey conducted in Great Britain showed that 69 per cent of English radio owners were dialing sponsored shows coming from the continent. A similar survey in 1935 showed 60 per cent of the radio homes were listening to commercial programs.[363]

Dygert goes on to point out that both British and American advertisers were using

361 Memo from F.P. Bishop of *The Times* to The London Press Exchange, 18 November 1931, held in H.A.T. LPE Archive, Box 1.

362 Crawford, William *The People's Food*, London, William Heinemann Ltd, 1938, pp. xi–xii.

363 Dygert, Warren B. *Radio as an Advertising Medium*, New York, McGraw-Hill Book Company, 1939, p. 232. Dygert is quoting from the journal, *Advertising Age*, 7 December 1936. The research which supports these statements is discussed in the next chapter.

this facility, and that "many large American advertising agencies have London branches which are said to place more than 50 per cent of all the advertising contracts from these continental stations".[364] He cites the Ford Motor Company, Goodrich Rubber, Colgate Dental Cream, Palmolive and Outdoor Girl Cosmetics as "some of the American advertisers that thus enter Britain".[365] Clearly the transatlantic operation of such agencies as JWT was largely responsible for this extension of advertising empires, and would have been based on demonstrable research such as that illustrated above. The attention to the European market by American advertising interests was considerable, and the Agencies' determination to explore that market may well have been fuelled by the fact that in 1934 the US Communications Act sought to regulate American radio by establishing the Federal Communications Commission,[366] which subjected the medium to more constraints than it had hitherto known, ironically at the very moment when completely *unregulated* commercial competition to the BBC was beginning its most fruitful phase. One of the key sections of the act, summarized by Siepmann, provided that:

> the wave lengths of the air are deeded in perpetuity to the people of America. They constitute a public domain to which the broadcaster is given conditional and temporary access, and once admitted into this domain, he may pursue profits for himself. The broadcaster may construct transmitters, studios, and so on, which, of course, are his private property. But they cannot be used except under a licence granted by the Commission, and subject to [certain] conditions ...[367]

As we have seen, there was, among US commentators on commercial broadcasting, a remarkable awareness of how the British system of radio regulation curtailed the power of advertisers in the rich field of potential offered by radio in the 1930s, as well as clearly articulated statements of how the regulations could be – and were being – circumvented. In 1938, Hettinger and Neff were noting some of the problems and their solutions awaiting the potential American advertiser:

> The merchandising of a radio program in Europe and in the US presents slightly different problems. Since commercial broadcasting is prohibited in many countries, most newspapers do not accept paid advertising announcing the program. On the other hand, many radio magazines are popular, even in countries where private broadcasting is non-existent. The more important of these enjoy a large circulation and are worthwhile media for the promotion of the advertiser's program. Counter and display cards, letters to dealers, mail inserts, and similar merchandising devices can be employed in most European countries just as they are in the US.[368]

So we see that American radio, evolving at approximately the same time as its British equivalent, approached the same issues of audience, content and finance with radically differing conclusions. At the same time it is clear that the outcome

---

364   Ibid., pp. 232–233.
365   Ibid.
366   Siepmann, pp. 16–19.
367   Ibid., p. 18.
368   Hettinger & Neff, p. 260.

within US broadcasting was not as unequivocal as popular history might have us recall. As Engelman has stated, the greatest years of commercial radio growth in the US were before the main development of commercial competition to the BBC, by which time American radio was seeing a growth in public radio:

> If commercial radio broadcasters in the United States made great strides during the consumer and advertising revolution of the 1920s, the crisis of the Great Depression enabled noncommercial broadcasters to mount a significant counteroffensive in the period 1930–1935.[369]

Thus "an examination of the interwar period dispels the myth that a consensus existed from the outset about the desirability of a predominantly commercial system of broadcasting".[370] Nevertheless once established, it was the formalisation of American commercial radio policies, as determined ultimately by the proven success and efficiency of the major advertising agencies in United States of the 1920s, that informed the evolution of British commercial radio – recorded in London for transmission from the Continent – during the 1930s. How this was translated into a coherent advertising policy and style, and how it achieved success in Britain through sponsored programming very much shaped on the American model, is the subject of the following chapter.

---

369   Engelman, p. 40.
370   Ibid., p. 11.

PART II

Production Issues

Chapter four

Radio for Sale: Sponsored Programming in British Radio during the 1930s

> *FX: Steam train leaving station:*
> *[Sung, with piano accompaniment]*
> *"We're off to Reading, hurrah, hurrah,*
> *At Huntley and Palmers to spend the day,*
> *We're longing to reach this wonderful town*
> *To taste their biscuits so crisp and brown."*[371]

Context

It is at this point necessary to examine the two principal practical issues confronting non-BBC broadcasters during the years 1930–39. These are identified as:

1. Revenue

2. Programme making

Thus the next two chapters examine firstly how the aims and objectives of American commercial radio were translated to a medium aimed at British consumers, and secondly, how the agencies involved with this process contributed to the practical making of programmes, within the context of the development of several rival recording technologies, explored by both Commercial and BBC interests alike.

The most significant pressure on entrepreneurs seeking to break the BBC monopoly in the 1930s was that of persuading potential British clients that radio had the ability to succeed as an advertising medium rivalling existing methods of marketing: print, poster and increasingly, the cinema. During the decade a sophisticated understanding of radio as a selling medium developed from the American model

---

371   Commercial, Radio Normandy, 1932. Author's collection.

discussed in the previous chapter, together with the necessary thriving industrial infrastructure that was in place, supporting European English language commercial programming aimed at undermining the BBC's monopoly. Further, radio was used by many major consumer brands successfully as an important part of sales campaigns, developing concepts of programme planning and targeting audiences which paved the way for today's frameworks for radio's audience-related decision-making processes. A key part of this study is material from the J. Walter Thompson archive and a 1935 survey of advertisers utilising selected commercial stations, conducted by Legion Information Services, and held by the BBC in its written archives at Caversham.

It is important to place the growth and scale of radio advertising during the decade within the context of other media of the time. In 1933 the American Bureau of Advertising published a pamphlet which examined the years 1928–33 and claimed that radio advertising still had some way to go to prove itself to potential clients:

Of the 5000 national advertisers who might use chain radio broadcast, a comparatively small percentage have tried the medium so far. No doubt as some suitable measure of coverage is approached, and the sphere of broadcast advertising is more clearly defined, new users of the medium will appear. Time, however, will continue to limit the number of broadcast advertisers as it does today. There are only a few "good" hours – in the middle of the evening – when the listening audience is at its greatest; and less than a hundred advertisers can compete for a share in the effective peak of circulation. This suggests that the demand for radio time in the "good" hours might be greater than the supply. There are indications, however, that the demand is already lessening. One of these is the decline in broadcast expenditure. In the last 6 months of 1932, expenditure in broadcast time dropped 28.5 per cent below the first half of the year, and stood 11.3 per cent below the corresponding period of 1931.[372]

In his unpublished memoir of 1994, Soper also identifies the issue of Radio's potential for advertising as a relatively new and untried medium, providing this context:

Most of JWT London's billing was spent in the Press in those days. I would guess the breakdown to be, roughly, 90 per cent press, 5 per cent Outdoor (Posters) 2 per cent Point-of-Sale material and 3 per cent Radio. Despite Radio's minority showing in the pre-war billing, it not only had great potential, as was already an achieved fact in the USA, but to all the London office rank and file, it was the number 1 home entertainment, and talking point. People stopped reading books, playing musical instruments or going out to the cinema for their amusement – instead they listened to the wireless.[373]

Notwithstanding the fact that print advertising gained by far the highest share, the

372 On the Air and Off – An Analysis of the Course of Broadcast Advertising from 1928 to 1933, "Prepared for the Exclusive Use of Bureau of Advertising Members". Bureau of Advertising, US, 1933, p. 3. WAC CAV File R34/959.
373 Soper, Sam My Life at JWT, unpublished memoir, J. Walter Thompson Archive, History of Advertising Trust, MSS1994, cat. 5.11.97.

growth in radio advertising expenditure is interesting. This is demonstrated in Kaldor and Silverman's survey of advertising in the years 1935 and 1938, published in 1948.[374] Their overall estimates, measured in millions of pounds, include Press (display and classified), Posters, Radio and Cinema, and may be summarised thus:

	1935	1938
Press: Display	42.8	42.3
Press: Classified	5.6	5.5
Posters & Transport: Space	4.2	4.4
Production	1.25	1.3
Radio (inc. production)	0.4	1.7
Film (inc Production)	0.55	0.7
Total	56.8	55.9

Given the relative consistency in the other media between the two sampled years, it will be seen that the impact of radio advertising was increasing significantly when it was curtailed by closure of the continental radio services due to the coming of the Second World War.

Early Examples of Sponsored Radio

The sophistication of the late 1930s advertising campaigns had, as we have seen in the previous chapter been born out of the American consumer explosion of the 1920s. While market forces, public service issues and the debate as to the funding of radio is seen as polarising British and US approaches to broadcasting, the subject was under scrutiny elsewhere, notably in Europe. The first scheduled radio broadcast in the world, referred to in my chapter, "Context", is claimed to be Idzerda's Dutch concert, transmitted from The Hague from 8.00 p.m. – 11.00 p.m. on 6 November 1919.[375] Significantly, it was a sponsored programme.

The early Hague experiments continued to encourage others, including Captain Leonard Plugge's Eiffel Tower broadcast of 1925 and there were further commercial experiments throughout the 1920s. In 1927 and 1928 the Kolster Brandes (KB) radio manufacturer sponsored a series of English concerts by the de Groot orchestra from Hilversum,[376] and from 1929 to 1931 there was an occasional series of record programmes broadcast from Radio Toulouse, sponsored by the Vocalion Record Company.[377]

In January 1930 an anonymous BBC internal memo commented on a programme sponsored by Decca Records on Radio Paris and transmitted with both French and English announcers:

> Announcements are made after every record, something like this: "You have just heard Such-and-Such, recorded on a Decca Record No.XXX. You are

374   Kaldor, Nicholas & Silverman, Rodney *A Statistical Analysis of Advertising Expenditure and the Revenue of the Press* Cambridge, Cambridge University Press, 1948.

375   Dutch Radio Museum pamphlet: *Steringa Idzerda*, pp. 1–3.

376   *Steringa Idzerda*, p. 7.

377   Briggs, Asa *The Golden Age of Wireless, Volume II, 1927–1939*, Oxford, Oxford University Press, 1995, p. 325.

now going to hear Such-and-Such, recorded on a Decca Record No. ZZ." The closing announcement is more or less like this: "Ladies and Gentlemen, you have been listening to a concert offered by the Decca Gramophone Company of London and Paris. The records you have heard broadcast have been selected from requests received during the past week, and our next concert, which will take place on Sunday afternoon next, will consist of records selected as the most popular from this week's post. We should like to hear from listeners and correspondence should be addressed to Radio Publicity Limited, – Regent Street, London …"[378]

This early style of "live" sponsored programming, with a presenter simply linking records was soon to give way to more complex recorded productions as the medium expanded. When, in January 1930, Leonard Plugge established the International Broadcasting Company, broadcasting regular sponsored programmes from a range of European stations, notably Radio Normandy in Fécamp and in 1933 Radio Luxembourg created a further outlet for commercial programming, the scene was set for a period in which sponsorship was to play a key part in English language radio from Europe – and in the popular cultural climate of Britain.

The Issue of Sponsorship

Through the first years of the 1930s there was a strong debate as to the merits of commercial broadcasting in Britain, similar although not as extensive as had been explored in the USA; *Wireless Magazine* carried a series of articles on the subject between 1930 and 1933, with considerable emphasis placed on the American model. The magazine claimed that the BBC itself could introduce sponsored programmes based on the lessons learned in the US, where many programmes of a "serious" nature carried little more than the sponsor's name, without undue interruption for advertising:

> Just imagine what a week of sponsored hours would sound like through a BBC station … The announcer says, "Now ladies and gentlemen, you are to be the guests of The Moonlight Soap Company. The Moonlight Symphony Orchestra will open the programme with …". That would be all the advertising; the rest would be a good programme.[379]

In the same year the BBC decided to give its audience a taste of what commercially supported broadcasting meant in programming terms. On New Year's Eve, 1930, an episode of *Amos 'n' Andy* was broadcast in a relay from the US. *Radio Times* issued the following justification:

> We announce this in advance because a broadcast by *Amos'n'Andy* is something of an event. These pretended negroes, who broadcast daily in the interest of a powerful toothpaste corporation, are the single most popular item in the American programmes … To hear *Amos'n'Andy* … will be to take a step nearer to solving the great riddle of those United States.[380]

As has been pointed out by Valeria Camporesi the BBC was inviting its listeners

---

378   BBC Memo, 28 January 1930. BBC Written Archives Centre, Caversham, WAC E2/2/1.
379   *Wireless Magazine* November 1930, p. 394.
380   *Radio Times*, 5 December 1930.

to judge this work as a study rather than as entertainment, inviting them "to a detached evaluation of a distant culture".[381] In its 1933 *Year Book,* the BBC addressed the issue of commercial radio directly by commissioning an article by the leading advertising agent Sir Charles Higham. Higham, together with William Crawford, was a major figure in the British advertising scene; it was therefore seen as an important vindication of non-commercial broadcasting that this giant should speak out AGAINST sponsored programming. Higham wrote that he believed "that eventually radio advertising in England will take its own place amongst media for selling goods" but that when it did "it will be in self defence", taking into account the actions of "foreign competition".[382] Higham's views, counter to the messages reaching London from New York, culminated in the idea that there would be no way of measuring the success of a radio advertising campaign:

> The advertiser ... has neither the guarantee that the sales talk which follows the "sponsored programme", will be listened to (it is more than likely that as soon as it begins, the listener will switch off), nor the knowledge that the people who *do* happen to be listening are the people to whom his product appeals, nor the assurance that even if they are, they are not being antagonised by the method of approach.[383]

As we have seen in the previous chapter, this argument had already been exploded in the US by Lord and Thomas's deal with Pepsodent over the *Amos'n'Andy* show in 1929. Higham compounded the error of his outdated understanding of the contemporary marketplace in his final paragraph:

> Advertising success cannot be built on such hit-and-miss methods. Every penny of the advertising appropriation must be directed to the right people, at the right time, in the right way. In the press, where I spend 95 per cent of my clients' appropriations, I can achieve all these ends. But "on-the-air" I haven't the slightest guarantee that I am achieving any of them.[384]

There is no doubt that, given the emergence of increasingly serious commercial opposition between 1930 and 1932, Higham's article was commissioned because his views represented exactly what the BBC – just moving into its shining new premises in Portland Place – wanted to hear and wanted to communicate to the world. It is however important to place Higham's comments in the context of his own prejudices. As Terry Nevett has explained:

> Although Higham kept abreast of new trends in the sphere of advertising, especially by trips to the United States, he was by no means always in sympathy with them. He believed the growing emphasis by agencies on research was a nonsense ... By the mid-1930s he no longer enjoyed his earlier dominance, perhaps because the new generation of advertising men and women, coming in increasing numbers from the universities, and sitting

381   Camporesi, Valeria *But We talk a Different Language. US "models" in the History of British Radio, 1922–1954.* Unpublished Ph.D thesis, University of Westminster, 1990, p. 89. This work was subsequently published in a revised form as *Mass Culture and National Traditions: The BBC and American Broadcasting 1922–1954,* Fucecchio, European Press Academic Publishing, 2000.

382   Higham, Sir Charles "Advertising on the Wireless", *BBC Year Book, 1933,* London, BBC, p. 59.

383   Ibid., pp. 59–60.

384   Ibid., p. 60.

professional examinations, were looking for something more sophisticated than Higham's old-fashioned blend of salesmanship and advertising evangelism.[385]

Sir William Crawford had reservations about radio as an advertising medium. In a telephone conversation in November 1935 with the newly appointed BBC Controller of Public Relations, Sir Stephen Tallents, he stated himself to be "as a listener ... altogether against radio advertising" and "convinced that the public would be very strongly against its introduction into England". He added that he found it difficult to sell radio space to his clients.[386] Nevertheless, in the same conversation, he admitted that Crawfords had themselves made two series of thirteen programmes for Bird's Custard, placed on Radio Luxembourg at a cost of £300 per fifteen minute episode. As Tallents reported in his transcript of the discussion, the success of audience response could not be denied:

> They run a competition in connection with it, in which the first letter opened on the following Wednesday morning with a correct list of singers in the programme wins £5, and there are also 10/- prizes. They get at present about 20,000 entries every Wednesday morning.[387]

As we have seen, the American model of radio as a sophisticated advertising medium had been in place since the early days; research was detailed and widespread and by 1931 there was a growing library of books on the subject in the US to which Higham and Crawford would have had access. Among these was *Broadcast Advertising* by Frank A. Arnold, Director of Development at NBC and Lecturer in Broadcast Advertising at the College of the City of New York. Arnold's writing, geared though it was to an American industry, contained many lessons for the British entrepreneurs. Fundamental was his statement of what he perceived as the four essentials of good sponsored programming: "First", he wrote, "it should be the best of its kind. Second, it should be fitted to the product. Third, it should be adapted to its audience, and fourth, it should occupy a suitable time."[388]

This last point was to prove of crucial importance to the success of English language commercial radio in the 1930s. It may therefore be claimed with some confidence that when the European commercial campaigns of those years began in earnest, they had as their basis a sophisticated body of background research gained from American experience in all areas of radio advertising, from audience evaluation to the relationship between product and programme. In 1938 Hettinger and Neff commented on the stringency with which Radio Luxembourg controlled its advertising:

> Because Radio Luxemburg [sic] is the principal outlet for radio advertising on the European continent, it has been particularly careful in the formulation of its advertising standards. Only 95 words of advertising copy are allowed on a 15-minute program, 160 on a 30-minute program and 190 words on

385 Nevett, T.R. *Advertising in Britain*, London, Heinemann, 1982, p. 146.
386 Crawford, Sir William, BBC telephone conversation transcript, 14 November 1935. WAC CAV R34/959.
387 Ibid.
388 Arnold, Frank A. *Broadcast Advertising – The Fourth Dimension*, New York, John Wiley & Sons, 1931, p. 87.

an hour's program. No commercial announcement must be longer than 40 words if in one language.[389]

Making Programmes

The production of sponsored broadcast material meant a major adjustment in the way many advertising agencies operated. Almost all programmes were pre-recorded in Britain and shipped out to the Continental stations for transmission. In these programmes the sponsor's message was usually integral to the overall content, which meant that the agencies had of necessity to become programme-makers as well as experts in their own field. In order to establish the expensive facilities necessary for such work, a considerable number of contracts were required, and as a result most commercial programming was inevitably produced by a relatively small number of major agencies. The IBC itself quickly established itself as a facilities house, offering sophisticated studios for hire. Towards the end of the decade, it boasted proudly that it had helped set up some of the agencies' radio services by this method:

> It needs a good deal of radio advertising to justify a complete department. Agencies with only one or two accounts on the air cannot economically take the step of forming one. To them particularly we offer a programme unit complete in every detail and rich in experience. Since its inception in its present form, our programme unit has been responsible for nearly five thousand broadcasts on behalf of advertisers. It is currently handling productions ranging from a single voice to a cast of dozens of artistes. Any advertising agent can place this highly-skilled and efficiently-equipped organisation at the disposal of his client at no higher cost than if he were producing programmes within his own Company.[390]

Outside of the IBC's own operation, the leading advertising agencies involved in programme-making for UK audiences were the London Press Exchange and the giant American J. Walter Thompson Organisation. Initially established in Mansion House Chambers, JWT moved into Bush House in the Aldwych in 1933. "Sam" Soper has given us a strong image of opulence in the new headquarters, an atmosphere of commercial success designed to breed confidence in its clients:

> For me after the Victorian atmosphere of Mansion House Chambers, just to be in the "ace" office block in London was a thrill. We were on the seventh floor – a huge space with rooms partitioned off all round the outside wall; each south wall had a window or two looking out over The Strand and were used by Senior Management. The other rooms on North, East and West walls were used by the Copywriters and Art Directors and by Departmental Managers ... Emerging from the lift on the 7th floor, you would walk into a carpeted reception room lit by two brass candelabras with matching wall lights. The carpeted room was lined with fitted oak furniture – a curved, glass-doored book case in front of which sat Miss Marsh, a pale-faced lady immaculately dressed, with beautifully waved hair in the style of the times.

---

389   Hettinger, Herman S. and Neff, Walter J. *Practical Radio Advertising*, New York, Prentice-Hall, 1938, p. 257.
390   *This is the IBC*, promotional booklet, 1938, author's collection.

She had a manner which was somewhat frigid towards staff and suppliers' representatives, but suitably deferential and delicately warming towards clients who might visit the company.[391]

Soper goes on to describe Bush as a vibrant environment in which star names such as Bebe Daniels, Ben Lyon, Vic Oliver, Max Miller, Debroy Somers and many others would "walk along our carpeted corridors to see Betty Stanley, our chief talent-buyer or Frank Lee, who I believe both 'bought' talent and directed the production under the elegant supervision of a monocled actor-manager of the British theatre world named Basil Foster. Later he was replaced by a radio news-reporter (from Canada I think) called Stanley Maxted."[392]

The necessity of recording material nurtured as a by-product the development of new technical facilities. JWT issued sampler records for clients, containing examples of programming of various types. Howard Thomas, then working for the London Press Exchange, produced programmes at the HMV recording studio at Abbey Road, while observing the progress made by the rival Thompson group – particularly towards the end of the 1930s – at Bush House:

> In 1939 J. Walter Thompson was leading the way ... by pioneering the Philips-Miller system of recording sound on metal tape.[sic] The BBC engineers had been experimenting with this revolutionary advance but they had failed to enthuse the programmers about its merits. Thompson's made their own decision and installed the equipment in their studios at Bush House. The capital cost was considerable but continuous recording on tape rapidly made savings in time and money. When the BBC took over Bush House in wartime for overseas broadcasting the JWT studios and tape-recorders became an immediate asset for the propaganda drive.[393]

The quality of the studios at Bush House is borne out by Soper in his memoir who frequently visited the "fully equipped recording studios in the basement of the South East Wing, where previously there had been a swimming pool. The studio contained two full-sized concert grand pianos, one a Chappell, the other a Steinway."[394]

The Nature of Products Advertised

The character of radio advertising, and the social environment within which it operated during the most successful years of pre-war commercial radio, may be assessed through the example of the J. Walter Thompson ledgers for the years 1936, 1937, 1938 and the first months of 1939, recently discovered in the Organisation's

---

391 Soper, pp. 19–20.

392 Ibid., pp. 25–26. Maxted had been involved in quality issues while Programme Director at the Canadian Broadcasting Commission prior to taking up his post at JWT. In 1933 he had entered into a debate on the standards of broadcast music with Professor CF Thiele, secretary of the Canadian Bandmasters' Association, who claimed that: "90 per cent of the radio music today is trash and jazz and the most degrading type of music." Speaking for CBC, Maxted had argued that "most people who listen will agree that there has been a steady improvement in the quality of music broadcast". (*World Radio*, Vol. XVII, No. 422, Friday 25 August 1933, p. 228).

393 Thomas, Howard *With an Independent Air*, London, Weidenfeld & Nicolson, 1977, p. 34.

394 Soper, p. 25.

Berkeley Square headquarters in London.[395] Analysis of this data shows what products were deemed appropriate for a radio market. The 1930's was a period of considerable unrest and uncertainty both at home and on the international scene. From the data available we may see how advertisers exploited the economic pressures as well as the climate of world-wide political uncertainty. This was already prevalent in billboard and press advertising; it is therefore not surprising that it spread into the field of commercial radio. J. Walter Thompson's books show a direct comparison between these forms. It is clear from these that most of the Organisation's biggest spending clients invested some of their budgets on radio advertising. Given the mood of the time, further analysis confirms that the brands which spent most heavily on radio advertising tended to be relatively affordable products aimed at the household or "quack" medicinal market. The term "night starvation" belongs to a Horlicks campaign, and in his privately printed memoir, George Butler, an Art Director for JWT from 1925–62 gives an insight into its origin:

> Like most good things in advertising, the phrase "night starvation" had disputed paternity. But my belief is that a copywriter called Basil Nicholson coined the phrase. At first, the client found the idea very hard to accept, but it developed into one of our most successful campaigns.[396]

Dyer draws attention to a notice which appeared in a 1931 edition of *Advertisers Weekly*, which demonstrates the awareness of the commercial sector of the possibilities for exploitation within the social climate of the time, in this case for the manufacturer of a brand of tonic wine (Wincarnis):

> Rising unemployment figures, it seemed, were inevitably reducing our market; yet we refused to be intimidated by this. Consideration of the matter showed that even those who drew unemployment benefit represented a potential market and one likely to be productive enough if approached in the right way. So instead of neglecting the unemployed, we visualized them as a prospective market of 2,500,000 people.[397]

Spending

Among the largest of the agencies' accounts were those of Reckitts, Horlicks, Pond's and Kraft. Brown and Polson concentrated their campaign on Custard Powder and Cornflour, two staples of home baking. On the other hand three of the largest spenders – Rowntrees at around £250,000 total per annum, Pond's at £130–150,000 total per annum and Horlicks at £200,000 total per annum – show differing approaches to radio advertising. Rowntree steadily increased their radio spending from under 10 per cent of total spend in 1936 to almost 15 per cent by 1939. Pond's remained constant in their broadcast budgeting, with a fifth of total spend allocated to radio during the period. Horlicks spent more than one third of their money on radio advertising, with a daily one-hour variety programme. Many of J. Walter Thompson's clients chose not to advertise on radio, probably because

395   J. Walter Thompson Archive, unpublished ledgers and accounts, kindly loaned by the Organisation.

396   Butler, George *Berlin, Bush House and Berkeley Square*, privately printed memoir edited by Firth, Jill from conversations, 1985, p. 28.

397   Ibid., p. 47.

in relation to press and outdoor advertising, the production costs were comparatively high: (for example out of every £5.00 spent by Horlicks on radio, £2.00 went on production costs. This against £1.00 in £10, or less, for press production.)[398]

The typical nature of the spending in radio in relation to total budgets of some major clients within the JWT rosta may be seen from the following table:[399]

Client [1936]	Total spend	Airtime	Radio production	Total radio
B&P	74,649	11,054	3,458	14,512
Horlicks	214,557	44,179	42,830	87,009
Ponds	148,840	17,945	12,059	30,004
Rowntree	251,953	20,569	12,218	32,787

Air time could vary widely, according to how much was purchased on any one station or the time of day; clients, via their agents, could place the same programme on a number of different stations. For example, the *Horlicks Picture House* programme was broadcast simultaneously at 4.00 p.m. each Sunday on Radio Luxembourg and Radio Normandy. In addition to this and its daily Teatime programmes, it also bought time on Normandy and Luxembourg in 1936 and 1937 at various times between 8.00 a.m. and 9.30 a.m. At the same time, production costs for Horlicks during this period show as being almost as high as air time. This may be explained by the fact that the company's policy was a high profile one, with top stars of the day featuring on many of its programmes. On Sunday 12 December 1937 *Horlicks Picture House* presented the following: Vic Oliver, Gene Gerrard, Betty Ann Davies, Webster Booth and Helen Raymond, together with compere Edwin Styles and the Horlicks All-Star Orchestra directed by Debroy Somers.[400]

In 1934 the IBC had countered a British press ban on publicity for its programmes by launching its own listings magazine, *Radio Pictorial*. From this time many of the major clients bought advertising space in the journal as well as on the air. For instance, the daily *Horlicks Tea Time Hour*, broadcast on weekdays on Radio Luxembourg and on Sundays on Radio Normandy between 4.00 p.m. and 5.00 p.m., was supplemented by a half-page cartoon-strip featuring a series of fictional "case studies" such as "Ames, the Fighting Parson" who "worked desperately hard in a poor, thickly populated parish". However, when things became too much for him, "night starvation" was diagnosed, and Horlicks provided the answer. This message was carried through into the radio programmes. The advertisement in *Radio Pictorial* thus served two purposes: it publicised the transmission at the same time as it sold the product.

The technique of using a strip cartoon to illustrate a story or a running argument was very widely used by us [at JWT]. We all got pretty good at it.

398 Findings based on figures in J. Walter Thompson Archive.
399 Ibid.
400 *Radio Pictorial*, 10 December 1937.

Sandy Mackendrick started as an Art Director doing Horlicks continuities with great skill. It made him a film director.[401]

The same double approach was utilised with Bird's Custard, as well as Rinso for its *Rinso Music Hall,* broadcast on Luxembourg and Normandy on Sunday evenings. Here the print approach was to produce a poster-like advertisement reminiscent in style of the layout of music-hall posters with which the audience of the time would have been familiar. A programme such as this, employing major stars of the time (Sunday 31 January 1937 boasted Turner Layton, Albert Whelan and Tessie O'Shea among others)[402] was costly in production terms, and required strong print back-up of this kind in order to confirm its standing on a day when the BBC was at its most vulnerable due to its Sunday policy. The issue of Sunday broadcasting – central to radio advertising's success, brought with it problems for some clients, among them Cadbury's, who were to become major users of the medium through the agency of the London Press Exchange. Howard Thomas, at that time a producer with LPE, recalls in his book *With an Independent Air*, the nerve-racking ordeal in 1937 of making a sample programme at Bournville in front of the firm's Board of Management, including George Cadbury, (Chairman), Dame Elizabeth Cadbury and Paul Cadbury, "whom I was told had just been elected to the Chair of the Sunday Observance League".[403] In the first instance Cadbury's turned down the idea of commercial broadcasting, but within a year had changed their view, and Thomas produced a series of programmes hosted by the Blackpool tower organist, Reginald Dixon.

This Saturday breakfast programme – *Cadbury Calling, music for all tastes, a new blend of entertainment* – went on the air in September 1937, and the opening notes came from the chimes of the Bournville carillon, playing *Early One Morning.*

Finally, in April 1939, Thomas succeeded in persuading Cadbury's to buy time in Radio Luxembourg's Sunday schedule.

Cadbury Opera House went on the air for twelve weeks, music from a different opera being performed every week. From an (imaginary) seat in a box, during the (imaginary) interval, we had gentle recommendations for Cadbury's Roses chocolates.[404]

The issue of Sunday observance was also overcome by Rowntree, another major firm of Quaker origin.

The company ... agreed to a suggestion made by J. Walter Thompson and began on consecutive Sundays to advertise its jellies on Radio Luxembourg. The board soon recognized the benefits of radio advertising, and decided to

401   Butler, p. 9. Alexander "Sandy" Mackendrick, born 1912 in Boston, USA. During the war he worked for the Ministry of Information, producing documentaries and newsreels as part of their Psychological Warfare Branch. In 1945 he joined Ealing Studios as a script writer, and produced his first film, *Whisky Galore* in 1949. Subsequent films included *The Ladykillers* (1955) and his study of Broadway megalomania, *Sweet Smell of Success* (1957).

402   *Radio Pictorial*, 22 January 1937.

403   Thomas, p. 6.

404   Ibid., p. 38.

promote cocoa and Black Magic across the airwaves, overriding Gilderdale's [CW Gilderdale, Director] objection to advertising on Sundays.[405] Study of the JWT archive material relating to radio advertising has revealed that no marked seasonal trend was noted for most of the brands advertised. A major exception to this however was the case of Sun-Maid Raisins. With this product the spend begins in September, continues in October and November and tails off again in December. This would seem to reflect a marketing campaign aimed at housewives making mince pies, puddings and cakes for Christmas. Otherwise overall spending through the year was noted as reflecting a business reality which holds today: that is a rise in the spring, followed by a tail off before another peak in summer, an autumnal dip and a further rise in the pre-Christmas period.

The manufacturers of larger, relatively expensive, so-called "luxury" goods seem from the JWT ledgers to have decided that the radio market was inappropriate. Singer Cars, for instance, began the sample period spending a proportion of their £20–25,000 annual advertising budget on radio, but very soon dropped out of the list, preferring to spend on press and outdoor advertising as the decade moved towards its close.

In 1936 the BBC employed RJE Silvey as part of its newly established Listener Research Group. Silvey was a crucial figure, since he had worked in the Commercial sector with the London Press Exchange, and brought with him much valuable information on the methods of agencies and commercial stations. Judging from material in the BBC's Written Archives at Caversham, Silvey was particularly active in his researches into Commercial Radio Advertising during 1937 and 1938. It is apparent from the nature of internal BBC communications that he was set the task of assessing if and by how much interest in commercial radio had been growing. In a memo dated 21 October 1937, to the BBC's Head of Public Relations, he reported on findings based on enquiries made with advertising agencies, from which he concluded that the amount spent by advertisers on buying airtime was moving dramatically upwards:

1934:   £30,000
1935:   £315,000
1936:   £630,000

Silvey adds that: "It is believed in well informed quarters that the 1937 figure may be very nearly double that of 1936".[406] He goes on to put the issue of radio advertising spending into proportion, pointing out that "it is interesting to compare the relative amounts spent on press and radio advertising. The total in the former is probably of the order of £15,000,000, while the latter, if the estimates I have received are reliable, is rather less than £1,500,000"[407] In another memo to Maurice Farquharson of the Listener Research Group, dated 4th February 1938 Silvey reports:

---

405 Fitzgerald, Robert *Rowntree and the Marketing Revolution 1862–1969*, Cambridge, Cambridge University Press, 1995, p. 313. In a footnote Fitzgerald cites meetings of Rowntree's York Board on 1, 12 and 26 March 1935, 28 May and 2 September 1935. Jellies were advertised on Radio Luxembourg from August 1935 and other products from November.

406 Memo, RJE Silvey to C.(PR) 21 October 1937. WAC E2/2/2.

407 Ibid.

The number and importance of advertisers using commercial radio is considerable. In this coming week on Sunday morning 14 advertisers will be broadcasting from Luxembourg and 12 from Normandie. [sic.] Most of these advertisers are of very well known products, and they include Lever Bros, Rowntrees, Stork Margerine, MacLeans, Carters Liver Pills, and J. Lyons and Co. 31 advertisers will be broadcasting from Luxembourg before 10.45 in the mornings next week. They include such firms as Horlicks, Phillips Dental Magnesia, Carters Liver Pills, Cadbury Bros, Milton, Andrews Liver Salts, Rowntrees, Brooke Bond Tea, Stork Margarine, Reckitts, and "Force" [breakfast cereal]. 38 advertisers will be broadcasting from Normandie before 10.45 a.m. next week. Among them are Horlicks, Drage, Carters Liver Pills, Milk of Magnesia, Phillips Dental Magnesia, Macleans, Odol, McDougalls Flour, Kolynos, Reckitts, Brooke Bond Tea, "Force", Glymiel Jelly, Borwicks Baking Powder and Wincarnis. These lists are significant not only because most of these firms would be most unlikely to use an advertising medium which they did not believe to be economically successful, but also because many of these firms have been using commercial radio for a number of years.[408]

Not all radio advertising took the form of sponsored programmes. There were also a certain number of "spots" sold. Unlike actual programme material, there is little remaining audible evidence of this, since the "spots" were usually read "live" by studio announcers, or transmitted in a similarly transient form; Ingersoll watches, for instance, sponsored "The Ingersoll Time Signal" on Radio Normandy. Two recorded examples survive however; these were made early in 1932 at Levy's Sound Studios, then situated in the Quadrant Arcade off Regent Street. The commercials, for Spink's Jewellers and Renis Face cream are 60 seconds and 90 seconds respectively, and took the form of straight "reads" by the late Stephen Williams, one of the first presenters on Radio Normandy and subsequently Radio Luxembourg. Given the social and economic climate (Britain had come off the gold standard in 1931), the Spink commercial has a topicality in that it invites listeners to sell their old gold jewellery and gain "record prices, owing to the enormous increase in the price of gold ... By so doing you will help yourself and help your country ..."[409] The announcements were highly successful, and continued on Radio Normandy for over a year.[410] The Renis Face Cream commercial is also a straight "read" by Stephen Williams, offering a free sample jar of the Cream to listeners who wrote to the firm's Great Stanhope Street headquarters. When interviewed shortly before his death in 1994, Williams recalled the occasionally serial nature of early commercials of this type, and the far-reaching effect of the medium's story-telling power on advertisers and listeners:

> We invented a romantic story concerning the product; Max Staniforth [Senior Announcer, Radio Normandy] started it off with the beginnings of

408   Memo, RJE Silvey to M. Farquharson, 4 February 1938. WAC R34/960.

409   Commercial, Spink and Son, February 1932, Radio Normandy.

410   Interview with Stephen Williams, 1994 conducted by Bickerton, Roger (Vintage Radio Programmes Collectors' Circle). Williams also writes of this in his article, "Pioneering Commercial Radio" in the *Journal of Advertising History*, Norwich, MCB University Press, Volume 10, No. 2, 1987, p. 10.

the story, "Long ago in the streets of Persepholis, a beautiful princess was being carried in her litter ..."[411]

The next Renis commercial would be by Williams, who continued the elaborate tale about a secret and near-miraculous beauty ungent, the secret of which was long-lost, until its recent rediscovery by archaeologists:

> "The ingredients have now been identified, purified and gathered together again and presented to the Ladies of Britain in the form of Renis Face Cream ..." and so on.

The storytelling style, with listeners gaining the latest instalment each time they tuned in has been developed much more recently by television, for example in Britain with the well-known Gold Blend coffee advertisement series of the 1990s, which has subsequently led to a whole genre of similar serial commercials. In his interview, Stephen Williams went on to underline the effectiveness of the Renis campaign:

> I think it's interesting to note that this preparation was so successful that it became a viable commercial proposition entirely on the back of Radio advertising and I believe was marketed for a good many years following our campaign from Radio Normandy. The success of the campaign also helped greatly in the development of radio advertising – commercial broadcasting – because we were able to prove that a product that was advertised only on the air and in no other medium at all could and would sell profitably to the public. Up to this time advertising agents had been very dubious about whether we could sell; they knew we could attract listeners, they knew we could engender interest, but they were very doubtful as to whether we could actually SELL anything. From that moment onwards I think one can safely say that radio advertising became a successful and recognised medium.[412]

The availability of "spot" advertisements such as this made radio as a medium available to smaller firms as well as to the large organisations, who were to seize the opportunities afforded by more sophisticated programming as the 1930's progressed.

Prompted by the developing sophistication of the Commercial stations' campaigns, the BBC commissioned its own survey from Legion Information Services,[413] examining the commercial activity on three of the Continental stations, Luxembourg, Normandy and Poste Parisien. The sample month was October 1935, and the survey reveals a huge number of advertisers and a wide range of air-time prices, presumably based on time of transmission. For instance on Luxembourg the makers of Brown and Polson's Cornflour bought 4 x 15 minute programmes for £480, while California Syrup of Figs bought the same amount of airtime on the same station for £220.

411 Ibid.
412 Ibid.
413 Legion Information Services Survey, October 1935, BBC Written Archives, Caversham WAC.

	Luxembourg	Normandy	Paris	Total
Transmission time	106.5 hours	238 hours	32.5 hours	377 hours
Estimated time sold	68.75 hours	114.5 hours	22 hours	202 hours
% of time sold	65	48	68	54
Spots	74	256	45	375
Estimated cost	£28,993	£13,298	£3,764	£46,055
No. of advertisers	57	61	18	136

Luxembourg had a major advantage over the IBC stations in that its pirated long wave frequency provided nationwide coverage of Britain throughout the 1930s, whereas Radio Normandy had only sporadic reception in the North of England. To its advertisers Normandy sought to counter this by claiming deliberately to "Target the prosperous South". Nevertheless these figures show Luxembourg was clearly far and away the most successful of the Continental stations, a factor that was crucial in its re-emergence after the war.

Perception of the Radio Audience

The success of Commercial programming in the 1930s was very much a partnership between the Agencies and the stations, and the latter part of the decade saw a major and concerted effort to convince advertisers that the medium of radio had "come of age" in this respect. Just how these two parts of the industry perceived the target audience, given the level of research undertaken by agencies from the 1920s onwards on behalf of clients is interesting. In 1938 the IBC issued a promotional gramophone record for potential advertisers, demonstrating how much expertise had been accumulated, in a set up "documentary" narrated by Bob Danvers-Walker, following a programme through from contract to air. In the same year the J. Walter Thompson Organisation issued a similar recording to prospective clients that is a fine period example of audience targeting – or as the announcer calls it, "programme architecture".[414] The record, entitled *There's Something of Importance in the Air* was narrated by a presenter with a distinctly "BBC" style of delivery, who announced that:

> The Radio Department of the J. Walter Thompson Company brings to your ears extracts from its principal programmes. Frankly we understand that you as a business man may not find all our programmes entertaining. You may say that the "selling talks" would not sell you. But we ask you to remember that quite deliberately we have avoided to try to entertain or "sell" men like you. Most of our programmes – like radio itself – are designed specifically for the great middle classes …[415]

This message is repeated throughout the recording; later the announcer again underlines the point:

> Though it may not suit your own particular taste, it is chosen by entertain-

---

414   J. Walter Thompson Sampler Record, *There's Something of Importance in the Air*, 1938, author's collection. CD Appendix (H) Track 1.
415   Ibid.

ment experts who know what appeals to the mass of people who buy the products. Entertainment linked to a sales message, presented in a highly dramatic and personal way, made possible by this new advertising medium – commercial broadcasting.[416]

The announcer might well have been talking to an "upper-class" BBC audience. His message however was that there was another band of listeners tuning in to other stations, consumers of a different style of programme altogether, and with a purchasing power which could be harnessed by radio. To study this material is to become aware of how the commercial possibilities of radio in Britain were understood and exploited before the Second World War. Near the decade's end Hettinger and Neff were able to conclude from the standpoint of interested American observers that:

> Radio advertising in Europe has been generally successful; its new and repeat business is growing in volume. Several programs on Radio Luxemburg are examples of what can be achieved. A contest for the name of a song produced 12,714 letters at an average cost of 5 cents per contact. In another case 33,000 samples of canned soup were distributed at an average cost of 1 cent each. An advertiser of hand lotion distributed 23,000 samples at a cost of approximately 1.5 cents per unit.[417]

To examine the memories of listeners is to understand how effective these policies proved. For all the vast spend that Horlicks invested in their nightly show, the commercial from the 1930's that almost everyone in Britain remembered was from a weekly programme, targeted carefully to a predominantly children's audience, evidence that a memorable and well-produced message broadcast at the right moment is measured in more than air-time. The League of Ovaltineys programme was broadcast from 1934 at 5.30 p.m. on Sunday evenings on Radio Luxembourg:[418]

> *We are the Ovaltineys, happy girls and boys,*
> *Make your request, we'll not refuse you,*
> *We are here just to amuse you.*
> *Would you like a song or story, will you share our joys?*
> *At games and sports we're more than keen,*
> *No merrier children can be seen;*
> *Because we all drink Ovaltine*
> *We're happy girls and boys.[419]*

Produced in J. Walter Thompson's Bush House basement studio, the programme achieved immortality through what might be legitimately claimed to be the most successful advertising jingle of all time. Decades later it can still be recalled and sung by several generations. After the war, the League of Ovaltineys programme was revived in precisely the same format, and the jingle was used on television during

---

416 Ibid.
417 Hettinger and Neff, p. 260.
418 Radio Luxembourg, *League of Ovaltineys* broadcast, 1938, author's collection. CD Appendix (H) Track 3.
419 Ibid.

the 1970s in a commercial. The original programme was built around Harry Hemsley, a child impersonator, and was peopled by children from stage schools. (Post-war, the popular entertainer Leslie Crowther was an "Ovaltiney".) In response to this success the rival London Press Exchange formed a rival "club" for its major client, Cadbury's produced by Howard Thomas. Called "The Cococubs" it was recorded on Saturday mornings at the HMV Studios, Abbey Road, St John's Wood, London.[420]

The placement of the Ovaltineys' programme was a deliberate response to audience research which will be discussed subsequently. The lessons of American campaigns once more bore fruit in the concept of creating a radio children's "domain" of which adults could approve, and which would be the focus of family listening at an appropriate time and day. In 1939 Warren B. Dygert of the American F.J. Low Agency, was to lend support to a policy which had by that time proved itself more than adequately on both sides of the Atlantic:

> The radio advertiser who wants to reach the juvenile audience market will do well today to select a type of program that has the parents' approval – if not their enthusiastic endorsement. Otherwise tremendous ill will and downright antagonism to the advertiser's product will ensue. It is characteristic of children that their interest soon wanes. If a product is to hold its position in a household, it needs a parent's endorsement after the child has introduced it.[421]

Dygert also advocated the concept of a club with membership rights and privileges, adding that "a feather, a badge, or a gilt button makes a boy an enthusiastic salesman and personal user, for a time, of any product that fits halfway into his daily life".[422]

Young subscribers to The League of Ovaltineys were issued upon joining with a rule book and a list of codes, together with other items which could change with membership status. An Ovaltineys comic was included free as a pull-out supplement to popular children's weeklies such as *The Target, The Dazzler, the Rattler, The Rocket* and *The Chuckler*, in addition to which there was a series of spin-off booklets including *The Ovaltineys' Book of Bedtime Stories* and *The Ovaltine Book of Nursery Rhymes*.

> *The League of Ovaltineys* was a fun venture, yet there was an element of military precision about it. There were secret codes, passwords, badges and greeting signals.One could move up through the ranks by getting new recruits. And senior members, who were awarded the Silver Star Badge, were told "Like an officer in the army, you will be in a position of authority. The younger members will look to you for guidance and instruction in the signs, signals and other activities of the League".[423]

Even before the League of Ovaltineys Leonard Plugge had created the International

420   Thomas, p. 34.

421   Dygert, Warren B. *Radio as an Advertising Medium*, New York, McGraw-Hill Book Company, 1939, p. 80.

422   Ibid.

423   Montague, Ron *When the Ovaltineys Sang*, Southend-on-Sea, privately printed pamphlet, 1993, p. 16.

Broadcasting Club for children, and in an amusing example of lighthearted confrontation, Plugge wrote to the BBC's Deputy Director-General, Vice-Admiral Charles Carpendale, making the BBC an Honorary Corporate member of the Club. Carpendale's deadpan response of 20th June 1933 is worth quoting here:

> My dear Plugge
>
> The Corporation is sensible of the honour which you confer upon it in enrolling it as a member of the International Broadcasting Club, but as it is felt that it would be undesirable for the Corporation to avail itself of the opportunity of joining in special Club broadcasts or request programmes and as the facilities for the announcements of children's birthdays and golden weddings appear rather personal than applicable to the Corporation's needs it is considered that the Corporation should not stand amongst your enrolled members.
>
> In thanking you, therefore, the card of membership is nevertheless returned.[424]

Notwithstanding the light-hearted nature of this exchange, it is clear that Plugge and the IBC were being true in their relating of audience policies to concepts of commercial research that were being explored on both sides of the Atlantic from the early to mid 1930s, concepts that would seriously damage the BBC in the remaining years of the decade. This chapter has explored the way American concepts of radio advertising and sponsorship were applied to expanding media fields targeting the British consumer during the 1930s. The development of research into audience habits, linked to a populist programming policy, aimed at a mass audience, and greatly influenced by US broadcasting strategies, provided within Britain at this time the basis for broadcast advertising, the lessons of which were to underpin the policies of UK commercial television programming at its advent two decades later.

Just as audience research grew in importance through the decade for both the commercial companies and the BBC, there was also a development in recording technology in the period which, explored for diverse reasons in the service of vested interests, was to change the nature of programme making. This is the subject of the next chapter.

---

424 BBC Written Archives, Caversham: E2/365/1: Foreign General – International Broadcasting Company file 1, 1930–33.

Chapter five

Recording Technologies and Strategies for British Radio Transmission Before the Second World War

For a few seconds there was only the hiss of the running of the steel tape. Then a whining cockney voice, vibrant with passion, echoed weirdly through the darkened room. Almost furtively Caird looked round at the faces. Which of them, he wondered, shared his own feeling of horror – almost of incredulity – as they listened to this voice of a dead man ...?[425]

Introduction

The evolution of recording for radio in Britain before the Second World War was closely connected to the differing needs of the BBC – transmitting from established bases in London and the Regions – and the commercial radio operators making programmes under the eye of sponsors on domestic soil which then of necessity required transportation to Continental transmission sites. The latter issue was particularly important; up to this time, radio had been principally a "live" medium, but as the influence of commercial radio grew, and sponsors demanded more famous personalities to take part in increasingly sophisticated popular broadcasts, recorded programming became the mainstay of output. The earliest material HAD been "live" and as the 1930s continued, the "sustaining" broadcasts, featuring a single presenter playing gramophone records remained a part of the policy of such stations as Luxembourg and Normandy (largely because such programmes were extremely cheap to broadcast). The smaller stations, or stations where only a limited amount of English language material was broadcast (EAQ, Madrid, Radio

---

425   Gielgud, Val and Marvell, Holt *Death at Broadcasting House*, London, Rich and Cowan, 1934, p. 44.

115

Ljubljana, Radio Côte d'Azur etc) continued with mainly "live" record-based programming through the decade. On the other hand the mass-audience stations required fare of a more elaborate kind to maintain their audience figures, and such artistes as George Robey, Geraldo and his Orchestra and Debroy Somers could only be captured by recorded means, mostly in London. As the 1930s progressed, mobile recording techniques were developed, notably with Radio Normandy's touring stage show, *Radio Normandy Calling*. A programme such as *The League of Ovaltineys* could only have been possible through recording. For its part the BBC was developing its Empire service, and issues of broadcasting to various time zones governed much of its policy-making regarding recording at this time. It is clear therefore that recording for broadcast was influenced by the specific requirements of both concerns, and these issues revolved around particular circumstances quite distinct from the production of gramophone records for public consumption. They embraced a varied range of technologies in an era when Germany was already developing the tape system (ultimately to become universal after the war), all based on the following criteria which individually or collectively affected both the BBC and the commercial stations transmitting populist programming from the Continent. These were:

- Quality of sound reproduction
- Durability
- The requirements of programming (duration, editability etc)
- Issues of portability
- Control of material

The purpose of this chapter is to examine the technologies for radio recording between 1930 and 1939 and to explore the practical philosophies upon which such technical strategies were based. I examine how recording in turn changed these philosophies.[426] The chapter investigates the development of the technologies vying for use as a broadcast medium; in doing so it makes clear that the imperatives of commercial radio and the practicalities of broadcasting content from a distant transmission source were major factors driving the exploration of the recording systems available. Of these there were three:

1. Magnetic
2. Disc
3. Film

---

426 I am grateful to Peter Copeland, former Conservation Manager at the British Library Sound Archive, the late Antony Askew, BBC Producer and Independent Recording Consultant and Dr Michael Biel, Professor of Radio and Television at Morehead University, Kentucky for discussion and insights into this subject. Much information has also been gained from oral history material featuring some of the pioneers of sound recording, lodged at the National Sound Archive at the British Library. Relevant web-pages consulted have been *The Chronology of Magnetic Recording* (http://www.ri.rutgers.edu/~dmorton/mrchrono. html) *Plan for the Preservation of Norwegian Sound Recordings*, chapter 5 (http://www.nbr.no/verneplan/lyd/english/e03.html), *Nagra Historical Account* (http://www.nagra.co./nagra/history.htm) and *Adventures in CyberSound: Recording on wire and Steel Ribbon* (http://www.cinemedia.net/SFCV-RM11-Annex/rnaughton/BLATTNER_STILLE.html).

These three technologies found their practical usage in British broadcasting through the following forms:

1. The Blattnerphone/Marconi-Stille system
2. The Cellulose Nitrate Disc (The "Watts" Disc)
3. The Philips-Miller Film System

I examine these methods of recording in turn, at the same time placing them in the context of both BBC and Commercial Radio usage during the years from 1930 up to the outbreak of the Second World War. As a matter of context, brief mention should be made of German developments in tape recording for radio broadcast prior to World War 2. Edward Pawley remembers visiting Berlin in the 1930s to witness a demonstration of a Magnetophon using paper tape impregnated with iron dust. He gives no date for this event, but goes on to mention that the tape frequently broke and "would clearly have no application in broadcasting until this problem had been resolved. A magnetic tape with a cellulose acetate base was first produced in Germany in 1934, but it was not applied to broadcasting on a significant scale until some years later."[427]

The principle of magnetic recording was arrived at as early as 1878, when Edison patented a magneto-mechanical system using a sheet of steel. Seven years later Charles Sumner Tainter also developed a magnetic recording device, and in 1887 Wilhelm Hedic of The Netherlands created a system using a tape which contained magnetic particles.[428] The following year, Oberlin Smith of Cincinnati suggested a magnetic recording machine which would use cotton or silk thread impregnated with steel dust.[429] The real breakthrough however was made by a Dane, Valdemar Poulsen (1869–1942) in 1898, when he built his Telegraphone, consisting of a length of steel piano wire wound around a drum. The device was intended for the recording of telegraphy transmissions; an electro-magnet tracked along the wire to record and reproduce audio signals. Poulsen demonstrated his invention at the Paris Universal Exhibition of 1900. A number of these machines were made in the United States, but were not marketed; it would be nearly a quarter of a century before the emerging medium of radio made the development of such a discovery relevant. A German engineer, Dr. Kurt Stille (1873–1957), created an improved version of Poulsen's invention in 1924, marketed as a dictating machine by the Vox Gramophone Company. Initially Stille – like Poulsen – used wire, later moving on to develop a metal tape. In 1925 Harold (later Sir Harold) Bishop and L.W. Hayes of the BBC's Engineering Department visited the Vox works in Berlin for a demonstration of the system, but found the fidelity to be considerably below the standard required for transmission.[430] The idea of "bottled programmes" – that is to say material which could be recorded and broadcast at a future date – was further debated in 1927 when the BBC became a Corporation. The reason for its initially slow development – particularly within world organisations such as the BBC – was only partially a technical and financial issue, as Asa Briggs has written:

427   Ibid., pp. 193–194.
428   Angus, Robert "75 Years of Magnetic Recording", in *High Fidelity*, US, March 1973.
429   *The Electrical World*, US, 8 September 1888.
430   Pawley, Edward *BBC Engineering 1922–72* London, BBC Publications, 1972.

"Live" broadcasting was greatly preferred, almost on moral grounds, to recorded broadcasting: it suggested to the listener, "this is it". Suggestions were made also that at the other side of the microphone if artists knew they were being recorded and retakes would be made, they would give mediocre performances. The Talks Department, which insisted on scripts that it could vet, went further and made an art form out of the scripted Talk (with a self-conscious capital T) delivered live. The art lay in properly relating writing to performance: what was natural had first to become artificial before it would sound natural again.[431]

Such thinking helped to justify the thought of recording "as an expensive luxury rather than a necessary component of news".[432] While the BBC initially felt it could afford to take a moral stance on the issue of recording, the competing commercial stations, recording sponsored programming in Britain for transmission from European broadcast sites, had an interest in developing recording techniques to the highest and most efficient standards of quality and durability. It is a further argument of this chapter that this competitive element in the use of the technology of the time actually accelerated development to the long-term benefit of pre-war radio broadcasting in general. That said, when the first exploratory moves were made, they were by the BBC, and the subject under tentative investigation was a variant of the Stille system.

The Blattnerphone/Marconi-Stille System

It was Louis Blattner, a German settled in England since the turn of the century, who was to take up Stille's idea of magnetic recording on steel and develop it to broadcast standards. Blattner was for a time the Manager of the Gaiety Cinema in Manchester, and had the reputation of something of a showman, using early versions of his recording machine as an attraction, giving the public the opportunity of paying to hear their own voice. It is believed that the title "Blattnerphone" originated with these demonstrations.[433] In the late 1920s The British Blattnerphone (Stille System) Company Ltd. was formed and studios were set up at Elstree, although its first machines were manufactured in Germany. In 1929, the BBC's Controller of Programmes, Admiral Sir Charles Carpendale and Noel Ashbridge, recently appointed as Director of BBC Technical Services witnessed a demonstration of the machine, and were sufficiently impressed to agree to a year's trial installation at Avenue House, Clapham. This was the headquarters of the BBC Research Department, formed originally from the former Marconi Company research group based at Writtle. Subsequently the machine was re-housed in Room 66, Savoy Hill at a royalty of £500. The BBC Year Book for 1932 (which covered the programme year from November 1 1930 to October 31 1931) claimed it to be: "in some ways the most important event of the year ..."[434]

The tape used in the original Blattnerphone system was steel, 6 mm wide and

---

431 Briggs, Asa *The BBC: The First Fifty Years*, Oxford, Oxford University Press,1985, p. 121.

432 Scannell, Paddy & Cardiff,David *A Social History of British Broadcasting 1922–1939: Serving the Nation*, Oxford, Blackwell, 1991, p. 118.

433 Askew, Antony, correspondence with author, 1999.

434 *BBC Year Book*, BBC, London, 1932, p. 101.

0.08 mm thick. A spool contained somewhat more than a mile of such tape, weighing 21 pounds. Travelling vertically through the heads at 5 feet per second this gave a playing time of 20 minutes. The device was cumbersome, driven by a dc motor, and its speed had to be regulated by observing a stroboscope and adjusting a sliding rheostat.[435] Uneven tape speed was a problem which plagued the early Blattnerphones, and continued to be a problem when a second generation of ac powered machines appeared in late 1932. These however had the advantage for programme makers in that they were capable of recording 32 minutes on a reduced width tape (3 mm), thus enabling half-hour programmes to be recorded on a single tape.

The machine was found initially to be unsuited to music recording, although it was useful for rehearsal purposes, due to the advantage of immediate playback. In March 1932, while broadcast equipment was being installed in the BBC's new headquarters in Portland Place, the Blattnerphone – together with a second machine to enable continuous recording – was re-sited on the seventh floor of Broadcasting House. On 23 May – just eight days after the change of premises – it was set an unexpected challenge. Amelia Earhart came to Broadcasting House soon after completing her transatlantic flight, and at extremely short notice there came a request that she should be recorded. The machine had not been fully set up, and was untested in its new site. Nevertheless the recording was a success, and went a long way towards proving the Blattnerphone – and recording – as an adjunct to the technology of wireless broadcasting.

The motive for the development of recording for broadcast became more insistent in December 1932, with the inauguration of the BBC's Empire Service; the requirement for "bottling" programmes for repeated transmissions across various time zones meant that demand for the machines was heavy, and maintenance became a problem. In spite of this – and the fact that tape editing was extremely laborious, the metal having to be either welded or soldered in the process – there is evidence that the use of recording had begun to change the way programmes were conceived. On Friday 13 January 1933 *Pieces of Tape*, a composite programme made up of items recorded during the year was broadcast, drawing an enthusiastic review from Leslie Baily, then the Radio Correspondent of *The Sunday Referee* and providing evidence that the technology was having an impact on programme-making:

> *Pieces of Tape*, the medley on Friday night of excerpts from programmes which have been recorded on the Blattnerphone at Broadcasting House was a most interesting programme. We shall hear a great deal more of the Blattnerphone. It has obvious possibilities as a means of introducing realistic sound-effects into radio plays, and the historical value of being able to store speeches, and music, and the sounds of events in this way must have been in the mind of every listener. I am told by a BBC engineer that nobody can tell how long it will be possible to preserve the Blattnerphone tapes, thirty miles of which are already stored away at Broadcasting House. Friday's programme was a

---

435   Godfrey, J.W. "The History of BBC Sound Recording", *BSRA Journal*, Vol. 6, No. 1, 1959 quoted in Pawley, p. 179.

selection from this library, and consisted of over 200 pieces of steel tape cut from the original reels and soldered together.[436] Baily's only reservation relates to the machine's ability to record music: "You probably noticed on Friday a certain amount of noise which especially obtruded itself during music. It is on speech, in fact, that the Blattnerphone is at present most effective. But improvements will be made."[437] The experiments continued and in the following year came *Stars in their Courses,* an edited programme featuring Irene Vanbrugh, Fay Compton, Sir Frank Benson and Matheson Lang.[438] In March 1933 the Marconi Company bought the rights to Blattnerphone. This was to see the start of a fruitful period of development, with a partnership between Marconi's for the mechanical design and the BBC Research Department for the electronics.[439] *The BBC Year Book* for 1934 contains an article entitled "The Application of Sound Recording to Broadcasting", in which is discussed the Blattner system alongside developments in disc recording. This will be examined later. It is clear however that at this time the BBC was thoroughly committed to the steel tape principle of recording: "It is probable … that whatever other [recording] system is used the Blattnerphone will serve as a supplement to it".[440]

There is an interesting aside on Blattnerphone recording in the 1934 novel *Death at Broadcasting House* by BBC producer Val Gielgud and Holt Marvell.[441] A murdered actor's last radio performance is captured on Blattnerphone tape, but even the police have to wait to listen to the evidence, "as the Blattnerphone machines were in particular demand for the Empire Service".[442] The book also gives a sense almost of superstition with which the recording process could be regarded:

> To Caird there had always seemed something repellent and almost indecent about the attempts of spiritualists to pierce the veil of the hypothetical after-life, and to drag back the voices of the dead to make suburban holidays and equivalent tomfooleries. Neither had he ever been able entirely to reconcile himself to the continued use, for purposes of entertainment, of the gramophone records of the voices of celebrated artists after their death. And though he had suggested the replay of this Blattnerphone record of Parsons's murder, now that he actually heard it, he experienced both fear and disgust, combined with an overwhelming conviction that the use of such a method must be unlucky and might well be something worse …[443]

436   Baily, Leslie "The Blattnerphone", *The Sunday Referee Literary and Entertainment Supplement*, 15 January 1933, p. 12.

437   Ibid.

438   Pawley, p. 182.

439   Ibid., p. 181.

440   *BBC Year Book 1934*, p. 418.

441   Holt Marvell was the pseudonym of Eric Maschwitz, originally an assistant in outside broadcasting, then editor of *Radio Times* who was moved by John Reith to become Head of the Variety Department, newly created in 1933 as a BBC response to the tide of populist programming coming from the Continent. Among other things, the charismatic and brilliant Maschwitz co-wrote the hit show, *Good Night Vienna*, and one of the great songs of the 1930s, *These Foolish Things*.

442   Gielgud and Marvell, p. 41.

443   Ibid., p. 44.

The CD Appendix contains an example of a Blattnerphone recording.[444] The BBC set Marconi the task of creating a new generation of machines – now named the Marconi-Stille process – in time for King George V's Jubilee in May 1935. By the end of the year there was a recording suite of six machines installed at Maida Vale, having outgrown the original premises at Broadcasting House. The Marconi-Stille machines built in consultation with the BBC were extremely reliable; Edward Pawley, in *BBC Engineering, 1922–1972* states that in a year's running, in which 1,957 hours of recordings were made, the percentage of breakdown time was 0.33 per cent, with none of this due to the machines themselves, mainly being attributed to tapes breaking at the joints.[445]

Direct Disc Recording

As we have seen, during the years 1930–39 broadcast recording technologies tended to overlap, and while Blattnerphone recordings were used within the BBC, other systems were being developed both there and within the Commercial Radio sector. Indeed there is no evidence to suggest that the Blattnerphone/Marconi-Stille systems were used in British broadcasting other than by the BBC. This was not true of the disc and film systems. Peter Copeland, former Conservation Manager at the British Library National Sound Archive has suggested that these technologies should not be seen as competing but as complementary.[446]

In the early part of the decade the BBC had formed a partnership with The Gramophone Company to enable the recording on disc of historic events. One of the first to be so recorded was on 21 January 1930, when King George V opened the London Naval Conference in the House of Lords. There were two major problems as far as the broadcasters were concerned. The first was financial: the system used was the same as that for making commercial recordings; the pressing process cost £50.00 per hour. The second issue was one of time: it was a lengthy process, taking in excess of 12 hours to accomplish.[447]

A further partnership was developed between the BBC and The British Homophone Company Ltd, enabling the cutting of soft wax discs. At a given moment a number of discs were set in motion together to record a programme or news item. The BBC Year Book for 1934 described the relative merits and problems attendant to this method:

> A fine cutting thread is used in the tracking of the recorder giving approxi-
> mately 150 revolutions to an inch of track, as compared with 84 revolutions
> in the standard record. This, together with slow-speed turn-tables running at
> 60 r.p.m., enables a 12-inch record to play for approximately 9 minutes. For
> immediate play-backs the Blattner system requires a little time (about half

---

444   CD Appendix (H) Track 4, *Sweeney Todd*, BBC Regional Programme, December 1934. Note: the recording has been transferred three times – from 78 rpm to 33 rpm, and subsequently to tape. There is another example of Blattnerphone recording on the web page created by the sound historian, Art Shifrin, (http://www.shifrin.net/audio/Marconi.htm).

445   Pawley, p. 182.

446   Copeland, Peter, former Conservation Manager, British Library Sound Archive, interviewed by this author, 5 January 2000.

447   Pawley, p. 183.

that taken for the recording) to re-wind the tape before running off again. The wax system is quicker than this, as the cutting head on a recording machine is changed for a specially designed pick-up which is tracked by the cutting mechanism and so can follow the grooves in the soft wax.[448]

There were variations available within the system:

Event duration	Speed	Grooves per inch
Up to 5 minutes	78 r.p.m.	80
Up to 7 minutes	78 r.p.m.	150
Up to 9 minutes	60 r.p.m.	150*

*Some depreciation of quality likely in the last minute of recording.[449]

The benefit of this system was that speculative recordings could be made at small cost, enabling broadcast decisions to be made and implemented quickly. This was particularly useful in respect of running commentaries, where highlights could be identified and less interesting sections rejected. The major problem was that one playback destroyed the soft wax recording. Thus it was necessary to make several waxes simultaneously, at least one being retained to make a pressing where the event was considered worth preserving. In 1934 – the last year the BBC operated this system in association with British Homophone and The Gramophone Company – more than 600 waxes were cut, and approximately 300 of these were processed to permanent discs.[450]

In the meantime, Cecil Watts, a musician and entrepreneur, had begun the development of a metal-based lacquer-coated disc, which was to revolutionise broadcast recording techniques. In a taped interview in the National Sound Archives' oral history section, Watts explained that the original impetus for the invention came in 1930, and combined two family enthusiasms – music and recording:

> My father was an enthusiast and expert on the Edison Bell phonograph. I'd been apprenticed as a piano tuner, so I was keen on tone values, sound, that sort of thing. The disc recording system came about because I became a musician and had various bands, and I longed for a play-back recording machine that would give an immediate play-back to rehearsing musicians.[451]

It is important to understand the nature of Watts' invention, and to compare it with conventional disc recording, in order to explain its attractiveness to programme-makers. In commercial recording, the initial wax disc was electroplated to create a "master". A "mother" was then made from the "master" by a second process of electroplating, and from this a number of working matrices or "stampers" from which the final commercial disc was pressed. The process was time-consuming, although the BBC did use it in certain cases where a permanent record of an historic event was required, or for some other reason it was necessary to retain a recording

448 *BBC Year Book 1934* BBC, London, pp. 418–419.

449 Ibid.

450 Pawley, p. 183.

451 Watts, Cecil, interview, British Library Sound Archive *Developments in Recorded Sound* Oral History collection, rec. 20 January 1961, ref. LP26453.

for posterity. Watts method – an aluminium-based cellulose-nitrate laquer-coated disc – enabled playback directly after recording; hence the term direct disc recording. The advantage of Watts' disc was that while it was soft enough to enable the recorder to cut, it was durable enough to withstand repeated play-backs of up to twenty times. The first Watts discs were cut from the centre outwards, which enabled swarf from the recording head's cutting of the lacquer to collect at the centre of the disc, out of the way of the head itself.

Watts' wife Agnes – later his biographer – was heavily involved in the firm and was also interviewed by the NSA, recalling how the business grew according to industry demand:

> He developed the first – very crude – machine over a period of months in a flat over 107 Shaftesbury Avenue. The first discs were hand-sprayed, but later they were dipped. Initially he had a little factory spread between two premises in Old Compton Street and Charing Cross Road. Later, when demand grew heavy, we moved to Cable House, Kew Green, where we had a combined house and office.[452]

Watts' company was named the Marguerite Sound Studios, later to become famous for its initials alone – MSS. The name "Marguerite" was a family one, and was used by Watts and his wife for their new venture, because it was believed to be lucky. For a number of years before the BBC showed interest in the system, the firm manufactured Acetate discs for Commercial radio companies such as the IBC and later Radio Publicity Ltd, the British agents for Radio Luxembourg, as Agnes Watts recalled that "we made records for advertising agencies making programmes to be broadcast from Fécamp and Luxembourg; this is what aroused the BBC's interest".[453] This is borne out by Edward Pawley who states:

> By the early 1930s Marguerite Sound Studios were taking on all kinds of recording commissions, such as advertisements for Radio Luxembourg. [This is imprecise, as Radio Luxembourg did not begin broadcasting until 1933. It is likely that Pawley is referring to initial use by the IBC, although certainly Luxembourg used Watts discs from the outset of broadcasting] The first approach from the BBC came in the autumn of 1933.[454]

The fact that discs could be cut in multiples was of value to the agencies, as it was for the IBC, in that it permitted syndication; it became common practice for recorded features to have a number of transmissions on various stations, and disc recording remained the most efficient way of facilitating this. The BBC obtained a trial machine on loan in April 1934, and after successful experimentation with the system a pair of Watts recorders were ordered for a channel at Maida Vale in June 1935, with a further four at a cost of £200 each in September. It is worth noting that in December 1934 the BBC Board agreed an allocation of £7,600 to develop recording generally. The discs came in two sizes, 12 inch (4.5 minutes recording/playback time, cost two shillings) and 13 inch (5 minutes recording/playback

---

452 Watts, Agnes, interview, British Library Sound Archive *Developments in Recorded Sound* Oral History collection, rec. 1984, no reference number available.

453 Ibid.

454 Pawley, p. 184.

time, cost three shillings). The increase in recording by BBC programme makers, using the Watts system may be judged by the following expenditure on discs:

1935: £   900
1936: £2,500
1937: £3,000

1939 saw the BBC using the Watts system at the rate of 25,000 discs a year.[455] With the disc technology came a new playback system; initially called "the Watts Desk". In August 1935 a Recorded Programmes Mixer was installed in Broadcasting House, consisting of three desks, giving access to up to six discs at a time. The degree of accuracy possible in such channels as these was extraordinary. In the mixing room a dial informed the operator of the number of grooves cut by the head as it moved over the disc, enabling the user to locate a specific sentence or even word by groove number. Pawley gives a graphic example of the precision thus available, at the recording of the Proclamation of the Accession of King George VI:

> The Garter King at Arms stammered over the phrase "our rightful liege Lord" but when the disc was reproduced it was possible to cut out the stammer and to reproduce the speech as it had been intended. Asa Briggs says that this story cannot be traced in the archives, but the present author remembers the recording very clearly.[456]

As is sometimes the case with inventions, a number of interests seem to have been developing the principle of the direct disc at about the same time. Professor Michael Biel recently discovered that the Speak-O-Phone company was demonstrating an uncoated aluminium system similar to early Watts experiments, in a St Louis department store in November 1928.[457] In America, the equivalent of Watts' research was being carried out by the Presto Recording Corporation in Brooklyn, N.Y. Their product – "The Presto Recording Disc", was devised in 1933 and advertised with what may be its first official announcement in *Radio Craft* magazine, dated October 1934:

> The Presto Disc
> For instantaneous recording. After years of research, we have developed a heavily coated disc that for quality of tone, fidelity and reproduction, and low surface noise, equals the commercial wax record. It is black in color, non-breakable, and non-inflammable ...[458]

This apparent coincidence forms part of what Brian Winston has named "supervening social necessities".[459] Winston argues that after the initial invention of a technology, its development or "second transformation" comes:

> not so much from the (socially conditioned) minds of technologists as from

455 Ibid., p. 186.
456 Ibid., p. 188.
457 Biel, Michael, Professor of Radio and Television, Morehead University, Kentucky, in correspondence with this author.
458 *Radio Craft*, October 1934, p. 238.
459 Winston, Brian *Media Technology and Society, A History: from the Telegraph to the Internet*, London, Routledge, 2003, pp. 5–8.

society itself. This transformation is, as it were, a concentration of the generalised social forces which have hitherto been determining the process of innovation … These generalised forces coalesce as a transforming agency …[460]

Thus the arrival of direct disc recording enhanced the development of mobile broadcasting. Pressure grew from journalists such as Richard Dimbleby and producers, among them Lawrence Gilliam, to take radio out of the studio using the new technology. Initially the only facilities for doing this were outside the BBC; In September 1934 Gilliam had to hire a mobile sound unit from a film company to record location-based "microphone snap-shots" for insertion into his feature about Londoners working on the Kent hop harvest, *Opping Oliday*.[461] Finally the BBC invested £1200 in its own mobile recording studio, a 30-cwt Morris van, its equipment powered by 24-V accumulators charged by a generator driven by the engine, and this initial unit, named M53, was first used to record part of Gilliam's feature, *Gale Warning* at Battersea Power Station in March 1935. The magazine *Wireless World* christened the unit "the BBC's Flying Squad".[462] From this point the BBC continued to develop mobile recording, and the 1937 *BBC Annual* referred to the fact that "a small fleet of recording vans has been designed and constructed for collecting programme material from all parts of the country for subsequent inclusion in the programmes".[463] As Scannell and Cardiff have pointed out, the vehicles were heavy and cumbersome, and their use as a rapid response tool for news was further impeded by "bureaucratic regulations governing three different sectors of BBC staff (engineers, drivers, producers)".[464]

Elsewhere in the world, major networks were converted to a new kind of programme making. In the United States for example, where the large nationals had not followed the lead of the smaller private stations in recorded programming, it was Herbert Morrison's dramatic commentary on the Hindenburg disaster – while testing the Presto Direct Disc system in the field on May 6 1937 – that began to break down resistance to recorded output at NBC. This event is chronicled in the US National Archives as part of an Inspection Report on the recordings:

> To test the practicability of recording an event on the scene of action and rushing the transcription back by plane for broadcast a few hours later, WLS, Prairie Farmer Station, Chicago, sent announcer Herbert Morrison and Engineer Charles Nehlsen to cover the first landing in 1937 of the "Hindenburg" at Lakehurst, N.J., on May 6th. As Morrison was describing its approach, the ship burst into flames and exploded. The men stayed on the job nearly three hours and recorded for radio the first eye-witness account of the great disaster. At the end of their recording, they caught a plane to Chicago in order that the account could be broadcast early on May 7th 1937.

460   Ibid., p. 6. Winston goes on to elaborate: "It is supervening social necessities of one kind or another which define the various different sorts of prototypes discernible in the historical record and which transform such prototypes into inventions" (Ibid., p. 7).

461   Felton, F. *The Radio Play. Its Techniques and Possibilities*, London, Sylvan Press, 1949, p. 99.

462   Pawley, p. 188.

463   *BBC Annual* 1937, p. 68.

464   Scannell & Cardiff, p. 123.

The National Broadcasting Company waived its rule against the broadcasting of records and sent this recording over 144 stations from coast to coast in the US.[465]

In UK commercial radio too developments moved towards the use of the outside broadcast recording, employing the Watts disc system. Radio Normandy used pictures of its outside broadcast recording units widely in the station's publicity material; the visual presence of the vans at locations around Britain was a valuable tool in establishing the company in listeners' consciousness. Roy Plomley, later to become famous for his BBC programme, *Desert Island Discs*, began his career in radio with the IBC and in 1936 he was put in charge of outside broadcast recording.[466] The first programme made for IBC stations by mobile unit was called *Radio Parade*, recorded under Plomley's direction on Sunday afternoons in a cinema in Kingston-upon-Thames. It quickly became popular and was subsequently sponsored by Stork Margarine. Initially the IBC had two mobile units, but this was expanded to three very soon, developing the touring show, *Radio Normandy Calling*. During 1937 Plomley was supervising an OB in Blackpool which was to underline the potential poignancy of the recording process:

> Between the time we recorded the show and the time it was due on air, the theatre burned down and all the scenery and costumes were destroyed, an event which made front page news all over the country. But there, on Radio Normandy, were Bertini and his Band, and the Five Sherry Brothers and Tessie O'Shea, and all the rest of the big cast, still performing on a stage that no longer existed.[467]

The use of recorded material from outside sources as opposed to live transmissions, gave commercial companies such as the IBC an advantage over the BBC in terms of flexibility. Many of the summer season variety shows recorded by the IBC, were also broadcast "live" by BBC radio. Plomley was charged with the task of planning a schedule so as to pre-empt the competition, by changing transmission dates, recalling that: "on several occasions we were able to put a show on air just a few days before it was broadcast by the BBC".[468]

In British radio the requirements of mobile recording with the onset of the war were to enhance the reputation of the Watts discs within the BBC. It is interesting to reflect on the later adherence to disc recording in the face of wartime and post-war developments in magnetic tape technology. (See below) Peter Copeland remembered being one of the last Technical operators in the BBC to be trained in use of the system as late as 1960.[469]

---

465   Stone, W.G., Inspection Report, 1 February 1938, US National Archives Accession PG.279 – Job No. 38–103, quoted in Biel, Michael J.*The Making and Use of Recordings in Broadcasting Before 1936,* pp 1002–3, Northwestern University, Evanston, Illinois, Ann Arbor, Michigan, UMI Dissertation Information Service.

466   Plomley, Roy, interview c. 1985 for radio programme, *Searching the Ether*, AIRC.

467   Plomley, Roy *Days Seemed Longer*, p. 147, London, Eyre Methuen, 1980. The CD Appendix contains a rare extract of Plomley's commentary recorded during the show.

468   Ibid., p. 148.

469   Copeland, Peter, in an interview with the author, 5 January 2000.

The Philips-Miller System

After a number of experiments by such as Hymmen, Berthon and Nublat into sound on film, in 1931 Dr. J.A. Miller of Flushing, N.Y., developed his Millerfilm system which became the basis of the Philips-Miller recording process, with tape and equipment manufactured by Philips in Eindhoven, Holland. This was a sound-only system, and its use was as a radio recording medium. The requirements of quality and instant play-back were answered at a stroke in this superior technical advance which, like the Watts discs, was picked up by both BBC and commercial companies alike, with the most widespread use initially among the latter.

The idea of film that required processing before broadcast clearly prevented the instant use of recorded work in play-back form. This was circumvented by having a groove or pattern cut in a cellulose base of film, coated with gelatine, on which was placed a skin of black mercuric oxide some three microns thick. A v-shaped cutter recorded sound signals by tracing a pattern in the oxide, leaving a transparent track down the centre of the film. This optical pattern could be "read" by a photo-electric cell. The result was the highest quality of recorded sound known before World War Two, even given advances then taking place in Germany.[470] The benefits and disadvantages of the Philips-Miller system – marketed as *Philimil* - may be summed up as these:

Benefit

High quality instant playback of up to 15 minutes per reel.

Disadvantages

1. P-M film was not erasable and therefore not reusable for recording.

2. Inspite of improvements in efficiency, it remained a costly system, partly because of (1).

3. Editing of the Philips-Miller film was somewhat problematic in that care was needed to prevent edits being audible. The techniques for avoiding this involved a time-consuming process of cutting the tape then painting over the splice with a black solution comparable to the original oxide, which attenuated the light comparatively slowly as it went past the photo-electric cell. Peter Copeland's explanation clarifies this further:

The technique – known as "blooping" – was rather like fading a volume control very quickly up and down, creating a 20 millisecond or so gap in the programme as the splice went through, which – if you chose the point of edit sensibly, that is to say between words or bars, you would possibly not notice it.[471]

4. It was argued that while its prime use would be for "bottling" programmes on the Empire Service, the increased quality would be negated and made irrelevant by the poor reception of Short Wave broadcasts.[472]

Nevertheless, the use of the system for classical music recording and other situations

---

470   A full technical description of the process is given by M.J.L. Pulling in "Sound Recording as applied to Broadcasting", *BBC Quarterly*, Vol. III, No. 2, July 1948.

471   Peter Copeland, author interview.

472   Askew, Antony, correspondence with this author.

where high quality reproduction was required, was unsurpassed in the late 1930s, as Pawley, writing in 1972, remarked that: "but for subsequent improvements in magnetic recording, the Philips-Miller system might well have remained the best recording system to this day".[473]

The CD appendix contains two orchestral examples which demonstrate through comparison the quality of the system.[474] It is interesting to consider the approaches of the BBC and its Commercial rivals in relation to this technology. Unlike the Blattnerphone, Marconi-Stille and the Cellulose Nitrate disc systems, Philips-Miller was not to the same extent developed in partnership between the BBC and its originator. A BBC Engineering Manual of 1942 bears out that: "the BBC had nothing to do with its development, the first machines being delivered in their fully-developed state in 1937 by their Dutch manufacturers, Messrs. Philips Lamps, Ltd".[475]

The BBC had begun experimental recordings with the film system in 1936.[476] However, Howard Thomas, then working for the London Press Exchange, and later to be a key figure in the development of Commercial Television, is correct in his assertion that the process was adopted more quickly by the Continental stations and their agents, when he states that: "the BBC engineers had been experimenting with this revolutionary advance but they had failed to enthuse the programmers about its merits".[477]

The *BBC Annual* 1937 also gives the impression that the commercial interests were leading the way in this field, mentioning as it does all three technologies then current:

> One employs cellulose-coated metal disks [sic], used chiefly for recording short items or components of a programme. Secondly there is the steel tape recording apparatus, which has recently been very much improved, [this is a reference to the Marconi-Stille machines which replaced the original Blattner-phones] used chiefly for complete recorded programmes for the Empire Service. The third system, at present only in an experimental stage (*so far as the Corporation is concerned*) [my italics] consists of a mechanical method of recording on celluloid strip, similar to that used for film.[478]

It is difficult to ascertain the extent of eventual BBC usage of the Philips-Miller system, although at its peak it would appear to have been considerable. Pawley

473 Pawley, p. 193.

474 CD Appendix (H) Track 6, Mozart, Symphony no. 39 (Minuet & Trio), London Philharmonic Orchestra, conducted by Thomas Beecham. Recorded in the Fierabendhaus of BASF, Ludwigshafen, 19 November 1936 on a K2 dc biased tape machine. CD Track 7: Mozart, Allelujah, Elizabeth Schumann, BBC Symphony Orchestra, conducted by Sir Henry Wood. Recorded in the Queen's Hall, London, 8 September 1936 on Philips-Miller film. There is actually no way of ascertaining the full quality of the Philips-Miller system today, since there are no surviving machines, and any recordings which still exist have been transferred at least once. Nevertheless comparison the two recordings demonstrates clearly that the the P-M technology was far in advance of the early tape being used by German sound recordists at the time.

475 *Engineering Division Training Manual, 1942*, London, BBC, p. 198.

476 *BBC Annual, 1937*, p. 68.

477 Thomas, Howard *With An Independent Air*, London, Weidenfeld & Nicolson, 1977, p. 34.

478 *BBC Annual 1937*, BBC, London, p. 68.

states that by April 1945, when the BBC was phasing out its use of the system, "at least one reproducing channel would have to be retained indefinitely to cope with the stock of Philips-Miller recordings (some 10,000)".[479] A programme of copying was instigated to transfer recordings considered of lasting value to disc, and later to tape. In 1963, the only *Philimil* films left in the archives were transferred to tape running at 7.5 inches per second by Rowena Taylor at Maida Vale, and the originals destroyed as a fire hazard.

The IBC stations, and later Radio Luxembourg had taken an early interest in the use of optical systems as a recording/playback medium, for reasons of durability as well as quality. The transporting of recorded programmes on discs from London studios to Continental broadcast sites brought with it obvious hazards. The progression from disc to Philips-Miller here came via the use of standard optical film sound recording. The well known broadcaster Bob Danvers-Walker was in charge of setting up many of the IBC stations, including Radio Normandy, and remembered the installation of play-back projectors at the station's studios in Fécamp:

> We had two Western Electric 35mm projectors as you would find in the projection room of a cinema. Programmes would be recorded using just the soundtrack: *The Horlicks Hour, The Ballito Stockings Hour, The Ovaltine Programme*: the major sponsors would have their programmes put onto this film. These were sent over from England, and we were not only the announcers, we were the engineers as well – we did everything![480]

The system was also used by the French staff at the station. In December 1933, *Wireless World* carried the headline "Film Recording at Fécamp":

> Radio Normandy (Fécamp) is now broadcasting concerts recorded on film. The recording equipment has been mounted on a special lorry which tours the principal towns, such as Havre, Rouen, and Dieppe, to "collect" concerts which the station will subsequently broadcast. It is stated that the scheme is designed to save land line costs and delays.[481]

Plomley confirms the use of 35mm film by both French and British broadcasters:

> A few of the programmes were recorded on the soundtrack of ordinary 35mm film, and were transmitted from a pair of soundheads which stood in the workshop. [See photograph] Sometimes French technicians would arrive to use them ... In those days the film used was nitrate stock, which was not merely inflammable but virtually explosive, but no safety regulations were observed. It was not unknown for someone to be seen winding back a reel with a lighted cigarette between his lips.[482]

---

479 Pawley, pp. 384–385.

480 Danvers-Walker, Bob, interview c. 1985 for radio programme, *Searching the Ether*, AIRC. Nichol, Richard (*Radio Luxembourg, The Station of the Stars*, London, Comet, 1983, p. 18) also mentions the use of film projectors in the programming making process: "In London sponsored programmes were recorded via an optical camera on to 35mm film – soundtrack only, of course – and the films sent out to Fécamp where they were laced up and broadcast, producing a sound quality far superior to that of the clumsy discs").

481 *Wireless World* 22 December 1933, p. 66.

482 Plomley, p. 112.

A similar optical system was later installed at Radio Luxembourg – slightly modified from the Radio Normandy prototype – in the Spring of 1934, supervised by a subsidiary of the Gaumont British Group. *The Sunday Referee*, owned by the group which also ran Gaumont British Pictures and for a time had sought to dominate English Language commercial radio (see Appendix A, Station Profiles), provided the technology which allowed programmes to be recorded optically of film sound track.[483] Nichol cites the effect the quality of film had on monitors. Just after 7.00 p.m. on 17 August 1934, BBC monitors at the BBC station at Tatsfield heard Christopher Stone introduce "live", a performance by the entertainer Ronald Frankau. The quality of what followed was good enough to give the impression that the singing – in addition to the announcement – was indeed "live".[484] Enquiries were made to the Post Office to ascertain if a landline had been granted to Radio Luxembourg. It was then discovered that Frankau had been on stage at the Prince of Wales Theatre in London, and no landline had been granted by the G.P.O. It was thus that "the Frankau concert was eventually deduced to have been recorded on film in the same way as many of the Radio Normandy programmes had been since 1932".[485]

The late Stephen Williams, interviewed shortly before his death in November 1994, was chief announcer on Luxembourg and remembered the system operating:

> They didn't like the Blattnerphone system, as it was too heavy, too big, too cumbersome ... so we went in for ordinary sound film ... What we did was install two systems by British Acoustics Ltd ... which operated on 35mm film cut in half lengthways so that it fed through the sound-heads on the single remaining line of sprocket-holes. That gave you a complete half-hour without any change at all and was easily transportable ... The first programme to be recorded in this way featured Carroll Gibbons, Olive Groves and Paul England.[486]

Williams remembered the system as being superceded by the Philips-Miller process in "about 1936". Certainly the P-M system was well established in Commercial radio by 1937 when the J. Walter Thompson Organisation opened a new studio, claiming it to be "the only one of its kind in Europe"[487] at Bush House, Aldwych, London.

> This system ... has the advantage that the record may be played back instantly, and at the opening demonstration Foster Richmond, the well-known singer, recorded an item which was reproduced through the loud speakers in the studio almost before he had time to sit down.[488]

Apart from his enthusiastic examination of the P-M system, the reporter notes that "in addition to a monitoring room there is a "dubbing" or editing room in which

---

483   Nichol, p. 33.

484   Ibid., pp. 32–33.

485   Ibid., p. 33.

486   Williams, Stephen interviewed by Bickerton, Roger, Autumn 1994, pub. in three parts in *The Historic Record and AV Collector*, Issues 39,40 and 41, April, June & October 1996.

487   Article, "New London Recording Studio: Specially Built for Recording Sponsored Programmes", *Newnes Practical Mechanics*, September 1937.

488   Ibid.

are a number of special disc recorders as well as sound-on-film recorders". Equally he is clearly impressed by the studio itself:

> The walls of the studio are panelled in such a way that the panels may be reversed, and one side is "quilted" to reduce echo, whilst the other side is panelled to provide echo, and thus any desired studio acoustics may be obtained in an instant.[489]

Situated above a swimming pool which had at one time been used by Bush House employees, the studio floor was "rubber-sprung ... built upon layers of rubber alternating with thick layers of cork down to a depth of 2 feet". Howard Thomas, at that time working for the rival London Press Exchange, recalls the Thompson Organisation's investment in this studio in his book, *With An Independent Air*, although he incorrectly refers to the Philips-Miller system as using metal tape. "Furthermore, the commercial radio commitment to pre-recording of programmes eventually influenced the BBC to yield in their devotion to live broadcasting and go over to recording."[490]

With the coming of war, the BBC was to be the beneficiary of Commercial radio investment. Howard Thomas observed that: "when the BBC took over Bush House in wartime for overseas broadcasting the JWT studios and tape-recorders [sic] became an immediate asset for the propaganda drive".[491] This is borne out by Peter Copeland:

> Before World War 11 there was only one Philips-Miller recording channel at the BBC. Then with the coming of war, suddenly realising with censorship of broadcasts and other phenomena coming in the political sense, the BBC understood that it was going to need a great deal more recording equipment than it had ever done before ... So round about September 1939 the BBC became aware that the commercial broadcasting organisations in London had got some Philips-Miller machines and they got their hands on them – I don't know if it was compulsory purchase or lease-lend – but they got their hands on them together with the staff who knew how to operate them, and those machines, which were redundant from the point of view of broadcasting from the Continent of course, became BBC-used machines.[492]

Pawley mentions "three ... machines taken over at the beginning of the war"[493] which are likely to be from the Commercial Studios. Martin Pulling, the BBC's Deputy Director of Engineering at the time remembered Philips-Miller channels at Maida Vale, London, as well as in Bristol and Manchester.[494]

Later Developments

The commercial companies in the last years of the decade began a move back to

---

489   Ibid.

490   Thomas, p. 34.

491   Ibid.

492   Copeland, Peter interviewed by this author.

493   Pawley, p. 385.

494   Pulling, M.J.L., interview in NSA *Developments in Recorded Sound* Oral History collection, August 1984, No catalogue Number.

disc recording, as did the BBC itself, although the Corporation's policy of detailed testing and customising of technology meant that this happened at a slower rate. In 1939 the IBC issued a marketing publication, *This is the IBC*. Here we find this description of how commercial programmes were made, including a comparison of the two technologies as they stood at the time. The following section was written by the IBC's Chief Engineer, Norman Angier. Angier had formerly been an employee in the Research Laboratories of The Gramophone Company Ltd (EMI) and subsequently Technical Recording Manager for Decca. He joined the IBC in 1938. His remarks give the clear sense of a moving away from the Philips-Miller process:

> At the time of introduction it appeared to offer many advantages over some methods of disc recording then in use. Improvements in disc recording have been so considerable since that this is no longer true ... A thorough examination of the two systems has convinced us that since the only purpose of transcriptions is to record advertising programmes, the advertiser is best served by using disc, which permits his programme to be recorded at the lowest cost consistent with the necessary standard of quality. Nevertheless, while we do not use the Philips-Miller system for recording, we maintain reproducing equipment at the station for those advertisers who wish to utilise it.[495]

The disc technology to which Angier refers is the new "Supercut" disc, introduced by MSS in 1938. Pawley describes this as to be "unbreakable, and to have a long playing life and an absolutely silent surface".[496] An interesting further comparison in the two rivals' recording technologies is in the speed of disc recording. Pawley states that before the war, 33.3 direct recordings "had proved a failure" in tests by the BBC.[497] The speed was not introduced by the Corporation until 1941. The BBC's *Engineering Division Training Manual* states two main disadvantages in the use of LP recording, the first being the requirement for new recording and playback apparatus.[498] If the implication here is one of capital investment in new technology, the second objection was a purely practical one: "Because of the greater number of 'words per groove' it is impossible, without further development, to lower the pick-up to the same degree of accuracy in, say, a continuous speech".[499]

On the other hand, where selectivity of material was not required, as in a variety show, this was less of an issue. Angier writes in 1939 that at IBC recording sessions "electrical transcription discs are recorded on a machine which is in effect a precision lathe, the turntable of which rotates at the exact speeds of 77.9 r.p.m. or 33.3 r.p.m".[500] It is easy to see how the LP, with its increased duration of 15 minutes, fitted the Commercial Companies' programming strategy very well, in that the majority of their broadcasts were of precisely this length.

495 Angier, Norman "Recording Commercial Radio Programmes", in *This is the IBC*, London, IBC, 1939.p. 14.
496 Pawley, p. 186.
497 Ibid., p. 187.
498 *Engineering Division Training Manual, 1942*, London, BBC, p. 197.
499 Ibid., p. 198.
500 Angier, Norman *This is the IBC*, p. 14.

The German invasion of Holland put an end to supplies of Philips-Miller film, and the system was never to reassert itself fully again. A similar problem affected the Blattner/Marconi-Stille process in that the steel tapes were manufactured in Sweden and at £20 for a fifteen minute reel in wartime, extensive usage became impracticable. Of the death of the *Philimil* process, Peter Copeland adds that: "it limped along for its niche applications where you either needed word-perfect editing, or you needed high fidelity, until the BBC developed its own disc cutting system using Watts' Cellulose Nitrate discs in 1944".[501]

In addition running costs for the Philips-Miller system were ten times as great as that of disc cutting.[502] The system was finally abandoned as a recording medium in October 1950, with the last four Marconi-Stille machines written off in 1952.[503] In 1945 the BBC acquired a German army Magnetophon Tonschreiber B magnetic tape recorder, and subsequently a Tonschreiber HTS broadcast standard machine.[504] Experimentation using these and subsequent machines led to the gradual adoption of tape as the pre-eminent recording medium.

Conclusion

The true revolution in tape recording came during the early years of the war, when the German engineers combined the technology already evolved, with a neglected discovery of some twenty years earlier – in 1921 – by two Americans, Carlson and Carpenter. The device – which became known as Ultra-Sonic Bias – enabled sound recordists to eliminate background noise whilst at the same time greatly reducing distortion and offering the potential of increasing the frequency range. Peter Copeland points out that, at the time of its original discovery, and for many years subsequently, there was little application for such quality enhancement: "No one could think of a technology for which it would be relevant. So the other media were leaping ahead and no one could think of a way of applying this invention to magnetic recording. The Germans did it."[505] Listeners at the BBC's monitoring station at Caversham near Reading during the war found themselves on occasion hearing Hitler broadcasting from two geographical sites at virtually the same time; clearly one of them was a recording, but the two transmissions were indistinguishable in terms of quality. This was the first clue that Germany was using a new and sophisticated recording technology, although the full answer was not discovered until the war was in its final stages. At that time Allied forces invaded Luxembourg, and discovered Magnetophon tape in the studios of Radio Luxembourg. Meanwhile British troops over-ran the factory of the Deutsche Grammophon Gesellschaft in Hamburg, where recordings of Hitler's speeches were stored for the posterity of the Third Reich.[506] Nevertheless it was not until plans for the BBC's high cultural Third Programme were being developed in 1946, that the idea of using a Magnetophon reproducing channel was actively discussed.

501   Ibid., p. 14.
502   Pawley, p. 384.
503   Ibid., p. 385.
504   Ibid., p. 387.
505   Copeland, Peter, interviewed by this author.
506   Ibid.

In the meantime BBC and Commercial interests during the 1930s explored recording from the standpoint of programming philosophies which in some ways were parallel and in others divergent. For the Corporation the requirement existed to "bottle" programmes for its Empire Service, and to meet the needs of an expansion in the radio day. In his 1934 book, *The Stuff of Radio* the drama producer Lance Sieveking foresaw a time when 24 hour broadcasting used recording to offer repeats of programmes at various times:

> It will be assumed that the listener who hears a play or talk at 4.00 a.m. will be asleep by 6.00 p.m., fourteen hours later. Therefore the same items will be given again on the same wave-length. The players and talkers of the first occasion will in many cases be in bed on the second occasion. Their performances, having been recorded and bottled, will be transmitted again without them.[507]

Likewise the Continental stations of necessity could only fully function with material pre-recorded either in their London studios, or at regional locations such as variety theatres, "bottled", often duplicated for syndication purposes, and shipped to the transmission sites.

At the same time within the BBC the pressure grew from journalists, and drama and features producers to develop a technology which could respond creatively to a sense of Place, and hold the "live" moment. The idea of capturing actuality, the eye-witness account, the essence of an event, became increasingly a vital factor in what made radio journalism different to newspapers, and the same idea of "getting fresh air into the microphone"[508] also influenced writers and producers of drama and features in the latter part of the decade. This thinking did not inform the programme making of the commercial companies, for whom recording was a utilitarian necessity rather than a consciously creative development which enhanced the art and craft of radio.

It may be seen that the development of recording for radio in Britain during the decade 1930–1940 was not solely along an arc of technical improvement. Each of the three technologies discussed answered certain specific needs of broadcasters. In this the various systems were the servants of corporate policy shaping the face of British broadcasting in both the Commercial and Public Service fields. Just as the Blattnerphone and Marconi-Stille machines enabled edited and "bottled" programming, offering the possibility of transmission across differing time-zones, so requirements of higher quality recording for orchestral music favoured the Philips-Miller system for a time. The lead taken by the Commercial companies in returning to disc recording in the last years of the decade reflected the practicalities of cost-saving, together with an improvement in sound recording and reproduction quality in this particular area. It was to be the coming of war which would develop the crucial element of portability of disc recording, making possible single presenter operation, and thus shaping much of the style of radio thereafter.

---

507 Sieveking, Lance *The Stuff of Radio*, London, Cassell, 1934, p. 406.
508 The phrase was widely used in later years; the author recalls its use often during his own BBC production training in the late 1960s.

PART III

Competition and Response

Chapter six

1928–1935

My reaction is why worry when 10 per cent of our listeners are affected? Are we so afraid of competition?[509]

Introduction

The necessity for commercial radio aimed at a British audience before the Second World War to transmit its programmes from a Continental base, produced many experiments on behalf of independent entrepreneurs during the 1920s and 1930s. Ultimately these efforts were to centre around the two most powerful and subsequently famous of the stations, Radio Luxembourg and Radio Normandy. Notwithstanding this fact, it is clear from an examination of BBC internal correspondence of the time[510] that numerous stations throughout Europe sold airtime to English language broadcasters, mostly on a test transmission basis, and that the BBC was monitoring these experiments closely. It is also clear that the ground prepared by these experiments led to the successes of the late 1930s in commercial terms. This section of the study examines the documentation related to developing and changing industry attitudes and policies, and assesses the debate inside the BBC and beyond around the threat from commercial radio, utilizing principally material contained in the BBC's Written Archives at Caversham, Reading.[511] Because of the complexity of the issues unfolding chronologically both within the BBC and internationally, the subject will be dealt with in three chapters. In this chapter I examine the unfolding scenario from 1928, when documentation within the BBC first demonstrates a serious awareness of commercial competition, up to 1935, at the time the Ullswater Committee gathered evidence which was to reaffirm the nature of the BBC's role as a Public Service Monopoly, while acknowledging that there were shortcomings in some of its policies which had alienated it from its audience. The third chapter in this section briefly examines the years of war, and

---

509   Note on BBC Internal Memo, 5 November 1928. BBC Written Archives, Caversham, WAC CAV E2/2/1.

510   BBC Written Archives, Caversham.

511   These archives contain no less than 15 files on the subject of sponsored programmes from 1928 to 1956.

the necessary changes which gave the BBC justifiable motives for a shift in the relationship with its audience. It is necessary first to explore in further detail the central issue of that alienation, mentioned earlier in this dissertation, namely the Corporation's controversial Sunday broadcasting policy, which largely eschewed populist programming in favour of strict sabbatarian principals.

Sunday

The *Radio Times* "National Programme" page for Sunday 7 April 1935 gives a good picture of what the BBC audience of the time could expect.[512] The station did not open until 10.30 a.m., when the first programme was the Weather for Farmers, followed by a 15 minute interlude. Thereafter the morning continued with part one of Bach's St Matthew Passion, some classical band music and a chamber recital by the Gershom Parkington String Quintet. Most of the afternoon was given over to the second part of the St Matthew Passion, followed by a talk "for the children" entitled "Joan and Betty's Bible Story". This took listeners to 4.55 p.m., when the series "Heroes of the Free Churches" reached episode 10, and dealt with the Quaker George Fox. At ten past five came "How to Read an Epistle", prior to the most daring piece of radio of the day, a performance of Sheridan's "The Rivals". Thereafter the diet of religious talks and chamber music resumed until close down with a Religious Epilogue at 10.45.

In fact the BBC's Sunday policy in the mid 1930s represented a *liberalising* of output compared to that of ten years previously, when *Radio Times* reported that the station did not open until 3.00 p.m. The first programme featured two hours of chamber music, then came The Children's Hour, after which the station closed down until after evening service at 8.30 p.m. At this point the BBC broadcast its own religious service, followed at 9.00 p.m. by an hour of light classical music and the news at 10.00 p.m. At 10.15 p.m. there was an interlude of classical piano music, with close down at 10.30 p.m.[513] The rule was that no broadcasting should be allowed to compete with religious activity; there were parts of the day when no radio was necessary or even desirable, given the perception of the broadcasters was that its entire audience *should* at such times be concentrating on their devotions. Between times an appropriately reverent mood must be maintained, in keeping with the sacredness of the day.

A further sample, exactly half way between the two examples cited,[514] confirms that as the 1930s began, the BBC Sunday was a sombre occasion indeed:

3.00 p.m.	Station opens. *Church Cantata (No.1)*. Bach
3.45 p.m.	*For the children* [Unspecified content]
4.15 p.m.	*The Wireless Military Band*
5.30 p.m.	*Piano Recital* [Saint-Saens, Schumann, Arensky]
6.00 p.m.	*Bible Reading: Paul, l l Corinthians, iii and iv*
6.15 p.m.	Close down
8.00 p.m.	*Salvation Army Service*. [Relay from The Queen's Hall]
8.45 p.m.	*The Week's Good Cause. The Bishop of London on behalf of St Margaret's House*

---

512   *Radio Times* 5 April 1935, p. 17.
513   *Radio Times* 29 March 1925.
514   *Radio Times* 28 March 1930, p. 769.

8.50 p.m.	*The News*
9.05 p.m.	*Orchestral Concert: The Wireless Symphony Orchestra, conducted by Sir Henry Wood.* [Programme of Beethoven, Mozart, Sibelius and Tchaikovsky]
10.30 p.m.	*Epilogue: "Tempting God"*

A major difference between 1925 and 1935 was that in the nineteen twenties wireless was new and novelty was all. Ten years had seen major changes in society. There was a growing tension; on the one hand there was what was seen as an out-moded 19th century sabbatarianism and a desire – particularly within the young and the working class – that the one day of rest should be a time to relax. On the other there were the advocates of strict Lord's Day Observance. In the April 1935 edition of *Radio Times* quoted above, an article was published by an American listener living in London, one H. Tosti Russell, who coined a new word to describe BBC programmes: "Decencysorship". This word, claimed Russell described:

> ... the means of respecting the apparent desire of the majority. But it also causes people who are not well acquainted with the BBC tradition to feel more than ever that Sunday is a very dull day in England, even on the air. From my own knowledge of the British, there are many who would enjoy livelier programmes on Sundays. But they undoubtedly approve of "decencysorship" rather than demand of those in control of programme alterations that would offend other listeners – a procedure that would go against the grain of the average Englishman because he would consider that it was not fair play. So on Sundays they philosophically tune in to Continental dance music.[515]

Reithian Ideals

The BBC's Director General, John Walsham Reith was in many ways the embodiment of such ideals, and the nature of his interpretation of those values in the BBC's Sunday broadcasting policy was a major factor in the radio crisis of the 1930s. Kenneth Wolfe has called Reith's attitude towards Sunday "almost superstitious".[516] Certainly, within the context of certain social attitudes towards The Lord's Day which might have been considered puritanical in other countries, his background was even stricter. A son of the Manse, whose father became Moderator of the General Assembly of the Free Church of Scotland, Reith believed that Sunday was an institution "which belonged to the maintenance of a Christian presence. He would defend the working man against being exploited and expose him to the best preaching which the churches could provide."[517] In 1960, eleven years before his death, he spoke of his childhood in a BBC Television interview conducted by John Freeman as part of the famous series *Face to Face*: "There was great love from my mother and father, but there was an austerity in my father's surroundings, and I never learnt that life was for living ... I don't know if that has come to me even yet".[518]

---

515   *Radio Times*, 5 April 1935, p. 12.
516   Wolfe, Kenneth M. *The Churches and the British Broadcasting Corporation, 1922–1956*, London, SCM Press, 1984, p. 63.
517   Ibid., p. 65.
518   Reith, J.C.W., interviewed by Freeman, John, *Face to Face*, BBC Television, 1960.

It was a background and an attitude which was to inform his thinking, and was set out in his 1924 book, *Broadcast over Britain*:

> The surrender of the principles of Sunday observance is fraught with danger, even if the Sabbath were made for man. The secularising of the day is one of the most significant and unfortunate trends of modern life ... The Sabbaths should be one of the invaluable assets of our existence – "quiet islands on the tossing sea of life"... It may simply amount to this, that certain things are not done on Sundays that are done during the rest of the week.[519]

It is clear from this that Reith's religious belief, when applied to programme schedules, would manifest itself in content which was imposed on the audience rather than evolve out of consultation. The broadcasting historian Leonard Miall has said that Reith's background created in him a fervour and a strict puritanism which went much further than the public institutionalised morality of the time: "On boards he made a point of asking applicants for BBC jobs whether they had attended church the previous Sunday. The Reithian sabbatarianism, in my view, was a lot less tolerant than that of the country as a whole."[520] On the other hand Desmond Hawkins[521] recalled a conversation with Reith in 1965 which revealed a sense of private morality and public morality:

> He said "I'm going to Windsor Races tomorrow, and I shall bet on every race on the card. But if I were your Director General I would STILL not allow the starting prices to be given on the radio. My concept is that Public life has to preserve certain standards; the individual may flout them if that is his wish, as long as he does it discreetly.'

Very early in the life of the British Broadcasting Company, Reith established the "Sunday Committee", a group of interdenominational churchmen whose role was to help the fledgling BBC to select its religious speakers. Within ten years the church had established a representative inside the BBC itself. The Committee grew into the more officially named Central Religious Advisory Committee, and in May 1933 Reith appointed the Rev. Frederick A. Iremonger as the Corporation's first Religious Director. Reith later defended the democratic nature of the process, claiming that the executive structure of the BBC prevented any kind of dictatorial dominance by an individual, and that decisions – including those affecting Sunday policy – were the result of a consensus.[522] On the other hand:

> I believe that a business of every sort depends on one man, whether he's executive chairman or chairman or general manager – it depends on one man for its success. I hold that still.

519   Reith, J.C.W. *Broadcast Over Britain*, London, Hodder and Stoughton, 1924, pp. 195–196.
520   Miall, Leonard, in an interview with the author, May 1997. Miall was the BBC's Washington Correspondent during the 1930s, and subsequently was involved with the re-establishment of Radio Luxembourg as an allied propaganda base in the closing months of the Second World War. He has written much about BBC personalities and history, and was adviser to Asa Briggs during the writing of *The BBC – The First Fifty Years* (Oxford, Oxford University Press, 1985).
521   Hawkins, interview with present author, 1998.
522   *Face to Face*, 1960.

Question: Even though that is so different from the Freedom of the Press, you still feel that one man should be solely responsible in broadcasting? Yes I do. I do.[523]

Public Service and Public Mood

Thus the BBC held a moral line between what was deemed acceptable and what was not in public behaviour based on Reithian principles rather than audience research. As early as 1930 this policy produced criticism among programme-makers who voiced their concern regarding the lack of information about public response to programmes. Val Gielgud, Director of Drama wrote at the time: "It must be of considerable disquiet to many people beside myself to think that it is quite possible that a very great deal of our money and time and effort may be expended on broadcasting into a void".[524] Nevertheless the climate of the time within the BBC meant that "Such ideas were dismissed as utopian by some of those who favoured them in principle and by others who openly declared them dangerous".[525]

Beyond the structure of the BBC there was criticism that the new Corporation was out of touch with the public mood, informed too often by a view at management level that its regional studios were less significant than their counterparts in London. When the features producer, A.E. (Archie) Harding made a New Year's Eve programme in 1933 containing material which produced a complaint from the Polish Ambassador, the judgment meted out by his Director-General was summary and telling:

> As Harding recalled it later, Sir John Reith had been magisterial. "You're a very dangerous man, Harding", he was reported as having decided. "I think you'd be better up in the North, where you can't do so much damage". In which opinion we see clearly enough how little was known about the North in Portland Place during the Depression years.[526]

As early as 1930 the accusation of being out of touch with the Public mood and taste was leveled by the journal *Wireless Magazine* which claimed: "The BBC stands condemned in the eyes of thousands of listeners as an organisation that simply will

---

523   Ibid.

524   Quoted in Silvey, R.J.E. *Who's Listening? The Story of BBC Audience Research* London, George Allen and Unwin, 1974, p. 14.

525   Ibid.

526   Bridson, D.G. *Prospero and Ariel, The Rise and Fall of Radio: a personal Recollection*, London, Gollancz, 1971, p. 22. Harding was to shape a Features Department in Manchester which pioneered many major programmes examining the experience and plight of the industrial North, with ground-breaking producers including Bridson himself and the young Joan Littlewood. Even so, some of these programmes, such as Bridson's poetic documentary, *Steel*, drew amusement from some of the steelworkers who were its subject. Scannell & Cardiff quote the Deputy Chairman of Hadfields Ltd, where outside broadcast recordings were made for the programme as saying that the programme "'was perhaps a little too much of a fantasy, but that [response] is only to be expected from a hard-headed people who spend most of their lives in the manufacture and manipulation of steel.' The *Daily Independent* was more blunt: 'Sheffield Laughed when BBC went Poetic over Steel' ran the headline, and the article went on the complain that all this poetry and word-spinning made the programme lack conviction." Scannell & Cardiff, *A Social History of British Broadcasting, Serving the Nation*, Blackwell, Oxford, 1991, p. 343.

not or cannot understand the meaning of entertainment".[527] In the same issue, the Editor invited listeners to write to the magazine if they felt the BBC would make better programmes as a commercial organisation:

> We invite you to write to *Wireless Magazine* if you are in favour of sponsored broadcasts. If your comments are favourable, we will pass them on to the BBC, for it is only by the pressure of public opinion that any change will be made in Savoy Hill's avowed policy.[528]

Set against such a populist tide, the BBC's Sunday policy of steadfast Sabbatarian "Britishness" was at odds with the message coming from other media. Its insistence that "Public Service Broadcasting" was defined by providing what was considered good for the audience rather than what the audience actually wanted opened it to competition from the Continent-based commercial stations which grew in number, output and success during the 1930s. The broadcaster Christopher Stone, who worked both for the BBC and its rivals at various times, defended the principle – albeit in somewhat mocking tones – in his book, *Christopher Stone Speaking*:

> The ideal of public service has been unequivocally adopted by the BBC, and so long as the present board of Governors and Director General are in control there is not the slightest fear that it will ever flag in the pursuit of its lofty mission, which is to keep or to put British Broadcasting at the head of all broadcasting in the world ... It is essential that all of us listeners should accept this lofty standard of public service as a standard which we wholeheartedly wish the BBC to maintain. Even if we switch off from talks or programmes of modern music or poetry readings we should be humble about our own shortcomings and proud that the flowers are there for others to pick.[529]

Stone goes on however to criticise the BBC for dividing society "into high-brows, middle-brows and low-brows", noting that "when it is catering for majorities its *nouveau riche* voice is unable to suppress a hint of snobbishness at times: an irritant of which it is no doubt quite unconscious".[530] Stone in many ways was the personification of the BBC dilemma; a broadcaster of great popular appeal, he was – almost uniquely – able to move between the BBC and its commercial rivals with apparent impunity for a number of years. In October 1932 however, Arthur Burrows, the BBC's first Director of Programmes, and by this time Secretary General of the Union Internationale de Radiodiffusion in Geneva, wrote to Major C.F. Atkinson at Broadcasting House:

> I spent the afternoon listening to the European broadcast programmes (Radio Paris, Christopher Stone presenting) ... I heard two programmes of gramophone records "sponsored" by an establishment in Brixton Road. A more disgusting display of musical depravity could not be conceived.[531]

527 Hunter, Alan S. *Wireless Magazine*, November 1930, p. 271.

528 Ibid.

529 Stone, Christopher *Christopher Stone Speaking*, London, Elkin Matthews and Marrot, 1933, pp. 157–158.

530 Ibid., pp. 159–160.

531 Letter, Burrows, A.R. to Atkinson, Major C.F. 10 October 1932. WAC CAV E2/2/1.

On the letter, in Reith's hand, is the comment: "I am beginning hesitantly to suggest that Stone's undoubted programme value here should no longer count against his other activities".[532]

Stone's career had begun in 1927, when he was substituted for his brother-in-law, Compton Mackenzie to introduce a morning recital of gramophone records on the BBC National Programme.[533] He quickly became extremely popular, and the BBC recognised his value in terms of audience appeal. Stone has been called "the first of the British 'disc jockeys' and thereby 'founder of a very exclusive profession' ".[534] However much Stone's audience-appeal made him a valuable asset, his increased association in the minds of listeners with the Commercial stations, and his public criticism of the Corporation's Sunday policy brought his career with the BBC to a close on 29 August 1934. On Radio Luxembourg however his popularity was continuing to rise. *The Sunday Referee*, at the time a key player in the development of Luxembourg, and the only British newspaper to publicise the Continental stations,[535] carried an article which reflected this in its edition of 5 August:

> Christopher Stone's recent broadcast from Luxembourg afforded an interesting opportunity to test the public interest in that station's Sunday transmissions, for Mr Stone invited his listeners to send for a copy of his magazine, "The Gramophone", in the current issue of which he makes this report:
>
> > In preparation we printed an extra 5,000 copies. Unfortunately, we had under-estimated the volume of appreciation; the analysis of the first 6,000 postcards was interesting insomuch as it proved the wide distribution of listeners. The London district naturally predominated with over 1,200, and Yorkshire came next with nearly 600, but very few counties were unrepresented, and the postcards came from as far afield as Ireland, Cornwall, the Isle of Man and North Scotland.[536]

It was a good demonstration of informal audience research, and also a clear message to potential advertisers of the power of popular radio on Sundays. In the same edition – indeed, immediately beneath this article, the paper's radio editor, Leslie Baily printed an attack on "The BBC Sunday":

> Some people deprecate Luxembourg's vogue, but it is one of the outstanding features of the radio situation today. I am sometimes asked what the BBC is doing about it. *The answer is nothing.* Some time ago they extended their programme hours to cover those of Luxembourg, and there was a slight

---

532 Ibid., Addendum.

533 Briggs, Asa *The BBC, The First Fifty Years*, p. 65.

534 Briggs, Asa *The History of Broadcasting in the United Kingdom, Volume II, The Golden Age of Wireless*, Oxford, Oxford University Press, 1995, p. 73. The quote is by Rex Palmer, in an interview with Stone during the programme, *These Radio Times*, broadcast on the BBC Light Programme on 25 April 1952.

535 See below, Appendix A.

536 *The Sunday Referee*, 5 August 1934, p. 13. It is worth noting here that *The Gramophone*, which survives and flourishes today as a journal of interest to collectors of principally classical music in recorded form, was founded by Compton Mackenzie, the brother-in-law of Christopher Stone. Mackenzie was also the magazine's first editor.

popularisation of material, but beyond this there will be no further conces-sions, I believe, so long as the BBC is under its present control.[537]

The criticism echoed a letter from a listener, "NMG" of Westward Ho!, published in *Radio Pictorial* of 8 June 1934:

> Surely the BBC could give us better radio fare on Sunday without destroying the religious associations of that day? As things are at present , we get – from Daventry National – nothing but unrelieved dullness until the concert at 9.30. The music which is played for us by various orchestras is uniformly proper and deadly in style – classical it may be, but it is not pleasant to listen to, except for the minority who are keen on such works – we have readings from the classics, Bach cantatas and missionary talks. The present Sunday pro-grammes may satisfy a very few, but the majority simply tune in to foreign stations, and so are enabled to hear something cheerful ...[538]

It is true to say that both these responses are taken from journals which actively supported commercial radio, and so must be read in that context. There was however a considerable groundswell of opinion which supported the views ex-pressed, both in the press and in the books of a number of respected media commentators during the 1930s.[539] In *Broadcasting in My Time*, published in 1935, Sydney Moseley launched a number of attacks on BBC policy, most noteworthy chapter being entitled "The Week-End Gaps":

> Nothing can better illustrate the need for some more effective control of the BBC than the long-continued contempt of public opinion in the matter of week-end broadcasts. The demand for a full Sunday programme arose directly broadcasting began. Indeed, listeners wanted something more than that: they wanted a full and varied *week-end* programme.[540]

537 Ibid. Leslie Baily was himself a journalist who moved between the BBC and Commercial interests. In 1933, while working for *The Sunday Referee*, he began compiling the highly successful series of BBC Archive-based programmes, *Scrapbook*. Freddie Grisewood presented, and the first edition, *Scrapbook for 1913*, began a sequence of programmes which included *Scrapbook for 1922*, broadcast to coincide with the BBC's 40th anniversary in 1962. The series finally ended in 1974. (See Paul Donovan, *The Radio Companion*, London, Grafton, 1992, p. 240.) The series also spawned two books, *Leslie Baily's BBC Scrapbooks* published by George Allen and Unwin, London, in 1966 (Volume 1 – 1896–1914) and 1968 (Volume 11 – 1918 – 1939). Baily's career included a radio play produced by Tyrone Guthrie, a period of time on the BBC staff, and scripts for films and television.

538 *Radio Pictorial*, 8 June 1934, p. 21.

539 See also Appendix A. The range of correspondence gathered by the present writer supports the general sense of listener dissatisfaction with BBC Sunday programming at the time.

540 Moseley, Sydney A. *Broadcasting in My Time*, London, Rich and Cowan, 1935, p. 160. Moseley claimed himself to be "Britain's First Radio Critic", (See Briggs 11, p. 490) and wrote on the subject in a number of Sunday papers as well as *Amateur Wireless*. His conversational and vernacular style is explained by the fact that he habitually used a dictation machine for his work. See also *The Private Diaries of Sydney Moseley*, London/Bournemouth, Max Parrish in Association with The Outspoken Press, 1960. As a matter of context, it should be noted that *Broadcasting in My Time* carried a dedication "To Isidore Ostrer, with personal regard and in recognition of his fight for British films and his vital help in my fight for British television". Ostrer, as shall be demonstrated later in this dissertation, ran Gaumont-British Pictures, and owned *The Sunday Referee*. He was a great supporter of Commercial Radio interests; *The Sunday Referee* and Gaumont British were linked to the development of Radio Paris and Radio Luxembourg in its early days in the most practical of ways as I shall demonstrate (See Appendix A, Pre-War Commercial Competition: The Stations).

Moseley found the whole concept of sabbatarianism incomprehensible: for him the idea of a day of rest which permitted none of the joys of God's world was so outdated as to be ludicrous:

Let us even concede the desirability of maintaining a certain Sabbath atmosphere. And even then, how can we possibly excuse the BBC for confining its tremendous service in the fetters of Victorian tradition? Why, the National Sunday League had fought the democratic fight to give the people legitimate Sunday entertainment before I was out of my boyhood! ... Yet here was this strangely mixed body of young men – some of whose "modern" ideas appalled even me! – holding up its hands in pious horror at the mere idea of giving listeners music and song and reasonable "entertainment" on Saturdays and Sundays![541]

Moseley's most remarkable claim was that letters received by him from listeners had changed their tone of late; initially he had received support from readers in his journalistic campaign for brighter Sunday broadcasts from the BBC. Latterly many of his correspondents had asked him not to pursue his pleas, "lest the BBC should take action at last and interfere with the reception of Continental programmes!"

The irony of it! There was the BBC, determined to "uplift" its listeners at all costs, and yet simply driving them, out of their boredom, to listen on Sundays to jazz and crooning and racing commentaries and heaven knows how many other foreign programme items which were, and still are, anathema to the Director-General as Sunday entertainment! The unbusiness-like BBC, in fact, lost so many customers by this obstinate Victorianism that it would certainly have been driven out of business had the Continental programmes been able to secure the licence fees of these dissatisfied listeners.[542]

Two years later, in *Radio is Changing Us*, D. Cleghorn Thomson provided a revealing and damning picture of Reith as a central part of the problem, using Broadcasting House itself as a metaphor for the man and his thinking. The building, he wrote, is "a cross between a liner and a lunatic asylum":

From the sombre Roman sacrificial altar-front with its Latin inscription in the entrance-hall, to the Director-General's private office, it all bears the stamp of a man with a complex make-up, but definite views and prejudices.[543]

---

541   Ibid.

542   Ibid., p. 162.

543   Cleghorn Thomson, D. *Radio Is Changing Us*, London, Watts and Co., 1937, p. 64. In a letter to the present writer, (18 February 1998) the late Dr. Desmond Hawkins, ex-Controller of the South West Region of the BBC and founder of the Natural History Unit, provided a vivid memory of David Cleghorn Thomson: "I knew him well in the mid-thirties, in unusual circumstances. In my early endeavours to establish myself as a freelance writer I met him as a literary adviser to Macmillans and radio critic on, I think, the News Chronicle. He had an attractive period house in Sussex but also maintained a flat in Charlotte Street (Fitzrovia) for occasions when he was detained overnight in London. There was a spartan spare room that he offered me (I was then camping out temporally with friends in Shepherds Bush). At that time he was a stylish dilettante of considerable charm, and considered probably homosexual. I was warned against accepting the offer but thought I could handle the risk, which in the event turned out to be no risk at all. He rarely spent a night there and it virtually became my home. I learned that he had been Controller of BBC Scotland, at a remarkably young age for such a job. He was the antithesis of everything Reith stood for, so I still wonder how he was appointed; he was very much in the aesthetic, Catholic, Highland tradition of Scotland, belonging to the circle of Moray MacLaren, Eric Linklater and Compton Mackenzie who sometimes turned up at 88 Charlotte Street.

Cleghorn Thomson went on to write about the "bewildering and labyrinthine corridors, a strange maze of passages where the uncouth swain … may well feel the 'shades of the prison-house" beginning to close around him". His most graphic description however was of the Director-General's own office:

It is redolent of the atmosphere of a panelled, centrally-heated Fifth-avenue Presbyterian manse study. A touch of stained glass, a portrait of the Chief's famous father, … and, let into the wall, a rather sentimental picture of one of those scenes from which old Scotia's grandeur keeps on springing. But it would be unfair to stop here. On the great desk at which Reith works there stands (or stood at one time) a small wooly lamb, mutely striving to remind him that he is a human being quite capable of unbending, and showing unexpected friskiness and simplicity on occasion. If Sir Stephen Tallents, who has rendered great service in the "projection of Empire", could only project this lamb throughout the staff, and even among the wider circle of listeners, some of the problems of the "unhappy ship" might not even arise for solution.[544]

The increasing popular impatience with the BBC's interpretation of its monopolistic role as the arbiter of taste and decency may be observed in many writings and satires. The parody of *Radio Parade of 1935* cited in the chapter "Culture at a Crisis", was one which carried with it the views of many, including some politicians. Cleghorn Thomson quotes Attlee in the House of Commons claiming that Reith:

tends to be dictatorial and a little impatient of criticism. Like many men of his great ability, he rather likes to be surrounded by "yes men". I think that he tends to rule a little by fear, and this only kills creative work.[545]

Cleghorn Thomson pushed home the comparison with Fascist leadership directly and unequivocally:

In subsequent debates, Sir Stafford Cripps, George Lansbury, and Lieut. Commander Fletcher further elaborated these unfavourable suggestions, plainly alleging Hitlerite methods, Goebbels's technique, and so forth, in no measured terms.[546]

It is clear that the BBC was full of division and hierarchical conflicts, as is borne out by Cardiff and Scannell:

In the mid-thirties the BBC was a troubled, unhappy place in which to work. It was riven by internal feuds and rivalries; by dissatisfactions with conditions and terms of employment, pay and promotion; by the lack of adequate mechanisms for bargaining and negotiating on these matters; by corporate meddling in the private affairs of staff members; … by the growing gaps between rulers and ruled within the institution.[547]

Reith undoubtedly got rid of him as totally unsuitable and installed the very opposite Rev. Melville Dinwiddie – a sort of Reith clone."

544 Ibid.
545 Ibid., pp. 67–68.
546 Ibid., p. 68.
547 Scannell, Paddy & Cardiff, David "Serving the Nation: Public Service Broadcasting Before the War", in *Popular Culture Past and Present*, ed. Waites, Bernard et al, Beckenham, Croom Helm, 1982, p. 171.

Awareness

Major C.F. Atkinson's memo of November 1928, from which the epigram cited at the start of this chapter is taken, is the earliest discovered evidence in BBC files of an awareness of commercial transmissions from Europe, aimed at British audiences. It identifies broadcasts from "Hilversum, Radio Paris, Scheveningen, Tour Eiffel and Radio-Belgique" as "the important sources of danger"[548] and foresees problems for the newly formed Corporation "if we don't do our utmost to stop this move".[549] Inspite of the final comment – supposedly from Reith – there was concern within the BBC until the outbreak of World War II regarding commercial incursion into its monopoly, and this concern was with the issue of advertising as a means of funding broadcasting as well as with the fragmentation of its audience. The last sentence in Atkinson's memo raises the fear that "with foreign and British advertisements flowing in, we shall find it difficult to resist pressure for our own system being opened to publicity".[550]

Atkinson's missive followed hard on a newspaper story, published on 4 November by the *Sunday Dispatch*, under the headline: "Brighter Wireless Challenge to BBC. Radio Threat to BBC Monopoly".

> The 10 million listeners in the British Isles – the majority of whom are dissatisfied with the wireless provender offered them by the BBC – will be immensely interested to learn that for the first time in its career the BBC is faced with the prospect of real and effective competition.[551]

Little is revealed beyond this, except that the "well known Peer", Gordon Sherry is planning to develop commercial radio broadcasting from Europe. In the week following the Sunday *Dispatch*'s article, the issue of broadcasting competition was dominating the British popular press. The *Daily Herald* developed the story in its edition of 5 November:

> Gordon Sherry, a very well known Peer, a theatrical producer and a composer told the *Daily Herald* yesterday that he is the chief financial broker in a scheme which is being presented to the public in the guise of a war against the State monopoly of British Broadcasting. Names cannot be divulged.[552]

The paper quotes Sherry as saying "We shall get our own back, one way or another". "All this, writes our Wireless Correspondent, points to an imitation of the American use of wireless for advertising purposes."[553] Research has yielded no clues to Lord Sherry's subsequent activities in this area. On the same day however the *Daily Express* reported that "a scheme for a Continental wireless station to broadcast a British programme every night to the British Isles is being widely canvassed".[554]

None of the papers reveal the location of the station, stating only that it is "an

---

548 Atkinson, November 1928, p. 1.

549 Ibid., p. 3.

550 Ibid., p. 3.

551 *Sunday Dispatch*, 4 November 1928, p. 1, WAC, CAV R34/960.

552 *Daily Herald*, 5 November 1928, p. 3, WAC CAV E2/2/1.

553 Ibid.

554 *Daily Express*, 5 November 1928, p. 5 WAC CAV E2/2/1.

important Continental station".[555] Given that Hilversum was already broadcasting Sunday concerts sponsored by the Kolster Brandes radio set manufacturer by this time, it is unlikely to be this station which was the subject of the newspapers conjecture. Briggs writes of "other broadcasts in 1929, 1930 and 1931 from Radio Toulouse",[556] and it may be here that Sherry was developing his interests. Once again targeting the Sunday audience, the Radio Toulouse transmissions represented the continuing experimental efforts of Leonard Plugge, and their success pointed to a strong potential in commercial radio, "evidenced by the fifteen hundred odd reception reports that flowed into the IBC offices at 11, Hallam Street, after each Sunday half-hour broadcast from Radio Toulouse".[557] Whether or not Sherry was linked to Plugge's work is not clear and from this point onwards, his name does not occur in the debate. Nevertheless his statement, the press coverage it provoked and Atkinson's memo points to a sense of real engagement with the subject in Britain at the time. From this point on, numerous files of documented monitoring demonstrate the BBC's awareness of commercial activity.

World Radio

The fact that such programmes could be advertised in a BBC journal, *World Radio*, added irony to the situation. In the climate of listener experimentation – searching the ether was a major pastime through the 1920s and 1930s, as listeners sought to tune to distant radio stations for the sheer fascination of the hunt – *World Radio*, formerly *The Radio Supplement*, had been founded in 1925. Established two years after the creation of *Radio Times*, its purpose was to widen awareness of overseas programmes. The trade press had objected to its existence, but nevertheless "it was expanded in 1932 to meet the special needs of Empire broadcasting".[558]

The interest in ether exploration at the end of the 1920s gave *World Radio* its main reason for existence. Compared to *Radio Times,* its circulation was modest; nevertheless as Briggs points out there is a marked rise between 1930 and 1931 which is not sustained thereafter:

	Radio Times	*World Radio*
1930	1,334,063	153,595
1931	1,575,151	181,513
1932	1,825,951	157,545

World Radio never again attained the weekly sales of 1931, finally ceasing publication in 1939.[559] The fact that in 1930 the journal was carrying listings which included sponsored programmes was one which raised issues for the BBC on two fronts: firstly, this was a BBC magazine, its subtitle being "The Official Foreign

---

555 Ibid.

556 Briggs II, p. 325.

557 *This is the IBC*, London, IBC, 1939, p. 3.

558 Briggs, II, p. 260.

559 Ibid., p. 261.

and Technical Journal of the BBC". To carry details of broadcasts containing commercial material aimed at a British radio audience could not therefore be appropriate. At the same time, the Corporation itself had commercial factors to consider in the sale of its magazines. At the foot of Atkinson's memo is an anonymous scribbled note pointing out "Incidentally we cannot afford to turn down legitimate adverts in *World Radio*".[560] In any event, it required considerable vigilance to sub edit every listing to check it for a sponsor's name; the magazine carried details of 34 foreign radio stations for seven days' programming each week. Mostly the information is terse and factual; occasionally however, there is a telling product name inserted. In the edition for 30 May 1930 we find from the Frankfurt-am-Main station there is at 6.30 p.m. on Sunday "A talk arranged by the Frankfurter Zeitung". Hilversum are broadcasting their "Kolster Brandes Orchestral Concert" at 5.40 p.m., and at 2.00 p.m. on Radio-Paris is "A Concert of Decca Records".[561] By 1933, details for such broadcasts had been cut to a simple "Sponsored programme".[562] Nearing the end of the decade – and the journal's life – *World Radio* carried full details of Radio Normandy's programmes, (steadfastly referring to it as "Radio-Normandie" in spite of its commercial Anglicization) but without sponsors' names.[563]

Captain Leonard Plugge, who founded the International Broadcasting Company in March 1930, had a foothold within *World Radio* in that he and his fellow directors had been under contract to the BBC through his company, Radio International Publicity Services Ltd., "to supply, translate and sub-edit foreign wireless programmes" for the journal.[564] This may explain an anonymous hand written comment on a BBC memo of July 1930 relating to the newly created International Broadcasting Company: "If it is Plugge, then we have some control over him".[565]

BBC Monitoring

Activity continued to increase, particularly on the part of Plugge's IBC. On 27 July, L.G Shuttleworth of the BBC's Tatsfield Monitoring station reported the following on the Brussels frequency:

> 20.58 Announcement in French and English: – This is the International Broadcasting Co., broadcasting a programme through the new high power Brussels station on 338 metres. The announcer then went on to say that by their correspondence the various kinds of programme were voted as follows. 46 per cent mixed programme, 37 per cent Light music. 17 per cent Classical music. The IBC would attempt to find a programme suitable for all tastes.[566]

One week later, Shuttleworth again monitored the IBC Brussels broadcast, at the end of which he noted: "23.40 Announcement: – 'That concludes the IBC

560 Note on Atkinson Memo, 28 January 1930, WAC CAV E2/2/1.
561 *World Radio* 30 May 1930, Vol. X no. 253, pp. 834–835. Author's collection.
562 *World Radio*, 25 August 1933, Vol. XVII, pp. xxiii–xxiii. Author's collection.
563 *World Radio* 25 February 1938, Vol. XXVI, No. 657, p. 26. Author's collection.
564 Briggs II, p. 326.
565 BBC Internal Memo, 16 July 1930. WAC CAV E2/365/1.
566 Reception Report from Tatsfield Monitoring Station, 28 July 1930. WAC CAV E2/365/1.

programme, and on Sunday next, the 10th August, another programme will be broadcast from Katowitz, Poland on 408 metres. Goodnight.'"[567] The same evening Shuttleworth picked up an English language programme from Toulouse which began at 10.40 p.m. with: "an announcement from Radio Toulouse on 779–3 Kc/s: A recital of gramophone records by the 'Vocalion Gramophone Co. of Hayes, Middlesex'."[568] On this occasion, Shuttleworth noted that there was no mention of the IBC in the broadcast. On 10 August, he monitored Katowitz, and picked up the IBC transmission from 10.40 p.m., including at 11.07 p.m., the following announcement:

> This is Katowitz on 408 metres broadcasting a programme by the International Broadcasting Co for the benefit of British listeners. This is the first of a series to be radiated from this station. The IBC would be pleased to receive any reports from British listeners concerning quality, modulation, fading and interference by morse or from other stations. Description of receiver used and in fact any other impression which may be noted. If the concerts are appreciated an increasing number of broadcasts will be attempted from the leading continental stations. The address of the IBC is 11, Hallam Street, W1, and all reports should be forwarded there.[569]

It was noted that Katowitz resumed its normal Polish language broadcasts at 11.38 p.m. Time and again Plugge was to be the source of Corporation irritation, and on 4 November 1931, Atkinson commented for the first time on an English language broadcast from a French station in Fécamp in the following terms:

> Radio Normandie is by way of being a freak station. It works on short wave but is receivable at quite good strength, particularly along the South coast of England, because it is near the coast of France, and the propagation of these short waves over the sea is quite good, even in daylight … It is therefore, quite a suitable medium for broadcasting advertisements to England, as although it would reach only a limited area, this particular area is fairly densely populated, and includes all the big towns round the South coast and the Isle of Wight district.[570]

Two weeks later, Atkinson sent another memo, this time to Admiral Carpendale, reporting that on 15 November, "these people sent out a programme sponsored by Philco Radio, an American firm selling receivers in this country. This was a blatant American affair, openly addressed to British listeners."[571] Again Atkinson's concern is for the future of the BBC's non-commercial position: "It seems to me that if we calmly allow this kind of thing to go on, sooner or later we shall be forced off the 'no advertising' standard, which, to my mind, would be disastrous".[572]

---

567 Reception Report from Tatsfield Monitoring Station, 5 August 1930. WAC CAV E2/365/1.

568 Ibid.

569 Reception Report from Tatsfield Monitoring Station, 10 August 1930. WAC CAV E2/365/1.

570 Atkinson, C.F., BBC Internal Memo, 4 November 1931, WAC CAV E2/365/1. At the end of the memo is the handwritten comment: "Added in D.G.'s letter to Post Office on general subject". D.G. is the Director General, Reith. Clearly the issue of Commercial broadcasting was under top level discussion by this time. The mentioned letter by Reith is not on file.

571 BBC Internal Memo, Atkinson, 16 November 1931. WAC CAV E2/365/1.

572 Ibid.

Radio Normandy was subsequently to switch its frequency to the Medium Wave, thus consolidating its Southern England reception. Of all the experiments by the IBC, it was Radio Normandy – initially Radio Fécamp and then Radio Normandie – that was to be the most successful and far reaching in its provocation of the BBC, and driving the Corporation to action within the International Broadcasting Union.

Attempts at Wavelength Legislation

The IBU had been set up in 1925 to serve the mutual interests of national broadcasters within Europe; within two years of the Fécamp reports, it was the initiation of Sunday broadcasts from Radio Luxembourg in the Spring of 1933 that incurred the greatest anger and activity, being as they were through the use of a pirated wavelength "in defiance of the IBU, the Post Office, and the BBC".[573] The International Broadcasting Union had always had a strong BBC presence; in 1930 Carpendale was elected its President for the sixth successive year, and at its Annual General Assembly near Laussanne in May 1930, its Council had resolved "that the Union should continue to work for the improvement of reception conditions in Europe, as regards both radio-electric and electrical interference, and for as simple and practical as possible a development of foreign relays ..."[574] In May and June 1933, the IBU held The European Broadcasting Conference in Lucerne, at which the allocation of broadcasting wavelengths was to be the central – and controversial – issue. This related specifically to the burgeoning commercial activity, and could not have been more topical. By April 1933, the continental English language output of sponsored programming on Sundays appeared as follows:

Radio Normandy	12 hours
Radio Paris	2.5 hours
Radio Toulouse	1.5 hours
Radio Côte d'Azur	1 hour[575]

A number of crucial resolutions affecting broadcasting of this kind were passed by the IBU at Lucerne, at the instigation of the BBC under Carpendale, and aimed at such stations as Normandy and Luxembourg:

1. The systematic diffusion [see Relay Exchanges, below] of programmes or messages, which are specifically intended for listeners in another country and which have been the object of a protest by the broadcasting organization of that country, constitutes an "inadmissible" act from the point of view of good international relations.

2. The Union can have nothing to do with any developments in the technical field of broadcasting which do not pay the most scrupulous attention to the rules established by international conventions ...

3. The Union cannot sympathise with any type of programme which is essentially based on the idea of commercial advertising in the international field ...

4. The transmission of international programmes by a national organization, which has not been internationally recognized, might give rise to such serious

---

573 Briggs II, p. 335.

574 *World Radio* 30 May 1930, Vol. X No. 253, p. 817. Author's collection.

575 Figures from Briggs II, p. 334.

difficulties and disturb the good understanding between nations so profoundly that the transmission of such programmes despite the absence of international recognition must be considered by the Union as an "inadmissible" element in European broadcasting.[576]

The effect of these resolutions was initially encouraging; Radio Paris, taken over by the French Government in April 1933, ceased sponsored programming in November of that year; by July, Radio Toulouse also stopped its activities for the time being. By August, *World Radio* was reporting a setback for Radio Normandy:

> The Lucerne Plan, together with the French Ferrié Plan, will affect the private stations in France, though the extent is not yet realized. Radio-Normandie (Fécamp) has been compelled to reduce its power to 700 watts, and other private stations are wondering how they will be affected.[577]

The international moves which led to the Lucerne agreement had been at the core of discussions during the fourth International Radio Telegraphic Conference, held in Madrid in September 1932, at which was created the International Telecommunications Union. The hope of many of the IBU members attending the Madrid conference was that many more wavelengths would become available, when in point of fact, "only four additional channels in the long wavebands were apportioned",[578] largely due to a stalemate caused by various National interests amongst members: "At Madrid, Biblical examples were used to support the claim of one service as against another, regardless of the technical aspects".[579]

Thus the wavelength issue remained unresolved, although agreement was confirmed in the case for "national sovereignty in broadcasting matters".[580] The IBU was handed the responsibility for arranging a subsequent conference to discuss this in detail, and the Lucerne Conference was the result. When the Lucerne Plan was put into operation, on 15 January 1934, the BBC retained its one long wavelength and increased its ten medium wavelengths to eleven.[581] Hopes for the control of the Foreign English language transmissions were not to be fulfilled and in reality, commercial broadcasting from Europe – and in particular France – extended rather than diminished between the Lucerne Conference and the Second World War. The new Paris station, Poste Parisien, already on the air from February 1932, began broadcasting in English as well as French from ultra-modern studios on the Champs Elysees in November 1933, Radio Lyon opened in 1936 and Toulouse was back on the air in 1938. Most damaging of all, in January 1934, Radio Luxembourg began transmitting on the Long Wavelength of 1,304 metres, which had been allotted at Lucerne to Radio Warsaw, but had not yet been activated.[582] By any standards, Luxembourg was by this action, branded as a "pirate".

576 Quoted by Briggs II, pp 333–334, from R.H. Coase: *British Broadcasting: A Study in Monopoly*, London, Longmans, 1950, pp. 111–112.
577 *World Radio* 25 August 1933, Vol. XVII, No. 422, p. 221. Author's collection.
578 Briggs II, p. 319.
579 Tomlinson, J.D. *The International Control of Radiocommunications*, Michigan, University of Michigan, 1945, p. 158.
580 Briggs II, p. 320.
581 Pamphlet: *Outstanding BBC Dates*, compiled by the BBC London Reference Library, Broadcasting House. 1960. Not commercially published, p. 22. Author's Collection.
582 Briggs II, p. 335.

Relay Exchanges

Alongside the development of "wireless" broadcasting (that is to say a *transmitted* signal), there was an area of the dissemination of radio which was to compound the problems of competition for the BBC. The idea of sending material down a telephone wire for public – as opposed to private – consumption, had been present from the 1890s, when the concept of the "Radiophone" had first been introduced. The device enabled subscribing listeners to hear a relay of a concert or a church service through a telephone. With the development of radio on a mass audience scale in the late 1920s and early 1930s, the idea of wired relays, under licence to the Post Office as controller of the lines, became a key issue in British radio. One of the most enthusiastic supporters of "Wired Broadcasting" was as we have noted already, the BBC's first Chief Engineer, P.P. Eckersley. After his acrimonious departure from the BBC in 1929, Eckersley developed Wire broadcasting until 1935, when opposition from radio manufacturers began to erode the further establishment of the scheme. The concept was a simple one; if a radio signal can be sent down a telephone wire to a loudspeaker in the listener's home, then vagaries of signal strength, fading and signal cross-over can be controlled and largely eliminated. Eckersley's experiments gave prospective listeners a choice of four programmes.[583] With the BBC offering two – the National and the Regional Services – the way was therefore open for competition on an equal technical quality basis. This – and the fact that a subscription to a relay service was cheap,[584] and therefore attractive to the poorer parts of society – was of crucial significance to the issue of commercial competition from the Continent. As Briggs has said:

> They [relay receivers] were bound to be used, in a free market, for the rediffusion of foreign commercial programmes if these programmes genuinely made an appeal to large numbers of listeners. The motive of the relay exchange owner was simple – to please the greatest possible number of subscribers.[585]

The growth of relay services in Britain during the first half of the 1930s was remarkable:[586]

	Exchanges	Subscribers
1931	132	43,889
1932	194	82,690
1935	343	233,554

The BBC found itself sharing relays with its commercial competitors; in 1931 the

---

583 Eckersley, P.P. Talk to the Ilford Radio Society, May 1958. Tape in the author's collection, supplied by Myles Eckersley, son of Peter Eckersley.

584 Eckersley, Myles *Prospero's Wireless*, Romsey, Myles Books, 1998, p. 237: "The charge for a Rediffusion set was one shilling a sixpence a week, plus an annual ten shilling broadcasting licence fee. A loudspeaker was an extra sixpence a week (or five pounds cash)." Myles Eckersley's biography of his father, Peter, is an invaluable resource, and has been supplemented in this study by generous help and conversations with the present author.

585 Ibid., p. 331.

586 Coase, R.H. *British Broadcasting: A Study in Monopoly*, London, Longmans, 1950, p. 76.

BBC reached agreement with two of the leading relay companies – Standard Radio Relay Services Ltd and Radio Central Exchanges Ltd – that they would relay only BBC programmes.[587] The scheme was thwarted when, after the General Election of 1931, Kingsley Wood, the new Postmaster General, refused to implement the agreement, arguing that:

> It would be unfair to impose restrictions on relay subscribers which were not imposed on the private owners of wireless sets. Most of the relay subscribers were, after all, listeners with limited means who should not be deprived of the freedom enjoyed by richer citizens. Wood did not add, as he might have done, that relay subscribers also constituted a section of the "mass electorate".[588]

The Post Office was in a difficult position; on one hand its principle in broadcasting was to sustain the BBC's monopoly, whilst on the other it sought to provide radio in areas of poor reception, which coincidentally frequently were also areas of less affluent population. Thus major relay subscription areas included Leicester, Derby, Nottingham, Sheffield, Middlesborough, Newcastle and Carlisle. For obvious reasons of reception, Wales – North and South – were "wired" and the city of Hull boasted "the most extensive wire network in Europe".[589] The *BBC Year Book* for 1933 contained articles on "Broadcasting and Advertising", and "Rediffusion". In the latter the anonymous writer claimed that the fact that the BBC "has set its face resolutely against devoting its programmes entirely to amusement ... has already resulted in an acknowledged improvement in public taste".[590] If they fell into the wrong hands the Wireless Exchanges could threaten this standard, with Continental stations using the relays to "produce their own programmes abroad on the existing American system ... The growth of wireless exchanges upon present lines must be viewed with concern by all who realize the power of broadcasting and who value the policy and achievements of the BBC".[591]

The development of the relay exchanges in the first part of the 1930s was a crucial fact in the advance of commercial radio in Britain before the Second World War. Now there was a guarantee that they were broadcasting their programmes into areas they had previously been unable to reach in extraordinary technical quality: "It was miraculous compared to an ordinary broadcast; the interference was negligible".[592] The technical innovation and the opportunity it gave for targeting, was explored by the IBC by aiming specific programmes at key areas. In January 1933, the BBC's North Regional Director sent a memo to the Corporation's Foreign Director stating that:

> The Liverpool municipality has been approached by the International Broadcasting Club ... to supply a statement of five hundred words about Liverpool, which could be used in a concert to be broadcast from Radio Normandie on

---

587 Briggs II, p. 332.
588 Ibid., p. 333.
589 Eckersley: *Prospero's Wireless*, pp. 238–239.
590 *BBC Year Book* 1933, BBC, p. 72.
591 Ibid.
592 Eckersley, P.P. Talk to Ilford Radio Society, May 1958.

26 February. As the result of our telephone conversations, the Town Clerk of Liverpool is recommending that no such statement should be sent, and there is no doubt that the Municipality will refuse to send one without bringing us into the picture.[593]

The memo goes on to add a post script to the effect that "since dictating this memo, I have been rung up by the Lord Mayor of Manchester. He has received a somewhat similar communication … It would seem fairly obvious that all the big cities, if not many smaller ones, are being approached."[594]

Examining editions of *Radio Pictorial* it is clear how such "local" broadcasts fitted into the schedule; the aim was to create interest within a specific locality, without disrupting programming or alienating listeners from other parts of the country. Such broadcasts were thus placed either at the start or the end of transmissions. For instance, Radio Normandy's schedule for Thursday, 9th May 1935 tells us that the last programme of the day – at 12 midnight – was a "Club concert for High and West Wycombe Listeners". The next day, at 4.30 p.m., the start of afternoon broadcasting from the station, there was a fifteen minute "Bournemouth, Weymouth, Southampton and Winchester Club Concert".[595] In this way, with the aid of new technology, the IBC sought to undermine (albeit in a relatively minor way) the BBC's prized Regional Service. Likewise, the Corporation's newly established Empire Service had already proved the subject of commercial parody.

Empire Services

On 19 December 1932 the BBC inaugurated its Empire Broadcasting Service from its Daventry Transmitter. The event was launched with considerable ceremony, with a "Round the Empire" programme on Christmas Day, a message from King George V and a special number of *World Radio*.[596] Even before the new service began, Plugge's IBC had responded with a new source of transmission, EAQ, Madrid, and a new and provocative name and call-sign: "This is the IBC Empire Short Wave programme, radiated by EAQ, Madrid".[597]

The Tatsfield Monitoring Station's Engineer-in-Charge, H.O. Griffiths communicated the information to L.W. Hayes on the BBC's Technical Committee, with the comment that "My staff are of the opinion that reasonable listeners could not mistake this for a BBC transmission".[598] Hayes however had originally noted the broadcasts as early as 22 October; thus Plugge's organization had pre-empted the BBC's Empire Service by just under two months. He held a different view to Griffiths on the issue of audience confusion:

> I am afraid I do not agree with Griffiths' remark that reasonable listeners would not mistake this for a BBC transmission. Even if they heard every word

593 BBC Internal Memo, 17 January 1933. WAC CAV E2/365/1.
594 Ibid.
595 *Radio Pictorial*, May, 1935, p. 27.
596 *Outstanding BBC Dates*, pp. 20–21.
597 BBC Internal Memo, Griffiths, H.O., Engineer-in-Charge, BBC Monitoring, Tatsfield, 2 January 1933. WAC CAV E2/365/2.
598 Ibid.

of the announcement, which they might not as they are listening on short waves, they might well think they had misheard "IBC" for "BBC". The only suggestion I can make is that they should drop the word "Empire" altogether, but I suppose it might be difficult for us to get them to do this.[599]

In fact this suggestion had already been made directly to Plugge on 10 November 1933. The letter, written by an unidentified BBC executive, is remarkably deferential in tone:

I am told that you are using the following formula in making announcements from your Empire Station:

"This is EAQ, the Empire Short Wave station Aranjuez ..."

This formula we find is causing some confusion with the one we employ in our Empire transmissions, and I wonder if you would be kind enough to consider introducing some change, which would make confusion impossible?[600]

The BBC's Written Archives contains no record of Plugge's reply, and the EAQ Empire Service announcements continued without change.

The IBC's tenancy was only a part of a much larger scheme by EAQ for worldwide English language transmissions of its own; in 1934 the station's programme magazine, *EAQ*, began publishing articles in English as well as Spanish. In its December edition, 1934, it published an article by A.E. Bear, European and Colonial Representative of the International Short Wave Club in London, whose words will have encouraged supporters of the IBC experiment, even though his article addressed the issue of programming of National cultural interest rather than the populist fare of Plugge's stations:

Short wave transmitters are now installed in most every country in the world ... The Spanish short wave station EAQ ranks among the most powerful and best heard stations in the world and has played a great part in making short wave listening and accomplished fact ... I suggest that the practice of announcing in English as well as Spanish should be extended to every transmission.[601]

The extending of this policy can be seen from a section from the November 1935 edition of the magazine, entitled "Programme Notes":

Commencing 5 September, EAQ transmissions where [sic] extended and our present schedule is as follows: transmission No.1, from 22.30 to 24.00 directed to Spanish residents in North America and Europe. Transmission No. 2, from Midnight to 00.30 the Popular programme for English speaking listeners in all parts of the world, and Transmission No. 3, from 00.30 to 0.2.30, dedicated to Spanish speaking listeners the world over. A note should be made of two variations in the above schedule. There is no English programme on Mondays, and the Sunday night transmission No. 2 is given

599   Hayes, L.W., BBC Internal Memo, 5 January 1934, Ibid.

600   Letter from unidentified BBC staff member to Captain Leonard Plugge, 10 November, 1933. WAC CAV E2/365/1.

601   Bear, A.E. *EAQ* Programme Magazine no. 27, December 1934, pp. 4–5.

over to the International Broadcasting Company for their weekly broad-cast.[602]

Griffiths' memo to Hayes mentions that he monitored EAQ "between the hours of midnight and 1 a.m. on Dec. 29th/30th, 28th/29th, and January 1st/2nd".[603] The January edition of EAQ confirms that on the 1st and 2nd of the month, IBC broadcasts were indeed scheduled, worded in Spanish: "24.00 a 1.00: Transmisión del programa especial, en inglés organizado por la 'International Broadcasting Co.'"[604]

That the BBC was unsuccessful in stopping the IBC using its "Empire Service" title is evidenced by a programme listing in *Radio Pictorial* as late as March 1937: "IBC Short-Wave Empire Transmissions. EAQ, Madrid 30.43 m., 9860 Kc/s. Time of Transmission. Sunday, 12 (midnight) – 12.30 a.m. Announcer: E.E. Allen".[605] The programme consisted of a 15 minute *Medley*:

She Shall Have Music ...	Sigler
Puttin' on the Ritz ...	Irving Berlin
Indian Love Call ...	Friml

and

March Winds and April Showers ...	Samuels[606]

This was followed at 12.15 a.m. by *The IBC Time Signal* and three further records, *Two Trumpet Toot* by Kern, *Dixieland* and finally *Burlington Bertie from Bow* by Hargreaves. The transmission ended at 12.30 a.m. with *The IBC Goodnight Melody* which closed all IBC stations at the end of the broadcasting day.[607]

The nature of the broadcasts – while appearing to be quite innocuous, raised an issue for the BBC; if listeners *were* mistaking these transmissions for the Corporation's Empire Service, then a misunderstanding of what that service stood for would arise. On the other hand, limited "leased" broadcasts of this sort were unlikely to reach a major audience, and there is no subsequent evidence that Hayes' concern was borne out. As with other irritants from the IBC, the Aranjuez programmes did little in real terms to jeopardize the BBC's relationship with its growing international audience.

From the IBC's point of view, they were an example of the company's policy of "keeping a wavelength warm".[608] On the same programme page in the edition of *Radio Pictorial* cited above, there are other examples of this: Between 9.30 p.m. and 10.00 p.m., Radio Ljubljana, 569.3 m., 527 Kc/s ("Announcer F. Miklavcic") broadcast two short programmes of records. On the same evening Radio Côte D'Azur (Juan-les Pins), 235.1m., 1276 Kc/s, transmitted its evening programme from 10.30 p.m. to 11.30 p.m., featuring light orchestra music suitable for dancing. In each case, the close down announcement included a suggestion to retune to the

602 *EAQ* No. 41, November 1935, p. 4.
603 Griffiths, 2 January 1933.
604 *EAQ*, No 19, January 1934, p. 32.
605 *Radio Pictorial* 27 March 1937, p. 32.
606 Ibid.
607 Ibid.
608 *This is the IBC*, London, IBC, 1939, p. 34.

other station at the appropriate time, and contained the increasingly familiar *IBC Goodnight Melody*.[609]

Potentials for Growth

As has been demonstrated above, throughout the 1930s BBC monitoring staff identified a number of IBC broadcasts of this sort; some developed into regular scheduled events, and were advertised in *Radio Pictorial*, while others, such as Radio Rome, were only temporary experiments. A BBC transmission reception report dated 22 October 1934, gives detailed information of how such programmes were structured:

19.00   This is Rome broadcasting on 420.8m. We are now broadcasting a programme of gramophone records by Jack Payne. This half-hour is dedicated to all our English speaking listeners.

19.05   Request made that people should listen to Radio Normandie every Sunday afternoon.

19.08   On his next record Jack Payne will play ...

19.11   His next rendering will be ...

19.15   IBC wish to thank all listeners for their reports on these concerts. Carry on the good work of sending reports.

19.18   That was Jack Payne playing ... Now they are going to play ...

19.21   For this half-hour's programme we are sending you some recordings of Jack Payne and his band. Here they are playing ...

19.25   We conclude the programme with "Some Memories of Jack Payne and his Band". Here it is.

19.28   Once again we come to the end of our programme, sent to you by Radio Rome at this time every week. May we jog your memory again about those reception postcards, if you have not already done so. Will you please send a postcard giving details of reception in your district. Mark your postcards "Radio Rome reception" and send them to the IBC, 11, Hallam Street, London, W.1. All listeners writing to the IBC will receive a programme of next week's transmission from Radio Rome. Goodbye, everybody.[610]

In a separate memo, the monitor, C.G. Graves adds that typically, the IBC are making these broadcasts as unsponsored; this fact supports the suggestion that the programmes were experiments and demonstrations to potential advertisers of the power of Continent-based stations carrying English language material:

The way I read it is that IBC, who are at present putting on unsponsored programmes from Rome are engaged upon ascertaining who their audience is. If they find that in reply to their requests they get quite a large number of replies from this country then I imagine they will move into sponsored programmes.[611]

---

609   Radio Pictorial, 27 March 1937, p. 32.

610   BBC Internal Memo, 22 October 1934. WAC CAV E2/365/2.

611   Graves, C.G. BBC Internal Memo, 30 October 1934. WAC CAV E2/365/2.

Ireland

In the meantime, an assault on the BBC monopoly came from another direction, when, on 6 February 1933, a new high power station opened in the Irish Free State. Radio Ath Luain broadcast initially on 413 metres at a power of 60 kilowatts; ironically, as a result of the Lucerne Conference, early in 1934 it changed its wavelength to 531 m. and actually increased its transmission power.[612] The station – which could be heard in London – became known as Radio Athlone, subsequently metamorphosing after the War as Radio Eireann. The licence to supply sponsored programmes had originally been granted to Athlone Radio Publicity Ltd.:

> The company booked one hour six nights a week for a year, with a booking fee of £60 an hour and an extra £1.10s. an hour for copyright fees. Each hour could be divided into three programme periods, if desired, and the amount of advertising was limited to 100 words per programme, which was roughly 5 per cent of the total time.[613]

The first sponsored broadcast was transmitted on 24 April 1933,[614] and the BBC had advanced notice of it from, of all people, Leonard Plugge. A BBC memo from a PW Darnell to the Director of Information and Publications, offers facts on the matter, adding "Captain Plugge ... gave me this information".[615] Plugge's intelligence was that the Directors of Athlone Radio Publicity were "an American, a Colonial and another connected with a publication known as *Smith's Weekly*".[616] In reply a memo states "*Smith's Weekly* is the *John Bull* of Australia controlled by a millionaire. They outbid IBC and are paying £25,000 for this one hour a week day. Plugge thinks it would be to our benefit to get control ... but I should say that a still longer view is to do nothing about it."[617] Within three months Radio Athlone's agreement with Athlone Radio Publicity had run into acrimonious difficulties, and the advertising contract was granted briefly to the IBC,[618] although not without criticism from the Irish listeners: "... Advertising programmes were heavily criticised in Ireland for being un-national, unworthy of the national station, and unfit to be transmitted to listeners abroad".[619]

Nevertheless, Radio Athlone was a legitimate station, recognized by the IBU, and as such the BBC was unable to protest too strongly about output which – although audible in Britain – could be argued to be aimed at a native Irish audience. In a letter of 15 July 1933, now missing, from the IBC to Reith, Plugge appears to have raised the issue of consistency regarding the interpretation of Lucerne. Judging from Carpendale's reply to the IBC, Plugge seems to have been arguing that if the BBC could accept Athlone, why could it not acknowledge the rights of his company

---

612 Gorham, Maurice *Forty Years of Irish Broadcasting*, Dublin, The Talbot Press, 1967, p. 86.
613 Ibid., p. 87.
614 Ibid.
615 BBC Internal Memo, 11 April 1933.
616 Ibid.
617 BBC Internal Memo, 11 April 1933.
618 The case of Radio Athlone is further explored in Appendix A.
619 Ibid., p. 88.

to broadcast from the Continent too? Reith passed the letter to Carpendale for reply:

> I need hardly point out that the case of your advertising programmes addressed to British listeners from French stations differs only in importance and not in principle from that of political exiles using the microphones of a neighbouring country to incite sympathisers at home. It is not material to this argument that these programmes are heard by (a) French listeners, and (b) listeners in other countries, and thus favour British external trade ... As to (b), it is only necessary to say that the Madrid Convention has laid down that the object of broadcasting, on the basis of which its facilities have been assigned, is to give a national service. The case of Athlone is not parallel with that of the French stations, as English is the normal and majority language in Ireland, whereas French stations broadcasting in English have no other object but a non-national one.[620]

Although the development of commercial broadcasting experiments did not continue at its initial rate beyond the middle of the decade, the assault on the BBC's monopoly continued unabated. A BBC memo by Isa Benzie dated 17 April 1936 notes the arrival of Juan-les-Pins as the latest French station advertising in English and with schedules published by the IBC. She adds that: "I believe that no one should say with confidence that there will not be further additions to French stations doing advertising within a relatively short time".[621]

From the pivotal year of 1935 until the end of the decade commercial radio – both in terms of advertising revenue and audience – reached a formidable peak of success and popularity, principally through programmes transmitted by Radio Luxembourg and Radio Normandy. This is the subject of the next chapter.

---

620 Carpendale, letter to Captain Leonard Plugge, 19 July 1933. WAC CAV E2/365/1.

621 ID Benzie: BBC Internal Memo, 17 April 1936, WAC CAV E2/2/1. Briggs refers to Benzie as "A key figure in the development of overseas broadcasting". She became the BBC's Foreign Director. (Briggs, II, p. 424)

Chapter seven

1935–1939

> *Turn off the wireless. Tune in to another station;*
> *To the tricks of variety or the rhythm of jazz.*
> *Let us roll back the carpet from the parlour floor*
> *And dance to the wireless through the open door.*[622]

1935

This chapter continues the examination of documentary evidence relating to the Public Service/Commercial broadcasting debate during the 1930s, focusing on the BBC's reaction to a diverse range of potential competition from British, European and American entrepreneurs in the light of the increasingly visible financial success of the two leaders in the field, Radios Normandy and Luxembourg. These events are set against the deterioration of international affairs – the Spanish Civil War and the rising shadow of World War – as the decade progressed. As in the previous chapter I shall utilize for this purpose original material contained in the BBC's Written Archives at Caversham. The year 1935 offers itself naturally as a point of division within this section in that it proved to be pivotal both in the immediate arguments surrounding issues of competition and monopoly in British radio at the time, and for the subsequent development of broadcasting in Britain. It was also the year of a General Election, and the successful campaign of Leonard Plugge as Conservative candidate for Chatham (see page 54) . The IBC sought to make Commercial Radio a political issue, just as the "Pirate" stations of the 1960s were to do thirty years later. The IBC issued a hand-out urging voters to lobby their prospective candidates on the matter:

HANDS OFF RADIO NORMANDY!

Ask your Parliamentary Candidate to give you a pledge to resist all interference with English programmes from the Continent. Insist on this before giving your vote. Act now in the name of freedom.[623]

---

622 Auden, W.H. and Isherwood, Christopher *The Ascent of F6*, Act II, Scene III, London, Faber & Faber, London, 1936, p. 102.

623 Ibid.

The BBC's Charter was due to expire on December 31st 1936, and in 1935 a committee under Lord Ullswater was appointed:

> to consider the constitution, control and finance of the broadcasting service in this country, and advise generally on the conditions under which the service, including broadcasting to the Empire, television broadcasting, and the system of wireless exchanges, should be conducted after the 31 December 1936.[624]

The Ullswater Committee sat through the summer of 1935, and received representations from all interested parties, including both the BBC and the IBC, although Reith was dismissive of the right of the latter even to be considered:

> The demand of the International Broadcasting Company Ltd. for constitutional recognition as part of the national system was amusing. It was not a broadcasting organisation at all, but an advertising agency which bought time from continental broadcasting organizations willing to sell it; it was not even the only one of its kind.[625]

Competition

The commercial stations deliberately set out to satisfy the audience most neglected by the BBC, that is to say the young and the working class who felt disenfranchised by the Corporation's Sunday policy. In 1935 Sunday listeners to Radio Normandy could tune in at 7.00 a.m. to an hour of light music, followed by records of Harry Roy's Dance Orchestra, and a schedule that included (usually in 15-minute programmes):

9.00	*The Smoking Concert: A Convivial Congregation with a Cigarette and a Song on their Lips* (Presented by Rizla Cigarettes)
9.15	*Hollywood Heroes* (Presented by the makers of Lux Toilet Soap)
9.30	*Alfredo Campoli and his Orchestra* (Presented by California Syrup of Figs)
9.45	*Extra! Music Behind the Headlines* (Presented by Preservine Soap)
& c.	

The evening schedule included Jessie Matthews in the *Horlicks Picture House*, *The Rinso Music Hall* (with Tommy Handley, shortly to begin his *ITMA* career with the BBC), *Advance Film News* (Sponsor, Associated British Cinemas) and Vaudeville (Sponsor, Western Sports Pools).[626] The IBC's claims for the audience attracted by these programmes were extravagant. For BBC staff such as Maurice Gorham, editor of *Radio Times* during the 1930s, it was a frustrating situation: "We did not believe all the figures these stations issued, and they would have taken a lot of believing, but we could not oppose them with any of our own".[627] Initially the BBC's response had been one of lofty superiority. Gorham remembered a programme board meeting after the King's Silver Jubilee at which it was reported by the Corporations' Controller of Programmes, Alan Dawnay how unaminous had been the praise of the BBC's coverage of the event, both by the press and the public,

624 Broadcasting Committee, 1935 Cmd 5091, vii.
625 Reith, J.C.W. *Into the Wind* London, Hodder and Stoughton, 1949, p. 228.
626 *Radio Pictorial*, April 1935, p. 17.
627 Gorham, Maurice *Sound and Fury, Twenty-one Years in the BBC*, London, Percival Marshall, 1948, p. 59.

adding: "... but of course that is not the final test. The real criterion is what we ourselves round this table think of our work."[628]

The nearest the BBC had itself come to any sort of objective examination of output was in the activities of the Programme Revision Committee, set up in 1934. The Committee, while noting that it reached its deliberations without any reliable data about audience and social habits, divided the Radio audience up notionally into four categories: the wireless trade, the "tap-listener", the occasional listener and the serious listener. As Scannell and Cardiff have said, the Committee did little more than tell the BBC what it wanted to hear:

> There was daytime listening for the trade who could demonstrate the quality of their goods to customers. The tap-listener was the sort that the BBC always discouraged and therefore "warranted no further special provision in pro- grammes". The occasional listener was catered for in the general balance of output as was the serious listener, whose needs were entitled to "the greatest measure of consideration". All in all, the committee concluded, without a shred of evidence in support, the existing ratios of programming were "about right".[629]

The Nature of Audience Research

The previous chapter described the arrival at the BBC in 1935 of Sir Stephen Tallents as Controller (Public Relations). Tallents had worked in Public Relations for the Post Office and the Empire Marketing Board. He understood matters of corporate image. His appointment was to bring "the public and the broadcasting authorities into closer touch".[630] Tallents understood the need for the lateral approach in gauging audiences and their requirements:

> We want to know more than we do about the habits and tastes of listeners in different parts of the country and at different times of the year ... As to people's habits, there is a lot of information to be got indirectly from indirect sources such as gas and electric light companies – even the water companies, for the water engineer at Portsmouth has just sent us a graph showing how everyone ceased to use water for cooking, washing etc while the broadcast of the King's funeral was on.[631]

In the year of Tallents' appointment the *Report of the Broadcasting Committee, 1935* was published under the Chairmanship of The Right Hon. The Viscount Ullswater, G.C.B., who was critical of the BBC's approach to Sunday broadcasting:

> We have little doubt that something has been lost in the past by a lack of attractiveness in the programmes broadcast on Sundays (apart from religious services). We think it an advantage that one of the alternative programmes should be of a lighter and more popular character than the other, and that

628 Ibid., p. 52.

629 Scannell Paddy & Cardiff, David *A Social History of British Broadcasting, 1922–1939*, Oxford, Blackwell, 1991, p. 233.

630 *Manchester Guardian*, 9 July 1935, p. 6.

631 Tallents, Sir Stephen in a letter to his son, quoted in Briggs, 11, p. 247. Briggs believes the letter to have been written in 1936.

the contrasting programme though in more serious mood should be of interest to a good proportion of thoughtful listeners.[632]

In October 1936, as we have seen, the Listener Research Department was finally established under R.J.E. Silvey, and one of the major tasks in its first months and years was a rigorous examination of how the BBC's Sunday policy compared to its continental rivals. A key part of their research revolved around how the young listener was catered for. On weekdays the BBC broadcast *The Children's Hour*, taking its title from poem by Longfellow which contains the lines:

> Between the dark and the daylight,
> When the night is beginning to lower,
> Comes a pause in the day's occupations,
> That is known as the Children's Hour.

The programme actually established itself in a 45 minute slot between 5.15 p.m. and the 6.00 p.m. news, and generally contained a mixture of music, plays and poetry. On Sundays, as has been seen, this mixture was replaced by Bible readings and religious talks. Silvey's Listener Research Department found unequivocal evidence that the Commercial stations won the battle of Sunday tea-time by filling a gap the BBC's policy prohibited it from doing itself, having created a demand for this programming for the rest of the week; a memo pointed out that "from 4.00 p.m. to 5.00 p.m. both Luxembourg and Normandie broadcast a *Horlicks Tea Hour*, and from 5.30 p.m. to 6.00 p.m. Luxembourg broadcasts the *Ovaltineys*, which is primarily a children's programme".[633] *The Ovaltineys' Concert Party* began in 1934, and resumed on Luxembourg after the war, finally ending in 1957. The programme was broadcast in conjunction with a club run by Radio Luxembourg, *The League of Ovaltineys,* (See chapter, "Radio for Sale") supplying merchandise and publications, which reached a peak membership of over five million.[634] Thus the BBC had literally handed its rivals the gift of an audience; having established an expectation in their listeners (in this case children), they then denied those listeners the same content on Sundays.

Commercial Radio Listener Research

In 1938 the IBC contracted the American research agency, Crossley Incorporated to carry out a survey which involved interviewing 5,785 listeners. Results were analysed by day and hour. The figures confirmed commercial growth: weekday figures showed that while only 30 per cent of the potential audience tuned in before 11.30 a.m., 64 per cent of that audience tuned to commercial stations. The share fell in the afternoons, when 44 per cent of sets were being used while only 36 per cent of the audience were listening to Commercial radio. Once again, however, the Sunday figures were the most dramatic; mornings demonstrated that 52 per cent of sets were working, with 82.1 per cent of the audience listening to European stations. After noon the number of sets working rose to 66 per cent and up to 6.00

632   *Report of the Broadcasting Committee, 1935*, Cmd. 5091, p. 31, paragraph 100.

633   Pegg, Mark *Broadcasting and Society 1918–1939*, Beckenham, Croom Helm, 1983, p. 126.

634   Hartley, Ian *Goodnight Children … Everywhere*, Southborough, Midas Books, 1983, p. 68.

p.m. 70.3 per cent of those sets were tuned to the Commercials. Of these the two most popular stations were Radio Normandy and Radio Luxembourg.

In 1939 Plugge's organisation published a booklet the aim of which was to "sell" commercial radio to potential sponsors. It was a sophisticated piece of publicity, creating the impression of a large-scale, efficiently-run organisation which understood completely the business of advertising on radio. In it, the IBC made claims for:

> A Research Department with its finger on the pulse of Radio Normandy's audience and ready to supply statistical information of every description on the distribution of the audience, listening habits, programme preferences, etc., a Department ready to examine all aspects of marketing and distribution.[635]

The IBC policy, according to the booklet, was to develop "sustainer" programmes alongside sponsored shows, with the aim of testing audience and potential sponsors' reactions at one and the same time.

> We offer services that we believe the listeners want but which are not yet proved suitable for sponsorship. With sustainers we adjust the balance of the broadcasting day so that a proper variety of listening is available. We put ourselves in the position to offer advertisers established programmes with an audience already gathered to them.[636]

The Radio Normandy signal was targeted as we have seen at "The Prosperous South" of England, which happily coincided with the station's transmitter range. The claim was that research was based on two main areas:

(1)   The IBC General Panel, based on listeners, "not necessarily regular patrons of Radio Normandy, who form a microcosm of listeners as a whole".

(2)   The International Broadcasting Club, set up by the IBC as a "Friends" organisation, paying a yearly subscription in return for publications and various other merchandise designed to aid publicity such as badges, cuff-links, tie pins etc, all bearing the company logo. This group was claimed to have a membership of one-third of a million, forming "a magnificent body of listeners to which questions of programme popularity can be referred in those cases where the problem is suitable".

(3)   Apparently there had been criticism that this was not representative in that "it must necessarily be composed of the poorer classes":This is a by-product of the fallacy that only C and D classes pay any attention to radio advertising. All surveys, no matter by whom, have shown this to be untrue, and that the penetration of radio advertising is sound in all classes. The incidence of ownership of telephones amongst the IBC Panel is 24 per cent. The penetration of the telephone in the C and D classes is quite small (the reason why

635   *This is the IBC*, IBC, London, 1939, p. 43. William E. Franklin was head of the IBC Research Department from 1935–39. He subsequently became Director of Overseas Research for the BBC, and in 1947 joined South African Research Services. He went on to found his own research company which carried out radio listenership surveys for the South African Broadcasting Corporation for 21 years.

636   Ibid., p. 24.

we do not use the telephone for surveys in England) so that it appears that the A and B classes must be fairly represented in the panel.[637]

Given the high rate of unemployment in Britain at the time, and the poorly-waged "working class" the idea that IBC listeners had disposable income was clearly an important matter for the Radio Normandy sales team.

Independent Audience Research

The facts had, however, been present from the beginning of the decade. In York R. Seebohm Rowntree carried out his own surveys through the decade into various aspects of social life. Rowntree, (1871–1954), chairman of the York-based Chocolate firm, was a philanthropist who dedicated his life to the study of social problems and welfare. The continuing research which was to culminate in his book, *Poverty and Progress*[638] centred around the social habits and conditions surrounding the people of York. His findings are based on returns from 388 local families. Taking weekends without differentiating between Saturdays and Sundays, he found that a total of 1,328 hours were spent listening to light music, dance music and variety, and 343 to plays, classical music and religious services. He also noted that it was usual for working class families to tune in to Radio Luxembourg on a Sunday morning and stay tuned to the station all day. The arrival of Relay companies opened up the station to 3,000 subscribers in York, and enabled Rowntree to have an accurate gauge of the most listened-to programmes. Leading the field was the *Littlewoods Pools Programme* from Luxembourg each Sunday at 1.30 p.m. It had a 100 per cent load against the BBC on the other channel.[639] Charles Siepmann of the BBC's Talks Department had seen the importance of Rowntree's work as early as 1930:

> I feel convinced that a statistical survey, i.e. anything in the nature of a mere numerical analysis of public opinion, whether widely or narrowly conceived, will prove futile and misleading. We are not out to count heads, but to collect a mass of information on which to base broad conclusions.[640]

Even Reith supported Siepmann when he consulted Rowntree about his methods of research in June 1930. Nevertheless this was not to say that, at that time, an enlightened BBC approach to audience research was at hand, as Briggs states:

> He [Reith] believed that … the introduction of regular listener research would inevitably have the effect of influencing, even of dictating, programme policy: in the distance he feared the shadowy shape of programme planning based on programme rating …[641]

It was to be six more years before the BBC was to make its first practical moves in Rowntree's direction. John Reith left the BBC at the end of June 1938, just under two years after the establishment of the Listener Research Committee. The follow-

637 Ibid., pp. 42–43.
638 Rowntree, R. Seebohm *Poverty and Progress*, London, Longmans, Green and Co., 1941, cited by Scannell & Cardiff, pp. 363–364.
639 Ibid.
640 BBC Internal Memo, C.A. Siepmann, BBC WAC, quoted in Pegg, p. 103.
641 Briggs II, p. 242.

ing year Sir William Crawford and H. Broadley produced a study of class habits, *The People's Food*. One of the most significant findings to come from its research was the disparity between eating times; working class "high tea" was usually taken between 5.00 p.m. and 5.30 p.m., while upper class "afternoon tea" was usually between 4.30 p.m. and 5.00 p.m. Working class listeners usually had "supper" between 9.00 p.m. and 9.30 p.m. while the upper class "dinner" generally occurred between 7.30 p.m. and 8.00 p.m. The book was the first to study such social habits in this way in relation to the world of the broadcaster:

> The hour of the tea-time meal is even more important to wireless broadcasters than breakfast and lunch. *The Children's Hour* must be fitted in between their return from school and tea-time or postponed until tea is well over. A programme of special interest to housewives will not secure its maximum listening public if it clashes with the preparation of tea or the washing up.[642]

Within months of Crawford and Broadley's book, the Second World War was to remove many of the criteria which had been used by programme makers, while at the same time, as Silvey has said, providing a boost for the cause of Audience Research.[643] Indeed the war redefined broadcasting in a way which was ultimately to the advantage of the BBC. Reshaped by the influences of the Allied Expeditionary Forces Programme with its strongly American and Canadian light entertainment bias and a situation which made Public Service Broadcasting a principle of national significance rather than an imposed dogma, the Corporation was able to escape from the embarrassment of an increasingly untenable public position by re-asserting itself as the true voice of a united country. At the same time it was able to use the opportunity to reshape programme policies after the war to reflect a more populist approach to programming. In 1948, Maurice Gorham, editor of *Radio Times*, and a man who had been an employee of the BBC from 1926 to 1947 wrote:

> From 1932 to 1939, when the war saved the BBC from itself, was the great Stuffed Shirt era, marked internally by paternalism run riot, bureaucracy of the most hierarchical type, an administration system that made productive work harder instead of easier, and a tendency to promote the most negative characters to be found amongst the staff. Externally it was similarly marked by aloofness, resentment of criticism, and a positive contempt for the listener, which was only finally to be broken down by the joint influence of Listener Research and the war.[644]

BBC Audience Research

The second part of the 1930s brought with it a change in perception within the BBC relating to the issue of research. Gorham noted the haphazard way decisions relating to programme-appeal were made:

> In programme-planning circles they talked easily about contrasts and alternatives, this kind of audience and that kind, successes and failures, good

---

642   Crawford, Sir William and Broadley, H. *The People's Food*, London, William Heinnemann Ltd, 1938, pp. 60–61.

643   Silvey pp. 112–113.

644   Gorham, p. 45.

programmes and bad; and it was all based on what the BBC officials themselves thought ... I was always longing for a little Listener Research ... Radio Normandie, Luxemburg [sic] and Athlone were getting some hold on the British public ...[645]

Robert Silvey's work in BBC Audience research was to focus increasingly on commercial radio, the growing threat it brought both to the BBC both in terms of audience loss, and the establishment of a possible status quo which established advertising revenue long term and a legitimate means of funding broadcasting. It would be hard to conceive of anyone better fitted for the job; he had been recruited from the London Press Exchange, one of the larger of the British advertising agencies, where he had been employed to write a survey of listening to European commercial stations:

> The LPE needed to have this kind of information, for its clients were being increasingly pressed by these stations to include radio advertising in their advertising appropriations ... the survey showed that the regular audiences for these stations were substantial and increasing.[646]

The Unit grew in turn out of the appointment of Sir Stephen Tallents as Director of Public Relations for the BBC in 1935, and the significance of this aspect of the BBC's pre-war development is clear from its decision "to elevate Public Relations to the status of a Division – parallel with the existing three Divisions: Programme, Engineering and Administration ..."[647] In the *BBC Annual 1937* an article under the title "Public Relations" gives a symptom of the thinking engendered by Tallents and his team:

> A "take it or leave it" attitude on the part of the BBC might well be fatal to the success of its programmes. The BBC wants listeners. It wants new and good listeners, and it is the special function of its public relations system to encourage the development of good and widespread listening by a variety of means.[648]

This is in distinct contrast to Reith's own words in the first *BBC Handbook* of 1928:

> The most careful tapping of public opinion cannot do more than afford data for consideration. It cannot, save in rare instances, give quite definite guidance; the preferences individually expressed cancel one another out as often as not and a proportion of the correspondence even praises or blames everything alike.[649]

It would be wrong however to suggest that the two statements represent a shift of opinion on behalf of Reith himself; nor would it be accurate to state that the BBC as a whole was totally in support of the democratization of listening. Indeed there were elements outside the Corporation during the mid 1930s which believed in the values of the old-style paternalism:

---

645 Gorham, p. 59.

646 Ibid., p. 16.

647 Ibid., p. 13.

648 *BBC Annual* 1937, BBC, London, p. 84.

649 Reith, J.C.W., Introduction, *BBC Year Book 1928*, BBC, London, p. 33.

The BBC ought never to be too anxious to please the public at all costs …
the promoter of entertainment who tries slavishly to follow public taste is
always left behind and it is the promoter with the courage and the insight to
lead the public tactfully towards new satisfactions who is rewarded in the
end.[650]

In a rejoinder to a memorandum submitted to the Ullswater Committee by the
Publishers' Association, Reith linked the idea of standards and response to the
requirements of popular taste to the issue of competition:

An examination of the International Broadcasting Company's programmes
will show whether or not the competition which the Corporation has to face
from sponsored programmes broadcast in English is likely to raise the
standard.[651]

Ullswater and Beyond

The BBC made representations of its own to the Committee; the Corporation's
General Advisory Council created a report as evidence on a range of issues, among
them that of Wireless Exchanges. As stated in the previous chapter, the BBC's
attempts to gain control of these through negotiations with the Post Office had
broken down, and the independence of the Exchanges created a technical loophole
whereby Commercial Stations could be broadcast in high quality down lines into
areas where they would have otherwise have had severe reception problems. The
Council's statement on this matter was unequivocal:

No commercial organisation should be allowed to destroy the unity of
programmes, and to introduce elements which have hitherto and with public
approval been deliberately excluded … We therefore feel strongly that in
future no Exchange should be allowed to transmit programmes inconsistent
with the general policy and principles followed in the programmes of the
Corporation and that to this end the Corporation should be given control
over the programme activities of all Wireless Exchange systems in the United
Kingdom. At the same time, we suggest that the technical work of the
Exchanges be undertaken by the Post Office.[652]

The Ullswater Committee supported this view virtually to the letter in its report,
although not without dissent from one of its members, Lord Selsdon, who favoured
the idea of the competition the exchanges offered and represented a significant body
of support amongst the mid-1930s British establishment for commercial alternatives against the BBC.[653]

---

650   *Yorkshire Post* 10 July 1935, quoted in Briggs: *The History of Broadcasting in the United Kingdom*,
      Volume II, *The Golden Age of Wireless*, Oxford, Oxford University Press, 1995, p. 247.

651   Reith, J.C.W., rejoinder to Memorandum by the Publishers' Association, 1935, quoted in Briggs II, p.
      456.

652   Report from the BBC General Advisory Council to the Ullswater Committee, June 1935, published in
      Briggs II, p. 451.

653   Boyle, Andrew *Only the Wind Will Listen: Reith of the BBC*, London, Hutchinson,1972, p. 273. In his
      former role as Postmaster General, Seldson, then Sir William Mitchell-Thompson, had angered Reith
      with his views and actions on a number of issues. (See also Boyle pp 169–174.)

The BBC generally emerged from the enquiry favourably in terms of the recommendations made by Ullswater, with its charter renewed for ten years. There were issues of criticism in the report, and suggestions that there should be a more varied representation among the governors – increased from five to seven (" 'homogeneity of age or opinion' were to be avoided"),[654] when placed beside the fact that the Corporation was "chided for the heaviness of its Sunday entertainment"[655] were judgements that it should respond to the challenge identified by Continental competition. The Report was published on 16 March 1936; a Government White Paper followed in June. In the meantime the matter of Wireless Exchanges had given rise to considerable debate. The idea of BBC control was put forward in The House of Commons as "cultural dictatorship".[656] Richard Law, who was to become Lord Coleraine, argued forcefully for the freedom of the Exchanges: "Are we to understand that the only way in which the Corporation can achieve a balanced and good programme is to have everybody in the country listening to the BBC's programme, and nothing else, all the time?"[657]

It was not a quality issue, Law maintained, but one of monopoly; it was not desirable that any one body should be in a position to dictate "not only what should be broadcast in this country, but to say what should be listened to, not by the country as a whole, but merely by the poor and less fortunate listeners".[658]

The Government White Paper supported most of Ullswater's recommendations; on this issue however, it did not, and the views of such as Law and Selsdon prevailed over the view of the greater number of the Committee. The Exchanges, which had their licences extended to the end of 1939, were not to be taken over by the BBC and the Post Office, as the Corporation had proposed, but were to retain their independence. The Government's provisions were that there should be a minimum standard of "efficiency in technical and other aspects", and that in the case of Exchanges which offered more than one listening option (the vast majority), must be a BBC programme during the Corporation's hours of broadcasting.[659]

Commercial Expansion

The decision was to have a crucial effect on the financial growth of Radio Luxembourg and Radio Normandy during the remaining years of the decade, in particular because it gave potential advertisers confidence that consumer demand in areas where Wireless Exchange services operated (particularly poorer areas) would continue to create opportunities for populist commercial broadcasting. On 7 October 1937, Robert Silvey sent a memo to Tallents quoting figures from an IBC audience survey of audiences for Radio Normandy in South East London and

---

654   Smith, Anthony *British Broadcasting*, Newton Abbot, David and Charles, 1974, p. 67.
655   Ibid.
656   Richard Law, Debate on the Report of the Broadcasting Committee, 29 April 1936, *Hansard*, vol. 31, col. 1008.
657   Ibid.
658   Ibid.
659   Cmd. 5207 (1936) *Broadcasting: Memorandum by the Postmaster-General on the Report of the Broadcasting Committee* quoted in Briggs II, p. 473.

Southampton, designed to show how these audiences had increased over one year:[660]

	1936	1937
Sunday		
Morning	22%	60%
Afternoon	32%	57%
Evening	24%	53%
Weekday		
Morning	15%	43%
Afternoon	9%	37%
Evening	2%	5%

Silvey was at pains to point out that the IBC did not reveal how their survey was conducted, and "these figures … must be taken with a considerable pinch of salt, but I think it very improbable that they do not represent a fairly substantial increase in listening to Radio Normandy in these towns, though not, of course, as great as is claimed".[661]

That summer Maurice Farquharson, on holiday in Normandy, had received a graphic illustration of the extent of investment that had become possible as Continental Commercial Radio gained in financial stature. Traveling through the small town of Caudebec-en-Caux, he came across the new headquarters, not yet opened, of Radio Normandy.[662] At this point, the station was still operating from its original cramped studios in Fécamp. The new premises represented considerable opulence in contrast, consisting as they did of "an extremely beautiful little period chateau, perhaps early eighteenth century, situated in a delightful garden on the river bank of the Seine".[663] Farquharson was able to gain access to the building, presumably because much of it was open to the public, including a restaurant. The studios, he observed, were on the "first and upper storeys", and "the only outward indication of the building's purpose as a broadcasting center is provided by the words 'Radio Normandie' in gilt letters on the entrance gateway". He was able to recommend the restaurant as "very good – almost certainly the best in the place", and this, together with the fact that Caudebec was noted as a beauty spot, very popular with visitors "will no doubt in themselves bring the company a certain amount of goodwill". It was only when he explored further that he realized that the Chateau premises were only for the French native broadcasts.

Up until this point, Radio Normandy's transmissions in English had been limited by the fact that all facilities had to be shared with the French broadcasters. With the growth in popularity from the mid 1930s onwards, a new arrangement had to be made, and Caudebec's chateau and grounds provided the answer. In direct contrast with the opulence of the chateau, Farquharson found the IBC studios at

660   Silvey, R.J.E. BBC Internal Memo: *Extent of Audience for Radio Advertising*, 27 October 1937. WAC CAV R34/960.

661   Ibid.

662   Farquharson, Maurice BBC Internal Memo to Stephen Tallents, 17 August 1937. WAC CAV E1/717.

663   Ibid.

"the bottom of the garden [in] a garage with two or three adjacent rooms. These bungalow studios are roofed with a sort of corrugated iron and are otherwise unimpressive." Gaining permission to look round, he noted that, utilitarian as the facilities were, they provided all the basic requirements of a radio station:

(1) A small studio with six gramophone turntables and microphone for announcer (there are two announcers); (2) gramophone record library (not yet stocked, but with large consignments ready to be unpacked); and (3) a room for apparatus, accumulators etc.[664]

Farquharson felt the sound proofing to be less than adequate but on the other hand "there will, of course, be no live artists to consider". Nearby, at Louvetot, a mile or so along the Yvetot Road, he was told, was Radio Normandy's new transmitter, not yet in use, but representing a major increase in power for the station.[665] What he does not mention, and probably did not know, was that the acquisition and development of the Caudebec site represented more that two years' work on behalf of the IBC and their Norman landlords; that premises – formerly "L'Hotel du Chateau", had originally been acquired in 1935, and the major refurbishment he saw was the product of that time as well as highly confident investment.[666]

From an examination of the files at the BBC's Written Archives at Caversham, it becomes clear that Farquharson, together with Stephen Tallents and Robert Silvey, was engaged in a major assessment exercise relating to Commercial competition to the BBC during the Autumn of 1937. Also in October we find an anonymous[667] BBC report which summarises activity in the area between 1934 and 1936. While acknowledging that there had been an increase in expenditure on all forms of advertising it adds that "neither the general nor the press advertising increases has been anything like so rapid as that in the radio advertising field".[668] The report goes on to clarify the position regarding stations currently broadcasting, a statement which can hardly have comforted the BBC after the efforts of Madrid and the Ullswater Committee. Radio Luxembourg, run by Radio Publicity (London) Ltd, and the International Broadcasting Company Ltd were of course, the chief players, the former operating services from Radio Normandy, Poste Parisien, Juan les Pins and Ljubljana. "The last named station is at present being 'kept warm' ... Radio Normandie [sic] also have an hour a week on EAQ Madrid short-wave, but these transmissions are 'temporarily discontinued'."[669]

Turning to the account of an American commentator, César Saerchinger, it is clear nevertheless that it was the activities of Radio Luxembourg – "a radio station à la Américaine" as he called it[670] – which drew the greatest attention internationally. Saerchinger's account nowhere mentions the IBC's operations, while referring to

664 Ibid.
665 Ibid.
666 Lhote, Francois, France Radio Club, interviewed by the author, August 1999.
667 Anonymous Internal BBC report, *Radio Advertising*, October 1937, WAC CAV R34/959. Almost certainly this was written by either Tallents or Silvey.
668 Ibid.
669 Ibid. The Spanish Civil War was at the time at its height.
670 Saerchinger, César, *Hello America! Radio Adventures in Europe*, Cambridge, Massachusetts, Houghton Mifflin, 1938, p. 361.

Luxembourg's "very name" as "anathema to the radio nabobs".[671] Significant as the activities of Wireless Publicity and the IBC were, they did not represent by any means the sum of commercial radio activity, as the report went on to point out:

> Radio Lyons on 215.4 metres does sponsored programmes in English. It is not known for certain who are the publicity agents for these programmes, but it is believed to be a French group.
>
> David Allen & Co., with whom P.P. Eckersley is associated, are running programmes on Radio Toulouse.
>
> Sponsored programmes are occasionally broadcast from Athlone.[672]

Speculation in the Shadow of War

The remainder of the report was more conjectural; David Allen and Plugge had both apparently been in negotiation with Vienna, seeking to broadcast sponsored programmes on short-wave. Eckersley was reported to have been in Skopje, Yugoslavia, negotiating a wavelength "for a station in the Irish Free State". It was not known whether this was for Athlone, at the time being badly jammed by a station at Palermo, or for a new enterprise. Additionally there were rumours of the commencement of short-wave broadcasting from Luxembourg, and experiments on Sark: "Here, however, the Postmaster-General has jurisdiction, and might be counted upon to disallow any such project". A further possibility was a new station in Lichtenstein: "It is, however, understood that the Posts and Telegraphs Lichtenstein are run by the Swiss P.T.T. If their authority there extends to broadcasting, it is believed to be unlikely that they would entertain sponsored programmes in English."[673]

Of all these rumours, the most substantive seems to have been that concerning the potential development of an Austrian English language commercial station. In April 1937 there had been correspondence between the BBC and the General Director of Austrian Radio, Oskar Czeija, relating to this matter. A letter from Czeija is missing from the files, but the reply to this letter – by Isa Benzie, Director of Foreign Affairs for the BBC – is extant, and it is clear from this that Plugge had been exploring the possibility of developing transmissions. After explaining to Czeija the nature of Plugge's activities, Benzie goes on to outline the recommendations of the Ullswater Committee and the British Government's response to its report:

> The Ullswater Committee (on broadcasting) recommended in its report last year "that the responsible Departments should take all the steps which are within their power, with a view to preventing the broadcasting from foreign stations of advertisement programmes intended for this country". The

---

671 Ibid. Saerchinger elaborates on the standard and success of Luxembourg briefly: "Its programmes are the most unexacting in Europe; it makes little pretence at cultural values; it gives the British low-brow what he thinks he wants, and apparently its efforts are crowned with success ... Having applied the 'American system' to the European scene, Luxembourg represents the single 100 per cent example of untrammelled private enterprise. Its inhabitants tolerate it, as the inhabitants of Monaco tolerate gambling, but there is no evidence that they like it." (Ibid., pp. 361–362.)

672 *Radio Advertising*, October 1937, p. 33.

673 Ibid.

Government remarked in the "White Paper" which set forth its views on the Ullswater Report: "the Government accept this recommendation".[674]

Benzie ends the letter with a statement which will have left Czeija with no doubt that to support Plugge or any other British entrepreneur in this way would be to offend both the BBC and the British Government: "The Corporation has always associated itself entirely with the view taken in official quarters of broadcast advertising in English from continental stations".[675] In the face of such unequivocal "guidance" it is perhaps not surprising that from this point onwards the Austrian issue receives no further mention. In any event Hitler's arrival in Vienna on 14 March 1938, confirming the "Anschluss", Germany's annexation of Austria, put the matter beyond discussion. On 16 June 1937, Sir Charles Carpendale wrote a letter to an undisclosed recipient, itemising more exploratory moves, among them two from Peter Eckersley:

> Eckersley has recently been to Copenhagen to try to purchase their long-wave transmitter (wave included!) to broadcast sponsored programmes in English – the offer was turned down for various reasons – one being that it left Denmark without a National Service![676]

With hindsight, the second paragraph in Carpendale's letter is startling: he notes that "Germany has had three separate missions last winter approaching first Goebbels, then Goering, then their Foreign Office to erect or purchase a station for sponsored programmes". The intelligence was that two of these representations had come from Plugge, the third, probably, from Eckersley. All were turned down. Hungary had also been approached, with the promise "that they would make a fortune, etc., especially by programmes sent on a Sunday". Then, adds Carpendale, "there is the Plugge-Austria business of which we know … So it looks like two opposing factors – Plugge and Eckersley and co., at work all over Europe".[677]

However apparent this fact must have seemed to Carpendale at the time, there were other possibilities of competitors emerging. Tantalisingly for the speculators, as the rewards of Commercial radio became more evident, so the deteriorating political climate in Europe put further development beyond incoming investors, so many of these ventures came to nothing. In the BBC Written Archives there is a remarkable document relating to this time, a typescript of an article published in November 1937 by *The Utrechtsch Dagblad*, and submitted in draft for information to the BBC. With supreme irony, particularly given its source, the article carries the headline: "Radio Invasion in Europe". The substance of the piece is an interview with Leo Y. Chertok, "the American financier who obtained world wide fame in September 1935, when he disputed the much talked-of oil concession in Abyssinia with the Standard Vacuum Oil Company, through which America was almost dragged into the Abyssinian incident".[678] Chertok claimed in the article that his

---

674 Letter from Isa Benzie, Director of Foreign Affairs, BBC, to Oskar Czeija, Generaldirektor, Oesterreich Radioverkehrs A.G., Johannesgasse 4b, Wien 1, 28 April 1937. WAC CAV E2/2/2 .

675 Ibid.

676 Carpendale, Sir Charles, Letter, 16 June 1937. WAC CAV E2/2/2.

677 Ibid.

678 Article, "Radio Invasion in Europe – New Syndicate Founded – Broadcasting in the Service of Advertising" *Utrechtsch Dagblad* , typescript dated 16 November 1937. To the typescript is added a

syndicate was negotiating in "21 European countries", among them France, Germany, Italy, Norway, Sweden, Denmark and the Netherlands. It would seem from the correspondent, that Chertok had not conducted sufficient research prior to the interview, on the morning of which he had received a letter which confirmed that Government control in Holland "would in no way consent to a commercialization ... a judgment which we – when Mr Chertok asked us about it – could fully support ... 'That is unfortunate', said Mr Chertok". The Radio Syndicate expected nevertheless to make its first broadcasts in Europe "within three months", backed by "millions of dollars worth of American advertising". Chertok, apparently thinking as the interview progressed, added "We must turn elsewhere, to Radio Luxembourg for example, although that station is to a great extent booked by English advertising firms, or Brussels; or if necessary we must erect a station in Scandinavia or Finland which will catch Holland".[679]

From this it would appear that the syndicate saw what the IBC and Radio Luxembourg had achieved beaming their signals into Britain as the blueprint for commercial radio across the whole continent. The programmes were to be planned "in the same manner as American coast-to-coast relays", with "gramophone and talky film records prepared in advance [in the syndicate's New York Studios] to be performed on a given date".[680] Furthermore, with great ambition "They will be recorded in 21 different languages. The idea is to give the same programme, for example, in twelve countries at the same time, each of course in the language of the country for which it is broadcast". The programmes would advertise everything "from cars to soap". The syndicate's headquarters were to be in Paris and London, with branch offices in the European capitals and with Vienna as the center for the Balcan [sic] States. Chertok was in Britain to locate a site for his operation, claiming to be in negotiation "for a London theatre, which we shall have to alter into a gigantic receiving station, and that will it is hoped be the first stone of a London Radio city. In this theatre the European spot programmes will be recorded in different languages." Asked how he could imagine the diverse European public "which presumably differs considerably from that of America", would react to such a scheme, he replied "Europe will react in the same way as America".[681]

It was pointed out that the existing concerns broadcasting Commercial radio into Britain had run up against strong opposition, not only from the BBC and the Post Office but from the Newspaper Proprietors' Association. The interviewer, who apparently equated the BBC with the British Government, ended with a salvo which was blandly deflected by Chertok:

It will be more difficult than you suppose, with the BBC and the NPA, in other words the Government and the press, against you, we concluded. "Oh",

---

note for BBC information: "Below is the report of an exclusive interview which one of our representatives had at the Savoy Hotel, London with Mr Leo Y. Chertok, the well known American financier, who was concerned with the Abyssinian oil concession. Mr Chertok has great plans in the Radio domain, as appears from the interview." WAC CAV R34/959.
679 Ibid.
680 Ibid.
681 Ibid.

said Mr Chertok with a broad smile, "we have capital, and difficulties are there to be overcome".[682]

No trace has been found of Chertok's plans thereafter. It may be that his thinking represents a lack of understanding of the worsening European political situation, but it was clearly fuelled by the tradition of American success-bred confidence (as with the J. Walter Thompson Organisation's work) in the European field up until that point. Likewise he had probably not appreciated the differences and complexities of a European culture as opposed to the US. Two years earlier, in the American advertising journal, *Shelf Space,* a journalist writing under the pseudonym of "Zoc" (short for Zoccola) had found the NPA's opposition to commercial radio to be incomprehensible, based on the US model, in which:

> as the radio advertising budget has increased, so has the advertiser spent more in the press ... It is pretty obvious that if a man is spending $5,000 on a programme, if he has booked Grace Moore or Maurice Chevalier he wants to tell the world about it and make sure of the maximum number of listeners, and to do this he has only the press on which to rely.[683] "Little wonder then", Zoccola concluded, "that advertisers in England have looked rather wistfully over the Atlantic ... [when] ... only the Continental stations have been willing to take their ready money".[684]

Three years after this article was published however, when Chertok was making his bullish statements about riding rough-shod over any problems in his path, British advertisers, in common with the rest of the country, were looking less wistfully West, and more anxiously East.

Formalised Audience Research

Robert Silvey continued to develop Listener Research through what he termed "Barometers", listening panels drawn from the general public, all of them volunteers. The first of these, created in September 1937, was significantly, given the issues of popularism current at the time, the Variety Barometer, consisting of 2,000 volunteers[685] and Silvey decided to put them to work almost immediately to measure current listener-response to the competition coming principally from Radios Normandy and Luxembourg. In his survey he asked for information relating to weekdays and Sundays separately. By February 1938, his figures were complete, and on the 4th he sent a memo Stephen Tallents, copied to Maurice Farquharson in the Public Relations Division:

> We know for certain that they all of them [members of the Variety Barometer] listen from time to time to our variety programmes, and there is evidence to suggest that they are a pretty typical sample of the public for light entertainment. Since it is generally agreed that light entertainment is the most

---

682 Ibid.

683 "They Call it Selling Space!", article in *Shelf Appeal,* October 1935, p. 25. WAC CAV R34/959.

684 Ibid.

685 Silvey, pp. 77–78. The campaign to find the volunteers was launched at the microphone during the "Music Hall" programme on 18 September 1937, and backed up with written material in *Radio Times.* 28,000 postcards were received, with 47,000 offers of help from which the 2,000 were chosen at random. (Silvey, p. 78.)

popular form of broadcasting (those who never listen to any light entertainment must be a very small minority of the listening public) we can even go further and say that the 2,000 are not unlikely to be a fairly good sample of the whole listening public.[686]

Silvey found that "22 per cent of these regularly listen to foreign stations on weekdays and 67 per cent on Sundays". Taking weekdays first, he noted that "the great bulk of foreign station listening is before 10.30 a.m". Radio Normandy was the most popular, closely followed by Radio Luxembourg, with the next most popular station being Radio Lyons, "less than a quarter as popular as either of the two former". He began his sample at 8.00 a.m. and ended at 10.30 a.m., and found that, of the whole 2,000 in the barometer, those regularly listening, as a percentage taken in half hour samples, broke down as follows:

8.00 a.m.	10 per cent
8.30 a.m.	11 per cent
9.00 a.m.	10 per cent
9.30 a.m.	8 per cent
10.00 a.m.	8 per cent
10.30 a.m.	5 per cent

His Sunday sampling began as on weekdays, at 8.00 a.m., but extended until 12.30 p.m., with the start of BBC transmissions. Of the 2,000 the Sunday percentages were as follows:

8.00 a.m.	5 per cent
8.30 a.m.	7 per cent
9.00 a.m.	15 per cent
9.30 a.m.	18 per cent
10.00 a.m.	24 per cent
10.30 a.m.	25 per cent
11.00 a.m.	27 per cent
11.30 a.m.	25 per cent
12.00 p.m.	25 per cent
12.30 p.m.	21 per cent[687]

This time the order of preference among listeners was different, and Silvey was able to provide percentages to prove it:

> The most popular station on Sundays is Luxembourg to which 46 per cent of the 2,000 say they listen regularly. The next most popular station is Normandie [sic] to which 30 per cent of the 2,000 say they regularly listen. The third most popular is Lyons which claims 12 per cent.[688]

Silvey also that month investigated Sunday listening via samples from two Relay services; the "load curves" were supplied to the BBC by exchanges in Bradford and Chelsea, and represented audience measurement on 1 March 1936 and 7 March 1937. His memo to Tallents, copy to Farquharson of 16 February 1938 drew attention to the fact that "although they are a bit out of date", BBC programme policy had not changed since the curves were created; the data therefore remained

686 Silvey, R.J.E., BBC Internal memo to Maurice Farquharson, 4 February 1938, "Audience for Foreign Programmes in the Mornings on Weekdays and Sundays", WAC CAV R34/960.

687 Ibid. It would have been interesting had Silvey extended his brief to compare listening figures on Sunday when there was direct competition for listeners.

688 Ibid.

relevant in terms of competition between the BBC and Commercial stations broadcast by the exchanges.[689]

The Bradford load curve, used by Silvey almost two years after the event is in fact unrepresentative of normal listening conditions; a major explosion at the Bradford Corporation Electricity Works on Monday 24 February had crippled the city and full supplies of electricity were not reinstated until Monday 2 March.[690] Thus during this time it would have been impossible to listen to mains-supply radios, while Radio Relays, relying as they did on telephone lines, would have remained unaffected. There is no evidence in Silvey's research to demonstrate that he was aware of this circumstance. There was, he said, "very considerable" demand for radio of one kind or another through the whole day from 9.00 a.m. until 11.30 p.m. The choice was between the BBC National Service and one continental station, which was subject to subscriber choice but which, according to Silvey was "usually Luxembourg". The peak listening for the day under scrutiny in 1936 was at 4.00 p.m. when "the King (Edward Vlll) spoke". (Edward had been proclaimed King on 21 January, at the death George V, who was buried at Windsor on 28 January) This was transmitted "on all services" (i.e. BBC networks). For the rest, the day was representative in its contrasting programming. Silvey's research claims surprisingly that the highest point in terms of listeners was between 8.00 p.m. and 9.00 p.m., and "this was the only time when the audience to our programme exceeded that of the foreign station". The BBC National Programme at this time was relaying a Roman Catholic church service from St. Mary Moorfields, Eldon Street, London EC2.[691] Meantime the Regional Service broadcast a Service from Hinde Street Methodist Church, Manchester Square, London W.1,[692] and the North Region transmitted devotions from St Michael and All Angels Parish Church, South Shields.[693] These services were followed at 8.45 p.m. by *The Week's Good Cause* and at 8.50 p.m. by The News. In other words there was nothing of specific

---

689   BBC Internal Memo, "Sunday Listening" from RJE Silvey to Sir Stephen Tallents, copy to Maurice Farquharson, 16 February 1938. WAC CAV R34/960.

690   *Yorkshire Observer*, Tuesday, 25 February 1936, p. 1. The paper carried dramatic photographs: "A serious explosion at the Bradford Corporation Electricity Works plunged the city into darkness last evening. Our picture shows the building ablaze." In its edition of Thursday, 27 February (p. 2) the paper went on to explore the implications of the accident for listeners, under the headline, "The Blow to Radio. Oh, for a Crystal Set!"(Ibid., p. 2.) The article pointed out that although battery receivers were available, they were not widely so; "It is difficult to obtain any statistics as to the relative number of battery and mains receivers in Bradford, but, judging by the sales of receivers I should imagine that 75 out of every 100 receivers in use are of the mains type. In the same way it can be estimated that there are about 200,000 radio listeners within the city boundary, and of these at least 150,000 would be without radio. The amount of listening done, therefore, would be comparable with that which was done in 1924." Although the correspondent does not taken into account Relay services, the point that this was an exceptional circumstance, is well made. Silvey's research nowhere demonstrates that he was aware of this, nor whether the date was chosen deliberately because of the reliance of the Relay Exchange (certainly this would have been an ideal opportunity to observe Relays at their maximum efficacy, although untypical of normal use.) *The Yorkshire Observer* for Monday 2 March reported that "barring unforeseen hitches ... the full supply for lighting and power will be available today – as promised on Friday". (p. 3).

691   *Radio Times*, Issue dated 28 February 1936, p. 18.

692   Ibid., p. 20.

693   Ibid., p. 23.

listener-interest to the citizens of Bradford to suggest a major pull away from the commercial competition at this time.[694] From 9.00 p.m. that evening the BBC National offered a light music programme from the Park Lane Hotel, but "this was only about half as attractive as the Luxembourg alternative".[695]

The Chelsea load curve of a year later represented in its sample "an almost exclusively working class audience", and like the Bradford curve showed considerable listener activity throughout the day, starting at 9.30 a.m. "At the time of our morning religious service about 30 per cent of their subscribers were listening – rather less than 10 per cent to the BBC and rather more than 20 per cent to Luxembourg."[696] From 11.00 a.m. until the end of the curve at 10.30 p.m., the audience fluctuated between 40 per cent and 60 per cent of the company's subscribers, but "the BBC alternative to Luxembourg never commands more than 12 per cent until the 8.00 p.m. – 10.30 p.m. period". As with Bradford, the BBC's evening religious programme achieved the maximum audience of 30 per cent, although the Luxembourg alternative was close to it at 28 per cent. Unlike Bradford however, the BBC was able to maintain its audience above the competition for the rest of the curve: "After 9.00 p.m. the Corporation's programme, which in this case was Galsworthy's *Old English*, commanded 33 per cent of the subscribers while the Luxembourg alternative remained at a steady 22 per cent".[697]

Robert Silvey's investigations during early 1938 also centred on advertisers using commercial radio. On 4 February he wrote to Tallents and Farquharson that "the evidence shows that the audience for foreign programmes in the mornings on weekdays and Sundays is both extensive and increasing".[698] He cites in support of this his own statistical enquiries, the observations of practitioners in radio advertising (notably the agencies), "after due allowance has been made for the fact that they are interested parties" and "the nature of and increase in users of time on commercial radio stations". He notes that "the number and importance of advertisers using commercial radio is considerable". For Silvey the significance of his findings was "not only because most of these firms would be most unlikely to use an advertising medium which they did not believe to be economic, but also because many of these firms have been using commercial radio for a number of years".

Radio at the Crossroads

There was one final international attempt to crush commercial opposition before the outbreak of war, prompted by the British Post Office and debated at the World Telecommunications Conference in Cairo.[699] The Engineer-in-Chief at the Post Office, Colonel Angwin tabled a motion in February 1938 to the First Subcommittee of the Technical Commission of the conference that:

---

694 In both the Bradford and the Chelsea curve, the BBC edges ahead of commercial competition at the time of the evening broadcast service. A possibility is that the listenership was affected at 8.00 p.m. by a number of children going to bed, but this is not acknowledged by Silvey.

695 BBC Internal Memo, 16 February 1938. WAC CAV R34/960.

696 Ibid.

697 Ibid.

698 Silvey, R.J.E., BBC Internal Memo, "Audience for Foreign Progammes in the Mornings on Weekdays and Sundays", to Sir Stephen Tallents, copy to Maurice Farquharson, 4 February 1938.

699 Briggs, II, pp. 339–340.

because of the difficulty of allocating to the broadcasting service between 150 and 500 kilocycles, a sufficient number of waves to allow each country in the European region to assure a satisfactory national service, no waves of this band may be used by a country in this region for transmissions in the nature of commercial publicity sent in any other language but the national language or languages of that country.[700]

Angwin went on to say that the British Parliament and Press were "aroused over this question". It is clear that the matter of stopping the continental stations was one which continued to cause considerable controversy. In a letter published in *The Spectator* of 11th February 1938, a reader voiced indignation:

> In answer to a question in the House yesterday, Mr Eden confessed that he had asked the French Government to suppress sponsored programmes in English from stations in France. I have no interest in the matter, either as an advertiser by these means or as a listener; but I think that the average Englishman deeply resents such official interference with his liberty to do what he likes with the apparatus for whose possession he pays the BBC 10s. a year.[701]

Angwin's resolution was passed by the Technical Subcommittee, but was subsequently reopened when the French delegate, who had been absent at the first meeting, objected. At the second vote, there was a tie, and under the Conference rules the resolution was deemed to have lapsed; thus the matter did not reach the Conference proper. It was clear that "France had successfully defended French commercial interests not only in France but in Luxembourg".[702]

From this point on, it became clear to BBC and Post Office representatives that arguments against commercial competition could prove disastrously counter-productive for the broadcasting status quo in Britain. There were those in government and elsewhere who were prepared to consider a new financial structure for broadcasting, based on the proven success of the commercial model supplied by the continental stations:

> Kingsley Wood, the former Postmaster-General and then Secretary of State for Air, was not averse to commercial broadcasting from inside Britain; Sir Robert Vansittart of the Foreign Office and Robert (later Lord) Boothby

---

700 Ibid.

701 Warburton, Eliot *The Spectator*, no. 2,720, 11 February 1938, p. 228. Mr Warburton gives his address as United Service Club, Pall Mall, S.W.1. The letter, under the headline, "The Right to Listen" goes on:"...His [i.e. "the average Englishman"] indignation grows when he hears it said that this action has been taken at the instance of certain newspapers, which fear the rivalry of radio as an advertising medium. ... Is it too late for this country to make it clear to the Foreign Office that we expect them to address themselves to the many great national interests that require all their attention at present, and not to trouble our good neighbours about relatively insignificant matters in the interests of a small section of our Press, which interests are, in this matter, opposed to those of the great majority of inhabitants of these islands? The BBC can have no interest in the matter, for, if advertisers, who pay for the bulk of the pabulum and the modicum of news in our popular Press, also provide our low-brows with the entertainment they want, the BBC can use its funds to put on the air that which it thinks good for us without any qualms that all parties are not getting what they want for their money. Advertisers <u>have</u> to conform to the wishes of their public!"

702 Briggs II, p. 340.

from the Conservative back benches, conscious of the stormy international scene, thought that Britain should sponsor advertising stations abroad from which British programmes could be disseminated; there were even voices in the Treasury hinting that the BBC's licence revenue was becoming insufficient to cover the amount required for the future development of television and overseas broadcasting, and that different ways of financing broadcasting might have to be considered. It is scarcely surprising that at the last pre-war international conference, held at Montreux in the spring of 1939, the Post Office delegates were instructed not to raise the advertising question and, if consulted by other delegations, were to discourage them also from raising it.[703]

The commercial radio star was at its zenith. In March 1938 a number of parties interested in advertising on radio commissioned an enquiry into audiences for foreign radio stations. The Incorporated Society of British Advertisers (ISBA) and the Institute of Incorporated Practitioners in Advertising (IIPA) were employed as auditors, with Professor Arnold Plant of the London School of Economics as Chairman. On 7 March, Tallents asked Silvey to investigate.[704] On 15 March, Silvey responded to Tallents' request.[705] His findings showed that the IBC had financed the project, and that before it even began "all the stations, other than the IBC, backed out because they realised that whatever the results of the investigation, it would inevitably be used primarily as sales talk for the IBC".[706] Negotiations on this point seem to have been long and fruitless, leaving, as Silvey pointed out "little time between the beginning of the investigation and the Summer Time [when the findings were to be published] for the carrying out of the fieldwork". It was thought that sixty investigators would be needed for house-to-house interviewing, and Silvey wryly added that "It is more than doubtful if anything like sixty honest investigators could be obtained at a moment's notice. Consequently this is likely to reflect very seriously on the quality of the work."[707]

The survey had ceased to have any real meaning as a general examination of commercial radio other than the IBC's interests. It was clear from letters and telephone calls received by the Corporation that interviewers already in the field were naming themselves as from the "BBC", when in fact no such investigation was being conducted. Approaches had been made to the IIPA requesting that the organization should "stress with their investigators the need to make sure that there is no misapprehension". Silvey was, however, doubtful: "I am not very confident about the result of this".[708]

In the event the *Survey of Listening to Sponsored Programmes* contained no major

703 Ibid., p. 341. The instruction to Post Office delegates to remain silent on the issue of advertising came directly from the BBC Deputy Director-General. [Memorandum cited by Briggs, dated 9 January 1939.]

704 Stephen Tallents to RJE Silvey: BBC Internal Memo, "Advertising Stations", 7 March 1938. WAC CAV R34/960.

705 Silvey, R.J.E., BBC Internal Memo, "Advertising Stations" 15 March 1938. WAC CAV R34/960.

706 Ibid.

707 Ibid.

708 Ibid.

revelations, whilst underlining what Silvey and his team already knew: that commercial stations maintained their domination of British listening on Sundays:

> Over 1 million households, it was estimated, were listening to Luxembourg between 1 o'clock and 2 o'clock on Sunday afternoons. The north-east of England, south Wales, and the London area provided the highest proportion of listeners – in that order. With minor exceptions, the BBC weekday service remained more popular than that of all foreign commercial stations combined, and British listening to foreign stations reached its peak when none of the Corporation's stations was transmitting.[709]

Independent of the survey, Silvey had proved to his own satisfaction in any case that by the time Europe began to move irrevocably towards war, the Commercial companies had demonstrated that the threat of the first half of the decade had turned to genuine and serious competition, with BBC output coming more and more under threat from Luxembourg, Normandy, Lyons and the other continental stations. What the IIPA survey controversy observed by him in 1938 seems to point to, is a growing distrust among the Commercial operators, and had it not been for the war, it is possible that conflict and increasingly acrimonious relations between the stations might have indirectly benefited the BBC.

In the meantime the BBC demonstrated its increasing interest in and growing awareness of the importance of radio audiences by commissioning Hilda Jennings and Winifred Gill of Bristol University to conduct "A Survey of the Social Effects of the Coming of Broadcasting".[710] The purpose of the work was "to discover the actual effects of this new public service [i.e. radio] on the quality of individual, family, and social life. Is it decreasing parochialism of outlook? Is it tending to produce only a docile, receptive listener, or is it increasing critical faculties and releasing creative energies?"[711] For the project "a working-class neighbourhood was selected in preference to one which was predominantly middle-class"[712] and "The neighbourhood chosen was a thickly-populated district of east Bristol".[713] One of the early tasks of Reith's successor, F.W. Ogilvie was to write an introduction to the report when it was published in July 1939:

> There is much talk of the influence of wireless, yet very little study has been made to determine in what that change consists ... Everywhere the listener has the material for observation in his own home and among his friends and fellow workers. Everywhere the student has it ready to hand in his own neighbourhood. I hope that this report will lure other observers and other students of social affairs to an important, fruitful, and so far all too neglected field of research.[714]

There is an irony in such a statement from the BBC, having come so late to the

---

709   Briggs II, p. 337.
710   Hilda Jennings and Winifred Gill, *Broadcasting in Everyday Life*, BBC, London, 1939.
711   Ibid., p. 7.
712   Ibid.
713   Ibid., p. 8.
714   Ibid., p. 5.

idea of audience analysis; there is also a significance in the timing of the report, coming as it did at such a crucial shift in the leadership of the BBC.

Question-forms were issued to individuals and families, to teachers and to over 800 senior schoolchildren in the neighbourhood. All information obtained was then analysed from the point of view of individual, family, and social life, and also its bearing on particular subjects, such as effects on musical appreciation, dialect, interest in world affairs, sport, religious and political life in the district.[715]

Figures varied according to the nature of the question asked. For instance, "Who chooses the programmes?" drew a response from 756 homes. An enquiry into the proportion of homes in which a specified musical instrument was played was answered by 819 households, and "What Children like listening to" was based on answers from 807 children. It is a notable characteristic of the Survey that at no point does it mention Commercial radio competition. Neither indeed does it speak of BBC programmes as such, preferring to concern itself more generally with "Broadcasting" and "Radio". Thus it sets itself as a sociological document rather than a partisan work, and so avoids awkward issues of audience preference beyond the BBC monopoly. The three questions cited above nevertheless provide us with interesting and surprising answers within the area under discussion. To summarise, the survey concluded that Programme selection out of a sample of 756 homes was conducted mostly by the father of the family, closely followed in the statistics by the family as a whole.[716] Regarding musical instruments played in households, out of 819 homes, almost half named the piano, and nearly the same number stated the harmonica.[717] Drawing a conclusion from this and supporting interviews, Jennings and Gill stated that "there seems no doubt that broadcasting has stimulated the amateur production of music while at the same time working a revolution in the attitude of the public towards the musician ... The leader of a dance-band inspires hero-worship. Every little boy who plays a mouth-organ dreams of 'getting on the air'. ... Pupils ask to be taught music heard on the air. There is a sale for songs popularized by broadcasting."[718]

It would be useful to know how much this desire was fuelled by listening to Continental stations. The BBC sponsored survey does not supply this information. Perhaps most interesting, given the nature of the present enquiry, was the response from 807 children to the question relating to their listening habits:

Variety:	750 votes
Music:	675 votes [the nature of the music is not specified]
Children's Hour:	575 votes
Boxing:	550 votes
Church Services:	475 votes
Football:	350 votes
Talks:	350 votes[719]

---

715   Ibid., p. 8.
716   Ibid., p. 23.
717   Ibid., p. 29.
718   Ibid., p. 18.
719   Ibid.

These figures supply us with a fascinating historical snapshot. That variety and music should prove most popular amongst the young is hardly surprising. That the Children's Hour, Boxing and Church Services should be shown to be so relatively close in voting, is on the face of initial findings more so. However given that most programming was chosen by the dominant male in the family, followed by the family as a whole, this finding should be qualified by the consideration that young people did not always have a voice in what was listened to.[720]

The Coming of War

On 20 June 1939 the new Director of Religious Broadcasting, Dr J.W. Welch chaired an informal conference at Broadcasting House, London at which "there was unanimous feeling in the group that the strict puritan Sunday could no longer be enforced and general agreement that this was to the good".[721] Nevertheless he felt that there should remain a clear distinction between Sunday programming and that for the rest of the week; in the words of the minutes from the meeting, any kind of output which would help listeners to "appreciate beauty, apprehend truth, and live fuller and more constructive lives should be welcomed and should find fullest expression (but not exclusive expression) in the specifically 'religious' items".[722] As Briggs has pointed out, "This new emphasis collided with the grim facts of 1938 and 1939 as much as with traditional BBC policies".[723]

Radio Times in the early months of 1939 demonstrates that some changes had been instigated. Broadcasting on Sundays now ran continuously from 9.30 p.m. throughout the day, ending, after the Epilogue, with the Shipping Forecast at 11.00 p.m. Within the output there was a noticeable increase in light music, although it could still hardly be called "popular". Between 4.00 p.m. and 6.00 p.m., the accent remained firmly on a blend of religious instruction and chamber music. That apart, *Radio Times* dated 20th January 1939 advertised that Doris Arnold would begin a new series "of her popular gramophone record programmes of favourite melodies – *These You Have Loved*".[724] The programme, first heard in November 1938, stayed as part of the Sunday schedule until 1977, while another, *The Week's Good Cause*, which started in 1926, still exists today, renamed as Radio 4 Appeal.[725] Thus we may examine in detail the style of programming at the end of the decade, and compare it with the radical change brought by the introduction of the Forces Programme, and how this metamorphosed into the Light Programme after the war. It becomes clear in examining these listings that the lessons of competition were not by any means fully acted on prior to the outbreak of war. On Sunday 5 March 1939, the National Programme opened at 9.25 a.m. with *A Religious Service* from Lichfield Cathedral, followed by a weather forecast and a fifteen minute silence before a programme of light orchestral music was broadcast. That the Forces

---

720   See Appendix A: Listeners – samples of correspondence.
721   Briggs II, pp. 606–607.
722   Ibid.
723   Ibid.
724   *Radio Times* 20 January 1939.
725   Appendix G contains comparative Sunday listings for the first Sunday in March in the years 1939,1943 and 1946.

programme on the other hand, on Sunday 7 March 1943 could open its transmissions at 6.00 a.m. with a programme entitled *Revielle – Cheerful Gramophone Records*, and at 8.00 a.m. feature half an hour of *Rhythm on Records* would have been unthinkable within the regime of just four years earlier.

With the coming of war, the BBC quickly mobilised its publicity to emphasise the nature of its role: here was a very real need for public service broadcasting, and the hastily issued "Supplementary Edition" of *Radio Times* dated September 4 sought to underline this fact to its readers:

> Radio will be one of the chief means of communication during the war. This has already been proved. The Government can speak to the people – news can reach the remotest village – instructions can be issued by the Ministries – warnings can be given of approaching attacks.[726]

At the same time, "programmes broadcast will be real, presented entertainment, studded with plays, musical comedies, features, talks: in fact ordinary broadcast programmes – only probably of a rather higher standard than those we know in peace!" To this was added a cautious caveat "if all goes well".[727]

Since coming to his job in the newly created Audience Research department in 1936, R.J.E. Silvey was employed for a remarkable amount of time in monitoring commercial radio activity. With Stephen Tallents and Maurice Farquharson, he was in a position to demonstrate to the BBC the nature and scale of commercial competition, and to identify how it had achieved its success. Given the volume of work generated in this area, the creation of his department points to a growing awareness within the BBC that audience-measurement mattered, and that the lessons learnt from agencies such as the J. Walter Thompson Organisation in the conduct of radio research for advertising ends could and should be applied to public service broadcasting. The fact of Silvey's appointment, and the further fact that he had been recruited from an advertising agency, is further evidence to support the view that the BBC's attitudes to audience research in the 1930s were informed by the threat caused by continental commercial stations. It was not to be until after the Second World War that it was to truly consolidate its position within the Corporation; that said, it should be added that there was never unanimity on the subject. As late as 1960, the producer Lionel Fielden was to write that "the real degradation of the BBC started with the invention of the hellish department which is called 'listener research' ".[728]

Much of the BBC's attitude to competition and response to it, an attitude which was to inform increasingly its position as a public service broadcaster in the latter years of the twentieth century, grew out of tensions in the 1930s caused by the

---

726 *Radio Times* 4 September 1939, p. 3.

727 Ibid.

728 Fielden, Lionel *The Natural Bent*, Andre Deutsch, London, 1960, pp. 108–109. Fielden goes on: "That Abominable Statistic is supposed to show 'what listeners *like* – and of course, what they like is the red-nosed comedian and the Wurlitzer Organ. But anyone who has studied the letters received by the BBC knows that (a) only Abominable people ever write to it, and (b) hardly a single letter is a valid criticism … For the broadcasting official there can be one rule only – to do what he believes to be good and to spare no trouble in the doing of it. Once he begins to follow what is supposed to be popular taste, he is on the road to stagnation."

exposure of its monopoly for the first time. Between the years 1935 and 1939 that attitude developed into a formal and structured response, differing dramatically from the unfocused awareness of competition from the continental stations which characterized the period from 1928 to the middle of 1935. In the event it was to be international conflict rather than policy that restored the BBC monopoly; we therefore must now explore the reasons for the demise of commercial radio, and finally briefly discuss its ultimate restoration in the post-war years. This is the subject of the next two chapters.

Chapter eight

1939–1945

Good night – and Happy Dreams[729]

Wartime Programming

The Second World War changed the face of British Broadcasting forever. Experimental programming by the BBC for the Forces began on 7 January 1940, stung into action once again by the IBC which had turned Radio Normandy into "Radio International" at the announcement of war, broadcasting to troops and issuing a free magazine, *Happy Listening* to British forces until the French Government closed the station down for security reasons. The story of the short life of Radio International and its pre-emptive initiative in Forces broadcasting is another fascinating example of the way in which commercial interests were able to act quickly and decisively to turn a situation to their advantage and score over the slower policy-making of the BBC.

In London, Leonard Plugge and executives of the International Broadcasting Company had been engaged in seeking government support for running their organisation as – ostensibly – a Forces Broadcasting service.[730] There had been little support from the War Office for this idea, so during the false calm of the autumn of 1939, the IBC, notably through its energetic continental director, George Shanks, began negotiations with the French government to reopen the Fécamp transmitter in the service of allied troops.[731] The proposal was that daytime programming was to be in English, from 7.00 a.m. until 8.00 p.m., when the

---

729 Plomley, Roy, from the IBC close down announcement. On the evening of Radio Normandy's last broadcast, this was broadcast as normal. From the author's personal archive.

730 Plomley, Roy *Days Seemed Longer*, London, Eyre Methuen, 1980, p. 165.

731 Ibid., p. 166. Plomley describes George Shanks as "the company's *éminence grise*: a tall, languid man of great charm, he had been a fellow-pilot of Plugge's during the First War. Of Anglo-French descent, he had spent much of his childhood in Czarist St Petersburg, and was blessed with a satisfactory financial background stemming from a celebrated champagne firm. Among a number of orders and decorations which had been bestowed on him was the richly-named papal one of Privy Chamberlain of Sword and Cape. His contacts were many and most useful."

transmitter was to be given over to Czech broadcasting for two hours, followed at 10.00 p.m. by a further two hours of transmissions by the Austrian Freedom Station, closing down at midnight.[732]

In fact the station was more accessible in England than in France, and British listeners continued to enjoy many of the familiar programmes and presentation staff. The IBC produced a new listings sheet, *Happy Listening*, (published for only two issues) carrying on each page the title: "Radio International: Broadcasting to the British Expeditionary Force in France". The title of the sheet was clearly designed to provide a continuity in British listeners' minds with Radio Normandy; Prior to 30 December 1938, Radio Normandy's listings in *Radio Pictorial* had carried the slogan, "For Brighter Radio". From this date onwards the slogan was replaced by the words, "Happy Listening".[733] Some former sponsors agreed to allow their programmes to be rebroadcast without the commercials; thus audiences were able to hear Carson Robison and his Pioneers, Charlie Kunz and Joe Loss just as before.[734] Christmas programmes from Radio International "included a message from Canon Pat McCormick at St Martin-in-the-Fields, piano music from Charlie Kunz, and 'singing and strumming' from Tessie O'Shea and George Formby".[735]

Opposition to Radio International came from Fernand Le Grand himself; having lost income from selling airtime to the International Broadcasting Company, he "now had his transmitter requisitioned by the government and handed over to the IBC for nothing ...".[736] Briggs writes that "fear of commercial interests as well as desire to entertain the troops galvanized the BBC, which won the dubious support both of Field Marshal Viscount Gort, the Commander-in-Chief of the BEF, and the French General Gamelin, both of whom were 'very much opposed to Fécamp' ".[737] Pressure mounted for the closure of Radio International, and shortly after the New Year Roy Plomley received the news that his work in France was over:

> I was recording *Tommy's Half Hour* every week at Poste Parisien, which was just like old times. During the afternoon of 3 January, George Busby came into the control cubicle, while I was recording, and told me that protests of the military authorities had taken effect and that all transmissions from Fécamp were to stop at once.[738]

Radio International ceased broadcasting accordingly on 3 January 1940.[739] The BBC began experimental Forces broadcasting on 7 January, "to be extended on 18 February to twelve hours a day – from 11.00 a.m. to 11. p.m".[740] *For the Forces* very soon expanded to provide a full service, based very much on research into

732 Ibid., pp. 166–167.

733 *Radio Pictorial*, 30 December 1938, p. 36.

734 *Happy Listening*, 8 December 1939, p. 5.

735 Briggs, Asa *The BBC, the First Fifty Years*, Oxford, Oxford University Press, 1985, p. 186.

736 Plomley, p. 168.

737 Briggs, *The BBC, The First Fifty Years*, p. 186.

738 Plomley, p. 172.

739 Montague, Ron *When the Ovaltineys Sang*, privately printed pamphlet to accompany *The Story of Radio* exhibition, Central Museum, Southend-on-Sea, June 1990, p. 26.

740 Briggs, *The BBC, The First Fifty Years*, p. 186.

audience requirements. By the middle of the war the Sunday page in *Radio Times* was showing home audiences a very different bill of fare to that to which they had been used in peace time. Opening at 7.00 a.m., the service provided record shows such as *Broadway Melodies* at noon, followed by *The Fred Allen Programme* "recorded in America by the Special Services Division of the United States War Department" and in the afternoon *Johnny Canuck's Review* produced by the Canadian Broadcasting Corporation. Later there was *Forces Choice* in which "Members of the fighting forces and of the Home Front who work behind them, come to the microphone with their choice of gramophone records". This was a form of democracy previously foreign to the BBC. At 7.10 p.m. came the popular comedy programme, *Happidrome* with Hal Miller, Gladys Ripley and Nosmo King.[741]

By early 1944, there was an increasing demand to make these programmes available for a domestic audience, and *Radio Times* for 25 February that year announced a modification to its schedules in the form of the General Forces Programme: "Why the BBC has decided from this current Sunday its service for troops overseas shall become the alternative programme in this country".[742] The answer quite simply was public pressure from the Home and Fighting Fronts combined, the *Radio Times* claimed: "… a common wish [among the Forces] to share their listening with the folks at home".[743]

May 1944 saw the Sunday output on the General Forces Programme strongly reflecting popular taste and relating its scheduling to audience listening habits. *Radio Times* for Sunday 12 May tells us that Tommy Handley's *ITMA* show was broadcast at 4.30 p.m. At 6.00 p.m. came *Variety Bandbox* with Bebe Daniels, Ted Ray and Geraldo and his Orchestra, (produced by Stephen Williams, one of the pioneer presenters on Radios Normandy and Luxembourg), and later in the evening a programme of Music Hall under the title *Palace of Varieties*.[744]

There could be no going back from this policy, and the BBC's solution, as the end of the war approached, was to turn the General Forces Programme into a new programme which was to preserve its character, alongside a Home Service which retained in an evolved form some of the qualities of the pre-war BBC. In July 1945, the Director General of the BBC, W.J. Haley announced six new British Regional Services and The Light Programme, as well as plans for a future Third Programme in which "operas, plays, discussions, features will be given the fullest time their content needs".[745] The message for the old guard was clear: taste would not be undermined by change, culture would not be sacrificed for populism. As for John Reith himself, a recollection by the late Frank Gillard shows him to have remained to his death, very much the man he had always been:

> When I became Managing Director of Radio in 1963, Reith invited me to lunch at the House of Lords, flattered me with clumsy praise that someone "of my calibre" (his phrase) had been selected to run BBC Radio, and then

741   *Radio Times*, 15 August 1943.
742   *Radio Times*, 25 February 1944.
743   Ibid.
744   *Radio Times*, 12 May 1944.
745   *Radio Times*, 27 July 1945.

launched his torpedo – "of course, Gillard, I shall expect you to restore my Sunday policy". I had to tell him frankly that his hope was unlikely to be realised, and my calibre-rating very quickly collapsed.[746]

The evidence demonstrates that while the BBC of the 1930s had a growing corporate understanding of the nature of the competition from the commercial stations broadcasting from the continent, it steadfastly resisted any major change to its programming, until the coming of war forced change through partnership with American and Canadian broadcasters. That the criticism was so widespread and so vocal, only make it all the more remarkable that the BBC's determination remained so unshakeable for so long. There can be no doubt that central to that determination was the spiritual presence – for some, even after his retirement in June 1938 – of John Reith.

How much the climate had changed by the early years of the war may be judged by an exchange between J.W. Welch, Director of Religious Broadcasting during the planning for a Forces Broadcasting Service, and A.P. Ryan, Liaison Officer for the BBC in its relationship with the Ministry of Information. Ryan had visited France to ascertain the broadcasting requirements of troops.[747]. It was clear that a "light" programme was what was needed, and when Welch complained at the subsequent abandonment of the Sunday policy, Ryan replied, "It is our duty as a public body enjoying monopoly rights from the State, to tackle our problems as vigorously and single-heartedly as we would if Fécamp was a commercial rival".[748]

Across the memo, in the hand of Frederick Ogilvie, Reith's successor as Director-General, are the words, "I agree with Ryan's Views".[749] Leslie Baily claims that:

> The first slap-up variety show on the sabbath was *Garrison Theatre* devised by Charles Shadwell and Harry Pepper, starring Jack Warner, on 18 February 1940: an important date in social history, marking the beginning of the end of treating Sunday as different from other days.[750]

In the event it is not an exaggeration to state that the coming of World War II saved the BBC from an increasingly embarrassing situation in two ways: firstly, it removed the continental stations almost at a stroke. Radio Luxembourg closed down in September 1939, with the untypical broadcasting of a march written by a Luxembourg composer and entitled *For Liberty*. Radio Normandy also closed, only to reopen briefly, as we have seen, as "Radio International".[751] Secondly the war brought with it crises for which the BBC was perfectly equipped. As Pegg has written:

> On 5 August 1914, British citizens probably discovered that war had been declared by reading a newspaper. On 3 September 1939, they almost certainly

746   Gillard, Frank, in a letter to the present author, 20 November 1996.
747   Briggs, Asa *The BBC, The First Fifty Years*, Oxford, Oxford University Press, 1985, p. 186.
748   Ibid., p. 187.
749   Ibid.
750   Baily, Leslie *Leslie Baily's BBC Scrapbooks, Volume Two, 1918–1939*, London, George Allen and Unwin, 1968, p. 157.
751   See Appendix A.

heard the news of the outbreak of hostilities from the Prime Minister himself.[752]

It was the BBC that the public turned to, and in its emergency edition of *Radio Times* published the day after the announcement of war, the Corporation pledged itself to provide all its audience required:

> There are obvious functions of radio during a war, and their vital importance is recognised by everyone. But there is another function that is nearly as important, and that is entertainment. Broadcasting can help to take our minds off the horrors of war as nothing else can.
>
> That is why the BBC has not been content to plan programmes consisting merely of gramophone records alternating with news.[753]

The war brought with it much internal reorganisation for the BBC. As part of it, Maurice Farquharson was appointed – on the recommendations of a committee led by Tallents – as Director of a new department entitled Home Intelligence.[754] For his part Silvey continued his researches, although with a different emphasis. In a memo of November 1939 entitled "The Public's Attitude Towards the BBC and the Extent of Listening to Foreign Stations"[755] he was responding to yet another request from Tallents. In doing so he utilised figures collected independently by the British Institute of Public Opinion in the course of one of its regular surveys. On 21 October they asked a cross section of the population the question, "Are you satisfied or dissatisfied with the way the BBC is doing its wartime job?" Silvey was able to pass on the fact that, according to the survey "48 per cent said they were satisfied, 35 per cent said they were dissatisfied, and the remainder either said they did not listen or had no opinion". A subsequent question, "Do you ever happen to listen to foreign stations?" brought an answer of necessity quite different to the one it would have drawn just a few weeks earlier. Silvey states:

> Rather more than half the persons asked said "yes". Men said "yes" rather more often than women; young people said "yes" rather more often than older people; people in the higher income groups tended to say "yes" rather more often than persons in the lower income groups.[756]

A third question, "Which foreign station did you listen to last?" provided data from which, when accumulated, it was possible to ascertain "an indication of the relative extent to which different foreign stations are heard. They show that no less than 50 per cent of those who listened to foreign stations (or nearly 27 per cent of the whole population) listen to Hamburg; second place was taken by Paris but only 10 per cent of those who listened to foreign stations listened to this; third place was Rome with 6 per cent and fourth Berlin with 5 per cent. Only 2 per cent said they listened to New York, and 1 per cent to Schenectady."[757]

---

752 Pegg, Mark *Broadcasting and Society 1918–1939*, Beckenham, Croom Helm, 1983, p. 218.

753 *Radio Times* Supplementary Issue, 4 September 1939, p. 3 (Author's collection).

754 Briggs II, p. 594.

755 Silvey, R.J.E., BBC Internal Memo, to Stephen Tallents, Copy to Maurice Farquarson as Director of Home Intelligence, 17 November 1939. WAC CAV R34/960.

756 Ibid.

757 Ibid.

The statistic relating to the Hamburg listenership is a chilling one, touching as it does on one of the broadcasting phenomena of the war, the extraordinary hold on the public imagination of the propaganda broadcasts of William Joyce, "Lord Haw-Haw" which emanated from that station. The BBC Monitoring Service observed that Joyce's Hamburg broadcasts had, as early as December 1939, created "a tradition of their own".[758]

The Coming of "The Light"

The immediate post-war BBC presided over by William Haley may be seen now as being the start of a system of broadcasting which would evolve along cultural strands, culminating just over twenty years later with the creation of Radios 1,2,3 and 4, and the subsequent development of broadcasting into the "branded" genre programming of the early 21st century. The removal of serendipity from radio listening which Reith had seen as a cornerstone of Public Service Broadcasting was perceived by many as a retrograde cultural step, although in truth in the early years of the era there continued to be a considerable amount of overlapping of programmes. To a certain extent this was deliberate; Haley saw the BBC networks of the mid 1940s as competing with one another. Each network would contain music, drama and features for instance, but with a different guiding overall policy which had pertained before the war, when "the listener had been 'plunged straight from popular to unpopular material, from highbrow to lowbrow and vice versa' ",[759] earning the BBC the reputation of being "didactic, arbitrary, and 'something of a governess' ".[760]

On 29 July 1945 peacetime broadcasting in Britain resumed with the Home and Regional Radio services of the BBC. On the same day the Forces Programme gave way to the newly named Light Programme. On 29 September 1946, the Third Programme was inaugurated, created initially as an evening service of uncompromisingly "highbrow" cultural speech and music. The Light Programme aimed to provide entertainment programming of a more populist nature, and the major force behind the early development of the network was Norman Collins, later to be a key figure in the development of commercial television. Collins it was who launched the continuingly successful *Woman's Hour* on 7 October 1946, the very day the British listener was introduced to another radio legend (albeit not so durable) in the form of *Dick Barton, Special Agent*. Indeed the year was one of numerous "firsts" including the first edition of *Housewives' Choice* and Wilfred Pickles's *Have a Go* both coming to the airwaves on 4 March (although Pickles was broadcast first only in the Northern Region, finally achieving national status from 10 September). This travelling quiz show, hosted by the genial Pickles with his wife Mabel "at the table", which was to run for more than twenty-one years, began its life under the producership of Philip Robinson. A subsequent producer was Stephen Williams, formerly one of commercial radio's pioneers on Radios Normandy and Luxembourg during the 1930s.

---

758 Briggs, Asa *The History of Broadcasting in the United Kingdom, Volume 3,The War of Words 1939–1945*, Oxford, Oxford University Press, 1995, p. 130.

759 Briggs, Asa *The BBC, The First Fifty Years*, p. 244, quoting Haley (uncited).

760 Ibid.

The changes were seen as far-reaching, and caused considerable controversy within the BBC. Briggs, quoting Sir Richard Maconachie, Controller of the Home Service in 1941, reminds us that:

> "Giving people what they want" had never been sound BBC doctrine, and Maconachie, with a great weight of personal and institutional experience behind him, put his trust in a forbidding general sanction ... "The principle of the assistant in a sweetshop being allowed to eat himself sick might apply".[761]

D.G. Bridson was later to write:

> The Forces Programme was the first attempt by the BBC to cater for a particular <u>category</u> of listener ... As the natural successor of the Forces Programme, the Light catered for those who wanted levity all the time, purely for background listening. If that was all one wanted retuning one's set was no longer necessary: one stayed tuned to the Light Programme hour by hour and day by day. Discriminating listeners, of course, continued to shop around ...[762]

The BBC had continued to debate the issue of commercial broadcasting through the war. In 1943 plans were put in place for a "popular" programme to counteract the threat of "sponsored programmes from our neighbours".[763] There was a concern that "American interests might become involved in Europe" after the war, and seek to "capture European markets, particularly in television".[764] Haley felt that the tripartite programme structure of Home, Light and Third would counter the audience hunger for such material as had caused so many problems before the war. In January 1944 he wrote:

> In time the provision of general contrast, the feeling of competition and choice in the BBC's programmes, should cause what present demand there is for commercially provided material to subside.[765]

Previous to this the idea of supporting popular, or "background" programming as it was called, with advertisements was even discussed within the BBC, Sir Noel Ashbridge suggesting in August 1943 the radical possibility of fixed slots "paid for at a rate varying with the time of the day ... Broadcasting would then in effect be on the same basis as a newspaper which has advertisements not connected with the text".[766] It is remarkable that Ashbridge, an elder statesman of the BBC, and a member of the original 2MT Writtle team, should have, in making this statement, having predicted the format of commercial television and radio funding which would not materialise in Britain for years.

---

761 Briggs, Asa *The History of Broadcasting in the United Kingdom, Vol. IV, Sound and Vision 1945–55*, Oxford, Oxford University Press, p. 48.

762 Bridson, D.G. *Prospero and Ariel, The Rise and Fall of Radio, A Personal Recollection*, London, Gollancz, 1971, pp. 178–179.

763 Briggs IV, p. 48.

764 Memo written by Maurice Gorham, 28 May 1948, quoted in Briggs IV, p. 48.

765 Haley, William quoted (uncited) in Briggs, *The BBC, the First Fifty Years*, p. 230.

766 Ashbridge, Noel, Note, 19 August 1943, quoted in Briggs IV, p. 49. Briggs also draws our attention to another BBC suggestion, put forward on 12 May 1943, that "dual system" should be employed, "allowing for 'official' and 'sponsored' programmes, both under the ultimate control of the BBC".

The Light Programme was generally well received when it commenced broadcasting, although some critics complained that it started too late in the morning, and there were a number of voices raised in regret at the withdrawal of the many popular American acts with which the public had become familiar during the war.[767] Briggs however states that within the Variety Department during 1945 and 1946 morale was low.[768] Restrictions on producers were considerable, and many staff, new to broadcasting after a number of years serving in the Forces, objected to the censorious nature of programme policy. British Society as it emerged after the war produced responses in its observers which rehearsed many of the class-ridden arguments of the pre-war years. Rose Macauley, a regular contributor to the Third Programme wrote in 1947 in the *BBC Quarterly*:

> I am aware that standards of good and bad are debatable, and that what is detestable to one person is often delightful to another … All the same, the broad fact remains that the mass of people in this country enjoy stuff that to the minority, and even to the majority in many other countries, seems wretched vulgar tawdry stuff.[769]

Ivor Brown, writing just over a year later in the same journal felt that, on the other hand, "there is no need whatever to be ashamed of escape entertainments and the more ordinary recreations. They have their place with the 'sucky sweet', the cup of tea, and the smoke".[770] The BBC's response to the commercial competition of the 1930s had taken more than five years of war to formulate itself into a broadcasting strategy. As it happened, changing circumstances and new media rules, particularly in France, were to mean that it would not be subject to competition on a similar scale for nearly twenty years. When that competition finally established itself as a regulated reality, it was within the context of an uneven media playing field which was riddled with political argument and compromise.

---

767   Briggs, *The BBC, the First Fifty Years*, p. 248.

768   Ibid.

769   Macaulay, Rose "Inquiry into Pleasures" in *BBC Quarterly*, Vol.II, No 1, April 1947, BBC, p. 36. It should be borne in mind that the *BBC Quarterly* was a journal which published the writings of producers, managers and senior BBC staff, leaning more towards the observation and discussion of a Reithian nature. The journal was started by William Haley in 1945 as a forum "for those who are professionally engaged in the art and science of broadcasting and its organisation". *BBC Yearbook, 1947*, BBC, p. 143.

770   Brown, Ivor "The World of Entertainment", in *BBC Quarterly*, Vol.III, No.2, July 1948, BBC, p. 72.

Chapter nine

Post War

It's smooth sailing, with the highly successful sound of Wonderful Radio London.[771]

This work's principal focus has been to explore the influence of commercial radio during the years of its pre-war challenge to the monopoly of the BBC in the 1930s, and the eventual changes in BBC policy towards generic broadcasting partly as a result of this pressure. In order to further demonstrate the long-term absorption of this form of radio, and the subsequent compromises forced on commercial – or "independent" – radio when it was eventually granted legal status in Britain in 1973, it will be useful to extend the story beyond the years covered by its central chronological period of concern. This chapter therefore provides evidence of the parallels between the 1930s and the 1960s in terms of competitive pressure on the BBC from commercial sources. It chronicles the culmination of generic BBC radio programming in 1967, and the regulatory impositions under which Independent Local Radio battled to survive from its birth in 1973 to the passing of the 1990 Broadcasting Act and beyond towards further deregulation introduced by the Communications Bill of 2003. In so doing, it demonstrates that the early pioneers of British commercial radio were the true instigators of change in a system which is still moving towards the establishment of commercial radio as a parallel competitor for domestic audience. Initially however we must explore historically the immediate post-war fate of the two principal stations which had attacked the BBC's monopoly and decimated its audience prior to hostilities: Radios Luxembourg and Normandy.

The Second World War put an end to commercial competition from Europe, and after the end of hostilities, the changing map of French broadcasting meant there could be no return to Plugge's media empire. As Raymond Kuhn has pointed out:

> The main concern for French politicians … was not so much to encourage consumer demand for radio, but to ensure that the medium would serve the objectives of the post-war state. The main provision of the immediate postwar

legislation was the confirmation of broadcasting as a state monopoly with public service goals, placed under the responsibility of a Minister of Information. The Liberation government thus legitimised the framework within which broadcasting in France was to develop and attain maturity: a state monopoly with a formal public service role, but in practice closely subordinated to the political interests of the government of the day.[772]

It will be seen from this that there could be no place for French stations such as the pre-war Radio Normandy, and if such an organisation could not exist domestically, there could be no foothold for international ventures such as the IBC. Such legislation did not apply in Luxembourg, resulting in the return of Radio Luxembourg as the sole English language commercial competition for the BBC in the immediate post-war years. Many popular innovations date from this period; *Opportunity Knocks* – later to become a hugely successful television series – was broadcast on Sunday afternoons, and also on Sundays, from 1948, Britain's first *Top Twenty* chart show became a radio sensation among the young, popular music-starved UK audience. The immediate post-war era of English language commercial radio begins with the dramatic story of the death and rebirth of Radio Luxembourg. It is important therefore to briefly examine the station's war-time history, and to explore failed attempts to re-establish Radio Normandy in a similar image to that of Luxembourg.

Radio Luxembourg

Although domestic transmissions continued from Luxembourg until the German forces over-ran the station in May 1940, English language broadcasting ended on 18 September 1939. As stated earlier, the last item was a patriotic march called "For Liberty", written by a Luxembourg composer. *The Daily Telegraph* reported that "It was played with considerable feeling, and the words were sung in none of Luxembourg's commercial languages, but in the national dialect which few but real Luxembourgers can understand".[773] Ironically the sheer power of its transmitters and their international capabilities drew attention towards the possibilities of radio as a weapon of war. As Wood explains, "The three 600ft masts on Junglinster Plain had opened the eyes of many to its potential for propaganda broadcasting".[774]

In the early hours of 10 May 1940, German forces invaded Holland, Belgium and Luxembourg. On the same day, Radio Luxembourg went off the air.[775] Tangye Lean reports that by 22 May "Luxembourg has been hooked up with the German radio".[776] The style of German propaganda quickly assumed a tone which was to become familiar:

> (To France): "French guns are powerless before the German mobile fortresses ..."

772 Kuhn, Raymond *The Media in France*, London, Routledge, 1995, p. 90.

773 *Daily Telegraph*, 23 September 1939, quoted in Asa Briggs, *The History of Broadcasting in the United Kingdom, Vol. II, The Golden Age of Wireless*, Oxford, Oxford University Press, 1995, p. 342.

774 Wood, James *The History of International Broadcasting*, London, Peregrinus/Science Museum, 1994, p. 45.

775 Lean, E. Tangye *Voices in the Darkness, The Story of the European Radio War*, London, Secker and Warburg, 1943, p. 111.

776 Ibid., p. 123.

(To Belgium): "Walloons, Reynaud has said that only a miracle can save France ... the English think only of saving their skins, and are fleeing in disorder to the Channel."[777]
The fact that Tangye Lean states that Luxembourg was "hooked up to German radio" implies that Luxembourg was used as a relay station, rather than as a "live" broadcasting base by the Germans between 1940 and 1944, a fact further confirmed by Frank Gillard: "William Joyce, 'Lord Haw-Haw', who broadcast Nazi propaganda to Britain from 1940 to 1945, did not speak from Radio Luxembourg, as has been suggested in some accounts. His station was Radio Hamburg, on the medium wave."[778]

Staff at Radio Luxembourg had prepared the station for its take-over by concealing programme material such as disc and film recordings. Nichol suggests that this prohibited Nazi propagandists from transmitting a more sophisticated message:

> Without all that authentic material – the discs and film recordings were of stage shows, orchestras and announcers – the German broadcasters were unable to present their output from the Grand Duchy as they would have wished. Armed with all the recordings the propaganda broadcasts could have been far more subtle and far more effective.[779]

The fact that Radio Luxembourg was captured twice – by the Germans in 1940, and by the American 12th Army in 1944 – without suffering significant damage to its broadcasting or transmission equipment, is an indication of how determined both German forces and allies were to keep this powerful tool available for propaganda purposes. Frank Gillard states that "the German defenders had planned to smash it up, but they left it too late. They only inflicted minor damage, relatively speaking, before they were over-run. I was there myself within a few hours."[780]
Leonard Miall has supplied the present author with a unique and dramatic document, prepared by officers of SHAEF in 1945, entitled *Radio Luxembourg, 10 September 1944 to 10 September 1945,* and chronicling the recapture of the station.[781] This states:

> On 1 September 1944 when the American Forces were approximately at Troyes, about 100 kilometers from Luxembourg, the Germans in Luxembourg began to panic and evacuate. On the morning of 1 September 1944 the Germans blew up the main control room in the basement of the studio building ... Transmissions by the Germans ceased on the same day ... On 1 September Matty Felten [former Chief Studio Engineer at Luxembourg] entered the studio premises and found them completely empty. He also went out to the transmitter and found it undamaged.[782]

In a remarkable exchange Felten persuaded the German skeleton guard left at the transmitter, whose orders had been to destroy it, to limit the damage to a

777   Ibid.
778   Gillard, Frank 20 November 1996 in correspondence with the present author.
779   Nichol, Richard *Radio Luxembourg, the Station of the Stars,* London, Comet,1993, p. 53.
780   Gillard correspondence.
781   This document is reproduced at length as Appendix F.
782   SHAEF, *Radio Luxembourg, Historical and Descriptive Review, 10 September 1944 to 10 September 1945,* PWD-SHAEF, 10 September 1945, p. 1.

destruction of the valves. "The German engineer, one Peterson, was amenable because he was indignant with the Germans for having failed to evacuate his furniture for him ..."[783] This was to prove crucial in the allied use of the station as was the fact that "on 9 September Felten went to Junglinster again and learned from one of the technicians that some time previously a stock of spare tubes [valves] had been moved to the Post Office warehouse in Morsch for safety from air bombardment".[784] On 10 September "units of the Fifth Armored [sic]. Division, First American Arm, arrived in Luxembourg City", and "on 23 September operation of the station was begun by relays from London and New York".[785] A day later "the production on the air of four 15-minute programs [sic] daily by the Twelfth Army Group personnel began".[786] These were "primarily tactical in nature".[787] Broadcasts were originally transmitted under the name "Radio Twelve-Twelve"[788] and included material aimed at the German troops and civilians, but not declaring itself as anti-Nazi, and purporting to be an underground German domestic station. Thus its reports gained trust and confidence within the enemy, which enabled it to have enormous propaganda effect.[789] Its daily programme, *Front Post* was on occasion supported by leaflet drops over the retreating German army. As Wood says:

> The role of "12–12" was to cause chaos, confusion, alarm, uncertainty and fear for what the future held for the German population. By reporting the false presence of tanks in the vicinity of Nuremberg and Ludwigshafen, the station caused panic in the streets. After 127 nights on the air, "12–12" disappeared without trace; it had served its purpose.[790]

Up until May 1945, the propaganda from Luxembourg had been jointly in the hands of British and American personnel, among them Leonard Miall, who had been formerly the BBC's Washington correspondent, and who was now directly involved in broadcasting to the fleeing enemy:

> I had been the chap in charge of the talks broadcast to Germany during the early part of the war from the BBC, and then in the middle I was seconded to a thing called The Political Warfare Executive, which was a secret department under the Foreign Office which ran the policy for propaganda, and I was sent on a mission to the United States to help correlate the BBC's broadcasting into Europe with that of America ... I came back to England towards the end of the war, and was then sent out to Luxembourg soon after we'd captured it, to broadcast to the German troops, who were then only about seven miles away, beginning to go into retreat.[791]

Miall remembered that the Germans had augmented the equipment on the station

783   Ibid.
784   Ibid., p. 3.
785   Ibid., p. 3.
786   Ibid.
787   Ibid. See Appendix F.
788   Wood, p. 83. The name came from the frequency: 1212 kHz.
789   Ibid.
790   Ibid.
791   Miall, Leonard, interviewed by the present author, May 1997.

with machinery which, in allied hands, was to advance post-war broadcasting technology:

> For instance, tape recording was very much a part of Luxembourg. The machines, later developed into what we know as Ampex recorders, were called Magnetophones. The premises otherwise were the same as had been used before the war and were subsequently used later by the Commercial operators. Very pleasant offices they were.[792]

When the war ended on 8 May 1945, the Allied forces remained in control of Luxembourg for some months, and according to the SHAEF document:

> In August 1945 the United States Press Service Headquarters and personnel were moved from Inveresk house, London, to Radio Luxembourg. Their monitoring service was thereupon consolidated with that of Radio Luxembourg to receive the news files from OWI, New York and other sources.[793]

Subsequent to this plans were put in motion to move programming for the American occupying forces to other stations.[794] It was however not until the Summer of 1946 that the station was returned to its owners, and Wood states that "during this time, it is believed that Churchill wanted to use it as a propaganda weapon against the Soviet Union".[795]

Radio Luxembourg's initial re-emergence as a peace-time English language broadcaster falls broadly into four phases: 1946–1955, 1955–64, 1964–67 and post 1967. These four phases link to:

1.   Post war "family" commercial broadcasting, resuming on Long Wave, with similarities to the pre-war model of sponsored programmes. (*The Ovaltineys* returned, remarkably the same as seven years earlier.) Sponsored quiz shows such as *Take Your Pick*, *Double Your Money* and *Opportunity Knocks* found large family audiences. From this period comes the famous *Horace Batchelor* broadcasts which for an immediate post-war audience defined the station in the memory as did *The Ovaltineys* for listeners up to 1939.

2.   After 1955, and the launch of Independent Television in Britain, many of these shows moved – with their hosts – to ITV. The impact of Commercial Television on the station was immeasurable, and Luxembourg became from this point increasingly a niche record-based station, with sponsorship moving to companies such as Capitol, Decca Group and EMI. Thus a disenfranchised youth audience was once again being nurtured, and the station was "DJ"led.[796]

3.   From 1964, with the coming of the offshore radio stations, Luxembourg's position became increasingly tenuous; now this of all stations, ironically, was having its own monopoly eroded until:

792   Ibid.
793   SHAEF document, p. 8 (Appendix F).
794   Ibid.
795   Wood, p. 83.
796   Barnard, Stephen *On the Radio, Music Radio in Britain*, Milton Keynes, Open University Press, 1989, p. 33. Barnard's book gives an excellent background to the latter years in particular of this subject.

4. 1967, and the launch of Radio 1 brought land-based popular music radio to a British youth audience for the first time. This fact, and the subsequent introduction of British commercial radio from 1973 contributed to the gradual marginalisation of Radio Luxembourg, which for a time broadcast via satellite to a dwindling audience until its English language service finally went off the air for the last time 30 December 1992.

Radio Normandy

As has already been discussed Radio Normandy ceased English language transmissions under this name on 7 September 1939, and continued to broadcast under the name "Radio International" until it closed down on 3 January 1940.[797] Taken over by the Havas News Agency, the station became a relay for French state programming, and this continued until 9 June 1940. At this point, with the German forces were closing in on Fécamp, orders were given to destroy both the transmitter and transmission valves. In fact only the valves were destroyed, and within five weeks of the Germans arriving at the Caudebec transmitter on 13 June, Radio Normandy was broadcasting Nazi propaganda.[798] Like Luxembourg, the station held significant potential as an instrument of war; however, its proximity to the coast made it vulnerable to naval bombardment. In May 1943 German engineers instigated a plan to camouflage the station's studios under earth-mounds, but severe damage was done during three bombardments during the summer of 1943, the most significant, on 13 August, scoring no less than 800 hits on the site.[799]

The Allied invasion of Europe began on 6 June 1944. Remarkably, given its position within an intensely contested area of hostility, the Caudebec transmitter and broadcasting facilities remained in the hands of the 7th German Army until 28 August, by which time Paris had been liberated. Prior to their final retreat from the area, the Nazi forces inflicted massive damage to the station buildings, burning the main structure, and blowing up the transmitter.[800] In January 1945 an American Forces mobile station began broadcasting from the site using the name "Radio Normandie". Transmissions ceased when military personnel based in the area left in April to support the final overthrow of Berlin.[801]

Changes in post-war French media law meant that the private stations could not function as they had during the 1930s. Meanwhile, in 1945, the founder of Radio Normandie, Fernand Legrand was arrested by the liberating forces and accused of having collaborated with the Germans. He was found guilty, and served a prison term of five months.[802] In the same year, a new relay transmitter was erected at Louvetot on the site of the old Radio Normandie antenna, but this was used simply to disseminate national state programming.[803]

---

797 See Appendix A.
798 Lhote, Francois, France Radio Club. Correspondence with author. M. Lhote's records show that German transmissions began on 27 July 1940.
799 Ibid.
800 *Le Courrier Cauchois*, 20 September 1997, p. 13.
801 Lhote correspondence.
802 le Sève correspondence.
803 Francois Lhote correspondence.

A final attempt at a post war partnership between the IBC and Radio Normandy occurred early in 1947. In January, John McMillan, assistant to Norman Collins, at that time Controller of the newly established Light Programme, wrote to Collins:

> I hear from a most reliable source that Plugge, who has been in New York for some time trying to buy a transmitter for Radio Normandy, has now got over the dollar difficulty, and a 50 kilowatt station is in the act of being loaded.
>
> The IBC people are finding negotiations with the French administration very tedious. It seems that they have no doubts as to the outcome, but they are continually having to start over again owing to ministerial changes.
>
> It is said – but I don't know how true this is – that they plan to operate the station on a twenty-four hour a day basis, using a lower-powered transmitter for the small hours of the night. All transmissions will be in English and directed to people living in the south of England.[804]

There is evidence of activity on Fernand Legrand's side at the same time, fuelled by war compensation. In a letter dated 19th February 1947 from Legrand to Emile Durand, the secretary of the Association des Auditeurs de Radio-Normandie, and held today in the Archives of the France Radio Club at Barentin, there is some hope, but also a realistic doubt:

> For the first time in a long while I have good news: our association, after several years of dormancy, has just cashed a cheque as compensation for 30 million francs … . I leave for Paris tomorrow and I will then get the latest news regarding Radio Normandie and its future status. People have talked about the rebirth of some commercial stations in France, and particularly Radio Normandie. If things go well, I might even be asked by the present owners of the Station, the Havas agency, to run such an operation. Of course, we are talking about a commercial repossession; if it were to be under State control, I think we would all agree to retire.[805]

Nothing came of these plans; in the early 1960s the State broadcaster ORTF used the Normandie transmitter to broadcast some regional programmes though even these ended after a year.[806] In 1974 the French media was reorganised and public service French radio came under the responsibility of a new programme company, Radio France.[807] At this point, Normandy was served by a state regional station,

---

804   BBC Memo, 14 January 1947, John McMillan to Norman Collins. WAC E1/717. Apart from its significance as evidence of post-war movement towards re-establishing Radio Normandy, the memo is of interest in other ways. Collins was to become Head of BBC Television in November 1947, (Briggs IV, p. 205) and was to become one of the most important figures in the creation of British Commercial Television (Howard Thomas, *With an Independent Air*, Weidenfeld and Nicolson , London, 1977, p. 144.) "Norman Collins with the backing of Sir Robert Renwick, Lord Bessborough and C.O. Stanley of Pye, triumphed in their lobbying and the Television Act became law in 1954. British uneasiness about an innovation like commercial television was ameliorated by a phrase coined by Norman Collins: 'Independent Television'." – Thomas. McMillan had joined the team establishing the Light Programme in 1945 after working for the Overseas Service.

805   Letter from Fernand Legrand to Emile Durand, 19 February 1947, held in the archives of the France Radio Club: Correspondence with Francois Lhote.

806   Ibid.

807   Kuhn, p. 92.

FR3, and although the 1945 transmitter was still in place, it was no longer used. The final act occurred in 1976, when the station was handed over to scrap dealers. The mast was dismantled and the last remnants of broadcasting equipment were either removed or destroyed.[808]

The Second Revolution

It remains to be discussed how post-war agitation for an alternative to BBC Public Service Radio eventually led to the removal of the British Radio monopoly. France was in fact without legalised commercial radio even longer than Britain: until after the Mitterand election victory of 1981, when increasing pressure from pirate stations such as Radio Riposte finally provoked a change in the law.[809] In new legislation, Kuhn states "the state monopoly in radio provision was comprehensively smashed. After 1981 the floodgates were opened to an apparently infinite number and astonishing variety of small, privately run, local stations. By the end of 1983 it was estimated that up to 850 were operating quite legally."[810]

Offshore Radio in the 1960s

On Sunday, 29 March 1964 Radio Caroline, the brainchild of a young Irish entrepreneur, Ronan O'Rahilly, made its first broadcast from international waters five miles off Harwich. There followed an explosion in such stations which radically changed the course of youth music-radio culture in Britain, and ultimately prompted the BBC to create Radio One in 1967. This was American-style, DJ-fronted popular music radio of a style largely unheard of in Britain, and directly confrontational to the BBC's post-war policy. That said, Caroline was not the first attempt to create alternative music stations from ships in the North Sea. In July 1958, Radio Mercur had broadcast to Denmark from a site off Copenhagen. Other stations came and went, notable survivors being Radio Syd, moored off the Baltic coast of Sweden, and Radio Veronica, off Scheveningen in the Hague, Holland.[811] Another exception was the creation of the land-based Manx Radio on the Isle of Man, run by Richard Meyer, formerly of the IBC, broadcasting from 1964 as Britain's first legal land-based commercial radio station, through a special dispensation of the Government. Permission was only granted on the understanding that its broadcast signal could not be picked up beyond the Island itself.[812]

The growth of pirate stations between 1964 and 1967 mirrored the development of Commercial radio in relation to the BBC during the 1930s. In 1966 National Opinion Polls Ltd carried out a series of surveys to estimate audience size, coming to the conclusion that 45 per cent of the population were listening either to an offshore station or Radio Luxembourg each week. In terms of the top six operators, audience figures broke down thus:

808 Lhote correspondence.
809 Kuhn, p. 99.
810 Ibid., p. 100.
811 Baron, Mike *Independent Radio*, Lavenham, Terence Dalton Ltd, 1975, pp. 36–37.
812 Skues, Keith *Pop Went the Pirates*, Sheffield, Lambs' Meadow Publications, 1994, p. 26.

Radio Luxembourg:	8,818,000 listeners
Radio Caroline:	8,818,000
Radio London:	8,140,000
Radio 390:	2,633,000
Radio England:	2,195,000
Britain Radio:	718,000[813]

The spectacular growth of the off-shore stations was abruptly ended on 13th June 1967, when the Marine, etc., Broadcasting (Offences) Bill received its third and final reading in the House of Lords. It had been a determined policy of the Labour Government under Harold Wilson that commercial broadcasting of any sort should not be permitted in the United Kingdom. The Bill took effect at midnight on the night of 14–15 August, and all but the defiant voice of Radio Caroline fell silent.

Meanwhile there were a number of highly successful Independent companies recording radio programmes in London for transmission by Radio Luxembourg. Among these was Ross Radio Productions, co-run by Monty Bailey-Watson and John Whitney. Companies such as these were busy and profitable. Ross at its peak was making 30 programmes per week, using the still extant IBC studios at 35 Portland Place. As John Whitney later recalled:

> The biggest of our shows was *People Are Funny*, which ran for six or seven years on Luxembourg. I once saw the legendary Leonard Plugge; he had a huge pink Buick, and – what impressed me most – a telephone on the dashboard! I can't imagine how it worked in those days, but for me, that was the symbol to aspire to – that was the potential reward of Commercial Radio.[814]

In 1964, the year of Radio Caroline's first broadcast, Whitney founded – with John – later Sir John – Gorst, The Local Radio Association, and actively began agitating for land-based commercial radio in the United Kingdom. The two men had first met during the 1950s, when Gorst had been working as the Advertising and Public Relations Manager for Pye, who had been sponsors of some of Ross Radio's Radio Luxembourg programmes. John Gorst, who became the Conservative member for Hendon North, was an important figure in the lobbying of Tory support for Independent radio, prior to the 1970 General Election. The LRA, together with Commercial Broadcasting Consultants, set up in 1966 by Tony Cadman and Hughie Green, was the principal advocate (other than the pirate off-shore operators) of commercial radio.

> One of our aims within the LRA was to meet the argument of the BBC that there were not enough medium wave frequencies to permit the creation of a Commercial Radio network. So we commissioned the Marconi Company to research a feasibility study, and this of course proved that there were sufficient frequencies available.[815]

The LRA put forward a proposal for a Local Radio Network which might one day

---

813   Baron, p. 45.

814   Whitney, John, in an interview with the author, August 1999.

815   Gorst, Sir John, in an interview with the author, November 2000.

number some 150 local stations, with an operating cost of £60,000 per year. The Association gave some indications of its house style, per hour:

Music:	39 minutes
News:	5 minutes
Other speech:	10 minutes
Advertising:	6–12 minutes[816]

> I went off to see Edward Short who was the Postmaster General for the Labour Party. And I went in front of him and he fumbled around in his drawer and produced a letter I'd written to him. And he said "If you're the man who wrote this letter, we're not interested. I'm sorry if I've wasted your time, but I felt I should say it to you, face to face."[817]

It would be a mistake to assume that the implementation of the Marine etc., Broadcasting (Offences Bill) on 14 August 1967 marked the end of pirate radio in Britain: it has continued in various forms to the present day. On the other hand, with the demise of most of the offshore stations and the coming of Radio 1 on 30 September, a direct result of agitation created by the pirates, the BBC regained its monopoly. It was to be only a temporary respite: the Conservative Party had pledged itself to initiate legal, land-based Commercial radio as part of its manifesto in the General Election of 1970. With an unexpected victory for Edward Heath's party, it became clear that sound broadcasting in Britain was about to experience its greatest upheaval since the creation of the BBC.

Regulated Radio

One of the paradoxes of the creation of land-based commercial radio in Britain was that over-regulation diluted the character of this new "voice", so long awaited. Far from the mavericks who had fought so hard in the 1930s and 1960s, the change of the Independent Television Authority to a regulator in charge of both television and radio – the Independent Broadcasting Authority – made the first era of Independent Local Radio curiously Reithian. It was also an extremely precarious time financially for those involved on the stations themselves:

> Independent Radio was not expected to survive. It came with the Heath Government of 1970, was ratified by the Broadcasting Act of 1972, and started in 1973. Then we walked slap into the miner's strike. So you had a very sickly child, commercially to start with. When the Wilson government came back in at the 1974 election, it was in their policy to abolish Independent Radio. It was only the report of the Annan Committee [1977] – and at the same time a growing realisation among Labour MPs that Labour voters listened to Independent Radio – that it ceased to be a political football.[818]

It seems highly probably that, had a Conservative party come to power earlier, commercial radio would have been legalised at least eight years before it was finally launched:

> Support for commercial radio was well enough developed in the Tory Party

---

816 Baron, p. 61.

817 Whitney, John, in an interview with the author.

818 Stoller, Tony, Chief Executive, The Radio Authority interviewed by this author, November 2000.

for one commentator to note that, had it not been for the victory of the Labour Party in 1964, "a Conservative Government would have introduced commercial radio within 12 to 18 months of the election".[819]

In the event the programmes on the new stations were a symptom of the regulation by which they were surrounded, and provide evidence of an Independent – rather than a Commercial – network. Tim Wall has written of this:

> In the Government's 1971 White Paper on broadcasting, the concept of independence allowed the new sector to be presented simultaneously as independent from the BBC's public corporate status, independent from the BBC's programming monopoly and London-centric organisation, independent from the commercial pressures of media conglomerates like those establishing themselves in North America, and independent from the influence of US – originated popular culture.[820]

With the shift of power from Harold Wilson's Labour Party to Edward Heath's Conservatives in the General Election of 1970, the nature of how this alternative broadcasting source was to be defined became a major issue. Tony Stoller, until 2003, Chief Executive of the Radio Authority, was Head of Radio Programming at the Independent Broadcasting Authority from 1977, and was charged with establishing this definition:

> The Heath Government came to power unexpectedly. It never expected to come to power. It had commercial radio as part of its platform, but because it did not expect to get into power, it hadn't thought it through, and it had no idea what to do. The route they found was to take the ITV model. Remember Commercial Television came late to Britain – 1955 – and it was conceived as a public service. When Independent Radio came along: "Well, we'll do it the same way". One of my jobs when I worked for the IBA was occasionally to write rude letters for example to somebody at the BBC who had described it as Commercial radio, and demonstrate that it was not, it was Independent radio.[821]

For the Conservative Government, the post of Minister of Posts and Telecommunications was held by Christopher Chataway, who invited representations for the establishment of commercially funded local radio stations. In January 1971 John Gorst took part in a debate on the Radio 4 *Analysis* programme, with – among others – Ian Trethowan, Managing Director of BBC Radio.[822] Much of the programme revolved around discussion between Gorst and Trethowan as to the nature of Commercial Radio in the future. Gorst's view was that there would need

---

819   Local Radio Workshop, Comedia Series No. 15, *Capital, Local Radio and Private Profit*, London, Comedia Publishing Group, 1983, p. 13 The quotation is from the *Daily Mail*, 10 February 1965.

820   Wall, Dr. Tim, "Policy, Pop and the Public: The Discourse of Regulation in British Commercial Radio" in *Journal of Radio Studies* Vol 7, no. 1, Spring 2000, pp. 181–182.

821   Stoller, Tony, interviewed by the author, November 2000.

822   Sir John Gorst subsequently recalled the importance of the fact that the debate was taking place on BBC Radio. "When I had previously attempted to get the matter aired on the BBC, the then Managing Director of BBC Radio, Frank Gillard had told me "The BBC cannot allow its microphones to be used in a discussion of its own interests". That of course was before the 1970 election." (Interview with the present author, November 2000.)

to be a subtle balance between audience satisfaction, profit and the ability "to satisfy ... governments that it's in the public interest in the broadest sense of the word", as well as advertisers. "There are many elements and if you get one of these elements out of balance then the whole ... pack of cards falls apart. But the listener is of course, the first one."[823]

In the view of Trethowan, the issue was that Commercial Radio could not be viable financially if it attempted to take on the BBC in a Public Service role. He believed that a programme policy heavily biased towards music "will leave no room – even if they could afford it commercially – for these stations to do really many of the minority programmes that our local stations do – programmes for immigrants, for the blind, for the elderly, or the education programmes we do. Would commercial radio, as one of our stations does, do a programme on archeology? You may say 'Why should they? They have to maximise the audience'."[824] Three years after the introduction of Independent Radio, Michael Barton, Managing Director of BBC Local Radio was to write that: "... commercial radio has given us an added stimulus to the job we are doing; but we believe ... that we have different roles to play".[825]

On 29 March 1971, the Government published *An Alternative Service of Broadcasting* with its proposal for 60 commercial stations, and a freeze on further development of BBC local radio. (Subsequently with the 1974 election restoring power to the Labour Party, the expansion of Independent Radio was frozen for a time at 19 stations.) The Sound Broadcasting Act of 1972 transformed the Independent Television Authority into the Independent Broadcasting Authority with John Thompson as its first Director of Radio.

The regulation set out by the IBA was strict and limiting, binding franchise bidders to a strong Public Service remit. Successful companies could not combine with other companies to run a chain of radio stations The Authority would encourage the production of "programmes of merit", and companies would have their commercial activities severely limited. There was to be a 15 per cent shareholding from the main competitor – the local newspaper – and a guaranteed seat on the board for that competitor. Stations would be limited in the changes they could make to schedules; furthermore the schedule was strictly monitored in respect of a requirement to provide a range of programming including education, religion, "meaningful speech" and a range of different kinds of music. Additionally stations would be mandated to carry Independent Radio News.

> It was part of something which was hugely in the image of the early 'seventies. It was part of the liberal consensus, part of the view that it was for public authorities and public services to provide things which the public ought to want. So in the end, Reithian.[826]

John Thompson, from the time of his installation at the IBA, was a key architect

823 Gorst, John, MP, Secretary of The Local Radio Association, *Analysis*, BBC Radio 4, Friday, 15 January 1971.

824 Trethowan, Ian Managing Director, BBC Radio, Ibid.

825 Barton, Michael *BBC Lunchtime Lecture: BBC Radio in the Community* 11th series, 26 October 1976, quoted in Briggs, Asa *The History of Broadcasting in the United Kingdom, Vol V: Competition 1955–74*, Oxford, Oxford University Press, 1995, p. 635.

826 Stoller, Tony Interviewed by the author, November 2000.

of Independent Local Radio, and in a 1975 article, *Who Owns Independent Local Radio?*[827] predicted an ideal which would take some years to achieve: "Inherent in the concept of Independent Local Radio is the proposition that ILR should be an additional, or alternative, service and that its ownership should allow it genuine independence among the media".[828] Thompson recalled the words of a document published by the Authority before the first ILR broadcasts, in which the nature of ownership and programme content were discussed:

> In every area, the Authority will be looking, above all, for men and women capable of running a lively and responsible radio station: one which will provide, in the words of the White Paper, "a truly public service ... combining popular programming with fostering a greater awareness of local affairs and involvement in the community".[829]

He went on to underline his understanding of the words "public service" in the context of commercially funded local radio: "In ILR, private enterprise means the initiative and commercial skills of the community itself, linked to provide local radio broadcasting of relevance and use for the locality being served".[830]

With these statements in mind it may be seen that the launch of the first two stations – both metropolitan – was untypical of the informing ethic behind ILR as perceived by Thompson. In October 1973, the London Broadcasting Company began transmissions, closely followed by Capital Radio, with John Whitney as Managing Director. It is clear that the Authority was strongly interventionist in terms of programme regulation; regional IBA officers monitored stations according to strict guidelines, rules for religious programming were stringently applied, and the nature of appropriate programming was frequently commented upon. For example a proposal to network a Chart show in 1979 to interested stations produced a stern statement to all companies under the heading, "A Networked 'Top 30' Programme":

> It has been drawn to our attention that a programme is being offered to all companies in a "Top 30" format for simultaneous broadcast on Sunday afternoons. We have been asked for the IBA's views. It seemed appropriate therefore to make these available to all companies.
>
> Section 4(I) (c) of the IBA Act requires the Authority to satisfy itself that
>
> "the programmes broadcast from different stations for reception in different localities do not consist of identical or similar material to an extent inconsistent with the character of the services as local sound broadcasting services."
>
> Clearly (with the IBA's active encouragement) there is likely to be some growth in the amount of shared programming. If that is not to go against the intention of the Act, though, it must be kept in proportion.
>
> Section 2(2) (c) of the Act gives "programmes of merit" as one category where the IBA should ensure a wide hearing for programmes. It might be

---

827   Thompson, John, "Who Owns Independent Local Radio?" in *Independent Broadcasting 8*, London, IBA, November 1975.

828   Ibid., p. 17.

829   Ibid.

830   Ibid., p. 19.

reasonable to add to this programme material which helped to broaden a company's schedule but which they could not necessarily produce themselves. It does not seem to us that a simultaneously broadcast "Top 30" programme would come into these categories. On the contrary, it might tend towards the sort of "networked pop" programme which goes against the spirit of ILR.

The IBA would therefore wish to discourage companies from broadcasting this type of programme in the "networked" form which has been suggested. If any company, after consideration, decides that it wishes to do so they are asked to consult Radio Division in advance.[831]

As a matter of context it should be recalled here that Radio Luxembourg had started broadcasting a *Top Twenty* show on Sundays in 1948, presented by Teddy Johnson. In "Pick of the Pops" Alan Freeman had broadcast a Top Ten in the early 1960s on the BBC Light Programme, later transferring to Radio 1. *The Network Chart Show*, initially presented by David "Kid" Jensen was eventually syndicated through the ILR network from 1984, sponsored initially by Nescafé, and gained a weekly audience of four million listeners.

The origins of the over-regulation of independent radio in the 1970s and 1980s may be found in what has been referred to as the "conveniently vague" nature of the new service in the 1972 Sound Broadcasting Act.[832] Commenting on the Bill, the labour MP Ivor Richards made the point that:

> What the Bill does in essence ... is to provide a legislative and legal framework within which the Independent Broadcasting Authority will exercise its discretions. Its discretions are wide; and its discretions are virtually unlimited.[833]

The two stools between which Independent Radio therefore fell were on one hand the suspicion that regulation would be interpreted so lightly as to be virtually non-existent, and on the other that over-caution on the part of the new regulator would stifle the medium's financial development, and prevent it from being truly *independent*. In March 1979, Lady Plowden, at that time Chairman of the IBA, gave a speech to the Cardiff Business Club in which she referred to "the full responsibility of independence".[834] She spoke of "two bodies co-existing, the Authority and the BBC, where the buck stops with the appointed trustees of the public interest".[835] The role of the Authority, and its attitude towards radio, may be seen to be that of an over-cautious parent anxious to prove that its child was adequately disciplined: "... Freedom can only be exercised within the broad confines of the social obligations accepted by the society in which we live, willingly accepted by broadcasters themselves".[836] It was the nature of Governmental compromise in the powers it invested in the Authority, together with the Authority's interpretation of its own responsibilities as the regulator of independent radio

---

831 IBA Statement, 11 January 1979.
832 Local Radio Workshop, Comedia Series no. 15, pp. 20–21.
833 Ibid. Ivor Richards, MP quoted (uncited).
834 19 March 1979. Published in *Independent Broadcasting 20*, London, IBA, June 1979, pp. 2–6.
835 Ibid., p. 5.
836 Ibid., p. 6.

which came close to bringing the fledgling sector of British broadcasting to its knees.

Notwithstanding this, there remained commentators who suspected the motives of politicians who looked "to the interests of its supporters in the world of industry and commerce"[837] in the creation of commercial radio:

> It is ... a cause for concern that a major political party should allow such an important and influential medium [as radio] to be placed in the hands of a *sectional* interest whose explicit and overriding concern is to make money rather than to develop radio in the interests of the *whole* community.[838]

Towards Commercial Radio Again

Increasingly through the early 1980s there was frustration at how what was perceived by the independent companies as excessive regulation was jeopardising the very existence of the network. In June 1984 a meeting of executives from the stations then on air was organised by the AIRC under Brian West near Heathrow Airport. Out of this "council of war"[839] came four key decisions:

1. To make public the Industry's frustration at the IBA's over regulation.

2. To demand an early substantial cut in rentals.

3. To press the Government for new legislation on commercial radio

4. To commission an independent report on the potential for creating many more stations under light regulation.[840]

For Brian West, and ILR company executives around the country, the achievement of these aims was crucial to the survival of the Industry:

> Within three months many of the IBA's petty rules were dispensed with; within six months rentals had been reduced by more than a third and within a year the independent report (*Radio Broadcasting in the UK* by The Economist Intelligence Unit) had shown that there was scope for real, rapid expansion and that light touch regulation was feasible and safe.[841]

The process which began at the Heathrow Conference culminated six years later in the 1990 Broadcasting Act, which enabled Independent Radio to be truly *commercial* for the first time, permitting among other things the creation of large groups of stations and national commercial radio. Furthermore – together with allowing the consolidation of ownership, the Act contained no positive programme requirements, ceasing to regard Commercial Radio as Public Service Broadcasting.[842]

The Act also saw the abolition of the Independent Broadcasting Authority, and the creation of The Radio Authority, a vital aspect of the regeneration of Commercial Radio, in that it made it possible to remove many regulations which had originated in television rather than radio. The IBA had been – effectively – a television

---

837   Local Radio Workshop, Comedia Series no. 15, p. 14.

838   Ibid.

839   Brian West, November 2000.

840   Ibid.

841   Ibid.

842   Stoller, Tony, November 2000.

regulator with responsibility for radio. Now, at last, private sector radio had its own – lighter touch – authority.

Thus ended a crucial but under-documented period in post-war radio history. The paradox that land-based British Commercial Radio could not initially define itself as the early pre-war pioneers would have understood, was resolved by the relative freedom created by the 1990 Broadcasting Act. Tim Wall has stated:

> Centrally ... the [Radio]Authority is being asked to organise broadcasting for profit-maximising stations, while mitigating against the market results that are seen to be formed by frequency famine, the size of British listening communities, and the models of commercial broadcasting utilized by station staff.[843]

In the Summer of 2002 the Labour Government published a draft of a new Communications Bill, expected to come into force during 2003. Regarding commercial radio – already in the throes of Digital and Internet development – further legislation was to bring more radical changes. A new body – Ofcom – was to be the regulator across all media, becoming operational in December 2003. Plans included the permitting of cross-media ownership, and even international ownership of radio stations and groups: what the British commercial sector craved most however was a move towards still greater deregulation. In this context, history gives us an essential perspective; we can see how from an early pre-war confidence in its identity – enhanced by its post-war continental and offshore presence and popularity – British commercial radio was later compelled to justify its existence through a role as a Public Service broadcaster, independent of the BBC, although essentially Reithian in character. Only in the last decade of the 20th century was it permitted to reinvent itself in a form close to its original image as conceived by the founding fathers of the Industry in the 1920s and 1930s, and the post-1945 commercial activists. In the first years of the 21st century government legislation continued to relax its grip, permitting increasing consolidation, and in 2004 the two largest commercial radio groups in the UK, GWR and Capital, merged to form a company the aspiration of which was for the first time to address the imbalance of power between commercial and BBC radio interests.

As has been stated earlier, Britain – almost uniquely among other countries – gained Commercial Television (1955) before land-based Commercial Radio. Given that private sector radio from 1973 to 1990 was based on the Independent Television model of Public Service, it is interesting to speculate what Commercial Television might have been like, had the reverse been true, with post-1990 Commercial Radio as the model. The revealing cultural witness of the pre-war commercial radio pioneers offers us a new sense of continuity from as early as the very creation of broadcasting in Britain to the present day. We are thus in a position better to place this important aspect of 20th century broadcasting within the overall landscape of radio studies.

---

843 Wall, Dr Tim *Journal of Radio Studies*, Spring 2000, p. 193.

Conclusion

It's time to say goodnight,
And it's time to close your eyes
Let's put out the light
'til the dawn breaks through the skies.
While long shadows creep
May your dreams be sweet and bright.
In a moment you'll be sound asleep.
It's time to say goodnight.[844]

The purpose of this book has been to demonstrate fully for the first time the influence of commercial radio in Britain during the years of its first major challenge to the monopoly of BBC public service broadcasting, that is to say 1930–39. I have tried to offer an alternative to other broadcasting histories of the period by claiming for commercial radio a more significant role in the development of broadcasting than has previously been suggested. By extension this work puts forward the premise that by providing this competition the pre-war commercial radio entrepreneurs had a long-term effect on the British broadcasting scene, ultimately forcing change in BBC programme policy.

The nature of the BBC changed crucially during the years 1930–1939, starting from a paternalistic idea of public service broadcasting which still held to the attitudes inherent in a statement in the 1928 *BBC Handbook* under the heading "Programme Policy":

> The broadcaster ... is necessarily the actual chooser of the programmes. A false step would be taken if, carried away by his sense of what the public needs, he supposes it to be the same as what the public wants. Often – curiously often, a pessimist would have to allow – the two coincide, but it does happen that they disagree.[845]

---

844 Lyric from Radio Luxembourg's close-down theme, 1938/39 (author's collection).
845 Article, "Programme Policy", *BBC Handbook 1928*, London, BBC, London, p. 71.

211

By the mid to late 1930s when commercial programming was making huge inroads into BBC Sunday policy, the Corporation was in a difficult and complex situation with respect to its still relatively strict sabbatarian principles. Although it found it hard to make major changes in the nature of its programmes until the coming of war provided a fitting justification to do so, the most notable acknowledgement of a requirement for change came in 1936 with the creation of a unit within the BBC to measure and examine the radio audience. That the person entrusted with the creation of this unit – Robert Silvey – had been absorbed into BBC service from the London Press Exchange, "one of the larger British advertising agents",[846] is remarkable proof of this. Silvey refers to the events leading to his move from the commercial to the public service sector as "almost conspiratorial".[847]

The concept of generic broadcasting in the BBC began to evolve with the coming of the Forces Programme in early 1940. Even the creation of this service, as we have seen, was as the direct result of the initiative of the IBC in establishing Radio International on the erstwhile Radio Normandy wavelength at a time when all other commercial competition against the BBC, including Radio Luxembourg, had closed down. It can therefore be claimed that the BBC was forced to redefine its idea of public service broadcasting as a direct result of explicit competition.

The influence within this competition of American models of radio developed progressively through the years 1930–39, due largely to the importation of styles and practices by – notably – the J. Walter Thompson Organisation. Proven US techniques of advertising targeting were applied to the British radio audience, seen not as listeners but potential purchasers of goods advertised. The concept of the sponsored programme dominated over the "spot" advert, and a growing sophistication of advertising policy in which radio was used as part of a larger campaign utilizing press coverage to complement the radio message is perceivable in the latter part of the decade. It will have been noted that the last years before war brought a number of US soap operas to the British audience through Radios Normandy and Luxembourg, including some, such as *Stella Dallas* which had run successfully on American radio for many years, and which was to be the subject of a high profile feature film starring Barbara Stanwyck.

It is interesting to note however that the agencies behind such programmes resisted an overtly American "sound" to the programmes. Soap operas were adapted to a British context rather than simply broadcasting them as heard by the US audience. Analysis of programme tapes from the time has shown a remarkable lack of American voices in British commercial radio. Mostly the accents were those of the British upper middle class, and the legendary Ovaltineys were stage school children whose voices gave a strong sense of social privilege. Nevertheless the stated aim of the agencies was to reach working class families and their children. Audiences were used to the authoritative "superior" voice of the broadcaster, and in this respect the BBC style crossed over to the presentation of the commercials. (Indeed the movement of Christopher Stone and others between BBC programmes and those made by the commercial entrepreneurs demonstrates a freelance ethic which

---

846   Silvey, R.J.E. *Who's Listening? The Story of BBC Audience Research*, London, George Allen and Unwin, 1974, p. 16.

847   Ibid., p. 17.

promoted a certain unity of style between the two.) At the same time the J. Walter Thompson promotional record, included on the CD Appendix, addresses itself to a very different class of person to the proposed audience to whom the advertising is directed. The wording is carefully chosen and defensive towards potential prejudice against the quality and nature of the programming.

There were certain elements which, while present in American commercial radio, could not of necessity be included in the British models, due to the nature of its transmission requirements. As programmes were mostly recorded in Britain and shipped to distant transmission locations, the broadcasting of such programmes as news and sport was not appropriate. That apart, the BBC was unassailably dominant in both these fields. Instead the agencies concentrated on a comforting mix of popular music, variety and show business-related programmes which proved to be highly acceptable to the target audience during times of domestic hardship and international tension. Complementing this style of programming, the advertising policy offered remedies for stress related conditions: headaches, constipation, liverishness, "night starvation" and so on.

Given the nature of the "programme architecture"[848] on the IBC stations and Radio Luxembourg, it might seem strange to claim that there was an innovative quality to the programmes. On the other hand, given the context of programming from the BBC at the time, there can be claimed to have been stylistic innovation in terms of a more "streamed" output, together with a relative relaxation of presentation styles.

The true technical contribution to broadcasting of the time however came out of the necessity to record programmes using the highest quality signal carrier; thus J. Walter Thompson's sophisticated Bush House radio studio, discussed previously, utilized advanced notions of acoustics as well as the technically innovative Philips-Miller recording process. Experiments in this field were being carried out even before the BBC's Empire Service made recording a necessity for the Corporation in 1932. Commercial operators were in the forefront of disc recording, both for commercials and programme content, as demonstrated in my chapter on recording technologies.[849] Audience measurement was clearly a major influence on broadcasting, seen as more of a social science from 1936 onwards as a result of American Advertising agency practice, and introduced as a tool which was complemented by the ability to reach an audience both on the air, and physically through the means of mobile recording technology. Radio Normandy's policy of recording live stage shows which it also sponsored, such as *Radio Normandy Calling* gave the station a high-profile physical presence which complemented strongly the listening experience.

An interesting aspect of this research has been listeners' responses to the advertisements; unlike commercial radio at the end of the twentieth century, where the too frequently poor quality of on-air advertisements seems to take very little account of the fact that a high proportion of listening time in each hour can be given over to commercials, audiences who remember the Continental transmissions often look

---

848 Ibid.
849 See above, "Recording Technologies and Strategies".

back as fondly on the sponsors' message as the programmes themselves.[850] This link was made stronger by the policy of enabling listeners to join radio clubs which carried branded product names, and offered in return for membership subscriptions branded merchandise. Thus while there was political and establishment opposition to the stations and their programmes, there was through the 1930s a growing loyalty and affection amongst large sections of the listening public which was to be mirrored in the 1960s by the responses to the ship-based pirate stations such as Radio Caroline and Radio London.

Commercial Radio established itself twice for British audiences, both at times of extreme financial difficulty. One system flourished, flouting any form of regulation and supplying programmes of overt populism, while the other, although legally sanctioned, struggled to assert itself due to over-regulation, in the process incidentally providing many programmes of lasting value[851] before being permitted to operate truly as a business at the expense of Public Service programming towards the end of the twentieth century. In addition, the requirement for Independent Radio as created in 1973 to reflect a local community rather than broadcast to a broader national audience as the pre-war stations and the 1960s "pirates" had done (to the extent that their transmission capabilities permitted) further limited the abilities of the stations to be truly commercial.

The BBC has been influenced, and has developed as a result of attacks on its former monopoly, only at times when the commercial sector has been permitted to offer influential competition from the standpoint of its own terms, in other words, providing a genuine alternative. The coming of Independent Television in 1955 has been acknowledged elsewhere as a moment of singular significance in the development of the BBC's relationship with its audience.[852] The historical evidence shows the key moments of BBC change to have come about as the result of exterior pressure on and threat to its monopoly in radio and television. The first of these attacks was from the commercial radio companies of the 1930s, and the aspirations of these companies grew from a concept of broadcasting which had begun to be practised even prior to the creation of the BBC. The experiments of the *Daily Mail* sponsored programmes of 1919, coming as they did from an improvised radio station on Lord Northcliffe's yacht, predated the activities of the "Pirate" stations

---

850 See Appendix C: "Samples of Listeners' Correspondence".

851 Notable were the radio drama productions by Hamish Wilson of Radio Clyde. Likewise in 1981 Swansea Sound's David Lucas produced *A Nation in His Hand*, a remarkable drama documentary which told the story of the 1904–05 religious revival in Wales. Musically, in the late 1970s Capital Radio's *Great Orchestras of the World* series broadcast concerts by the Vienna Philharmonic Orchestra, The London Symphony Orchestra and the Berlin Philharmonic Orchestra, among others.

852 Forman, Sir Denis, Joint Managing Director and later Chairman of ATV recalled the impact of Commercial Television in 1955 on the BBC thus: "There was no feeling [within the BBC] for the big audience. So when ITV introduced programmes like *I Love Lucy* and *The Army Game*, we had no difficulty in taking the BBC's ratings away from them. In particular *Sunday Night at the London Palladium* put to bed any BBC attempt at Variety for good and all. In response they pulled themselves up to their full height and said, "this is rather disgraceful, what's happening on the other channel; we must carry on as we always have done and not be upset …". In the end of course they changed, but the BBC would have changed far more slowly had it not been for ITV giving it a shot in the arm." (Interviewed in *Auntie, The Inside Story, Part Two – Growing Pains, 1945–1960*, 3BM TV Productions for BBC 1, 1997.)

of the 1960s, and were the inspiration and early training ground for such broadcasters as Stephen Williams, paving the way as they did for the more sophisticated programming ideas of Leonard Plugge and others. The importance of marketing commercial products and targeting appropriate audiences led to audience research, and the necessity for broadcasting material from remote sites helped to develop recording technology. These practical necessities in turn were absorbed and further explored by the BBC. Commercial broadcasting in Britain has played a role which deserves more recognition in retrospective studies of broadcasting in the United Kingdom, with greater acknowledgement that the contribution of independent sector populist radio driven by a commercial imperative from the earliest days of British radio is an important – and thus far undervalued – aspect of the nation's broadcasting history.

BIBLIOGRAPHY

Bibliography

Written texts

Advertiser's Weekly, 20 February 1936.

Angus, Robert "75 Years of Magnetic Recording", in *High Fidelity*, US, March 1973.

Arnold, Frank A. *Broadcast Advertising, The Fourth Dimension*, New York, John Wiley and Sons, 1931.

Auden, W.H. and Isherwood, Christopher *The Ascent of F6* London, Faber & Faber, London, 1936.

Bailey, Peter "Making Sense of Music Hall" in *Music Hall, The Business of Pleasure* ed. Bailey, Peter, Milton Keynes, Open University Press, 1983.

Baily, Leslie *Leslie Baily's BBC Scrapbooks, Volume 2: 1918–1939*, London, George Allen & Unwin, 1968.

Baker, W.J. *A History of the Marconi Company*, London, Methuen, 1970.

Baldwin, Stanley *On England, and Other Addresses*, London, Philip Allan, 1926.

Baron, Mike *Independent Radio, The Story of Independent Radio in the United Kingdom*, Lavenham, Terence Dalton Ltd.

Barnard, Stephen *On the Radio, Music Radio in Britain*, Milton Keynes, Open University Press, 1989.

Barnouw, Erik *A Tower in Babel, A History of Broadcasting in the United States to 1933*, New York, Oxford University Press, 1966.

BBC Annual, 1937, London, BBC.

BBC Hand Book, 1928, London, BBC.

BBC Hand Book, 1929, London, BBC.

BBC Year Book, 1933, London, BBC.

BBC Hand Book 1940, London, BBC.

BBC Quarterly, Vol.III, No. 2, July 1948.

BBC Quarterly, Vol.II, No 1, April 1947, BBC.

BBC Written Archives, Caversham: E2/365/1: Foreign General – International Broadcasting Company file 1, 1930–33.

BBC Year Book 1932, BBC, London, BBC.

BBC Year Book 1934, London, BBC.

BBC Year Book, 1947, London, BBC.

Beck, Alan *The Invisible Play, BBC Radio Drama 1922–1928*, Canterbury, Sound Journal CD Book, 2000.

Bell, P.M.H., *France and Britain 1900–1940: Entente & Estrangement*, London, Longman, 1996.

Berkman, Dave "The Not Quite So Inevitable Origins of Commercial Broadcasting in America" in *Journal of Advertising History* Vol. 10, No. 1, 1987.

Felton, F. *The Radio Play. Its Techniques and Possibilities*, London, Sylvan Press, 1949.

Biel, Michael J. *The Making and Use of Recordings in Broadcasting Before 1936*, pp. 1002/3, Northwestern University, Evanston, Illinois, Ann Arbor, Michigan, UMI Dissertation Information Service.

Black, Peter *The Biggest Aspidistra in the World, A Personal Celebration of 50 Years of the BBC*, London, BBC, 1972.

Boyle, Andrew *Only the Wind Will Listen: Reith of the BBC*, London, Hutchinson, 1972.

Bridson, D.G. *Prospero and Ariel, The Rise and Fall of Radio, A Personal Recollection*, London, Gollancz, 1971.

Briggs, Asa *The BBC, the First Fifty Years*, Oxford, Oxford University Press, 1985.

Briggs, Asa *History of Broadcasting in the United Kingdom, Vol. I, The Birth of Broadcasting 1896–1927*, Oxford, Oxford University Press, 1995.

Briggs, Asa *The History of Broadcasting in the United Kingdom, Vol. II, The Golden Age of Wireless, 1927–1939*, Oxford, Oxford University Press, 1995.

Briggs, Asa *The History of Broadcasting in the United Kingdom, Volume 3, The War of Words 1939–1945*, Oxford, Oxford University Press, 1995.

Briggs, Asa *The History of Broadcasting in the United Kingdom, Vol. IV, Sound and Vision 1945–55*, Oxford, Oxford University Press.

Brochand, Christian *Histoire Generale de la Radio et de la Television en France. Volume 1: 1921–1944*, Paris, Le Documentation Francaise, 1994.

Bulletin des Lois, Journal Officiel no 23582, 14 December 1923.

Bulletin des Lois, Journal Officiel no. 29798, 31 December 1926.

Burrows, A.R. *The Story of Broadcasting*, London, Cassell, 1924.

Butler, George *Berlin, Bush House and Berkeley Square*, privately printed memoir edited by Firth, Jill from conversations, 1985.

Cardiff, David "The Serious and the Popular: aspects of the evolution of style in the radio talk, 1928–1939" in Collins, Richard (ed.) *Media, Culture and Society, A Critical Reader*, London, Sage Publications, 1986.

Carey, John *The Intellectuals and the Masses, Pride and Prejudice among the Literary Intelligensia, 1880–1939*, London, Faber, 1992.

Camporesi, Valeria *But We Talk a Different Language. US "models" in the History of British Radio, 1922–1954*. Unpublished Ph.D thesis, University of Westminster, 1990, subsequently published in a revised form as *Mass Culture and National Traditions: The BBC and American Broadcasting 1922–1954*, Fucecchio, European Press Academic Publishing, 2000.

Cazenave, F. *Les Radio Libres*, Paris, PUF, 1980.

Cleghorn Thomson, D. *Radio is Changing Us*, London, Watts, 1937.

Cmd. 1822 (1923) Wireless Broadcasting Licence by the Postmaster-General to the British Broadcasting Company Limited.

Cmd. 1951 (1923), *Broadcasting Committee Report* (The Sykes Committee Report).

Cmd. 2599, *Report of The Broadcasting Committee, 1925*, published 1926.

Cmd. 5091, *Report of The Broadcasting Committee, 1935*, Coase, R.H. *British Broadcasting, A Study in Monopoly*, London, The London School of Economics/Longmans, Green & Co., 1950.

Cobban, Alfred *A History of Modern France, Volume Three*, London, Jonathan Cape, 1965.

Cole, G.D.H. and M.I. *The Condition of Britain*, London, Gollancz, 1937.

Cook Batsford, Brian *The Britain of Brian Cook*, London, Batsford, 1987.

Cox, Jim *The Great Radio Soap Operas*, Jefferson, North Carolina, McFarland & Company, 1999.

Crawford, William *The People's Food*, London, William Heinnemann Ltd, 1938.

Crisell, Andrew *Understanding Radio*, London, Routledge, 1994.

Crisell, Andrew *An Introductory History of British Broadcasting*, London, Routledge, 1997.

Curran, James and Seaton, Jean *Power Without Responsibility, The Press and Broadcasting in Britain*, London, Routledge, 1997.

Daily Express, The, 5 November 1928.

Daily Herald, The, 5 November 1928.

Day, Gary "Culture, Criticism and Consumerism" in *Literature and Culture in Modern Britain, Volume Two, 1930–1955*, ed. Day, Gary London, Longman, 1997.

Donovan, Paul *The Radio Companion*, London, Grafton, 1992, p. 240.

Donzelot, Jacques *The Policing of Families*, London, Hutchinson, 1980.

Douglas, George H. *The Early Days of Broadcasting*, Jefferson, North Carolina, McFarland & Company, Inc., 1987.

Douglas, Susan J. *Listening In, Radio and the American Imagination from Amos 'n' Andy and Edward R. Murrow to Wolfman Jack and Howard Stern*, New York, Times Books, 1999.

Duval, Rene *Histoire de la Radio en France*, Paris, editions Alain Moreau, 1979.

Dyer, Gillian *Advertising as Communication*, London, Routledge, 1982.

Dygert, Warren B. *Radio as an Advertising Medium*, New York, McGraw-Hill Book Company, 1939.

EAQ Programme Magazine, No. 1, June 1932.

EAQ Programme Magazine No 19, January 1934.

EAQ Programme Magazine No.2 7, December 1934.

EAQ Programme Magazine No. 41, November 1935.

Eckersley, Myles *Prospero's Wireless*, Romsey, Myles Books, 1997.

Eckersley, P.P. *The Power Behind the Microphone*, London, The Scientific Book Club, 1942.

Eckersley, Roger *The BBC and All That*, London, Samson Low, Marston & Co. Ltd. 1946.

Electrical World, The, US, 8 September 1888.

Ellis, John "British Cinema as Performance Art, *Brief Encounter* and *Radio Parade of 1935* and the circumstances of film exhibition", in *British Cinema, Past and Present* (ed.) Ashby, Justine and Higson, Andrew, London, Routledge, 2000.

Emery, Walter B. *National and International Systems of Broadcasting – their History, Operation and Control*, Michigan, Michigan State University Press, 1969.

Engelman Ralph *Public Radio and Television in America, A Political History*, California, Sage, 1996.

Engineering Division Training Manual, 1942, London, BBC.

Fernadez, Francisco Jose Montes: *The Origins of Overseas Broadcasting in Spain*, Madrid, RTVE, 1988.

Fielden, Lionel *The Natural Bent*, London, Andre Deutsch, 1960.

Fitzgerald, Robert *Rowntree and the Marketing Revolution 1862–1969*, Cambridge, Cambridge University Press, 1995.

Foster, Andy & Furst, Steve *Radio Comedy 1938–1968*, London, Virgin, 1996.

Furth, Charles *Life Since 1900*, London, Batsford, 1956.

Giddings, Robert "John Reith and the Rise of Radio", from *Literature and Culture in Modern Britain, Volume 1, 1900–1929*, ed. Bloom, Clive, London, Longman, 1993.

Gielgud, Val and Marvell, Holt *Death at Broadcasting House*, London, Rich and Cowan, 1934.

Gifford, Denis *The Golden Age of Radio*, London, B.T. Batsford Ltd, 1985.

Giradeau, Emile, *Souvenirs de Longue Vie*, Berger-Levrault, Paris, 1968.

Gorham, Maurice *Sound and Fury, Twenty One Years in the BBC*, London, Percival Marshall, 1948.

Gorham, Maurice *Forty Years of Irish Broadcasting*, Dublin, The Talbot Press, 1967.

Guardian, The, 2 May 1983.

Guidance for Producers 1948 BBC booklet, facsimile published London, BBC, 1997.

Happy Listening, 8 December 1939.

Hartley, Ian *Goodnight Children … Everywhere*, Southborough, Midas Books, 1983.

Head, Sydney *Broadcasting in America*, New York, Houghton Mifflin Co., 1956.

Hennessey, Brian *Savoy Hill, The Early Years of British Broadcasting*, Romford, Ian Henry Publications, 1996.

Hettinger, Hermann S. and Neff, Walter J. *Practical Radio Advertising*, New York, Prentice-Hall, 1938.

Hill, Jonathan *Radio! Radio!*, Bampton, Sunrise Press, 1996.

Historic Record and AV Collector, The, Issues 39, 40 and 41, April, June & October 1996.

Newnes Practical Mechanics, September 1937.

Hobsbawm, Eric *The Age of Extremes*, London, Michael Joseph, 1994.

IBC Programme Sheet, The, 12 June 1938, The International Broadcasting Company.

Jeffery, Tom "A Place in the Nation: The Lower Middle Class in England", in Koshar,Rudy (ed.), *Splintered Classes, Politics, and the Lower Middle Classes in Interwar Europe*, New York, Holmes and Meier, 1990.

Jennings, Hilda and Gill, Winifred *Broadcasting in Everyday Life, A Survey of the Social Effects of the Coming of Broadcasting*, London, BBC, 1939.

Journal of Advertising History, Norwich, MCB University Press, Volume 10, No. 2, 1987.

Legion Information Services Survey, October 1935, BBC Written Archives, Caversham WAC.

J. Walter Thompson Archive, unpublished ledgers and accounts.

Kaldor, Nicholas & Silverman, Rodney *A Statistical Analysis of Advertising Expenditure and the Revenue of the Press*, Cambridge, Cambridge University Press, 1948.

Keillor, Garrison *Radio Romance*, London, Faber and Faber, 1993.

Kerwin, Jerome *The Control of Radio*, Chicago, University of Chicago Press, 1934.

Kuhn, Raymond *The Media in France*, Routledge, London, 1995 October 1945.

Klugmann, James "The Crisis of the Thirties: A View from the Left", in *Culture and Crisis in Britain in the '30s*, (ed.) Clark, Jon, Heinnemann, Margot, Margolies, David and Snee, Carole, London, Lawrence and Wishart, 1979.

Lacey, Kate "Radio in the Great Depression, Promotional Culture, Public Service and Propaganda", in Hilmes, Michele and Loviglio, Jason (ed.) *Radio Reader*, London/New York, Routledge, 2002.

Leavis, F.R. *Mass Civilisation and Minority Culture*, London, The Minority Press, 1930.

Lemaitre, Jean, *Allo! Allo! Ici Radio Normandie*, Fécamp, L. Durand & Fils, 1984.

Journal of Advertising History, Volume 10, Number 2, 1987.

Lenthall, Bruce "Public Intellectuals Decry Depression-era Radio, Mass culture and Modern America", in Hilmes, Michele and Loviglio, Jason (ed.) *Radio Reader*, London/New York, Routledge, 2002.

Lewis, C.A. *Broadcasting from Within*, London, George Newnes, Ltd, 1924.

Listener, The, 18 January 1933.

Listener, The, 25 January 1933.

Local Radio Workshop, *Capital, Local Radio and Private Profit*, Comedia Series No. 15, London, Comedia Publishing Group/Local Radio Workshop, 1983.

Low, Rachael *Film Making in 1930s Britain*, London, George Allen and Unwin, 1985.

McDonnell, James *Public Service Broadcasting, A Reader*, London, Routledge, 1991.

McIntyre, Ian *The Expense of Glory, A Life of John Reith*, London, Harper Collins, 1993.

Manchester Guardian, The, 9 July 1935.

Marwick, Arthur *Class: Image and Reality in Britain, France and the USA Since 1930*, Manchester, Manchester University Press, 1980.

Mathias, P. *The First Industrial Nation*, London, Methuen, 1971.

Meadel, Cecile *Histoire de la Radio des Années Trente*, Paris, Anthropos/INA, 1994.

Media Culture and Society, Volume 10, No. 1, January 1988.

Miall, Leonard *Inside the BBC*, London, Weidenfeld & Nicolson, London, 1994.

Middlemas, Keith *Politics in Industrial Society*, London, Andre Deutsch, 1980.

Montague, Ron *When the Ovaltineys Sang*, Southend-on-Sea, privately printed pamphlet, 1993.

Moores, Shaun, " 'The Box on the Dresser': memories of early radio and everyday life", in *Media Culture and Society*, Volume 10, No. 1, January 1988.

Moseley, Sydney A. *Broadcasting in My Time*, London, Rich and Cowan.

Moseley, Sydney *The Private Diaries of Sydney Moseley*, London/Bournemouth, Max Parrish in Association with The Outspoken Press, 1960.

Nevett, T.R. *Advertising in Britain, A History*, London/Norwich, Heinemann/The History of Advertising Trust, 1982.

Neville, Peter, *France 1914–69 – The Three Republics*, London, Hodder and Stoughton, 1995.

New York Times, 26 May 1935.

Nichols, Richard *Radio Luxembourg, The Station of the Stars*, London, Comet, 1983.

Offshore Echos Magazine, no. 105, London, June 1996.

Outstanding BBC Dates, unpublished fact sheet, London, BBC Reference Library, Broadcasting House, 1954.

Paris Vous Parle, no. 7 December 1964, Paris, ORTF.

Paulu, Burton *British Broadcasting: Radio and Television in the United Kingdom*, Minneapolis, University of Minnesota Press, 1956.

Pawley, Edward *BBC Engineering 1922–72*, London, BBC Publications, 1972.

Pegg, Mark *Broadcasting and Society, 1918–1939*, Beckenham, Croom Helm, 1983.

Plomley, Roy *Days Seemed Longer, Early Years of a Broadcaster*, London, Eyre Methuen, 1980.

Priestley, J.B. *English Journey*, London, William Heinemann, 1934.

Radio Craft, October 1934.

Radio-Magazine, no. 136, 23 May 1926.

Radio Pictorial, 8 June 1934.

Radio Pictorial, 19 October 1934.

Radio Pictorial, 5 April 1935.

Radio Pictorial, 3 May 1935.

Radio Pictorial, 13 December 1935.

Radio Pictorial, 23 December 1936.

Radio Pictorial, 22 January 1937.

Radio Pictorial, 27 March 1937.

Radio Pictorial, 11 June 1937.

Radio Pictorial, 10 December 1937.

Radio Pictorial, 4 March 1938.

Radio Pictorial, 18 March 1938.

Radio Pictorial, 6 May 1938.

Radio Pictorial, 30 December 1938.

Radio Pictorial, 18 August 1939.

Radio Times, 4 September 1939.

Radio Times, 28 May 1926.

Radio Times, 5 December 1930.

Radio Times, 29 March 1925.

Radio Times, 28 March 1930.

Radio Times, 5 April 1935.

Radio Times, 28 February 1936.

Radio Times, 20 January 1939.

Radio Times, 3 March 1939.

Radio Times, Supplementary Issue, 4 September 1939.

Radio Times, 5 March 1943.

Radio Times, 15 August 1943.

Radio Times, 25 February 1944.

Radio Times, 12 May 1944.

Radio Times, 27 July 1945.

Radio Times, 1 March 1946.

Recapture of Radio Luxembourg, The unpublished document, Supreme Headquarters, Allied Expeditionary Force, 1945.

Reith, J.C.W. *Broadcast Over Britain*, London, Hodder and Stoughton, 1924.

Reith, J.C.W., *Personality and Career*, London, George Newnes, 1925.

Reith, J.C.W. *Into the Wind*, London, Hodder & Stoughton, 1949.

Richards, Jeffrey *Films and British National Identity*, Manchester, Manchester University Press, 1997.

Roberts, Robert *The Classic Slum*, Manchester, Manchester University Press, 1971.

Robertson, Patrick *The New Shell Book of Firsts*, London, Headline, 1994.

Rodger, Ian *Radio Drama*, London, MacMillan, 1982.

Rowntree, R. Seebohm *Poverty and Progress*, London, Longmans, Green and Co., 1941.

Saerchinger, César, *Hello America! Radio Adventures in Europe*, Boston, Houghton Mifflin, 1938.

Scannell, "Broadcasting and the Politics of Unemployment 1930–1935" in Richard Collins et al, (eds.) *Media, Culture and Society – A Critical Reader*, London Sage, 1986.

Scannell, Paddy and Cardiff, David "Serving the Nation: Public Service Broadcasting Before the War", in *Popular Culture Past and Present*, ed. Waites, Bernard et al, Croom Helm, Beckenham, 1982.

Scannell, Paddy and Cardiff, David *A Social History of British Broadcasting, 1922–1939, Serving the Nation*, Oxford, Blackwell, 1991.

Scientific American, Vol. 127, No 1, July 1922.

Seaman, L.C.B. *Life in Britain Between the Wars*, London, Batsford, 1970.

Shelf Appeal, October 1935.

Siepmann, Charles A. *Radio, Television and Society*, New York, Oxford University Press, 1950.

Sieveking, Lance *The Stuff of Radio*, London, Cassell, 1934.

Silvey, Robert *Who's Listening? The Story of BBC Audience Research*, London, George Allen & Unwin, London, 1974.

Skues, Keith *Pop Went the Pirates, an Illustrated History of Pirate Radio*, Sheffield, Lambs Meadow Publications, 1994.

Smith, Anthony *British Broadcasting*, Newton Abbot, David and Charles, 1974.

Smulyan, Susan *Selling Radio, The Commercialisation of American Broadcasting, 1920–1934*, Washington D.C., Smithsonian Institution Press, 1994.

Snagge, John and Barsley, Michael *Those Vintage Years of Radio*, London, Pitman, 1972.

Soper, Sam, Press Production Controller, J. Walter Thompson, London *My Life at JWT*, unpublished memoir 1994, manuscript held in J. Walter Thompson Archive, History of Advertising Trust, Mss1994/cat.5.11.97.

Spectator, The, no. 2,720, 11 February 1938.

Steringa Idzerda, pamphlet published by the Dutch Museum of Broadcasting, Hilversum.

Stevenson, John *Social Conditions in Britain Between the Wars*, London, Penguin, 1977.

Stone, Christopher *Christopher Stone Speaking*, London, Elkin, Mathews & Marrot Ltd, 1933.

Stuart, Charles (ed.) *The Reith Diaries*, London, Collins, 1975.

Sunday Dispatch, 4 November 1928, p. 1, WAC, CAV R34/960.

Sunday Referee, The, 8 January 1933.

Sunday Referee, The, 5 August 1934.

Sweeney, Kevin B. "How Radio Advertising Developed", in *Advertising Age*, 7 December 1964.

Temps, Le, 24 March 1923.

This is the IBC, promotional booklet, London, IBC, 1939.

Thomas, Howard *With an Independent Air, Encounters during a Lifetime of Broadcasting*, London, Weidenfeld & Nicolson, 1977

Tint, Herbert *France Since 1918*, London, Batsford, 1970.

Tomlinson, Charles *The Way in and Other Poems*, Oxford, Oxford University Press, 1974, reprinted in *Collected Poems*, Oxford, Oxford University Press, 1985.

Tomlinson, J.D. *The International Control of Radiocommunications*, Michigan, University of Michigan, 1945.

Treasure, Dr. J.A.P. Group Chairman, JWT Co. Ltd, *The History of British Advertising Agencies 1875 –1939*, Jubilee Lecture to Edinburgh University Commerce Graduates' Association, 1976, Edinburgh, Scottish Academic Press, 1977.

Turner, E.S. *The Shocking History of Advertising*, London, Michael Joseph Ltd, 1952.

Vaile, Roland S. "The Use of Advertising During Depression" in *Harvard Business Review*, April 1927, reprinted in *Journal of Advertising History*, No. 4. February 1981.

Wander, Tim, *2MT Writtle, The Birth of British Broadcasting*, Stowmarket, Cappella, 1988.

Wild, Paul "Recreation in Rochdale, 1900–40", in *Working Class Culture, Studies in History and Theory*, ed. Clarke, John et al, London, Hutchinson, 1980, p. 149.

Williams, Raymond *Television: Technology and Cultural Form*, London, Fontana, 1974.

Winston, Brian, *Media Technology and Society, a History: From the Telegraph to the Internet*, London, Routledge, 2003.

Wireless Magazine, November 1930.

Wireless World, 13 October 1933.

Wireless World, 22 December 1933.

Wolfe, Kenneth M. *The Churches and the British Broadcasting Corporation, 1922–1956, The Politics of Broadcast Religion*, London, SCM Press, 1984.

World Radio, 30 May 1930, Vol. X, No. 253.

World Radio, 25 August 1933, Vol. XVII, pp. xxiii–xxiii.

World Radio, 25 February 1938, Vol. XXVI, No. 657.

World Radio, 30 May 1930, Vol. X, No. 253.

World Radio 25 August 1933, Vol. XVII, No. 422.

Wright, Patrick *On Living in an Old Country*, London, Verso, 1985.

Yorkshire Observer, Tuesday, 25 February 1936.

Yorkshire Observer, Monday, 2 March 1936.

Websites

Adventures in CyberSound: Recording on Wire and Steel Ribbon. Accessed April 1999. (http://www.cinemedia.net/SFCV-RM11-Annex/rnaughton/BLATTNER_STILLE.html)

Chronology of Magnetic Recording Accessed June 1999. (http://www.ri.rutgers.edu/~dmorton/mrchrono.html)

Nagra Historical Account (http://www.nagra.co/nagra/history.htm)

Plan for the Preservation of Norwegian Sound Recordings, chapter 5. Accessed June 1999. (http://www.nbr.no/verneplan/lyd/english/e03.html

Simeon, Pascal *T.S.F. et Rediffusion: La Radio a Lyon, ses Debuts,son Histoir*. Accessed May 2002. (http://pascalsimeon.free.fr/radioly.htm)

Recordings

Allelujah, Mozart. Elizabeth Schumann/Henry Wood and the BBC Symphony Orchestra, 8 September 1936, Queens Hall, London, Philips-Miller recording. Collection of Seán Street, donated by Antony Askew.

Carroll Levis and His Discoveries, Radio Luxembourg, February 1937. Collection of Seán Street, donated by Andrew Emmerson.

IBC Goodnight Melody from *Searching the Ether*, Audio cassette in the series, "Radio Nostalgia", RN8, STEMRA, Holland, 1982. First broadcast on the ILR Programme Sharing Scheme, 1982, distributed by the AIRC.

It's Time to Say Goodnight, Radio Luxembourg close-down theme: from *The Early Pirates*, Audio Cassette in the series, "Radio Nostalgia" RN7, STEMRA, Holland, 1981.

Laugh and Grow Fit, Joe Murgatroyd and Poppet. Radio Normandy, 1936, Collection of Seán Street, donated by Billie Love.

Poste Parisien Gong, and commercial from *Les Radios Privées d'avant-guerre: Radio-Cité, Poste Parisien de 1935 à 1940*, Commercial CD, EPM Musique, Paris 983012, 1994.

Radio Normandy Calling Radio Normandy disc recording, later transferred to tape, 1937. Collection of Seán Street, donated by Andrew Emmerson.

Radio Normandy Wavelength change, 1934. Collection of Seán Street, donated by Raymond Welch-Bartram.

Sweeney Todd, Blattnerphone recording, later transferred to disc, BBC Regional Programme, 1934. Collection of Seán Street, donated by Antony Askew.

Symphony No. 39, Minuet and Trio, Mozart, Thomas Beecham and the London Philharmonic Orchestra, 19 November 1936, live recording at BASF, Ludwigshafen, Germany, K2 dc biased tape recorder. Collection of Seán Street, donated by Antony Askew.

The First Pirate, feature, King, Brian, (Producer) BBC Radio 4, 14 January 2000. Collection of Seán Street, donated by Ken Garner.

The League of Ovaltineys, Radio Luxembourg, 1938. Collection of Seán Street, donated by Andrew Emmerson.

There's Something of Importance in the Air, J. Walter Thompson Sampler Record, 1938. Collection of Seán Street, donated by Andrew Emmerson.

Tune In (Holmes/Sarony), Radio Luxembourg Theme, Jack Payne and His Band, from Audio Cassette, *Stars of the Radio*, MCI Spoken Word, GAGDMC001, 1994

Vox Publicity Products, promotional recording presented by Christopher Stone, Circa Spring 1934. Collection of Seán Street, donated by Raymond Welch-Bartram.

We Can't Let You Broadcast That, Long Norman. Recorded 16 September 1933, Columbia Records, CA 13302, reissued 1989, Conifer Records, MCHD 163 as part of the compilation, *Radio Days*.

APPENDICES

Appendix A

Commercial Competition – the Stations

Tune in RADIO LYONS! You can rely on something interesting from this new station on Sundays and weekdays. The wavelength is 215 metres – not far below BBC's National, on medium wave-band.[853]

The sheer quantity of programming reaching British listeners from the Continent and Ireland in the latter, increasingly sophisticated phase of pre-war commercial radio from 1935 to 1939, was significant in a number of ways. It provided output which, although varying from station to station in terms of day-to-day coverage, in every case attacked the BBC Sunday policy. From 1936 it became increasingly clear to the BBC that stopping the broadcasts was not going to be possible, at the same time as the deteriorating international situation and its responsibilities at home were increasing.[854] The Anglo-continental partnership provided income for the radio stations themselves; this was particularly important the French "Postes-Privés" from 1935, when the Depression from which Britain was starting to emerge was striking France with full force.

For the British audience what amounted to a virtual network provided choice in listening. Sustaining programmes varied from station to station. On the other hand, agencies would buy airtime on different stations to transmit the same programme at an alternative time. For example in 1937, listeners could choose whether to listen to the serial dramatisation of Sax Rohmer's "Fu Manchu", sponsored by Milk of Magnesia, each Sunday either on Radio Luxembourg at 7.00 p.m. or on Radio Lyons at 10.15 p.m., the sponsoring buying advertising space in *Radio Pictorial* to alert readers to the fact.[855] The makers of Carters' Little Liver Pills likewise bought time on Luxembourg, Normandy and Poste Parisien during the summer of 1938

853 *Radio Pictorial*, 15 January 1937, p. 34.

854 Briggs, Asa *The History of Broadcasting in the United Kingdom, Volume II, The Golden Age of Wireless*, Oxford, Oxford University Press, 1995, p. 338. Briggs points out that the anti-commercial radio lobby aimed at France was constantly thwarted by what he calls "the kaleidoscopic French governments of the 1930s". No one government remained in power long enough to see through its legislation.

855 *Radio Pictorial*, 10 December 1937, p. 24.

for its *Carter's Caravan* programme of "Songs, Drama and Music", spreading content – and its message throughout the week:

Radio Luxembourg:	11.15 a.m. Sunday, 8.45 a.m. Monday, 8.30 a.m. Thursday
Radio Normandy:	2.45 p.m. Sunday, 9.00 a.m. Monday, 10.15 a.m. Tuesday, 10.15 a.m. Thursday
Poste Parisien:	10.30 a.m. Sunday, 9.15 a.m. Friday[856]

At the coming of war, the American model of commercial radio was confidently operating across Europe in English, and by 1938, US style soap operas had become a part of daytime broadcasting on Radios Normandy and Luxembourg. This development in itself provides us with speculation as to how the culture of broadcasting might have changed, had circumstances permitted competition to continue. The private radio stations which sold air time to British commercial broadcasters during the 1930s were a vital part of the process by which populist programming challenged the BBC's monopoly. In addition, these stations had existences independent of their English language function, as domestic broadcasters in their own right. Most of them did not survive the Second World War; post-war French government legislation prevented the return of "Les postes-privés" and their existence up until 1939 provides an ideal opportunity to examine commercial radio at the time and a glimpse at a lost era of European broadcasting. The International Broadcasting Company's policy, particularly in the years up to 1934, was to initially test station performance by buying small amounts airtime of half an hour to an hour; in some cases, as with Poste Parisien (see below) this led to further more significant development. In others the experiments were abandoned. In the pages of *Radio Pictorial* Radio Barcelona, Valencia, San Sebastian, Union Radio, Madrid, Radio Ljubljana and Rome all make appearances in the listings pages for brief periods, always providing a routine diet of records of light music. (We have seen in the section of this book on BBC response how the Corporation was actively monitoring these transmissions.) This appendix examines these stations, both from the point of view of their creation and domestic policy, and the way they were used by British agencies and broadcasters. I concentrate here on the stations whose partnership with British commercial companies was actively nurtured and which had a significant impact either on the pattern of listening in Britain, or the cultural and technical debate of the time – or both. I will begin this exploration with Radio Athlone, given that it was somewhat exceptional to the norm of commercial concerns of the time, being the only station to broadcast into Britain from the *west* as opposed to the Continent of Europe.

Radio Athlone

Part one of my examination of the BBC's response to commercial pressure discusses the case of Radio Athlone briefly in relation to the Corporation's reaction. Radio Athlone presents a unique case: a State-run broadcaster, initially part-funded by licence fees and part by customs duties. Its opening on 6 February 1933, had been attended by de Valera, at the time President of the Executive Council, accompanied

---

856   *Radio Pictorial*, 6 May 1938, p. 25.

by Sean T. O'Kelly, then Vice-President of the Executive Council, and a future President of Ireland, and Sean MacEntee, the Minister of Finance. The launch was announced by *The Sunday Referee* the previous day under the headline, "Ireland's New Radio Station":

> The new wireless station at Moydrum, Athlone, which will be formally opened tomorrow night by President de Valera, will be one of the most powerful in Europe. It cost £75,000 to build, and incorporates every recent improvement and advance in radio science.[857]

From the start it was a powerful station – 60kW, although this was later increased. (See below). A growing awareness of the Continental commercial radio developments was well established in Ireland from 1930 and this led in 1932 to the issue of advertisements by the Dail inviting applications from interested parties to supply sponsored programmes.[858] We have seen how the initial contract to run the station as a part-commercial enterprise had been granted to Radio Athlone Publicity, funded by the Australian magazine, *Smith's Weekly* which had initially outbid the International Broadcasting Company for the concession in the Spring of 1933, with the first sponsored programmes being broadcast in April. Because of the new and unknown nature of Athlone Radio Publicity, the Government obtained a guarantee from the New Ireland Asurance Company Ltd, covering payments to December 1933.[859] In the event this was to prove a shrewd decision. By June problems were beginning to develop in the partnership, with Athlone Publicity complaining that they were not receiving adequate service from the broadcaster in technical terms. Nevertheless in the August edition of *Wireless Magazine* there were positive words from the company through "W.J. Hernan, who is in charge of the Dublin office".[860] The account gave much cause for commercial optimism:

> One large radio manufacturer already sponsoring programmes through French stations has arranged sixty-seven high-class concerts through Athlone. A group of prominent British advertising agents have prepared a report which is favourable to sponsoring, and so it is unlikely that there will be shortage of material.[861]

Even as this article was going to press, things came to a head between Athlone Radio Publicity and the Government, the company failing to make the advance payment for its next period of the concession; A.R.P. prompted "vanished from the scene".[862] When Athlone Radio Publicity failed to deliver to its promise, The New Irish Assurance Company took over the financial running of the station, appointing the IBC briefly in April 1934 as its agent.[863] Gorham states that:

> It proved very difficult to sell time at the full rate on Radio Athlone. So the advertising programmes and the products they advertised were mostly cheap:

857   *The Sunday Referee*, 5 February 1933, p. 12.
858   Gorham, Maurice *Forty Years of Irish Broadcasting*, Dublin, Talbot Press, 1967, p. 87.
859   Gorham, p. 87.
860   *Wireless World*, August 1933, p. 52.
861   Ibid.
862   Ibid.
863   Gorham, pp. 87–88.

record programmes – and not always very new records – advertising patent medicines and cosmetics were typical of the fare. Only the Hospitals Trust, the body that ran the famous Irish Hospitals Sweepstakes, continued to put on programmes of a higher standard.[864]

After only a few weeks, the contract with the IBC was dropped, and the Irish government made a decision in May 1935 that no non-Irish advertisers would be permitted to sponsor programmes. The only advertiser on Athlone became the Hospitals Trust, which bought half-an-hour each weekday at a pro rata rate of £60.00 per hour.[865] In January 1937 transmitter power was increased to 100kW, the most that was permitted to Ireland by international agreement.[866] By this time the Hospitals Trust programmes, now extended to an hour per evening between 9.30 p.m. and 10.30 p.m. seven nights a week, were being listed in *Radio Pictorial*, "programming devised, arranged and produced by Irish Radio Productions, Hibernian Bank Chambers, St. Andrew Street, Dublin". The material consisted of gramophone records, and on certain evenings, recordings of horse racing commentary.[867] The journal billed the output as "On the Air – Radio Athlone!" surrounding the words with the symbols of a shamrock, a horse shoe and a black cat.[868]

From the end of that year, the station became known as "Radio Eireann" although little else appears to have changed in the *Radio Pictorial* weekly listing, apart from the headline: "Radio Eireann for Luck".[869] In the last published edition of *Radio Pictorial* the format remains unchanged,[870] demonstrating that after the early experiments with commercial radio, the pre-war situation in Ireland was remarkably stable.

EAQ Madrid

Some examination of the development of EAQ Madrid has been undertaken earlier in this book. Given that the station – although never fully developed by the IBC as an English language outlet for programming – became the highest profile of the broadcasters offering an English concession outside of France and Luxembourg, more should be said here of its origins. Significantly it was a Short Wave broadcaster with the express purpose of providing an international service; it was thus of interest to Leonard Plugge's organisation as a potentially global extension of commercial broadcasting. In the event this did not happen, and English transmissions by the IBC remained at no more than half an hour on Sundays between 12 midnight and

864   Ibid., p. 88. In fact, Gorham's comment of "patent medicines and cosmetics" could be applied to a great many of the IBC's sponsorship deals elsewhere in their growing empire, as well as those struck by the agencies who were also making sponsored programmes at the time.

865   Gorham, p. 91.

866   Gorham, p. 105.

867   *Radio Pictorial* 10 December 1937, p. 35. Gorham states that "Disc recording was installed in November 1936", p. 104.

868   *Radio Pictorial*, 10 December 1937, p. 35.

869   *Radio Pictorial*, 18 March 1938, p. 36. The name-change seems to have been fuelled by popular sentiment rather than any official policy. Gorham states that the public referred to the station as "Radio Eireann", and "The new name was habitually used in inter-departmental memoranda and in the Dail, but it was not legally recognised until it was adopted as the name of the joint television and sound broadcasting authority in the Act of 1960". (Gorham, pp. 105–106.)

870   *Radio Pictorial*, 18 August 1939, p. 38.

12.30 a.m., although consistent from late 1932 to the outbreak of the Spanish Civil War in July 1936. It is also true to say that by naming this nominal output as "The IBC Empire Service", Plugge was seeking, as so often, to undermine the BBC which on 19 December 1932 had launched its own Empire Service. A key text in understanding the development of EAQ from a Spanish perspective is *The Origins of Overseas Broadcasting in Spain* by Francisco Jose Montes Fernadez, and in particular his chapter on EAQ.[871]

The development of the station grew out of the creation of Radiodifusion Iberoamericana by the Spanish broadcaster Transradio Central in Madrid, with the intention of establishing a Spanish radio World Service. New studios began operating on 14 April 1932 and were connected by landline to the large 20kW Aranjuez transmitter 50 kilometres from the city.[872] Fernandez states that there were two aerials, "one directed towards South America, the other towards North America".[873] The official inauguration of the station was in May 1932, and in its first issue, the *EAQ Magazine* described the event:

> On Saturday 21 May the studio of this important station was officially opened in the presence of the President of the Republic, don Niceto Alcala Zamora, accompanied by the minister of state, senor Zulueta, and other dignatories. They were received by the President of the Administration, senor Setuian, the counsellors don Jose Asensio and don Manuel Escolano, the director general senor Villanueva [don Alberto Villanueva Labayen] and five executives from RIA. After some preliminary words in Spanish and English, spoken by senor Villanueva, the President of the Republic made a short but notable speech which was translated and broadcast immediately afterwards in English.[874]

The schedule of EAQ , which Fernandez describes as being "basically made up of musical features, information, entertainment and cultural bulletins",[875] was transmitted principally in the late evening and earlier morning hours, Spanish time, in order to reach overseas time-zones at appropriate listening times. In addition "on Saturdays ... there was a special programme in Castillian Spanish of more than two hours duration aimed at the Canary Islands, Guinea and Continental Europe from 6.00 p.m. – 8.00 p.m., mostly consisting of musical items".[876] He further states that:

> One of the sources of income for EAQ was selling programme time to interested parties who would in turn use the time for their own benefit. For example, the Protestant religious community for a certain period bought broadcast time to disseminate its doctrine by means of recordings in English.[877]

871   Francisco Jose Montes Fernadez: *The Origins of Overseas Broadcasting in Spain*, Madrid, RTVE, 1988. I am also grateful to Snr. Fernandez for much helpful material supplied in correspondence.

872   Fernandez, p. 104.

873   Ibid.

874   EAQ Magazine, Number 1, June 1932, pp. 1–2.

875   Fernandez, pp. 110–111.

876   Ibid., p. 111.

877   Ibid., p. 110.

In the first two and half years of the station's career, the IBC, was able to avail itself of EAQ's requirement to fill air time and build funds, by buying airtime on alternate evenings. For a time IBC broadcasts in 1934 were coming from two Madrid stations – EAQ (30 metres Short Wave) and Union Radio (274 metres Medium Wave) on an alternate nightly basis. The broadcasts were both introduced by the IBC announcer, H. Gordon Box. On other evenings the same announcer could be heard on Radio San Sebastian (Monday, 1.00 a.m. – 2.00 a.m.), Radio Barcelona (Wednesday, 1.00 a.m. – 2.00 a.m.) and Radio Valencia (Friday, 1.00 a.m. – 2.00 a.m.)[878] In every case, the broadcasts consisted of Box playing gramophone records. In November 1935 however transmissions grew more sophisticated due to the success of the station, and consequent investment, and in November 1935 were divided into three schedules:

Transmission 1: 10.30 p.m. – 12 midnight, directed at Spanish speakers in North America and Europe.
Transmission 2: 12.midnight – 12.30 a.m.:popular programmes for English speakers worldwide.
Transmission 3: 12.30 a.m. – 2.30 a.m., directed at all Spanish listeners, worldwide.[879]

The concession to the IBC was from this point granted on Sundays only in place of the Spanish-originated English language material. In 1935, EAQ expanded its output in other fields, and IBC transmissions were limited to Sunday until the outbreak of the Spanish Civil War. In January 1937 *Radio Pictorial*'s continental correspondent pointed to a radically changed situation, and a developing political/propaganda purpose behind broadcasting in the region:

> Before the upheaval Spain only had one short-wave station in Madrid. Nowadays there are large numbers of stations, some in Barcelona, others in or near Madrid, another at Seville, Burgos, etc. After midnight the very latest war reports can be heard from both sides, and some of the stations have the bulletins read by Englishmen.[880]

Inspite of the darkening European situation, it appears that the International Broadcasting Company did not relinquish its hopes of restarting and developing programmes from EAQ Madrid. The IBC produced its own slim programme sheet, independent of *Radio Pictorial*, for International Broadcasting Club Members. As late as mid-June 1938, the sheet is listing "IBC Short-Wave Empire Transmissions: EAQ Madrid, Announcer EE Allen. Transmissions Temporally Suspended".[881]

Poste Parisien

Poste Parisien, billed in *Radio Pictorial* up to May 1938 as "The Paris Station, Poste Parisien", although never a truly international station in the sense of EAQ, came to see itself as having a substantial audience outside its native France.[882] La Poste Parisien – originally La Poste Petit Parisien – was the fourth French radio station

878 *Radio Pictorial*, 19 October 1934, pp. 22–25.
879 Ibid.
880 Gulliland, A.A. "Europe's Short-Wave Secrets", *Radio Pictorial*, 22 January 1937, pp. 11–12.
881 *The IBC Programme Sheet*, 12 June 1938, The International Broadcasting Company, p. 6.
882 A 1937 poster in the author's collection proclaims: "Le poste Parisien – le poste français que le monde écoute".

to open, and the first European station owned entirely by a newspaper.[883] Paul Dupuy, Managing Director of the journal, *Le Petit Parisien* was a strong force in its early years, succeeded after his death in 1927 by his son Pierre, who retained a place on the station's board even after it was floated by the creation of la Compagnie d'energie Radioelectrique in 1929, a move which was to transform Poste Parisien into one of the most famous commercial broadcasters in Europe. The birth of the station was inspired by a visit Dupuy the elder and some colleagues made to the United States where they experienced some of the early commercial radio experiments; while there they purchased a 500 watts Western Electric transmitter, which was set up at new studios, initially at 18, rue d'Enghien in Paris, within the premises of the newspaper itself. Unauthorised broadcasting began on 3 July 1923[884] and was ratified on 23 May 1924 by de Loucheur, the PTT minister in Poincaré's government of the first part of that year. From the start Poste Parien sought to be international; in its early years, the station had a Anglo-French bias; Duval quotes the journal *L'Antenne* reporting the station's identification: "'Poste Parisien: Allo, ici poste du Petit Parisien (348m)', a male speaker, who then repeats the announcement in English. The start of transmissions is announced in French and English, as is the close down."[885]

On 25 October 1929 the flotation of the station, raising 5,500,000 francs through the sale of 50,000 shares at 100 francs each,[886] led to the creation of an ultra-modern studio complex on the Champs Elysees, and a 60 kW transmitter which made Poste Parisien one of the most powerful broadcasters in France. The new studios conformed to the very latest acoustical knowledge.[887] Roy Plomley, visiting Poste Parisien in 1932 referred to it in his autobiography as "the smartest of the private stations operating in Paris ... the studios were modern, the equipment was superb, and there was a pleasant atmosphere of chic".[888] The main auditorium consisted of a concert hall 200 metres square by 6 metres high. In addition two smaller studios provided facilities for more intimate musical ensembles, record presentations and speech programming. Listening rooms, technical control centres and artistes' "green rooms" completed the complex.[889] On 25 April 1932,[890] the new studios were opened in the presence of the President of the Republic, Paul Doumer;[891] it was a significant moment for radio in France. Duval suggests the relaunch of Poste Parisien to be "the birth of modern radio in France".[892] Rare recordings of the

883 Duval, Rene *Histoire de la Radio en France*, Paris, Editions Alain Moreau, 1979, p. 103.
884 Brochand, Christian *Histoire Generale de la Radio et de la Television en France Volume 1, 1921–1944* Paris, La Documentation Francaise, 1994, p. 204.
885 *L'Antenne*, September 1927, quoted in Duval, p. 104.
886 Duval, p. 105.
887 Ibid., p. 107.
888 Plomley, Roy *Days Seemed Longer*, London, Eyre Methuen, 1980, p. 115.
889 Ibid.
890 Broadcasting House in London was opened on 20 May.
891 One of Doumer's last engagements. On 10 May he was assassinated while attending a charity event at the Rothschild Foundation by a Belarussian émigré called Gorguloff, who shot Doumer while he was talking to the novelist, Claude Farrere. Doumer died of his wounds 14 hours later. Gorguloff was later declared insane. (Alfred Cobban: *A History of Modern France Volume 3, France of the Republics*, Jonathan Cape, London, 1965, pp. 133–134.)

station's French output during the 1930s predict station identification practices which survived World War Two. For example the programme punctuation of "The Poste Parisien Gong"[893] was later to become the trademark of Radio Luxembourg's English language transmissions.

The dual language policy, no doubt instigated by the English director – and chief announcer – of the station, Douglas Pollock,[894] was to grow consistently during the 1930s in partnership with the IBC. As has been stated, it was the policy of the IBC to begin a concession by broadcasting in English for a short time each week, and to measure public response in the United Kingdom, "as happened in the case of Poste Parisien, which was transmitting in English for eighteen hours a week by the outbreak of war".[895] A comparison between IBC broadcasts as advertised in *Radio Pictorial* magazine from 1934 and 1938 respectively will illustrate this point. On Sunday, 21 October 1934, IBC transmissions from Poste Parisien began at 5.00 p.m. with a programme of light orchestral music on gramophone records. The subsequent schedule was as follows:

5.30 p.m.	*Another Wonderful Symington's Soups Film Star Competition Broadcast* [Sound tracks from actual films, featuring favourite film stars in their most popular numbers.]
6.00 p.m.	*Orchestral Concert* [Gramophone Records, including Luigini: Ballet Egyptien, Oscar Strauss: Waltz Dream etc.]
6.30 p.m.	*Socapools' Broadcast* [Gramophone Records, including Lehar: You are my Heart's Delight, Wallace: Old Father Thames, etc.]
7.00 p.m.	Close Down
10.30 p.m.	*William S. Murphy's (Edinburgh) Broadcast* [Gramophone Records, including Romberg: The New Moon, Posford: Goodnight Vienna, etc. Note: Murphy was a Football Pools company.]
11.00 p.m.	*Wincarnis Concert: "Broadway Hits"* Specially Recorded in New York by the Wincarnis Broadway Boys
11.15 p.m.	*Strang's Football Pools Broadcast* [Gramophone Records, including Romberg: Deep in my Heart Dear (The Student Prince, Lohr, Little Grey Home in the West, etc.]
11.45 p.m.	Close down[896]

In *Radio Pictorial* dated 6th May 1938, we find that Poste Parisien is being marketed in a different way. The logo frames the station name in a circle, over the Eiffel Tower. It is however relatively small, and the anglicised version of the name, "Paris Broadcasting Station" takes precedence, together with the slogan, "Gay like Paris". The schedule for Sunday 8th May divides output between morning (9.00 a.m. – 11.00 a.m.) and early evening (5.00 p.m. – 7.00 p.m.). Although only slightly longer than the 1934 transmission, the latter schedule shows a more sophisticated

---

892   Ibid., p. 131.

893   CD Appendix (H) track 8. Poste Parisien "Gong" followed by commercial, broadcast 2 November 1937. *Les radios Privées d'avant Guerre*, EPM Musique, 983012–3.

894   Duval, p. 104.

895   Plomley, p. 124.

896   *Radio Pictorial*, 19 October 1934, p. 21.

approach to audience requirements. The morning output, all gramophone records, is a series of fifteen minute programmes (Station Announcer, John Sullivan), only some of which are sponsored. The 5.00 p.m. – 7.00 p.m. slot is however quite different:

5.00 p.m.	*Horlicks Picture House* MC: Ben Lyon, with June Clyde, Vic Oliver, Leslie Kentish, the Rhythm Brothers and The Horlicks All-Star Orchestra under Debroy Somers.
6.00 p.m.	*Lux Radio Theatre*
6.30 p.m.	*Rinso Radio Revue* Featuring Jack Hylton and His Band, Al and Bob Harvey, Tommy Handley, The Henderson Twins, Sam Browne, Alice Mann, Peggy Dell, Compered by Eddie Pola.
7.00 p.m.	Close Down[897]

It can be seen from this schedule that production effort has clearly been invested in parts of the schedule which have been identified as being of maximum significance in audience terms, with productions by agencies, aimed at times of maximum audience. Meanwhile the morning output has been delivered at minimum cost to the producing company (the IBC) while endeavouring to demonstrate to potential advertisers the power of radio as a medium for publicity.

Radio Méditerrannée (Radio-Côte d'Azur/Nice Juan-les-Pins)

Founded originally in the Municipal Casino at Juan-les-Pins, the station went through two name changes before arriving at Radio Méditerranée, although its IBC transmissions were consistently billed in Britain as emanating from "Radio Côte d'Azur (Juan-les Pins)" Under its first name of Juan-le-Pins, it began broadcasting in 1927, financed by L'Association Radiophonique de la Côte d'Azur. On 25 July 1930, the society was formally constituted, and from this point the station became known as Radio-Côte d'Azur. By 1931 its domestic programming came under attack for its poor quality of content. Brochand claims this to have been a debate surrounding Les Poste Privés in general at the time, but the Nice station in particular.[898] Criticism of the output is encapsulated in an article in the journal, *La Parole Libre*, of August 1931:

> The society running Nice Juan-les Pins seem to take all the considerable financial gain from commercial radio, but they do not repay this with quality. There is minimum effort put into improving their programmes … It is always the way with private stations, who consider radio to be an affair to make money out of with minimum effort. Radio is throwing its seed to the winds in the hopes of harvesting money.[899]

These views – which would undoubtedly have gained the support of the BBC – would have seemed more justifiable still towards the end of the decade. In the meantime – in 1935 – the French government revealed plans to operate a state

---

897 *Radio Pictorial*, 6 May 1938, p. 32.

898 Brochand, p. 181.

899 Paul Dermée, writing in *La Parole Libre, 2 August 1931*, quoted in Brochand, p. 181.

station from Nice using the title Radio-Côte d'Azur, and demanding that the private station change its name to avoid confusion.[900] From this point it became known as Radio-Méditerranée. In March 1938, the station was taken over by La Société Informations et Transmissions (SIT), led by Max Brusset, a member of George Mandel's cabinet in 1934 and 1940. Nearly six thousand shares were sold, and at the same time Brusset entered into negotiations with the International Broadcasting Company in London. Brochand sees here the probability that the French station was about to move into major development on an international scale, "playing the English commercial card".[901] Late in 1938, Radio Méditerranée obtained a loan of nearly three million francs from the IBC.[902] The purpose of the loan is not clear, but given developments elsewhere it may be that the loaned moneys would have been used to build new transmitters and studios for mutual benefit. In the event the war ended any further activity within a few months.

An examination of programme schedules drawn from *Radio Pictorial* provides an interesting profile of English language programming from the station. In October 1934, the magazine lists a two and a half hour broadcast on Sunday, 21 October from Radio Côte d'Azur (Juan-les-Pins) on 240 metres at a transmitter strength of 10kW, presented by "Miss Leo Bailet, Announcer",[903] and advertised in *Radio Pictorial* in a way which clearly sought to capitalise on the romantic location of the station: "Tune in on Sundays to the Sunny South".[904] The "programmes" were three half-hour broadcasts of gramophone records – *Organ Recital*, *Light Orchestral Music* and *Choral Selections* consecutively, until midnight. Thereafter there was an hour of gramophone records of *Dance Music* followed at 1.00 a.m. by the IBC Goodnight Melody and close down. (Appendix H – CD Track 12.) No advertising is listed, and no further transmissions from the station are scheduled for the rest of the week. The same journal, dated 10 December 1937, shows little change, other than the name and wavelength: "Radio Méditerranée [sic] (Juan-les-Pins), 235.m". Programmes remain confined to Sunday (12 December), and run from 10.30 p.m. – 1.00 a.m., no sponsorship is listed and the schedule, utilising gramophone records exclusively, runs thus:

10.30 p.m.	*Variety*
11.00 p.m.	*Tunes from Here and There*
11.30 p.m.	*Light Orchestral Concert*
12.30 a.m.	*Dance Music*
1.00 a.m.	IBC *Goodnight Melody* and Close Down.[905]

Examination of *Radio Pictorial* magazines through the first half of 1938 reveal no programme listings for the station. By August 1939 however, the station has a considerable presence. In *Radio Pictorial* dated 18 August 1939, it is listed as "Radio Mediterranean (Juan-les-Pins), 227 metres" and sustains a nightly schedule, usually

---

900   Brochand, pp. 212–213.

901   Ibid., p. 213.

902   Documentation Radio-France, no. 82.

903   *Radio Pictorial*, 19 October 1934, p. 22.

904   Ibid., p. 39.

905   *Radio Pictorial*, 10 December 1937, p. 32.

starting at 9.15 p.m., and running for an hour on Monday, Wednesday and Saturday, and approximately two hours on Sunday, Tuesday, Thursday and Friday. The announcer remains Leo Bailet, and intriguingly, no transmitter strength is listed. Relatively short as the transmissions are, they are notable for the increase in ambition, and a sense of providing sampling for audiences as an aid to measurement for possible further development. Programme durations were now mostly divided into fifteen minute segments, and the range of material stretched beyond the mere playing of records. Three times during the week, there was a "transcribed relay from The Coconut Grove, Hollywood". It seems likely that this was a syndicated programme; however, it is clearly an attempt to demonstrate "real" content. Tuesday evening featured a fifty minute unspecified performance by the Monte Carlo Symphony Orchestra, and on Tuesdays and Fridays, from 10.30 p.m. – 11.00 p.m., there was "Dance music relayed from the Sporting Club, Monte Carlo". These schedules, and the investment discussions between Brusset's company and the IBC, suggest that "Radio Mediterranean" could well have been, but for the War, the next major Anglo-Continental radio adventure.

Radio-Lyon (Radio Lyons)

Under its director and founder, Adolphe Anglade, Radio-Lyon began broadcasting from studios at 39, rue de Marseille, Lyon, on 1 September 1924.[906] The station continued to celebrate throughout its life the fact that it was the first French radio station to be built outside Paris: "The First Regional Broadcasting Station".[907] From 15 August 1926, it was administered by Radio-Lyon Transmissions, the company being formally constituted on 21 February 1927. There followed a series of complex domestic negotiations relating to ownership, issues which were finally resolved on 19 March 1928, when work towards financial control on the part of la société Radio-Lyon Emissions produced a flotation which sold shares which securing a total of 1,600,000 francs. The majority of these shares were bought back by Pierre Laval, soon to attain political power and attract ultimate controversy as a prominent member of the Vichy government. From this point on Laval was in control of the station, with the support of the founder, the journalist Adolphe Anglade, who was publicly named as the legal administrator of the Society.[908] In October 1934, the Society received permission to establish a new 25kW transmitter

906   Brochand, p. 209.

907   Gulliland, A.A. "Radio Lyons as I saw it" *Radio Pictorial*, 11 June 1937, p. 7.

908   Brochand, p. 210. See also Raymond Kuhn: *The Media in France*, Routledge, London, 1995 p. 86 and Asa Briggs: *The History of Broadcasting in the United Kingdom Volume II: The Golden Age of Wireless 1927–1939*, Oxford University Press, Oxford, 1995, p. 337. Pierre Laval (1883–1945) was a senator in the French government of Raymond Poincaré at the time of the Radio-Lyon purchase. Having begun his political career on the left, he subsequently moved to the extreme right. He became premier for the first time in January 1931, and returned to the post several times. His most notable role was to be in French foreign policy, and he played a significant although complex and controversial role in the notorious Vichy Government under German occupation firstly under Pétain in 1940, and subsequently as "chief of Government" in 1942. Escaping to Switzerland and thence to Spain in 1945, he returned to France later that year to stand trial for treason. He was sentenced to death, and after a failed attempt at suicide, was shot by firing squad on 15 October 1945. See also P.M.H. Bell: *France and Britain 1900–1940: Entente & Estrangement*, London, Longman, 1996, pp. 189–192 & pp. 194–197, and Peter Neville: *France 1914–69 – The Three Republics*, London, Hodder and Stoughton, 1995, pp. 64–67 and pp. 90–92.

at La Tour-de-Salvagny,[909] in the village of Dardilly, although broadcasting using the facility did not commence until 5 October 1935.

Clearly the considerable power of the transmitter was an attraction to English language broadcasters, and broadcasts began in the autumn of 1936. In its edition of December 1936, *Radio Pictorial* announced the broadcasts under the banner, "Radio Lyons Calling".[910] From this point until the coming of the war, and consequent close down, the station was referred to, anglicised, as "Radio Lyons", the pun being underlined by its marketing symbol of three lions superimposed on a broadcasting dial. The sole British agency for Radio Lyons English language concession was Broadcast Advertising Ltd, of 50, Pall Mall, London SW1, with a programme department at Vox, 10a, Soho Square, London W1.[911] This makes the station's English output interesting in that it is generated by a company other than Wireless Publicity (Radio Luxembourg), J. Walter Thompson or the IBC. From the start, the policy of Broadcast Advertising seems to have been one of creating its own personality broadcasters. In *Radio Pictorial*, 23 December 1936, there is a full page article on "The Man Behind the Golden Voice of Radio Lyons", Tony Melrose. At this point, the station was only broadcasting on Sunday, and the article sought to establish Melrose as a romantic figure, whose voice would be worth tuning in for in its own right.

> Distinguished, intelligent, charming – with a life of remarkable adventures behind him – such is Tony Melrose, director of the new Radio Lyons, and the man whose golden voice has captured the imagination of every listener to this new French station.[912]

The concept of the "Golden Voice" became a continuing marketing ploy; during January 1937, Radio Lyons expanded its output to a daily English service, although content was sparse apart from Sundays. On the same page as the Melrose article is published what may be considered to be one of the earliest examples of a radio popular music "chart", under the title, "Results of Radio Lyons Popularity Contest". The list consisted of twelve recordings of the day, numbered in order of popularity, and with the number of the previous week's placing in brackets after the title:

1	*In a Monastery Garden*	(No. 8)
2	*Request Record*	(No. 6)
3	*Toselli's Serenade*	(No. 7)
4	*Laughing Irish Eyes*	(No. 2)
5	*Huppertz's Poem*	(No. 3)
6	*The New Sow*	(No.11)
7	*Albert and the Lion*	(No. 4)
8	*Sarah, the Sgt. Major's Daughter*	(No. 5)
9	*Oxford Street March*	(No. 1)
10	*The Way You Look Tonight*	(No. 9)

909 Simeon, Pascal *T.S.F. et Rediffusion: La Radio à Lyon, ses Debuts, son Histoire*, http://pascalsimeon.free.fr/radioly.htm

910 *Radio Pictorial*, 23 December 1936, p. 28.

911 Ibid., 18 March 1938, p. 30.

912 Ibid., 23 December 1936, p. 14.

240

11	*Sousa's Marches*	(No.12)	
12	*Organ Grinder's Swing*	(No.10)	[913]

Campbell's soups sponsored a daily broadcast entitled "Film Time" thirty minute programme presented by "Your Man on the Set", featuring "interesting gossip from the film studios" at 4.30 p.m. Initially on certain days this was the ONLY programme to come from Radio Lyons, and there was aggressive marketing of "The Mystery Man of Radio Lyons", featuring photographs of the anonymous broadcaster in a mask.[914] By June 1937, Lyons was carrying six hours of evening programmes – fully sponsored – on Sundays, and two hours, from 10.00 p.m. – midnight for the rest of the week.[915] "The Man on the Set" had by this time been reduced to one broadcast per week – on Saturday evening at 10.30 p.m. Other "mystery voices had been added to the output however, including "The Night Watchman", (nightly, 11.30 p.m. – 11.55 p.m.) and "The Stage Door Lounger", (Monday night, 11.00 p.m.: "Theatre gossip, music and news brought to you by our theatre correspondent").[916] The same issue carried an article – "Radio Lyons as I saw it" – by *Radio Pictorial*'s French correspondent A.A. Gulliland, who introduced readers to yet another personality in the form of station announcer, Gerald Carnes, seeking to give the impression of the traditional eccentric Englishman abroad:

> Gerald Carnes is the great sensation in Lyons at the moment. As he has only been there since December, people have not yet had time to get entirely used to the sight of a young and tall man walking the street in brilliant sunshine with a black hat and – an umbrella! Carefully rolled, it is true, but nevertheless an umbrella. In the cafes they speak of the "mad Anglais" – but the black hat and the umbrella remain.[917]

Programme timings remained set to the pattern of output established by June 1937 through until the outbreak of war. *Radio Pictorial* dated 18 August 1939, shows a programme schedule of somewhat less ambition, but with the notable addition of "Radio Lyons Calling – Introducing Winners of the Radio Lyons Calling Amateur Talent Competitions, and Jan Ralfini and his band in hits and highlights from our roadshow".[918]

Radio-Toulouse

Radio-Toulouse plays a key part in the story of English language commercial broadcasts from the continent, in that it was the first station to broadcast sponsored programmes regularly to Britain from France in 1928, shortly after the illegal boosting of its transmitter strength to 60kW during that year. These were the record programmes, sponsored by Vox Records, and presented by Christopher Stone, monitored by the BBC at Tatsfield. It was to continue to play its part

913   Ibid.
914   Ibid., 15 January 1937, p. 28.
915   Ibid., 11 June 1937, p. 26.
916   Ibid.
917   Ibid., p. 7.
918   Ibid, 18 August 1939, p. 38.

intermittently during the 1930s, largely through the significant figure of its director, Jacques Tremoulet who, with his business partner, Louis Kierzkowski, was the aggressive guiding light of the station through turbullent years of change and mixed fortunes.

The station began broadcasting on 15 April 1925 with a modest 1.5kW transmitter, and studios at Villa Schmidt, rue Monié, Toulouse.[919] From this point there is a clear ambition to build a larger signal:

1926	2kW
1927	3kW
1928	5kW, then 8kW then 60kW[920]

In 1926, Radio Toulouse had clashed with the wavelength of the BBC's Sheffield station; the two stations adjusted their transmissions slightly and continued side by side.[921] It was part of an issue that was growing at the time as more and more stations came on air, and the matter of wavelength allocation was addressed in The Geneva Plan of the same year.[922]

During the mid 1920s the domestic popularity of Radio-Toulouse appears to have revolved around its station announcer, Jean Roy, who emerges from contemporary documentation as something of a cult figure at this time, largely due to his idiosyncratic pronunciation. This was parodied in the media press, one journalist commenting: "Mr Roy has such a personal manner of speaking and interpreting texts, that he is listened to by all Europe". The journalist then goes on to give examples of Roy's presentation style: "Ici rrrédio Toulouseu ... Pérris-capitale-de-la-Frrrance ..."[923]

The cause of French private radio in general, and Radio Toulouse in particular was given appropriate voice in the magazine, *Le Radiogramme*, which was published by Tremoulet as a support for his private radio interests. In 1927, the journal published a letter from a listener in Nantes. Whether or not the letter was genuine is unclear; nevertheless it was typical of the anti-state radio propaganda generated by the magazine at the time:

> Mr Roy has asked for responses to the broadcast of 23 October last. It is my pleasure to give you my impressions. The programme was better and the quality of the content as satisfactory as anything anywhere. The quality of the transmission was wonderful ... In sum it was an excellent programme, a success right down the line. Bravo Radio-Toulouse! You have blown away the howlings of the PTT. I could compare listening to their extracts from "Manon" broadcast from Marseilles. It was lamentable![924]

Meanwhile spasmodic English programming was coming from the station, organ-

919   Brochand, p. 206.

920   Ibid., p. 208.

921   BBC Written Archives, Caversham, WAC, R13/365/1. See also Scannell, Paddy and Cardiff, David *A Social History of British Broadcasting, 1922–1939*, Oxford, Blackwell,1991, p. 318.

922   Ibid. See also Eckersley, P.P. *The Power Behind the Microphone* , London, The Scientific Book Club, 1942 pp. 81–103. Briggs, Asa *The History of Broadcasting in the United Kingdom, Volume 1: The Birth of Broadcasting 1896–1927*, Oxford, Oxford University Press, 1995, pp. 290–294.

923   *Radio-Magazine*, no. 136, 23 May 1926, quoted in Duval, p. 165.

924   Letter to *Le Radiogramme* no. 157, 6 November 1927, quoted in Duval, pp. 169–170.

ised by the IBC Briggs mentions broadcasts from Radio-Toulouse – in addition to those of 1929 – in 1930 and 1931, and points out that in April 1933, when the IBC began its own programme listings sheet, it included Radio Toulouse with one and a half hours of programmes on Sunday.[925] Prior to this, radio listings in *The Sunday Referee* provide evidence of IBC involvement on the station through January and February 1933 with *The IBC Half Hour*, "(Danvers-Walker, Announcer)".[926]

On 5 April 1933, the Villa Schmidt studios were destroyed by fire, an event which Brochand describes as "providential", permitting as it did the move to better premises at 64 boulevard Carnot, and the replacement of ageing equipment using insurance funding.[927] The station quickly resumed its transmissions, on 1 July 1933, although with a government-enforced reduction in transmitter power of 8kW. English-language broadcasts ceased until 1937; in the meantime Tremoulet began searching elsewhere to explore his international ambitions, turning his attention to the fledgling Radio-Luxembourg. (See below.) Meanwhile one of the many changes of French government at the time, brought André Mallarmé to the post of Minister of Posts, Telegraphy and Telephony in early 1934, and he immediately gave authorisation for a 60kW transmitter, based at St. Agnan. Duval suggests that, "after Poste Parisien, Radio-Toulouse was the most powerful private station in France, and Jacques Tremoulet the builder of truly a radio empire".[928] As early as 1928, Tremoulet was among the first French radio entrepreneurs to show interest in the developing media situation in Luxembourg, and was to ensure co-operation between Radio-Toulouse and Radio Luxembourg in its French language transmissions through the 1930s.[929]

When an English concession was renewed at Toulouse, it was with a different company and on a considerably expanded basis, in a partnership with the British advertising agency, WED Allen, who had struck up a business relation with Peter Eckersley in the hope of building a similar empire to that of the IBC, or better still, of creating their own totally English-language commercial station based on Continental soil.[930] The Allen agency was operated by three brothers, Bill, Sam and Geoffrey, and they and Eckersley were energetically pursuing the project through 1937 and 1938:

> He [Peter Eckersley] and the Allen brothers travelled to Paris and back no fewer than ten different times in one year. Between trips to Paris, he travelled to Berlin, Copenhagen, Dublin, Ljubljana, Juan-les-Pins, Toulouse, Vienna, Rome, Brussels and Andorra, making enquiries from foreign commercial broadcasters about their willingness to accept the programmes.[931]

The Allen group's commercial concession on Radio-Toulouse started in 1937, with an inaugural address by Winston Churchill, followed by a talk by Eckersley.[932]

925   Briggs, Asa *The History of Broadcasting in the United Kingdom, Volume II: The Golden Age of Wireless, 1927–1939*, Oxford, Oxford University Press, pp. 525 and 334.

926   *The Sunday Referee*, 8 January 1933, p. 13.

927   Brochand, p. 209.

928   Duval, p. 208.

929   Ibid., p. 254.

930   Eckersley, Myles, *Prospero's Wireless*, Romsey, Myles Books, 1998, p. 395.

931   Ibid.

Radio Pictorial of 10 December 1937 lists daily programmes from Toulouse, including a request programme, *Yours For the Asking* ("Write to Radio Toulouse, 23 Buckingham Gate, London SW1 and ask them to include your favourite tune").[933] The wavelength was 328.6 metres, and station personnel were listed as "Compere, Joslyn Mainprice, Announcer, Allan Rose". Saturday and Sunday programming ran from 4.00 p.m. until 11.15 p.m., while weekday transmissions were limited to one hour, from 10.15 p.m. – 11.15 p.m. Mostly the output is gramophone records, and little advertising is named, with the exception of *Feen-a-Mint Fanfare*:

> Presenting Fans of the Stars, no.9. Polly Ward, introducing talent selected from her fan mail. Another £10 prize will be awarded for the best criticism of these programmes. Listen-in for full particulars. Presented by the proprietors of Feen-a-Mint, Thames House, London SW1.[934]

The same journal's listing for 4 March and 18 March 1938 show one hour's reduction in broadcasting on Saturday and Sunday, beginning at 5.30 p.m. Output remained mostly gramophone record shows, apart from Horlicks Picture House (J. Walter Thompson) from 10.15 p.m. – 11.15 p.m. on Sunday evening and Saturday programmes of football results and dividend news sponsored by International Sporting Pools Ltd and Empire Pools respectively. Programming information is stated as being supplied by "David Allen and Sons, Limited, 23, Buckingham Gate, London SW1".[935] By May 1938 however, the station disappeared from *Radio Pictorial*'s listings and did not reappear thereafter.

Radio Normandy

The role of Radio Fécamp – subsequently Radio Normandie (Normandy) – in the history of English language commercial radio is crucial to this study.[936] As has been stated above, the first reference to a radio interest in Normandy came from the broadcast greeting from Radio Paris on 24 December 1923, to celebrate the founding of a local radio club which, on 1 January 1924 became "The Association of Normandy Radio Listeners".[937] The true father of Radio Normandie was Fernand Le Grand, director of the Benedictine, the factory producing the famous

932 Ibid. See also Briggs II, p. 337.

933 *Radio Pictorial* 10 December 1937, p. 38.

934 Ibid.

935 *Radio Pictorial* 4 March/18 March 1938, p. 38.

936 The present writer is indebted to Pierre Denis le Sève, grandson of one of the founders of Radio Normandie, René Legros, for information about the station's early years. A correspondence has been carried out from 1996–2001, and has yielded many insights. M. le Sève has himself had a distinguished career in broadcasting, and at the time of this research was a features producer for the BBC's French Service, based in Bush House, London. His father was an engineer, and among his notable achievements was the installation in 1892 of electric lighting in Fécamp, making it the first town in France to possess it. (le Sève correspondence.) A correspondence has also been conducted with André Briand, who at the time of initial contact, in 1996, was 89, and the last surviving member of the French staff of Radio Normandie. Another key source has been a privately published booklet, *Allo! Allo! Ici Radio Normandie*, by Lemaitre, Jean, late president of L'Association des Amis du Vieux-Fécamp. (Pub. Fécamp, L.Durand & Fils, 1984.) Francois Lhote, of the France Radio Club has also supplied advice, information and material on this important station.

937 Le Sève correspondence.

liqueur first developed by the monks of the Benedictine monastery in the town. It was the major industry in Fécamp, and Le Grand's father was the founder.

Fernand Le Grand had been one of the first of "Les Sans Filistes" (See Appendix B) in the area, a friend of Edouard Branly, one of the early pioneers of radio technology, [938] and he became the president of the Association at its foundation. A strong and controversial character, he was "very authoritarian and would not take any opposition".[939] With Legros, Le Grand made the first transmissions from Fécamp in 1924, the irregular broadcasts using the call sign, EF 8 1C,[940] initially from the home of Legros, 11, place du Genéral Leclerc, then from part of the Benedictine Monastery in place de l'Hotel de Ville,[941] and finally from Le Grand's home, Villa Vincelli La Grandière, adjacent to The Benedictine.[942] As the enterprise grew, Le Grand converted his home more formerly into a radio station, turning the drawing room into a studio and investing considerable amounts of money in the increase of transmitter power. Reception reports were received from Rouen, Le Havre, Dieppe and the south of England.[943] In 1928 advertising began, and in the following year (18 February) a government decree formally recognized the right of the station to broadcast, and transmissions began to be subsidized by Fécamp Town Council and Chamber of Commerce.[944] A new transmitter of 250 watts was established outside the town (the original having been on the roof of Villa Vincelli La Grandière), enabling the station to be heard throughout the region,[945] and prompting a name change from "Radio Fécamp" to "Radio Normandie".[946] At this point, Le Grand and Legros developed additional studios in rue George Cuvier, and their enterprise came to the attention of Captain Leonard Plugge, driving through the town in late 1930. Plugge had recently formed the International Broadcasting Company, having conducted experiments in commercial broadcasting through the 1920s from Radio Paris and Radio Toulouse. In a personal account of Plugge's pioneering work, Stephen Williams, one of the first two English announcers on Radio Normandy, provides a delightful picture of the informality of the first business exchanges:

> One day ... driving from Dieppe to Deauville ... he stopped for an aperitif at the Café Colonnes in the small fishing town of Fécamp ... He heard that the youngest of the directors of Benedictine, M. Fernand Le Grand, was a keen wireless amateur with a small wireless transmitter in his living room ... Captain Plugge and M. Le Grand met over a bottle of Benedictine in the

938   Wander, Tim *2MT Writtle, The Birth of British Broadcasting*, Stowmarket, Cappella Publications, 1988, p. 125. Wander describes Branly's achievement thus: "In 1890 in Paris [he] invented his historic coherer detector, where he connected a battery across metal filings ... The fall in resistance of the filings allowed current (i.e. radio waves) to pass, and this was recorded on a morse printer."
939   Le Sève correspondence.
940   Brochand, p. 219, Le Sève correspondence.
941   Le Sève correspondence.
942   Brochand, p. 218.
943   Le Sève correspondence.
944   Ibid.
945   Lemaitre, p. 6.
946   Ibid., p. 7.

drawing room with the wireless set. They soon fixed up a deal. Le Grand would allow Plugge to use his transmitter to broadcast in English at certain times of the day and Plugge would pay him 200 francs an hour. [947]

Ironically Plugge, who was responsible for an earlier English language commercial broadcast, from Radio Paris in 1925 (see below) had begun developing his ideas of purchasing airtime from European broadcasters after forming Radio International Services Ltd in 1927, a company which supplied the BBC with details of foreign broadcasts for publication in *World Radio*.[948]

Williams' account states that immediately after his conversation with Le Grand, Plugge set off to arrange funds with a branch of Lloyds Bank at Le Havre. There he met the Chief Cashier, William Evelyn Kingswell, "obtained some cash and then asked Kingswell if he knew anyone who could go over to Fécamp, take some gramophone records, make up a little list and broadcast on Sundays for an hour or two in English. Kingswell said 'I might do it myself' – and he did!"[949]

Brochand suggests that it is possible to trace the period of the commencement of major British financial interest in the station: "The capital of Radio Normandie which had stood at 100,000 francs in April 1930, had risen by the 21 March 1931 to 500,000 francs ..."[950] He goes on to cite Plugge and the IBC as the new investors; there was some local opposition to foreign investment in the station, and the IBC overcame this by working initially and briefly under the umbrella of a French company, Etablissements Kraemer.[951] Plugge next sought to gain publicity from the British press for the venture, but met with hostility[952] – with the exception of one newspaper, *The Sunday Referee*, a populist sporting weekly owned by Isidore Ostrer of the Gaumont British Picture Corporation.[953] The favourable response from the paper was largely due to the presence on its staff of Valentine Smith, the recently appointed Circulation and Distribution manager, who in 1928, while working for the *Daily Mail*, had chartered a yacht to advertise the paper's insurance scheme through speakers as it cruised round the British coast. The "presenter" of

947 Williams, Stephen, "Pioneering Commercial Radio the 'D-I-Y' Way", *Journal of Advertising History* Volume 10, Number 2, 1987, p. 8. See also Stephen Williams, interviewed by Bickerton, Roger for "The Stephen Williams Story", in *The Historic Record and AV Collector Quarterly*, Issue number 39, April 1996, p. 36.

948 Bickerton, p. 36.

949 Ibid., pp. 36–37.

950 Brochand, p. 220.

951 Ibid.

952 Briggs, Volume II, p. 332: "In the conflict of conceptions the BBC had the full support of the press, which sent deputations on its own account to the Post Office to protest against foreign commercial broadcasts. It also agreed through the Newspaper Proprietors' Association and the Newspaper Society that newspapers would not make use of foreign stations for advertising or publicity purposes". See also *Advertisers' Weekly*, 22 December 1932 and 23 February 1933, cited by Briggs. (Ibid.)

953 Williams, Stephen *Journal of Advertising History*, p. 8. As a result of its publicity and involvement, the *Sunday Referee* was expelled from the N.P.A. in February 1933. It rejoined the Association in November 1934. (Briggs II, p. 334) and from that point involvement with commercial stations ceased. The need to publicise the increasingly active continental radio scene was met by the creation of *Radio Pictorial* in January 1934, published by Bernard Jones Publications Ltd of 37–38, Chancery Lane, Holborn, London W.C. 2. This journal subsequently became the only major source of information for British Listeners on the stations' broadcasts.

this output had been a young Stephen Williams, who had also worked for the *Daily Mail*, and who had moved to the *Sunday Referee* with Smith.[954] Both men were highly enthusiastic about the possibilities of commercial radio, and a weekly page of publicity for the station was established. Plugge employed Stephen Williams and Max Staniforth, former Head of Publicity for Argentine State Railways, and gave them the task "of launching M. Le Grand's half-kilowatt drawing room wireless set as five kilowatt Radio Normandy, the first regular English language commercial broadcasting station selling British goods to British listeners".[955] The crucial element of publicity – mostly lacking in Plugge's earlier experiments during the 1920s – ensured that a considerable audience became aware of the station's work; the IBC and the *Sunday Referee* jointly launched "The International Broadcasting Club". As Stephen Williams later recalled: "Within three weeks nearly 50,000 applications had been received at the *Sunday Referee* offices and in less than three months more than a quarter of a million names were on the books".[956]

Meanwhile the station continued to enjoy considerable success in the French domestic market: in October 1932, programmes for children began "with Tante Francine, the first woman announcer, and Oncle Roland. Tens of thousands of children joined the radio club".[957] Towards the end of 1932, Stephen Williams left the IBC to become Director of Programmes for Radio Publicity, a new broadcasting company founded by a Frenchman, Jacques Gonat, but operating from London. The Company commenced broadcasting on Radio Paris, and subsequently transferred its output to Radio Luxembourg when the French government acquired the station for the development of its national radio network in December 1993 (see below). When this event occurred the old Radio Paris wavelength (206 metres) was taken over by Radio Normandy.[958] After Williams' departure, new members of the English-language staff arrived and further developed IBC interests at Normandy and elsewhere, among them Bob Danvers-Walker and Roy Plomley.

Programming on Radio Normandy was by 1936 – in keeping with broadcasts on other Continental stations run by the IBC and others – largely recorded in London (see above, Radio For Sale). This was augmented by Outside Broadcast recordings, among them the "Radio Normandy Calling" review which toured British theatres, and frequently compered by Roy Plomley.[959] There were a number of "live sustaining" transmissions broadcast from the station in France however, and notable among these was a daily keep fit feature which was broadcast on the station from 1936 to 1939. This featured the variety act, "Joe Murgatroyd and Poppet", and was entitled *Laugh and Grow Fit*. The couple, who took accommodation in rue George Cuvier, wrote, performed and presented the programmes "live" six days a week at 7.45 a.m. Although the broadcasts were almost all "live", the present writer has been able to obtain rare copies of some of the few recordings made by "Joe Murgatroyd and Poppet" through the generous help of their daughter, Billie

954   Ibid., pp. 7–8.
955   Ibid., p. 9.
956   Ibid.
957   Le Sève correspondence.
958   CD Appendix (H) track 9 – Radio Normandy wavelength-change announcement, 1934.
959   Roy Plomley, *Days Seemed Longer*, Eyre Methuen, London, 1980, p. 142.

Love,[960] who has also helped with explanatory information regarding the survival of these documents, unique in the history of the period.

> My mother played the piano for ten songs per programme, each with parodied words to fit the exercises (which were genuine), and my father interpolating Yorkshire stories and quips. Every three months, they went to Paris to record, in one day, a week's programmes, so that they could have a week's holiday. They received extensive fan-mail which I remember, for during the second year of their work there, I was taken to France to go to school in Fécamp, and I helped them to sort the mail.[961]

Love recalls the "cultured tones" of announcer David Davies, as well as other English announcers including Richard Gale, Johnny Evans and Hilary Wontner. "The technical engineer was Cliff Sandall and the station manager was George Busby. The programmes were mostly sponsored by Halex Toothbrushes and Kolynos Toothpaste."[962]

In 1939, Pierre Legros, son of René Legros, set up a new and powerful transmitter on the Caux Plateau, and a government decree permitted Radio Normandy to move its studios to premises adjacent to the giant 170 metre transmission mast at Louvetot, above Caudebec. (The Chateau de Caudebec.)[963] "Now the station could be heard throughout France and the South of England."[964] The new station was indeed spectacular. Opening in June 1939, it prompted an enthusiastic article in the magazine *L'illustration*, which claimed "It has taken its place amongst the greatest French stations":

> A castle has been bought in Caudebec-en-Caux, where all the administrative and broadcasting services in French and English have been centralised. For the English broadcasts, indeed, are only operated by English technicians. Some kilometres from there, between Caudebec-en-Caux and Yvetot, at Louvetot, we find the technical installations and the broadcasting mast looking like a pyramid held on its top. An architectural grouping, Norman style in the best taste has been carried out there. If the metallic mast was not there to give the reasoning [sic] to the group of villas and to the castle of Louvetot, we could believe that this complex is a private town-planners trial done by artists with a brilliant eclecticism.[965]

960 CD Appendix (H) track 10. Joe Murgatroyd and Poppet, "Laugh and Grow Fit". Radio Normandy, 1938 .

961 Love, Billie, correspondence with the present author.

962 *Radio Pictorial* 18 August 1939, p. 33.

963 le Seve correspondence.

964 Ibid. It was just prior to this that the BBC's Maurice Farquharson had visited the new site, and had supplied his colleagues with a graphic account of the opulence afforded by successful commercial radio.

965 Chenevier, R. "A Radiophonic Film, the Birth and the Story of Radio Normandy", *L'illustration*, 17 June, 1939, reprinted in translation in *Offshore Echos* number 105, June 1996, p. 55.

By August 1939, "Joe Murgatroyd and Poppet" had been replaced each morning by Eric Egan, "Radio Normandy's Ambassador of Physical Fitness", who presented a fifteen-minute programme, *Doing the Daily Dozen* at 7.00 a.m., Monday to Friday. By now Radio Normandy was broadcasting fifteen hours of heavily sponsored English language programming every Sunday, beginning at 7.00 a.m., with breaks for French programmes between 11.45 a.m. – 1.30 p.m., and 7.30 p.m. – 10.00 p.m., closing down at 1.00 p.m. The amount of popular drama on the station is noteworthy; the schedule for Sunday, 20 August 1939 included at 7.00 p.m., an episode "in a series of exciting weekly dramas of crime and detection" featuring "one of the late Edgar Wallace's famous characters brought to life. (Presented by Milk of Magnesia)", followed at 7.15 p.m. by *Love Scenes – No 7: The Queen was in the Parlour* by Noel Coward, with Lilian Harrison and Jack Raine (Presented by Coty, England Ltd).[966] Weekday programming ran continuously from 7.00 a.m. until 6.00 p.m., when six hours of French programmes were broadcast by Le Grand's station, after which a further hour of late-night dance music ended the day in English at 1.00 a.m.[967]

Syndicated programming from agencies such as JWT meant that some of the more elaborate speech content could be heard on a number of stations, as has been stated, the most significant cross-overs occurring between Normandy and Luxembourg. Such material included fifteen-minute soap operas aimed at the housewife listener; US-style soaps began broadcasting on Radio Luxembourg and on Radio Normandy during 1938 and 1939, broadcast consecutively on weekday afternoons thus:

2.45 p.m.	*Young Widow Jones*: A moving human story of a woman's heart and a woman's love. Living in the small town of Appleton, Peggy Jones, in her twenties, with two children to support, ponders long on the question of what she owes to her children and what she owes to herself. A story of joy and despair, life and love as we all know it. (Presented by Milk of Magnesia)
3.00 p.m.	*Backstage Wife*: The drama of Mary Noble, a little provincial girl, who married Brian Noble, London's most handsome and popular star, dream sweetheart of a million other women. Hers is the story of struggle to hold the love of her famous husband; of what it means to be the wife of a famous star; of the intrigues, the joys and sorrows that face one in the complicated life backstage of the theatre (Presented by Phillips Magnesia Beauty Creams).
3.15 p.m.	*Stella Dallas*: A continuation of the famous story of a mother whose love for her daughter was the uppermost thought of her life (Sponsored by California Syrup of Figs).[968]

All three of these soaps were American imports, although they were remade for an English audience.[969] The American sponsors, Sterling Drugs, owned the products which were advertised in the British programmes. Indeed, the NBC broadcasts

---

966 Ibid.

967 *Radio Pictorial* 18 August 1939, p. 33.

968 Ibid.

969 See also Gifford, Denis *The Golden Age of Radio*, London, B.T. Batsford Ltd, 1985, pp. 27, 276 & 318.

carried the same names.[970] The weekday trend towards popular drama continued later in the afternoon with further examples of the genre, this time British-developed soaps, although strongly based on the American model, each lasting fifteen minutes, and separated by sustaining music shows:

4.00 p.m.   *Love in an Attic*: the happy-go-lucky artist and his wife invite you to share their ups and downs. (Presented by "Bisurated" Magnesia) ...

4.45 p.m.   *Marmaduke Brown*: The lovable, eccentric inventor and his patient wife, Matilda. (Presented by Phillips' Dental Magnesia)[971]

The scheduling of the programmes, aimed at the younger housewife at home, and the content, that of long-suffering spouses, supporting male "achievers" tell us much about mass media perceptions of women's role in 1930s society. 5.30 p.m. on Monday 21 August, saw the start of a new adventure serial in the mould of *Dick Barton, Special Agent*, and pre-dating the famous BBC series by nearly seven years:

> *Vic Samson, Special Investigator*. The first instalment of an exciting new series of programmes for the children, which will be given every week, Monday to Friday at this time. (Presented by Quaker Wheat and Quaker Rice.)[972]

The last transmission of *Vic Samson* was 7 September 1939, four days after the declaration of war.[973] It was also the last day of Radio Normandy. The station closed down at 1.00 a.m.[974] for the last time, Roy Plomley reading the end-of-day message which accompanied the *IBC Goodnight Melody* as usual.[975] The transmitter was handed over to the French government, officially marking the end of the station, and of pre-war English language commercial radio. As stated above the renamed "Radio International" succeeded Radio Normandy and broadcast until 3

---

970   Cox, Jim *The Great Radio Soap Operas*, Jefferson, North Carolina, McFarland & Company, 1999, pp. 15, 230 & 287. The American version of *Young Widow Jones* was *Young Widder Brown*. This ran from 1938 until 1956 on NBC, as did *Stella Dallas*. *Backstage Wife* began on NBC in August 1935, transferring to CBS in 1955 where it remained for the last four years of its existence, finally coming off the air on 2 January 1959 (Ibid.) Citing as I do in the text, the billing epigraphs for these programmes in their British forms, it is worth including here their American epigraphs:
Young Widder Brown
We present the moving human drama of a woman's heart and a woman's love – YOUNG WIDDER BROWN. In the little town of Simpsonville, attractive Ellen Brown, with two children to support, faces the question of what she owes to them and what she owes to herself. Here's the story of love and life as we all know it.
Backstage Wife
We present BACKSTAGE WIFE, the story of Mary Noble, a little Iowa girl who married one of America's most handsome actors, Larry Noble, matinee idol of a million other women – the story of what it means to be the wife of a famous star.
Stella Dallas
STELLA DALLAS! – The true-to-life story of mother love and sacrifice in which Stella Dallas saw her beloved daughter Laurel marry into wealth and society and, realizing the difference in their tastes and worlds, went out of Laurel's life. These episodes in the later life of Stella Dallas are based on the famous novel of that name by Olive Higgins Prouty and are written by Anne Hummert.
(Ibid).

971   *Radio Pictorial*, 18 August 1939, p. 33.

972   Ibid.

973   Lemaitre, pp. 12–13.

974   Ibid.

975   CD Appendix (H) track 11.

February 1940, four days before the BBC's Allied Expeditionary Forces Service began broadcasting.

Radio Paris

This significant Long Wave broadcaster began its existence as the Levallois Experimental Station, founded by the Radio Club of France on 25 May 1921. The name originated from the fact that the first transmitter was situated on the roof of the Levallois factory of the Société Français Radioélectrique (S.F.R.). This was later moved to a new site, at 84, rue de Landy à Clichy, the studios being situated at 84, boulevard Haussmann. It is not easy to set the precise date for its beginning as a commercial broadcaster: the main founder of the station, Emile Giradeau, claims this to be 6 November 1922,[976] while a publicity document in the archives of Radio France and dating from 1929 states the start as being 5 days earlier, on 1 November.[977] At its opening it was known as "Radiola", changing its name to "Radio Paris" in 1924.[978] It was as Radio Paris that the station broadcast Leonard Plugge's first experiment in English language commercial radio, a fifteen-minute fashion talk sponsored by Selfridges; with no advance publicity, the programme is said to have received only three reception reports from listeners.[979] As with its original French beginnings, the start of major English language developments on the station are problematic. Stephen Williams states:

> My personal interest in Radio Normandy faded when its teething troubles diminished, and quite soon I was asked to take on the job of running a similar English language programme service from Radio Paris, the principal broadcasting station in France, well established and very well equipped, with a power fifteen times greater than that of Radio Normandy. My transfer meant severing all connection with Captain Plugge and his International Broadcasting Company and a loosening of my ties with the *Sunday Referee*, for I became Directeur-général of Radio Publicity, a British company, chaired by a Frenchman (M. Jacques Gonat) and operating in Paris.[980]

Williams provides no date for this move. An article in *The Sunday Referee* dated 8 January 1933 states that "remarkable enthusiasm has been aroused among wireless listeners throughout the country by the initial broadcast last Sunday of the *Sunday Referee Orchestra*" on Radio Paris.[981] This would put the first involvement of the paper as being 1 January. The same issue implies a partnership with the IBC, stating in an article entitled "IBC's plans for 1933": "Mr Williams ... is now in Paris, announcing from 4 to 5 on Sunday afternoons during the SUNDAY REFEREE concert from Radio Paris and from 7–8 in the evening during the Gaumont-British *Film Fans' Hour*".[982] The programmes are listed under a heading which reads "Today's special Transmission by the International Broadcasting Company of London".[983] One week later however, there is a remarkable change: "This week's

976 Giradeau, Emile *Souvenirs de Longue Vie*, Berger-Levrault, Paris, 1968, p. 196.

977 Documentation Radio France number 84.

978 Brochand, p. 199.

979 Baron, Mike *Independent Radio*, Lavenham,Terence Dalton, 1975, p. 12.

980 Williams, *Journal of Advertising History*, p. 10.

981 *The Sunday Referee* 8 January 1933, p. 5.

982 Ibid., p. 13.

IBC Programmes" are listed as coming from Radio Normandy and Radio Toulouse. Radio Paris transmissions in English are not included, but are displayed in two separate special boxes:

> *Tea-Time Variety*. 4.0 p.m. – 5.0 p.m. *"Sunday Referee"* Hour of Non-Stop Variety. Music by Lazarus Goldschmidt and the "Sunday Referee' Orchestra. Stephen H.C. Williams announcing ...

> ... *Film Fans' Hour*. Gaumont-British Picture Corporation's concert. Musical Programme by Roy Fox and his Band. Jessie Matthews, Sonnie Hale and Stephen H.C. Williams announcing.[984]

There is no named production company, but it is clear from this that the IBC is not involved in the broadcasts. This is a symptom of an extremely complex argument relating to the concession for Radio Paris, and subsequently Radio Luxembourg, which will be examined in more detail below. What appears to be the case is that Plugge sought to persuade advertisers and the public that the IBC had a stake in the stations when in fact this was not the case.[985]

As has already been stated the *Sunday Referee's* proprietor was Isidore Ostrer, who held interests in British-Gaumont Pictures; on 8 January, and the paper had advertised the following week's programming with a feature article:

> Next Sunday Roy Fox and his dance band will fly to Paris in a specially chartered aeroplane in order to play during the *Film Fans' Hour*. The items will include several new numbers, and afterwards the band will return to England in time for their initial performance the following evening at the Kit Cat Restaurant, Haymarket, S.W.[986]

It would seem from the evidence that the *Sunday Referee* was seeking to establish itself at the start of 1933 as an aggressive presence in Commercial radio;[987] in spite

---

983   Ibid.

984   Ibid., 15 January 1933, p. 12.

985   See Bickerton, Roger, interview with Stephen Williams in "The Stephen Williams Story", *The Historic Record and AV Collector*, no. 39, April 1996, pp. 33 and 36. Later, due apparently to a misunderstanding between the two sister companies, Radio Publicity, (London) and Wireless Publicity (Universal) a limited amount of IBC programming was included on Luxembourg. See below in the Radio Luxembourg profile.

986   Ibid., 8 January 1933, p. 5.

987   The American marketing trade journal, *Shelf Life* (October 1935) carried an article about Radio advertising in which Ostrer's adventure in Commercial Radio with the *Sunday Referee* was discussed thus: "The only British newspaper ever to use the air for itself, and to associate itself with radio in any form is the *Sunday Referee*, one of Isidore Ostrer's most difficult and worrying properties. When Ostrer first bought the *Referee* from Sir Oswald Stoll, its circulation hovered around the not very robust figure of 20,000. The change of management and new money might have boosted it up a little more, but the figure was still far too uncomfortable for a national Sunday paper. So the *Referee* bought an hour (4–5) every Sunday from Radio Paris (now taken over by French interests) and used it profitably to send its own sales up to something like 160,000 in a little over a year. It published every Sunday a full programme of sponsored programmes from continental stations. Just what would have happened if the paper could have stood the pace for a few years longer is too difficult to speculate about. But the pace was indeed strenuous – after several warnings the *Referee* was finally expelled from the Newspaper Proprietors' Association ..." In fact the article is as we have seen, strictly inaccurate in claiming that no newspaper had been involved with radio up to this point; see Chapters 1, 2 and 6 for the involvement of the *Daily Mail* in early radio sponsorship. That said, this was before the true structure of British radio had been evolved.

of Williams' statement regarding "loosening ... my ties with the *Sunday Referee*", his involvement in these developments remained significant, due to the partnership between Gonat's company, Radio Publicity (Universal), the Associate company of Radio Publicity (London) and the newspaper. Meanwhile the French Government had begun moves to purchase Radio Paris as the central station in its proposed new state-run national radio service. As early as December 1932 Henri Queuille, the PTT Minister, had come to an agreement in principle with the directors of the station, and a contract was signed on 27 January 1933.[988] Negotiations continued through the year to agree a final hand-over date, the interim providing time for the station's private owners and their partners to seek an alternative to the station to continue commercial broadcasting; this coincided with the development of the existing private station in Luxembourg. (See below.) On 3 December 1933, Stephen Williams introduced the *Sunday Referee* programmes, transmitting "live" from both stations from both stations simultaneously. (See below.) Radio Paris re-opened under State control at 9.00 p.m. on 17 December.

Radio Luxembourg

The extent of the *Sunday Referee*'s aspirations in radio at this time may be judged from the leader column in its issue dated 26 November 1933:

> Next week we take over what is perhaps the finest radio station in Europe – Radio Luxembourg – and it will be available to all those advertisers who recognise that broadcast publicity is a sales force which cannot be ignored.[989]

On the day of the launch, the paper publicised the programmes in its Radio Supplement:

> Today marks the beginning of a new era in Sunday radio entertainment with the initial broadcast from the high-powered Luxembourg station of the Sunday Referee concert, the *Film Fans' Hour* and other sponsored concerts under the aegis of this newspaper. For more than two years now the Sunday Referee has been striving continuously for better and brighter Sunday radio for listeners in Great Britain, and today's inauguration will set the seal on yet a further advance in these efforts.[990]

Later in the same article the paper explains its novel solution to the problem of losing its audience as a result of the change-over: "In order that regular listeners to Paris may be notified of the change-over of the *Sunday Referee* programme the Luxembourg concerts will be relayed through Radio Paris".[991] Stephen Williams later explained his role in the process, interspersing programmes with the announcement, "This is Radio Paris and Radio Luxembourg", and advising the audience that from Sunday 10 December, the English broadcasts would be coming from Radio Luxembourg only, and adding:

> Since, at the moment, both stations were broadcasting exactly the same thing at different positions on the dial, listeners could identify Radio Luxembourg's position by moving down the scale until they heard my voice again. "Have

---

988 Brochand, p. 201.

989 The *Sunday Referee*, 26 November 1933, p. 6.

990 Ibid., 3 December 1933, p. 18.

991 Ibid.

you got it?" I asked repeatedly, "Well that's where you will find all our programmes from next Sunday onwards, so do please remember the dial reading and mark it if you can".[992]

It is necessary at this point to clarify the complex relationship between the IBC and Radio Luxembourg. Apparently, through a reading of contemporary publicity that the launch of Luxembourg had been postponed from the summer of 1933, and that the IBC had re-established its relationship with Williams' company and was to play its part in the English-language concession at Radio Luxembourg. The first official announcement of Radio Luxembourg's transmissions in English came from an IBC poster, giving the Hallam Street address and announcing Sunday 4 June as the first day of broadcasting. [993] This in fact is misleading. Although Richard Nichols' book[994] repeatedly refers to the connections between the IBC and Luxembourg, Stephen Williams insists that Plugge's company was not to any great extent "involved in supplying programmes or successful in obtaining the English language concession (although Plugge tried to represent it as having a contract with Radio Luxembourg)".

The beginnings of what was to become the most famous commercial radio station in Europe had been, as with so many of the French stations of the time, a purely amateur project. In 1920 an inaugural meeting of L'Association des Amies de TSF "had been held in a room a the Café Jacoby, in place d'Etoile, Luxembourg".[995] In 1924, the principal members of the Association, led by François Anen, a radio technician, set up a small transmitter of 100 watts in Anen's house on rue Beaumont. Two years later the Luxembourg government voted to subsidise the station to make overseas broadcasts – concerts of military music and theatre, performed in the Luxembourg dialect.[996] In 1928 Jacques Tremoulet, director of Radio Toulouse, sold the Luxembourg station the old Toulouse 3kW transmitter, and the movement towards major development began; in 1929 a powerful board was set up, including Anen, but also with Tremoulet, Henri Etienne, ex- editor of the influential French media journal *L'Antenne*, the French millionaire businessman, Raoul Fernandez as well as Girardeau of Radio Paris.[997] This formidable group proposed a new high-power station for the Grand Duchy, to be run by a group born out of their partnership and entitled Compagnie Luxembourgoise de Radiodiffusion, and on 19 December 1929 it was approved in principle by the Luxembourg government. In January 1930, the modest transmission from rue Beaumont ended,[998] and M. Dupont, Director General of Finance for Luxembourg

---

992   Williams, Stephen, "Pioneering Commercial Radio the 'D-I-Y' Way", *Journal of Advertising History*, Volume 10, Number 2, 1987, p. 11.

993   IBC flyer: "The most powerful broadcasting station in Europe for British Advertisers … The new station which will be the most powerful in Europe is available for British sponsored programmes. For full details and rates apply to International Broadcasting co., Ltd …" Reproduced in Nichols, Richard *Radio Luxembourg, the Station of the Stars*, London, Comet, 1983, p. 29.

994   Ibid.

995   Duval, p. 254.

996   Ibid.

997   Brochand, p. 257, Duval, p. 254.

998   Nichols, p. 13.

signed the statute approving the new station on 20 August 1930.[999] The document was a long one, running to 18 articles, two of which are particularly worthy of note:

> Article 1: The station will be used for the diffusion of an elevated standard of intellectual programme, as well as news and information both general and specific. It will nevertheless allow the concession of advertising.

> Article 2: The power of the transmitter will be not less than 100kW.[1000]

Other stipulations were that the wavelength should be those allocated to Luxembourg at the 1929 Prague conference, any other wavelengths to be by international agreement.[1001]

On 31 October 1931 *Wireless World* reported the establishment of a giant new transmitter on the Junglinster Plateau in Luxembourg, sponsored with French money. The source soon became clear; official sources in Paris stated that Raoul Fernandez, a member of the board of the Compagnie Luxembourgoise de Radiodiffusion had been awarded the Légion d'Honneur for obtaining the concession for the transmitter "entirely under French control".[1002] When the transmitter began testing using 200kW of power in January 1933, it was not on any agreed medium wavelength but on 1250 metres, a long wavelength to which it was not entitled, switching on 15 March 1933 to 1191 LW.[1003] The broadcasts were said to be experimental; however they were still being transmitted in the same format by October, when *Wireless World* noted that:

> To the casual observer they do not bear the mark of "experimental". Luxembourg describes these transmissions as experimental because this station dares not start broadcasting officially on its present wavelength, as this lies in a band reserved for non-public services and can only be used by broadcasting stations after sanction by the countries concerned, and this sanction is lacking.[1004]

Broadcasts were beamed to a number of European countries on specific days of the week, as Nichols states:

Monday	Italy
Tuesday	Belgium
Wednesday	Luxembourg
Thursday	Germany
Friday	Holland
Saturday/Sunday	Britain[1005]

The broadcasts in English began on Sundays at 7.00 p.m. and ended at 11.00 p.m. The content was somewhat subdued – a range of light orchestral music punctuated by talks and news bulletins. What alarmed the BBC and the British Post Office was

---

999   Duval, p. 256.

1000 Annexes aux statuts de la Compagnie Luxembourgoise de Radiodiffusion, Memorial no.45, quoted in Duval, p. 256.

1001 Nichols, p. 13.

1002 *Wireless World* 31 October 1931, cited by Nichols, p. 15.

1003 Nichols, p. 19.

1004 "Radio Luxembourg, An International Broadcasting Problem", *Wireless World*, 13 October 1933, p. 300.

1005 Nichols, p. 19.

the fact that the huge power of the Junglinster transmitter enabled the signal to be heard clearly all over Britain.[1006] We may understand with hindsight that the "experimental" transmissions were in preparation for the move of the Radio Paris broadcasts – also on Long Wave – to Luxembourg later in the year. Complaints to the Luxembourg government were to no avail; the response was that the Compagnie Luxembourgoise de Radiodiffusion, who sold the concession to the British entrepreneurs, was a private concern outside of their control.[1007] Yet the ultimate flaunting of international wavelength regulation was still to come. In May and June 1933 the International Broadcasting Union had held the European Broadcasting Conference in Lucerne. At this conference, Luxembourg applied for a Long Wavelength but was denied.[1008] The Lucerne Plan was due to be implented in January 1934. Meanwhile *Wireless World* in October 1933 questioned the rights and powers of the IBU itself:

> We are inclined to attach much importance to the Union Internationale de Radiodiffusion, but this body is the official expert to the International Union of the Postal Administrations of Europe in all matters regarding broadcasting, and no more. There are even members of the Broadcasters' union who at one time hoped that they would have authority to arbitrate in cases where any broadcasting station might start direct propaganda against the existing Government in a neighbouring country. These hopes have long since been shattered, and it is therefore excusable to ask why the International Broadcasting Union should pass a resolution against Luxembourg whilst no such action is taken against larger countries which are similarly offending.[1009]

The anonymous reporter – using the pseudonym "Wandering Wave", visited both the Junglinster transmitter and the studios, observing "the massive door to the transmitter. The design ... suggests that Luxembourg will encircle the world ..."[1010] Entering the building he found: "... one of Europe's most beautifully laid out broadcasting transmitters working with 200kW in the aerial and ample space provided for the addition of a powerful short-wave transmitter".[1011] He also noticed that "at the beginning of September there were no signs of any possible changes to adapt the transmitter to the medium wavelength prescribed for it under the Lucerne Plan". Visiting the studios at Villa Louvigny in Luxembourg City, he commented: "A series of beautiful new studios have just been completed. Plans are prepared for the building of a large concert hall to act as a studio as well."[1012] In December 1933 the same journal stated the Brussels *Soir* newspaper as reporting that Luxembourg was planning to deliberately flout any attempts to curb its power:

> Radio Luxembourg will refuse to surrender to the Lucerne plan, which required the station to withdraw its long wave and give up two thirds of its

---

1006 Ibid.
1007 Ibid., p. 25.
1008 Briggs, II, p. 334.
1009 *Wireless World*, 13 October 1933, p. 300.
1010 Ibid.
1011 Ibid.
1012 Ibid.

power. The French influences behind the company, it is stated, will triumph as the International Broadcasting Union "has no punitive power".[1013]

By this time as we have seen, two months after the English transmissions had begun there, Luxembourg took over illegally the wavelength of 1304 metres which had been allotted to Warsaw at the Lucerne conference but which had not at the time been taken up.[1014] This effectively made the station a "pirate" in a sense that none of the other continental broadcasters were; it also as Nichols says, had far-reaching effects on the way wavelength regulation was observed – and not observed – for the rest of the century.[1015] *Radio Pictorial* for 19 October 1934 reported the station firmly ensconced the 1304 metres wavelength broadcasting from 12.30 p.m. – 3.45 p.m. on Sunday, ("Announcers S.H.C. Williams and H. Gee") and from 9.00 p.m. – 9.45 p.m. the same evening.[1016] Programmes were sponsored by the Irish Hospitals Sweepstakes, (12.30 p.m. – 1.00 p.m.) Ballito Stockings, (2.00 p.m. – 2.30 p.m.) Vernons' Football Pools (2.30 p.m. – 3.00 p.m.), Wincarnis Wine (3.30 p.m. – 3.45 p.m.), and then for the evening transmission Snowfire make up (9.00 p.m. – 9.15 p.m.) and Symington Soups (9.15 p.m. – 9.45 p.m.) It is noteworthy that there is no mention of programmes sponsored by the *Sunday Referee*. By this time the boycotts put in place by the Newspaper Proprietors Association – including the banning of use of dedicated Newspaper Trains for distribution – had taken effect, and the paper capitulated and abandoned radio. In 1935 it rejoined the N.P.A. and was eventually absorbed into the *News Chronicle*.[1017] *Radio Pictorial* was in any case more than a replacement, and in November 1935, the Communist *Daily Worker*, ironically began publicising commercial content, proclaiming "no other daily newspaper in Britain gives the Luxembourg programme. The *Daily Worker* is now able to fill the gaps".[1018]

It will be seen from the 1934 timings in *Radio Pictorial* that transmissions from Luxembourg by the mid 1930s were still relatively modest in duration and content; the greatest change was to come in early 1936 when a take-over of the British concession was to change the whole sound and character of the station. Williams hints at this in his *Journal of Advertising History* article when he states, "… towards the end of the 'thirties big business interests began to enter the commercial radio field and there was little or no place for individual enthusiasts of the do-it-yourself persuasion".[1019]

Nichols inaccurately explains the background to the events of February 1936 thus: "Radio Luxembourg had been growing rather dissatisfied … since it was clear that the IBC, as middlemen, were performing a task which could easily be handled by the radio station itself, with a resulting increase in revenue".[1020] In point of fact the IBC was only involved in a minor capacity, and through a curious misunder-

1013 *Brussels Soir* reported in *Wireless World*, 22 December 1933, p. 66.

1014 Briggs, p. 335.

1015 Nichols, p. 25.

1016 *Radio Pictorial* 19 October 1934, p. 21.

1017 Williams, p. 12.

1018 *Daily Worker*, 29 November 1935, quoted in Briggs, II, p. 336.

1019 Williams, p. 12.

1020 Nichols, p. 38.

standing between the two branches of Radio Publicity, the true concessionaire. In his interview/ article, "The Stephen Williams Story", Roger Bickerton gives Williams' account:

> Relations between the IBC and Compagnie Luxembourgeoise de Rediffusion (CLR) which owned the station, had been frosty to say the least. Radio Publicity (London) Ltd – the English language concession company – of which Stephen was "Directeur-Général" was well aware of this, but the sales manager of the associate company, Radio Publicity (Universal) Ltd, was not. The result was that RP (U) and the IBC came to some sort of arrangement whereby RL spare time on, e.g. early Sunday morning and occasionally on weekdays, could be made available to clients of IBC.[1021]

The break between Radio Publicity and Radio Luxembourg came about suddenly, on Sunday, 16 February 1936, and was at the instigation of CLR, who "had decided to revoke the concession to Radio Publicity (London) forthwith and to operate through a new agent, Wireless Publicity Ltd".[1022] In its edition of 20 February 1936, *Advertiser's Weekly* broke the news, although the speed of events seem to have caused considerable confusion:

> The Very Strange Affair of Radio Luxembourg: New Company Claims Exclusive Rights for all Advertising Time.

> Strange events have been happening at Radio Luxembourg. First hints of these developments were given last week in *Advertiser's Weekly*, when reference was made to a "mystery radio advertising station" which had been advertising for staff. The name of Mr. Maurice Skitt of Harold Whitehead and staff was given as being one of the principals involved ... Mr Skitt has been appointed as general manager of Wireless Publicity Ltd, a new company which, states a letter from the station director of Radio Luxembourg, has secured exclusive rights for all advertising time on Radio Luxembourg. Wireless Publicity has offices in Electra House, Victoria Embankment. Meanwhile, what is the situation regarding the IBC and Radio Publicity (Universal), Ltd, both of whom are responsible for selling Luxembourg time in this country? An official of IBC said he had no statement to make, but that his company was continuing to supply programmes for British advertisers to the station. Mr. W.J. Collins of Radio Publicity (Universal) Ltd., said "This news is a great surprise to me. I have received no notification whatever that our contract has been terminated ..."[1023]

Williams was replaced almost overnight as resident announcer by S.P. Ogden Smith. Nichols states that "from this day forward the IBC lost the concession to sell airtime on Radio Luxembourg, and despite a high-powered breach of contract court case later in the year (which they lost), the rift was never mended".[1024] This again, is inaccurate, since the IBC at no time held the concession. The court action

1021 Bickerton/Williams, p. 37.
1022 Ibid.
1023 *Advertiser's Weekly*, 20 February 1936, p. 261.
1024 Nichols, p. 39.

was between Radio Publicity (London) and Compagnie Luxembourgeoise de Rediffusion.[1025] Roy Plomley briefly alludes to the incident:

> A fierce legal battle was fought over the English concession, and at one time two rival teams of English announcers were in the Duchy, strictly forbidden to speak to each other. The winners of the battle, Wireless Publicity, still hold the concession today. [1980] [1026]

To make the position absolutely clear, Radio Luxembourg programmes billed in *Radio Pictorial* latterly carried the announcement: "Information supplied by Wireless Publicity, Ltd., Electra House, Victoria Embankment, W.C.2. Sole Agents in the British Empire".[1027]

The years 1936 to 1939 were to see the dominance of Radio Luxembourg in the Commercial Radio sector, an expansion into daily programming and complete dominance of British Sunday listening. *Quaker Quarter Hour*, featuring *Carroll Levis and his Radio Discoveries*, *The Horlicks Picture House* and most famously *The League of Ovaltineys* completed commercial radio's supremacy over the BBC between 1936 and 1939.[1028] The station had its own theme tune, *Tune In*[1029] recorded by Jack Payne (formerly the director of the BBC Band) and even allowed itself the occasional broadcast of light classical music – if the sponsor wished it. On Sunday 20 August 1939, Sir Thomas Beecham conducted the London Philharmonic Orchestra. The programme was sponsored by Beecham's Pills Ltd.[1030]

Radio Luxembourg ceased its pre-war transmissions 18 days after the official declaration of hostilities. Having impressed itself indelibly on the broadcasting map of the decade, it was to be the only commercial radio station to resume English-language broadcasts in 1945. It was however to be events beyond the Second World War, rather than the war itself, which would bring this to pass. Notably in France, as Cécile Meadel has written, legislation "would remove completely the chaos of the situation in radio, to the point that the production of programmes that had been the responsibility of the stations, was placed within the guardianship of the State".[1031]

The solitary return of Radio Luxembourg on 1945, and its survival as a major force in Commercial English language broadcasting through the 1950s and early 1960s provided the only witness to a pre-war broadcasting climate which profoundly affected both the debate on Public Service Broadcasting, and listener attitudes to available programming.

1025 Bickerton/Williams, p. 37.

1026 Plomley, p. 124.

1027 *Radio Pictorial*, 6 May 1938, p. 29.

1028 *Radio Pictorial*, 10 December 1937 (p. 25), 6 May 1938 (p. 24), 18 August 1939 (p. 29).

1029 CD Appendix (H) Track 12.

1030 *Radio Pictorial*, 18 August 1939. Thomas Beecham was a member of the Beecham family, manufacturers of Beecham's Pills.

1031 Meadel, Cécile *Histoire de la Radio des Années Trente*, Paris, Anthropos/INA,1994, p. 12.

French Radio in the 1930s – Control and Chaos

In reality, the complaints from certain elements of the English press against our transmissions are essentially commercial; these newspapers do not like to see English clients continuing to pay some millions of francs to our stations for their advertising, diverting income away from English press accounts. [1032]

Economic, Social and Political Issues

The growth of commercial radio in Britain during the 1930s relied on the cooperation of private companies across Europe; Wireless Publicity and the International Broadcasting Company built their campaigns on the purchase of air-time from domestic stations anxious to boost profits beyond the confines of their home areas. A crucial factor for the IBC was the use of French stations which were perceived as the bedrock for of a commercial radio network aimed at the British listener. There is no doubt that the greatest level of European participation with the British companies at this time came from French stations. This was to change after the Second World War, leaving Radio Luxembourg as the single competitor to post-war BBC programmes. In the meantime France remained the ally of English language Commercial radio interests. Here, therefore, I set the Anglo-Continental partnerships within the political, social and economic context of France during the 1930s.

The administration of a new and ambitiously expanding medium in France after the end of the First World War has to be seen within the *zeitgeist* of an extraordinary era in French politics. It was a period in which private interest and national good seemed at times, for some politicians, to be interchangeable, and when Governments sometimes changed three times in a year, making any sense of cohesive policy

---

[1032] Gentin, François, Minister of Posts, Telegraphy and Telephony, France, memo, 31 January, 1938. Documentation Radio France number 102.

development nigh impossible. Before considering the nature of broadcasting legislation in France before the Second World War therefore, it is necessary to examine significant economic, social and political issues in the history of the 1930s which relate to the development of a partnership with English commercial radio entrepreneurs at the time. I begin by examining this aspect of the issue, and demonstrate that political instability and resulting ministerial inertia within France during the decade relevant to this study was a crucial element in the failure to curb commercial transmissions to the United Kingdom.

Among factors relevant to the search by domestic broadcasters for an audience beyond France was that of population. As Neville has said, "the French population, at around 40 millions barely changed between 1870 and 1940".[1033] At the same time, he goes on:

> Until the end of the Second World War ... France was still a largely agrarian society. Indeed the 1936 census showed that 37 per cent of the working population was still engaged in farming or allied occupations (by comparison Britain had this figure back in 1800).[1034]

There was also considerable financial instability during the period; between 1924 and 1926 there was a major economic crisis in France, caused by a number of factors. Principal among these were the cost of post-war reconstruction, the inability of an impoverished Germany to pay war reparations and a general unwillingness on the part of both government and the public to contemplate the raising of funds through higher taxation. In two years the French franc collapsed catastrophically:[1035]

French Franc	Value to £ sterling
December 1924	90
December 1925	130
July 1926	240

It was through the brilliance of Raymond Poincaré and his Government of "National Salvation" that by 1929, the year of the Wall Street Crash, a recovery had been achieved in France. Ironically in that year Poincaré's health failed, and he was forced to retire.[1036] There were no politicians of his stature to replace him as the new decade opened. For a time the French recovery cushioned the country against the deepening international recession but as Cobban has written, "The apparent immunity of France from world economic diseases was ... an illusion".[1037] By 1933 there were 1,300,000 unemployed, "and both agriculture and industry were in difficulties".[1038]

Attempts at reducing government expenditure failed time after time through the defeat of the proposals of successive Ministers of Finance, leading to political chaos.

1033 Neville, Peter *France 1914–69 – The Three Republics*, London, Hodder and Stoughton, 1995, p. 144.
1034 Ibid.
1035 Ibid., pp. 36–37.
1036 Ibid., pp. 38–39.
1037 Cobban, Alfred *A History of Modern France, Volume Three*, London, Jonathan Cape, 1965, p. 134.
1038 Ibid.

France saw three changes of government in 1932, four in 1933, two in 1934 and two in 1935.[1039] As a result of the combination of economic problems and resultant governmental instability, there came about a growing polarisation between Right and Left, with the Right wing flourishing during the middle of the decade, its strong Neo-Fascist core at the heart of the major rioting in Paris on 6 February 1934, in which twelve people died.[1040] The Communist party regrouped in the following year, and 1935 saw the creation of the Front Populaire, an alliance between Communists, Socialists and Radicals which came to power in the election of April 1936.[1041] Historians agree that the year 1935 was a significant one in the economic conditions of Britain and France; in the former economic recovery had been largely achieved, while in the latter the economy had reached its lowest ebb, and "British political stability was the converse of French turmoil and division".[1042]

In the ferment of French domestic political life, radio grew in importance as the decade proceeded. Kuhn states that the medium was first used in an election campaign in 1932, and was a factor in the Left's election success of 1936, when it was used by the leaders of the Popular Front.[1043] Concern regarding the political bias of private stations grew, as political figures became involved with commercial radio interests; as a result there were those that questioned the political bias and impartiality of news bulletins on such stations.[1044]

Anglo-French Discord

Two events occurred in 1935 which reduced the relationship between Britain and France to its lowest point since the beginning of the century.[1045] These events, the tide of popular Anglophobia which resulted, may be seen as a contributory factor in the French inability – or lack of desire – to respond to British complaints regarding air-time sales to British companies.

In June 1935 Britain signed an agreement with Germany which reduced the limits to the growth of the German navy which had been imposed at the Treaty of Versailles in 1919. Then in October of the same year, Mussolini's fascist troops marched into Ethiopia. In a pact between the British Foreign Secretary, Sir Samuel Hoare, and the French Prime Minister, Pierre Laval, a plan of appeasement was drawn up which would permit Italy to keep its conquered territories. This caused uproar in the British government, and Hoare resigned. With his resignation, the pact collapsed, and although Italy's occupation of Ethiopia was not reversed (indeed by May 1936 it was consolidated)[1046] Anglo-French relations were further damaged.

As a result of these two events, a period of deep distrust grew up between the two

---

1039 Bell, P.M.H. *France and Britain 1900–1940, Entente and Estrangement*, London, Longman, 1996, p. 171.
1040 Tint, Herbert *France Since 1918*, London, Batsford, 1970, p. 54.
1041 Ibid., p. 61.
1042 Bell, p. 172.
1043 Kuhn, Raymond *The Media in France*, London, Routledge, 1995, pp. 85–86.
1044 Ibid., p. 85.
1045 Bell, p. 201.
1046 Ibid., p. 197.

countries, and this manifested itself politically, culturally and in popular opinion. The views of a number of French writers during the 1930s show a growing sense of doubt in the English character. In 1931 André Siegfried's *La Crise Brittanique au Xxe Siècle* claimed that "the mental laziness of the English is extraordinary: they do not like to weary themselves with thought".[1047] Siegfried saw the ruling classes as setting a bad example to the rest of the country "because it was not gentlemanly to work too hard or to do anything very well. Even British political stability, which Siegfried thought was the envy of the world, contributed to the country's inertia.[1048] In 1933 the novelist Jules Romains published a remarkable interpretation of the British conscience, or rather the conscience of a small but influential part of the British nation, speaking of "perpetual idealism" to be found in:

> their natural tendency to be deeply moved by an exhortation or an objection made in the name of a moral ideal or moral law; all material interests are then abruptly set aside. It is, you might say, the legacy of the Puritans and of Cromwell.[1049]

As Bell comments, "This sentiment, Romains believed, was present in no more than three million people, but if those three million felt strongly enough, then Britain and the Empire would follow".[1050] Romains might have been describing the Reithian principle of Public Service Broadcasting at the time. Similar views were expressed André Maurois in *Les Anglais* (1935). In fact these were all writers who were sympathetic to the British, and yet they all identified a central issue, that Britain was a world power in decline, looking to allies across the Atlantic for help, whilst seeing Europe, physically so close, as a culturally distant place. "To crown everything, an influential minority among this extraordinary people was likely at any moment to seize on a moral issue and push aside all material interests – including, very probably, the interests of France."[1051]

After the political controversies of 1935 French attitudes towards Britain hardened; writing in 1954, M.F. Guyard summarised the general view at the time thus: "A people of hypocrites must of course form a hypocritical nation".[1052] The French press launched a savage attack on Britain through the autumn of 1935, which the British Ambassador described as being "of unrivalled bitterness".[1053] Reasoned resentment based on justly criticised errors in British foreign policy now combined with a popular escalation of Anglophobia fuelled by the popular and extreme press. Notable amongst these attacks were three articles by Henri Béraud published in the weekly journal *Gringoire*, under the title, "Faut-il réduire L'Angleterre en esclavage?". ("Must England be reduced to slavery?") Béraud cited as many examples of anti-French attitudes through history, countered by the great heroes

---

1047 Siegfried, André *La Crise Britannique au xxe Siècle*, 1931 quoted in Bell, p. 199.

1048 Ibid.

1049 Romains, Jules *Problèmes Européennes*, 1933, quoted in Bell, pp. 200–201. Romains' most famous work was to be *Les Hommes de Bonne Volonté*, a vast sequence of 27 novels published between 1932 nd 1946, which chronicled French society and the events of the first three decades of the century.

1050 Ibid., p. 201.

1051 Ibid., p. 201.

1052 Guyard, M.M. *L'Image de la Grande-Bretagne dans le Roman Français*, 1954, quoted in Bell, p. 202.

1053 Bell, p. 202.

of his nation, Joan of Arc, Crillon, Jean Bart, Robespierre and Napoleon among them. He was sceptical about British motives even as allies, as in the Great War: "The English fought with us. But it is by no means certain that they fought for us ... When I see England upholding, with the Bible in one hand and the Covenant in the other, the cause of the weak or righteous principles, I cannot help thinking that her own interests are involved."[1054] His conclusion could hardly have been more unequivocal: "I say that I hate this people ... I say and I repeat that England must be reduced to slavery, since in truth the nature of the Empire lies in oppressing and humiliating other peoples".[1055]

The riots in France in 1934 and the perception of a country in complete political disarray had brought the French reputation down in British eyes; now the reverse was true, and relations between the two countries reached their nadir in 1936, although regaining some sort of equitable balance as the shadow of war grew darker through the rest of the decade. Indeed the collapse of successive French governments seemed to undermine the political confidence of the nation from the end of 1936, and as Tint observes, "increasingly demoralised, the French were soon to make no international move at all without British agreement".[1056] In the summer of 1938 Paris gave the British King and Queen a warm welcome during a state visit to cement the Entente Cordiale which would have been unthinkable two years previously.[1057] (It was however an "Entente" which Tint refers to as being of "deceptive warmth".)[1058] In the climate of mutual suspicion and irritation, at a time when the numerous French governments made any kind of continuity of relations with the outside world extremely difficult, it becomes clear that British attempts during the mid-1930s to gain co-operation in the maintenance of its domestic broadcasting monopoly would be met at best by an inability to act and at worst by a determination not to do so.

State and Private Broadcasting

The failure of the BBC, although aided and supported by the Post Office and the British press, to end the commercial threat to monopoly broadcasting coming from the continent requires exploration. With the support of the IBU, voiced through the Madrid and Lucerne agreements, it would appear that the power and will existed to curtail any such competition with relative ease. Notwithstanding, it was only the outbreak of war which eradicated the problem – albeit temporally – for the Corporation.

It is important to establish the curious nature of French radio legislation before the Second World War: as Kuhn has said, although formally there was a state monopoly "in the transmission and reception of radio-electric signals of any kind"[1059] which had been established in 1923, in practical terms licences were granted to a number

1054 Béraud, Henri "Faut-il réduire l'Angleterre en Esclavage?" originally published in three instalments in *Gringoire*, and subsequently appearing in pamphlet form, 1935, quoted in Bell, pp. 202–203.

1055 Ibid.

1056 Tint, p. 64.

1057 Ibid., p. 68.

1058 Ibid.

1059 Kuhn, p. 84.

of private stations (Les Postes Privés) on the understanding that their transmissions did not interfere with those of state broadcasters. The whole was administered by the Ministry of Post, Telegraphy and Telephony (PTT), the name also applied to state-run stations. Although technically in breach of the state monopoly, private radio was permitted provided the state retained overall control: "Yet private radio was tolerated by the authorities only as a provisional concession; it was not allowed to broadcast as of right".[1060]

France had seen many early experiments in radio. As early as 1910 there had been attempts to determine the relationship between Government and private stations, their control and operation both domestically and internationally.[1061] This had taken the form of a decree establishing members of various Ministries, Marine, War, Colonies, Foreign Affairs, Commerce and Industry, Public Works and Posts and Telegraphs, and included experiments in transmission and reception.[1062] Technical advances included a radio link between Paris and the United states in 1915, and trans-Atlantic telephone service using radio waves initiated by the Administration of Posts and Telegraphs in 1916.[1063] It would appear from such sophisticated early thinking and policy-making that France therefore would be in a position to exercise an equally sophisticated control over the developing medium. In reality the condoning of the stations' transmissions during the late 1920s and early 1930s "was dictated by a double powerlessness to contain the explosion of the [private radio] phenomenon and to respond to the demands of listeners".[1064] Private and state-run broadcasters developed side by side in "almost anarchic conditions, punctuated by attempts on the part of the postal administration to establish overall control".[1065] Radio Tour-Eiffel, the first radio station in France, began transmissions on 24 December 1921. Less than a year later, on 6 November 1922, the first private station, Radio Paris, originally named Radiola, opened, with studios on boulevard Haussmann, and funded by a syndicate of electrical firms. A few months later, on 23 November 1923, the government sought to reaffirm its control over broadcasting by the issue of a decree providing for three classes of radio stations:

1   Stations created by government departments to be used in connection with the official business of the state and educational material, community programming and content relating to public utilities.

2   Government stations transmitting more general content aimed at a broad public.

3   Private stations transmitting programming similar to (2). The station owners would be licensed by the government, to whom they would pay a fee for being allowed to operate.[1066]

1060 Ibid.

1061 *Bulletin des Lois, Journal Officiel* No. 1506, 30 April 1910, pp. 1166–1167.

1062 Emery, Walter B. *National and International Systems of Broadcasting – their History, Operation and Control*, Michigan, Michigan State University Press, 1969, p. 239.

1063 *Paris Vous Parle*, no. 7 December 1964, ORTF Paris, p. 2.

1064 Cazenave, F. *Les Radio Libres*, Paris, PUF, 1980, pp. 19–20.

1065 Kuhn, p. 84.

1066 *Bulletin des Lois, Journal Officiel* no. 23582, 14 December 1923, pp. 3466–3474.

In fact by issuing this decree, the government was only ratifying a state of affairs which had created itself a year earlier in the establishment of Radiola alongside Radio-Tour Eiffel. Indeed, a newspaper report of March 1923, nine months prior to the publication of the decree, noted three transmissions available to Paris listeners, two coming from the Eiffel Tower on separate frequencies. One contained a musical concert and weather reports, the other offered an education programme, broadcasting under the name "Station de l'Ecole Supérieure des PTT", and featured coverage of a lecture by a professor of political science. The third choice was from Radiola, with a schedule including news, stock market reports and piano music.[1067] Thus a status quo had been established *prior* to official legislation which successive pre-war French governments found impossible to reverse before the end of the German occupation.[1068] As a further attempt at regaining lost ground, on 28 December 1926, the government under President Raymond Poincaré introduced a decree which sought to consolidate the regulation of private station operation, as well setting up a provision for a national French radio network.[1069] In 1928 14 state stations opened, alongside 13 private stations. Among the latter were a number which were to carry English language transmissions: Le Poste Parisien, Radio Lyon, Radio Juan-les-Pins, Radio Toulouse and Radio Paris. In 1933 Radio Normandie was also added officially to the list, although it had begun transmissions prior to this date.[1070] Intense rivalry existed between the two systems, characterized by Brochand as "La guerre des stations".[1071] This fierce competition was exacerbated by the fact that a radio receiving licence was not introduced in France until 1933; prior to this, public service radio accepted advertising in part funding.[1072] As part of the legislation of that year, a national state-run radio service was instigated, utilising a number of the PTT stations. As part of this operation, the government bought the previously private Radio Paris (Radiola).[1073] This event was to prove crucial in the development of English language commercial broadcasting. Radio Paris had been broadcasting English language commercial programming for a year, on behalf of the English company, Wireless Publicity Ltd, chaired by a Frenchman, Jacques Gonat and with the broadcaster Stephen Williams as its Director and Chief Announcer. The closure of Radio Paris as far as Wireless Publicity was concerned, coincided with the opening of a new, powerful radio station, largely funded by French interests, in Luxembourg.

Les Sans-filistes

The real origins of the conflict between official policy and the reality of the developing private/state radio map of France may be traced to the unique role of radio amateurs, "les sans-filistes" ("radio fans") up to 1930. It is certainly true that

1067 *Le Temps*, 24 March 1923, p. 5.

1068 Kuhn, p. 84.

1069 *Bulletin des Lois, Journal Officiel* no. 29798, 31 December 1926, p. 6135.

1070 Cazenave, p. 19.

1071 Brochand, Christian *Histoire Generale de la Radio et de la Television en France. Volume 1: 1921–1944*, Paris, Le Documentation Francaise, 1994, p. 9.

1072 Cazenave, p. 20.

1073 Brochand, p. 316.

radio was seized on by amateurs with specialist technical knowledge in advance of
formalised scheduled programming in a number of countries, including Britain.
Briggs cites a petition to the Postmaster-General in December 1921 signed "by
representatives of sixty-three wireless societies with over 3,000 members".[1074] In
France however, the role of the societies or "clubs" remained pro-active in terms
of the creation of radio after formalised broadcasting began. These groups of
enthusiasts were not content to listen. Their formation and continuance was, as
Brochand has said, a result of "their ambition to have a share in the joys of radio"
and the "principles of broadcasting".[1075] The earliest Radio Club in France was the
Société Française d'études de TSF, founded in 1914. Other clubs included:

Le Radio-club de France	1920
La société SFR	1921
Le Radio-club du nord de la France	1922
Le Radio-club de Marsekille et du Midi	1922
Le Radio-club de Cannes	1923
Le Radio-Club de Clichy	1924[1076]

Formed as they were of private individuals, it was understandable that out of their
enthusiasm should come an impetus for private radio stations. The clubs were
responsible in a very direct way for the early impetus that led to the development
of radio transmissions. It was Le Radio-Club de France that had created Radiola
in late 1922, and on Christmas Eve, 1923, the station announcer of what had by
now been renamed "Radio Paris" , Marcel Laporte, broadcast a message to a group
of sixteen enthusiasts, meeting in the Normandy town of Fécamp: "At this very
moment in Fécamp, in one of the best restaurants in town, the Radio Club of
Fécamp is being set up".[1077]

The growth of the clubs continued into the mid 1930s; frequently smaller groups
of "les sans-filistes" were grouped into regional confederations. Thus in 1935 La
Fédération des radio-clubs du Massif central, founded in 1933, numbered 16 clubs,
two with memberships of 3,000.[1078] In some areas the interest was extraordinary:
out of the Radio-Club of Fécamp with its sixteen initial members in 1923, by 1928
had grown Le Fédération des radio-clubs de Normandy, actively sustaining private
radio, and supported by eight clubs with a total membership of 15,000.[1079]

Notwithstanding the active involvement of radio amateurs in the medium through
the 1920s, the subsequent growth of radio listening in France during the mid to
late 1930s was of a very different order to that of Britain. Kuhn states that "in 1938
there were over 4 million radio sets in France, compared with only 1.9 million at
the start of 1935".[1080] In Britain the number of licences issued in 1935 was

1074 Briggs, Asa *The Birth of Broadcasting 1896–1927*, Oxford, Oxford University Press, 1995, p. 46.

1075 Brochand, p. 346.

1076 Brochand, pp. 345–346.

1077 *Illustration* magazine, 17 June 1939, reproduced in *Offshore Echos Magazine*, no. 105, London, June
     1996, p. 53.

1078 *TSF Revue* 27 January 1935, cited in Brochand, p. 349.

1079 Ibid., cited in Brochand, p. 348.

1080 Kuhn, p. 84.

7,403,109, a figure which had risen in 1938 to 8,856,494.[1081] Thus we may see that in the three years after 1935, the number of radio consumers in Britain was reaching a relative plateau, while in France the period saw maximum growth. Additionally, as Cécile Meadel has written, the year 1933 was of major significance in French radio: "This was the moment when the efforts of the amateurs, so long present and active at the start, were exhausted, and the efficiency of the 'professional' took their place; from now on it was less and less the work of volunteers".[1082]

It is clear that for Radio Normandie and private French stations like it with good reception possibilities in the south of England "its potential British audience was larger than its French equivalent"[1083] and as the decade drew towards its close increasingly powerful business imperatives were developing the commercial possibilities of the medium, in France as in Britain, although in both cases operating within the context of an uneasy, and in the case of France, an inconsistent relationship with the State.

French Response to British Complaints

The French authorities received numerous demands from the BBC and its supporters to act on the issue of English language transmissions from French radio stations, or stations with French interests during the 1930s. Initially the response was swift, and apparently authoritative. As Brochand has stated: "Various ministers of PTT addressed the issue in emphatic memoranda, to no effect, while the English continued to protest".[1084] In 1933 for instance, the relevant minister, Andre Laurent-Eynac:

> demanded that Radio Normandie conformed to the authorised technical requirements limiting their transmission power, thus resulting, in practical terms, in the prevention of making their listeners a part of British territory. The station did not budge.[1085]

Subsequently similar demands were sent to Radio Côte d'Azur and Poste Parisien, stating that it was forbidden to transmit advertising material from France in a foreign language, and that the client should be acquainted with this rule.[1086] This produced no result beyond Radio Normandie's response that "it would put an end to all advertising if the ruling was general".[1087] In the event nothing was achieved and "the English grievances emanating from the BBC and the British press continued to arrive at the Ministry of Foreign Affairs".[1088] By 1938 the inability (or lack of will) of French regulators to break the deadlock with Radio Normandie was being disguised by an irritation, not with the broadcasters in France but with

1081 Pegg, Mark *Broadcasting and Society 1918–1939* Beckenham, Croom Helm, 1983, p. 7.
1082 Meadel, Cécile *Histoire de la Radio des Années Trente*. Paris, Anthropos/INA, 1994, p. 13.
1083 Kuhn, p. 85.
1084 Brochand, p. 498.
1085 Ibid.
1086 Ibid.
1087 Ibid.
1088 Ibid.

the British complainants: "Our transmissions in the English language in no way contain political propaganda and in no way justify complaints of this order …".[1089]

A major factor in the failure to address the problem was the complex political situation in France throughout the 1930s. Between 1930 and 1939 there were no less than 24 changes of government,[1090] and out of this came both a lack of political will and an inconsistency of sustained policy development, making enforceable legislation almost impossible. In addition there were matters of vested interests among politicians which called into doubt the sincerity of any apparent intentions to comply with British complaints. Four of the governments during the decade for example were led by Pierre Laval, who was in power in 1931, 1932 and 1935, and Laval "had a stake in Radio-Lyon".[1091] Likewise Max Brusset, an assistant to Georges Mandel, who in 1935 was the PTT Minister in Laval's administration was the leader of the commercial group which ran Radio Méditerranée, broadcasting from Nice. The station – using the name "Radio-Côte d'Azur, Juan-Les Pins" sold airtime to Leonard's Plugge's IBC. Writing of the period under review Brochand adds that: "The ministerial instability of the third and fourth republics corresponded to a directorial instability, if one excepts the Vichy Regime and the period immediately before it".[1092]

At times towards the end of the decade, when the relationship between the two countries improved, an agreement to ban the partnership between commercial operators came close to being achieved. In April 1937, the Socialist politician Emile Courrière attacked the commercial companies: "The existence of the private stations, behind which we find in every case the influence of a politician, a newspaper or an advertising agency cannot be justified".[1093]

Then in June the Government of the Popular Front collapsed, to be replaced by the Radical administration of Camille Chautemps, a politician "well fitted to follow a policy of hesitating compromises".[1094] By December, *The Times* was reporting that the Chautemps administration, in the form of the Minister of Posts and Telegraphs, F. Gentin, was on the point of issuing a decree banning English language sponsored programmes from French stations.[1095] However in January 1938, the Government fell, and the incoming Minister, Lebas in the new administration led by Leon Blum, did not choose to pass the decree.[1096] In April the Posts and Telegraphs Committee of the French Chamber delivered a report which supported the broadcasts, but as Briggs states "Nothing came of its report".[1097] The reason behind this failure was yet another change of government in that month,

---

1089 Internal Memo, Department of PTT, 31 January 1938. Documentation Radio France, no. 102.

1090 Brochand, pp. 677–678.

1091 Kuhn, p. 86.

1092 Brochand, p. 675.

1093 Quoted in Meadel, p. 139.

1094 Cobban, p. 164.

1095 *The Times*, 28 December 1937, quoted in Briggs, *The Golden Age of Wireless*, Oxford, Oxford University Press, 1995, p. 338.

1096 Ibid., and Brochand, p. 678.

1097 Briggs, *Golden Age*, p. 338.

and the beginning of the Deladier administration which was to last through the rest of the year and through 1939.[1098]

Just at the time when BBC Sunday policy gave English commercial interests an opportunity to develop an audience, in France the initial impetus of the radio-clubs, leading to the movement for private radio provided the principle vehicle to reach that audience. This was set against subsequent governments' inability to control the system, and the stations' need to stimulate revenue, created a platform from which to reach that audience. The active partnership between certain French private stations and English entrepreneurs, was crucial to the success of this enterprise.

1098 Brochand, pp. 678–679.

Appendix C

Samples of Listeners' Correspondence

During the research for this work, correspondences have been entered into as the result of placing requests for memories in a number of journals and newspapers, including *Radio Bygones*, *The Stage*, *Ariel* and *Prospero*. What follows are extracts from these.

A number of correspondents recalled building radios.

Philip Marsh, Esher Surrey

My most vivid memories of the early "wireless" age was in the mid-20s watching my father make early sets on the kitchen table. He was a physicist and knew what was what. Valves, condensers and wires going everywhere, with him poised above the apparatus with soldering iron at the ready. What excitement when he finally switched the radio on, and all the valves glowed with mysterious orange light; quite magical.

*

B.R. Curtis, Stalbridge, Dorset

My father used to build his own radio sets in those days, and we could always obtain excellent reception of Normandy on these comparatively simple sets using the long wire aerial stretching down the garden that most people had in those days. It wasn't until 1938 that we actually had a factory-built Cossor Super Het. Receiver ... In 1938 two of the top programmes were a weekly show by Gracie Fields recorded in the Scala Theatre in london and sponsored by Fairy Soap. George Formby also had a weekly programme sponsored by Feen-a-Mint. There was much more variety to the programmes than there is to today's Commercial Radio.

[Mr Curtis also gave an example of commercial radio successfully competing with the BBC in terms of sports news.]

On Saturdays the Football Results of all the English and Scottish leagues were broadcast from 5.00 p.m., usually sponsored by the Football Pools companies. The BBC never used to broadcast these until 6.15 p.m.

*

John Black, Tonbridge, Kent

I built several radio receivers from thrown out gear from relatives. I was an illicit listener to Radios Normandie, Luxembourg and Lyon around 1937–39. I was 16 at the end of 1938 and in view of Matriculation exams in 1939 probably didn't listen much then. After going to bed, using the bedspring as aerial and the very new 15 amp socket earth I used to listen on headphones. My strongest memory is of a serial on Radio Lyon of *Fu Manchu*, and of course *The Ovaltineys* on Luxembourg.

*

J. Land, Nottingham

I was an engineer for Quaker Oats in the mid '30s and I remember our company advertised on one of the European stations featuring *Carroll Levis and his Discoveries*, a talent show recorded once a month at the Empire Leicester Square on Sundays, but broadcast each week.

[The programme, produced by the Lord and Thomas agency, was extremely popular, and was broadcast on Radio Luxembourg, Radio Normandy and Radio Lyons. It returned on Radio Luxembourg after the war. CD Appendix, Track 13.]

*

Norman Burton, formerly of Bury, Lancashire, subsequently settled in Revesby, New South Wales, Australia.

I recall programmes from Radio Normandy in 1938 when I was rooming and used to listen to the station at night. Programmes ran for a quarter of an hour and we had OK Sauce, with Master OK, the Saucy Boy, and there was Bolemium Bill who did a spiel for protective clothing ... A programme scheduled to go on Luxembourg but denied by the outbreak of war was the Kotex programme. Now as feminine hygiene products hadn't long emerged from the dark recesses of the back of the shop in the retail business, it would have been interesting to see what effect with would have had on listeners, but in the event it never happened ... The BBC programmes on Sunday were pretty solemn things ... In Germany they had "Strength through Joy", in the UK we had "Strength through Misery"!

*

For many correspondents jingles and theme tunes remain in the memory most.

Richard Mayne, London

Your appeal in *Ariel* brought back days of Sunday boredom in the 1930s when BBC radio (National and Regional programmes) became a desert of chamber music. I'd like it now; but to a child it was deadly. So the family used to tune in to Radio Normandy. I recall two programmes with indulgent affection. One was *Twisted Tunes* in which a former cowboy actor called Eddie Pola used to find likenesses between popular tunes of the day and their melodic sources in the classics. The other favourite – for which it was essential to come in from the garden or the bonfire – featured the adventures of a Biggles-like or Dick Barton prototype who flew around with a female sidekick called Barbara. His name escapes me, but Barbara's cropped up almost every week as the hero cried "Contact, Barbara!" when about to rev up and take off at the end of each episode ... [The programme was *Vic Samson – Special Investigator*. See 'Station Profiles: Radio Luxembourg.] And of course I'm still word-perfect on the *Ovaltineys'* theme song. All of which goes to show that only jingles are memorable. But we never drank Ovaltine.

*

P.S. Elliott, Ferndown, Dorset

I remember Eddie Pola's programme. In it the presenter identified popular songs whose tunes had been borrowed from the classics. Its flavour can be judged from its introductory song which went something like this:

> "Your tune is my tune and my tune can be yours,
> 'Though Liszt may have written it
> And I'm admitting it,
> Why don't we write it once more?"

Apart from this the thing I remember best are three singing commercials. Most people will have heard "We are the Ovaltineys" but there was also one for another hot drink:

> "You will be healthy, happy and wealthy,
> If you start with Horlicks each day ..."

The third was "Vernon's Pools are here again", sung to the tune of "Happy Days are here again".

*

Desmond Hawkins, Blandford, Dorset

The Ovaltineys jingle was infectious. It still comes uninvited into my mind at times. To most of us it was quite a new thing. The radio jingle was probably the most potent weapon: even those who didn't listen to Luxembourg must have somehow picked up the *Ovaltineys'* jingle and installed it on their social map. I am sure no high Court judge would have dared to feign ignorance of it!

[See CD Appendix track 3 for this famous jingle]

*

Peter Good, Derby, Derbyshire

My father came from a family influenced by the Anglo-Catholic revival of the 1890s and Sundays during my childhood were restrained, and if the wireless was used, it was for BBC programmes only. Radio Luxembourg was at its most popular on Sundays because it offered lighter entertainment, and although the station was forbidden on Sundays in our home, the neighbour played their set very loudly, and Radio Luxembourg was heard over a number of gardens during the summer months. I used to listen with envy to the latest dance tunes coming through the hedgerow ...

... Signature tunes were a must, as a form of product identity, but the only one I can recall was "With a Little Co-operation from You" which, understandably, was used by the Co-op ...

... Reception on the Long Wave was better than that which generations lived with when 208 was The Station of the Stars on Medium Wave, and for the Midlands Luxembourg was the loudest of all the commercial stations broadcasting from the Continent. Late in 1938 my father purchased a different radio (second-hand). It was one of the models now regarded as a classic, by E.K. Cole (Ekco) and for a while we persevered in tuning to Poste Parisien and Radio Toulouse, but our aerial could not bring in a very strong signal from such places. Probably they were received better on the South coast.

*

Norman Frost, Poole, Dorset

I have one memory. It is of a programme on Normandy by Joe Murgatroyd and Poppet, which was broadcast as far as I can remember each week day at seven in the morning, and consisted of a light-hearted version of musical physical training.

[See Appendix A,"Station Profiles": Radio Normandy and CD Appendix, track 10.]

*

Don Turner, Colchester, Essex

We listened to Luxembourg from the start in 1933 on Sundays to escape what my father called "Bark Kantatas" on the BBC. It was years before I found out what he meant.

Appendix D

Broadcasters

Anumber of distinguished broadcasters worked on the Continental stations. All have now died. Some however, left accounts of their time in the 1930s, and these help us to gain a vivid picture of the era and the nature of the working conditions. Notable amongst these accounts are those of Roy Plomley, Bob Danvers-Walker and Stephen Williams. Transcripts of interviews with them, as well as with Max Staniforth and Bernard McNab, have been collected from a number of sources, and extracts are included below.

Leonard Plugge's Eccentricity – Max Staniforth

He was in the bath when I visited him, and he had five telephones along the side all in different colours – blue, green, pink and so on. I remember it was about the time that yo-yos first arrived from America, because Plugge, inevitably, had one of the first.[1099]

Radio Toulouse – Max Staniforth

The announcer sat in a room directly below the assistant whose job was to put on each record. The only way you could communicate with him was via an iron girder which hung on a rope from the ceiling. When it was time for the next record, we hit this thing with a spoon or something large and metal. We never explained what was going on to the listeners of course. I suppose they just accepted that French radio required this regular clang.[1100]

Radio Normandy, beginnings – Max Staniforth

We were supposed to give the impression that the IBC was this enormous affair with lots and lots of studios. The "Radio Orchestra" was actually one of the dance bands of the time, and our comedian, who had a made-up name, was taken from the records of a real comedian who either didn't know or didn't mind. We could have been sued, I imagine, over and over again … .

… Plugge would send the list of sponsors and I was usually left to invent the actual advertising for them. Occasionally he would ring up and dictate a particular slogan or introduction requested by the sponsor. The first one? I think it was Spinks of Piccadilly who were advertising for any old gold, jewellery, medals – things like that. We did Dunlop's, I remember, and Palethorpe's sausages were regulars.[1101]

1099 Wainwright, Martin, interview *The Guardian*, 2 May 1983, p. 11.

1100 Ibid.

1101 Ibid.

Radio Normandy and the IBC – Bob Danvers-Walker

The studio as such – it was a hayloft over a stable, sloping roof, the walls padded with an old carpet or sections of carpet to dampen the sound. We were right beneath the bell tower of the Benedictine structure, which was a most ornate building. Down below where the coach and horses used to be was now converted by the French people into an office for their little typists, secretaries and so on. And in the middle of that floor they had one of those old blackjack stoves, a cast iron thing with a chimney going up through the centre of the roof, and every once in a while they would off-load coal into this thing – there was no sound proofing as such, so whenever we opened the microphone to stop the clatter of typewriters and also their loading of coal … we would have to open the door and call down and say "Silence si vous plait!" [sic] And then we would open the microphone, make our announcements, particularly when the all-important commercial was going over, finish this, put on a gramophone record and then say "Merci" and they would hammer away at their typewriters, or heap the coals on the fire …

… The success of these things was fantastic. The South of England was our stamping ground. That was when people used to – what was called – "search the ether". This was twiddle the old knobs of their set, and pick up stations from all over the Continent. The better the set, the further they could range) so that when they heard these English programmes, particularly at times when the BBC was not on the air, they would tune in to these things like crazy. Because we were putting out the kind of things that Radio 1 now – and local Commercial Radio – now puts out, all the pop music from beginning to end of the present times, but it did expand and in no time at all, from those earliest beginnings it grew into literally an empire. Now ultimately, during the nine years that I was there until the war killed it, I was responsible for installing and establishing commercial radio programmes from 9 different stations. Well now apart from Fécamp, there was Toulouse – they sent me down to the south of France – there was Poste Parisien in Paris, there was Radio Lyons. Then the Spanish circuit opened up, with, what was it? 1933/34? Before the Spanish Civil War, because I was there two revolutions before it! In Madrid. And that was a hairy-chested moment I don't mind telling you. So there was Radio Madrid, San Sebastian, Valencia and Barcelona. Being responsible for all those was quite a thing, and by the time the war happened – "when war broke out" – the commercial radio network was an intensely important one. And we had by that time entered into the field of recorded programmes. That was when the company formed its subsidiary, The Universal Programmes Corporation, and ultimately I was brought over then to engage in the presentation of these more elaborate productions. They were first of all on gramophone records – acetates, non-breakable records – and also – oh yes, film! 35 mm film. Because we had installed in Radio Normandy Western Electric sound heads – two cinema projectors, just as you'd find in the projection room of a cinema. Enormous great things! Because the soundtrack on there was the only part of the 35mm film used – just the soundtrack. And so programmes would be recorded, and it was "Horlicks Hour", "The Ovaltineys", "The Ballito Stockings Programme" and many of the major sponsors would have their programmes put on to this film. And so these things would be sent over. Well we had then to become – because we were not only just the announcers, we were also the engineers, we were also the programme designers, we had to do the office work, we had to do everything! It was work – eat – sleep, work – eat – sleep, that was the pattern of our thing, and the loss of announcers who had come over there thinking they were only going to be announcers, they saw no joy in life at all, and they used to fall by the wayside, we used to send them back in shiploads![1102]

Roy Plomley

I was interviewed by the boss – the General Manager – Richard Meyer, who became my boss, and a very good radio man indeed. And he listened to my idea. And he said it's absolutely splendid but we haven't got the technical resources, and its much, much too expensive. But having got that

1102 Howell, Dave and Thompson, Alan *Searching the Ether*, Audio cassette in the series, "Radio Nostalgia", no. 8, STEMRA, Holland, 1982. First broadcast on the ILR Programming sharing Scheme, 1982, distributed by the AIRC.

out of the way, he then gave me some time and began talking about Commercial Radio and its problems, and I was naturally interested, and he said that one of the problems was that there were just four chaps living in this small community – this small northern French fishing port called Fécamp and in the winter things got a bit morose. There was no English colony, they were on their own and there were crises of temperament and alcohol and it was terribly hard to keep staff. "And in fact", he said "we're minus an announcer at the moment. Do you happen to know anybody?" And I said, "Well, there's me". Because I happened to be out of work at the time as young actors spend most of their time out of work, and he said "Well fine, you shall have an audition". So I was sent a day or two later to the UPC studios, which was the production unit of the IBC, recording studios in Kilburn High Road; it had been the studios used by a disc firm called "Sterno" which had gone off the market, and I found that there were three others waiting for the audition, and I thought "Well this is no good, I thought it was just going to be me, if there's competition I'm going to be out for a start". One was an actor called Peter Bennett, and there was a man who said he had been the Paris representative of *Punch* (and to this day I cannot understand why *Punch* should have needed a Paris representative) and then there was a man whose name I forget but who afterwards ran a recording studio in London. And I went into the studio in my turn, and they gave me some stuff and some ad. announcements to make, and the man taking the audition was Tom Ronald, who afterwards became one of the senior Light Entertainment producers in the BBC, and had done his stint for years on Radio Normandy. And at the end of it when I'd done my stint he came out of the control room and said "Thank you very much", and I said "Thank you very much", and I went home. And when I got home there was a telephone call: why hadn't I waited? They wanted to talk to me? So I went back the next day and they said they wanted to make a record; they'd liked what I'd done but they wanted to make a disc to play to the bosses, but the recording channel had broken down so they sent me to a recording studio in Baker Street and I got the job. And off I went to Fécamp … At Normandy, we put the transmitter on, we pulled all the switches, and whatever, to get the thing going – we were right away from the French part of the business, they were across the road, and there were only four of us to do the whole 75 hours a week, and there were only one or two of us on duty at a time and we were on our own. We did our own light engineering, our own running repairs, we played our own discs, got our own discs off the shelves and put them away again, we chattered away, we wrote – or ad-libbed – most of the stuff, and providing you stayed reasonably sober and providing you sounded as if you enjoyed it, you were all right.[1103]

Poste Parisien – Roy Plomley

I was on my own, I had an office in the Champs-Elysees, I had an expense account, and – except on Sundays, when I had to work quite hard – I just had half-an-hour's transmission a day in the evening, from half-past-ten, to eleven, either I'd play records from the studio, or I compered the cabaret from a Paris night club. It was a pleasant job. I rather wish I had it now! But obviously I was ambitious, and after about six months they suggested I went to London and became a producer. And I produced programmes for Radio Normandy, Poste Parisien and, well, occasionally some of our stuff got on to Luxembourg too, although they mostly worked independently.[1104]

IBC Outside Broadcasts – Roy Plomley

I became the OB man. We had a lot of Outside Broadcasts. This was a development that happened in about 1937, we had our first IBC Outside Broadcast truck. It was very heavy, with a lot of equipment in it to do what could now be done with a small tape recorder. And then afterwards we had a more elaborate one; these lorries were put up on jacks and wax discs were cut, outside in the alley. And we recorded in cinemas, we recorded cinema organ programmes, with instrumentalists and soloists, and we recorded specially-staged variety shows from cinemas. We had our own road-show on the air, touring, *Radio Normandy Calling*, and I used to follow that round, we

1103 Ibid.
1104 Ibid.

used to judge the amateur talent competition on a Thursday night, and then record a half-hour show on Fridays. We went all round the country with that including some dates in the Midland where they couldn't receive Radio Normandy, because Radio Normandy blanketed the "prosperous South" – that was our advertising slogan – and indeed reception was terrifically good in the South, in wasn't bad in the North, but it was disastrous in the Midlands, and at the Midlands dates we used to play they used to look at the posters and say "Radio Normandy? What's that then?"[1105]

Programme Production from Disc – Roy Plomley

You had this control table with six turntables on it, and some of it was a little bit hairy. For example, when you were doing sponsored stuff, which carried money and money of course was what the programme was about, you might for example be finishing the signature tune of a fully recorded programme. When that came to an end you had to whip off the needle, and then you would do a station identification, which was "Radio Normandy broadcasting on a wavelength of ... whatever it was", having given the station identification signal, which was hitting four notes on a little xylophone which was sitting on the control desk, then give a time signal, which was a little bit approximate – you hit a gong, giving the time off a clock on the wall, which wasn't a very accurate clock. We then whipped on the next disc which was the signature tune for the following programme; we then had to fade that out and then cross-fade to some recorded dialogue from London, and from that dialogue, which was introducing a disc we had to go to that disc. And while that disc was playing we had to put away the disc we'd been using and lay out the next two or three discs we had to use. We were only using bits and pieces, we were going in and out on chalk marks and whatever. You had to keep your wits about you.[1106]

Bernard McNab
[In charge of putting on the discs for the soap operas on Radio Luxembourg]

Stella Dallas. That was the famous one. It was two sides of a sixteen-inch thirty three and a third. And it meant about thirty five minutes one side, twenty five minutes the other side. And while we did the flip-over, we did the commercial station announcement, and then put the other side on. We thought we were quids in. One day we thought we've got this "Stella Dallas" going for a long time, we'll put the needle on, and we'll go down to the little café on the corner and have ourselves a glass of beer or coffee, and we'd timed our watches, so we thought, "We'll come back and we'll be all right" in time to turn the record over. And when we came up the stairs we heard a little repeating noise, and it said "Stop, don't shoot, Stop, don't shoot, Stop, don't shoot", and we rushed in, and there was the thing about a third through the side, and it had stuck in a groove! So we faded it out quickly, we turned the record over, put on the second, because we were going to run short of time. Nobody noticed anything going wrong.[1107]

Max Staniforth

On one occasion I did a spell at Radio Paris, where the highlight of the week was an entire programme sponsored by Decca and announced by Christopher Stone (Stone was one of the best-known BBC announcers who eventually forfeited his contract because of his work for the foreign stations). To begin with, Stone came over to Paris himself but Decca soon realised that it was easier and cheaper to make a record of him – there were no tape-recorders then – and so there was I, happily introducing Stone, and signalling a technician to put on the record. So far so good – until one awful Sunday when I did my little introduction, sat back and heard Stone begin in his beautiful tones: "Good morning Ladies and Gentlemen ... click ... gentlemen ... click ... gentlemen ... click ... gentlemen ... click ... gentlemen ... ." We were exposed. There was nothing we could do.[1108]

1105 Ibid.

1106 Ibid.

1107 Ibid.

Bob Danvers-Walker

You have to visualise the whole orchestra – Mantovani and solo artistes – coming in to a studio to make a series of programmes, and all the announcing of the items and of course the commercial in the middle of the programme, all that had to go onto this gramophone record. Everything had to be right. You couldn't stub your tongue and then start again. You'd literally have the whole thing right from the beginning, and start again. You can imagine what an announcer – particularly right at the end – when he'd have to say "This programme has come to you through the courtesy of D.D.D ...." and you made a boo boo – a mess-up – of that announcement, you'd have to go right back and start again with "In a Monastery Garden" or heaven knows what.[1109]

The Closing of Radio International – Bob Danvers-Walker

This was virtually the death-knell of Radio Normandy. At Radio International I was responsible for pumping out some pretty hefty replies to Dr Goebbels, the Nazi Minister of Propaganda, and Lord Haw Haw, who was pumping out propoganda from their end, and I had provide counter-blasts. They were very successful, which may be measured by the fact that German aircraft used to line up, to enable them to get their navigation right, (it sounds unbelievable) they used to take a sort of cross-reference between Radio Normandy, Radio Calais and the BBC on one of their wavelengths, and then they would know where they were. This is absolutely true – for planting magnetic mines in Le Havre Harbour. And so the French rapidly caught on to this, as to how this particular station was HELPING the Germans in their war-effort, and they said, "That's it, we're going to close it down". And that was the finish of it.[1110]

1108 *The Guardian*, 2 May 1983. See CD Appendix Track 2 for a recording of Stone presenting a promotion for Vox publicity. The recording also contains Carroll Gibbons, the Two Leslies and Mr Goolden, editor of the *Sunday Referee*.

1109 *Searching the Ether*.

1110 Ibid.

From *Personality and Career*

By J.C.W. Reith

In 1924, John Reith was invited to speak to the pupils of Gresham's School, in Norfolk, the public school he had himself attended from the age of 15. He chose as his subject, *Personality and Career*. The text was published the following year with a foreword by Sir Auckland Geddes. The following is an extract from this text:

> If anybody tries to teach you that religion is a sort of added accomplishment, tell him to think again. It is an integral part of life. Religion grows out of human nature, born of its need, inspired by its greatness, limited by its restrictions. It is the supreme factor. Man is best occupied in striving to perfect that which in itself is an efflux from the Divinity, his own soul; and after all, we are told that the Kingdom of Heaven is within us. His highest labour is found in the search for truth, and, although truth abstract and immutable is unattainable, he must still go on searching. Truth, like everything else in this world, is relative. I have said that our intelligence is bounded and conditioned, and so it is. We know full well that there are vast changes of vibrations which we cannot perceive as sound or colour, or in any other way. We hear that what we previously considered as the most solid or material substances are but faults and bubbles in the universal ether which pervades everything. Ether, by the way, is a fascinating study, contradictory, mathematically proved, but a mental conception only. There seems to be some extraordinary connection between it and the workings of Omnipotence, as of both we read that all things consist and are upheld, and that in both we live and move and have our being. The universe, as we understand it, is immaterial, and our thoughts, which we consider immaterial, may be the most material things about us, and may stand when everything else is dissolved.[1111]

1111 Reith, J.C.W., *Personality and Career*, London, George Newnes, 1925, p. 5.

Appendix F

The Recapture of Radio Luxembourg

Radio Luxembourg's history is remarkable in many ways, not least because during the Second World War it was taken by opposing forces on two occasions without significant damage, its preservation being due to its extremely high value as a propaganda weapon of war. The following document was issued by Supreme Headquarters, Allied Expeditionary Force, as an account of the allied recapture of the station. It is reproduced here because it forms a crucial link between the station's military and civil careers. It is also a remarkably dramatic account in its own right. I am grateful to Leonard Miall, who was among the first civilians to be attached to the operation to relaunch Radio Luxembourg as an Allied propaganda weapon, for supplying me with this unique document.

*

PWD – SHAEF

CD-USFET

10 September 1945

RADIO LUXEMBOURG
Historical Review, 10 September 1944 to 10 September 1945

CHRONOLOGICAL

Up to September 1939 Radio Luxembourg was operated by a private commercial company which built the station under a franchise contract from the Luxembourg Government under which the Government received a royalty.

On 1 September 1939 the Luxembourg Government required the transmitter to go off the air to avoid any charges by the Germans of the breaches of neutrality during the war.

On May 1940 the Germans took military occupation of Luxembourg and took possession of the station. Until September 1944 the Germans used Radio Luxembourg as a major outlet of the German network. They employed many of the Luxembourg civilian technicians who were familiar with the station. However, Ferdinand Scholtes, the former Chief Transmitter Engineer, and Matty Felten, former Chief Studio Engineer, refused to work for the Germans and after various experiences obtained work in Luxembourg City as radio repairmen.

In May 1944 the Government in Exile of the Grand Duchy of Luxembourg delivered to PWD, SHAEF in London a letter authorizing the Supreme Commander to take over and use Radio Luxembourg as long as required by the military situation.

On 1 September 1944 when the American forces were approximately at Troyes, about 100 kilometers from Luxembourg, the Germans in Luxembourg began to panic and evacuate.

On the morning of 1 September 1944 the Germans blew up the main control room in the basement of the studio building and began to pack up all valuable instruments and belongings for evacuation.

Transmissions by the Germans ceased on the same day and most of the German civilians evacuated the transmitter without damaging it, leaving only a small skeleton guard.

On 1 September Matty Felten entered the studio premises and found them completely empty. He also went out to the transmitter and found it undamaged.

However, he learned from one of the technicians living in Junglinster that it was the plan of the Germans to blow up the transmitter before the Americans arrived. He suggested to the technician that the German Chief Engineer, still on the premises, should be persuaded to dissuade the Germans from blowing up the transmitter and should limit the damage to destruction of the tubes, on the ground this would be sufficient to prevent transmission for at least six months. The German Engineer, one Peterson, was amenable because he was indignant with the Germans for having failed to evacuate his furniture for him from the cottage on the transmitter premises when they left. Some time between that date and the arrival of the Americans this plan was carried out. All the tubes and other equipment were left in place. The glass portions of the largest tubes were broken with hammers and the smaller tubes and a large stock of spare tubes were shot through with bullets. No other damage was done.

On 2 September elements of the Wehrmacht took possession of the studio and transmitter premises and remained in possession until 10 September when they fled.

On 9 September Felten went to Junglinster again and learned from one of the technicians that some time previously a stock of spare tubes had been moved to the Post Office warehouse in Morsch for safety from air bombardment.

During the progress of Twelfth Army Group across France after D-Day, Colonel Clifford R. Powell, Assistant PW Officer, Twelfth Army Group had prepared plans for the taking of the Luxembourg studio and transmitter. These were completed while the PW Detachment, Twelfth Army Group were in camp at St. Saveur in August 1944.

On 10 September 1944 units of the Fifth Armored Division, First American Army, arrived in Luxembourg City. Together with them were Jacques Arouet of OWI and Wendell Gibbs of OSS, Civilian Intelligence interrogators for PW Division, Twelfth Army Group, selected by Colonel Powell. Gibbs was acquainted with Radio Luxembourg before the war in private business. Arouet and Gibbs consulted the local burgomaster. He referred them to Felten who brought them to the studio and found it completely vacated.

No further damage had been done beyond the explosion of 1 September although apparently preparations had been made for further destruction in the control room but nowhere close. Felten, the technicians whom he called together, and military personnel, removed approximately 50 kilos of dynamite charges and 25 caps and fuses from the control room. They then proceeded to clean up the building which had been left in disorder. The Germans had removed some of the amplifiers from the studio control rooms but nothing else.

A large stock of phonograph records and an extensive music library, all in complete disorder, were found in the station.

On 11 September Morris Pierce of OWI, attached to PW Division, Twelfth Army Group, arrived in Luxembourg City. Pierce and Arouet, in a jeep, took Felten and Scholtes to the neighbourhood of the transmitter. They learned there were still some Germans in Junglinster.

They thereupon proceeded to the Headquarters, Fifth Armored Division, where the Commanding General assigned a platoon of tanks and a detail of engineers to take the transmitter, in accordance with the plan prepared by Colonel Powell.

Early in the morning of 12 September the assigned force accompanied by Pierce proceeded to the transmitter, the approaches to which had been mined. One of the tanks was blown up by a mine with some loss of life but there were no Germans at the transmitter.

Felten learned that the stock of spare tubes at Mersch had been removed two weeks previously to the Post Office warehouse at Diekirch. On 13 September Felten and Pierce proceeded to Diekirch and found the stock of tubes intact. The next day, 14 September, three trucks with machine-gun escort brought the tubes from Diekirch to Junglinster.

As soon as the transmitter was taken the radio program production unit of PW Detachment, Twelfth Army Group, headed by Capt. Hans Habe, and Robert Colwell of OWI then stationed at Verdun began the planning and writing of tactical programs to be produced at Luxembourg by Twelfth Army Group.

On 16 September Colonel Powell arrived but the method of operating the station had not yet been determined.

On 17 September electric current was turned on at the transmitter and carrier wave was put on the air without modulation.

On 18 September PWD, SHAEF sent a crew consisting of John J. H. Peyser for Program operation, Irving Berenson for Administration and Mr. Fountain for Fiscal affairs, to the station, and on 20 September PWD, SHAEF sent William H. Hale as Chief of Station and Don V. Drenner as Chief Engineer. On that date Gibbs left.

On 23 September operation of the station was begun by relays from London and New York.

On 26 September, Hans Habe and radio program production group of PW Division, Twelfth Army Group arrived at the station from Verdun. The next day the production on the air of four 15 minute programs daily by Twelfth Army Group personnel began.

These programs were primarily tactical in nature, addressed to the German troops and to civilians in the immediate combat zone. The programs were:

1   "Story of the Day", based on front line intelligence, exposing weakness in units of the German Army facing Twelfth Army Group units.

2   "Letter Bag", consisting of readings from letters captured in German mail bags, field post offices or headquarters.

3   "Frontpost", based on the small newspaper of that name distributed by air to the German troops.

4   A "Leaflet Show", based on appeals to specific German units to encourage surrender.

In most of these programs use was also made of field recordings containing brief interviews with German prisoners of war and civilians.

On 3 October the Chief of Staff, SHAEF, issued a directive placing the station under the control of PWD, SHAEF for operation. This was based on the principle that although the transmitter is physically in the area of Twelfth Army Group, its signal was heard in the areas of all three Army Groups and was heard over all the western half of Germany. Therefore, it was concluded that for uniformity of guidance for output received by listeners over the entire area, especially in strategic broadcasts, policy and output should be under direct control of SHAEF instead of under any of the Army Groups.

Programs to be later produced by SHAEF personnel were to be particularly strategic in nature addressed to the German population behind the combat zone and ultimately to German civilians in occupied areas.

Early in October 1944, local programs in the Luxembourg dialect produced by a commission appointed by the Luxembourg Government was commenced.

All programs were produced by Twelfth Army Group or by the Luxembourg Government, as well as those produced by SHAEF personnel were to be subject to approval by SHAEF under SHAEF policy guidance and directives.

It was early found that the use of local electric current by the transmitter reduced the quantity of power available to other users to such an extent that the local streetcar line was obliged to suspend operation while the station was on the air. Generation of power at the transmitter was therefore switched to the diesel engines which were intact. Fuel oil was supplied by the U.S. Army.

On 15 October 1944, PWD, SHAEF (Main) designated the personnel assigned or attached for duty by it in connection with the operation of the station as "Radio Luxembourg Detachment of PWD, SHAEF".

The studio facilities of Radio Luxembourg were extremely limited as the previous commercial operation of the station was almost entirely confined to the playing of recordings. They were prepared in London by agencies of the commercial advertisers and shipped to Luxembourg and were supplemented by musical recordings from the station library. There were only two small speaker-studios with corresponding control rooms and one medium sized music studio large enough for an orchestra of 40 pieces without provision for audience. It was early determined that additional studio facilities would be necessary for satisfactory news operation. At the end of the north wing of the main building there is a low stone hexagonal tower known as the powder magazine, the only remnant of the ancient fortification on the site. This was preserved as an historical monument dating to the 16th century. It was determined to put the interior of this space to modern use by improving it with two additional small speaker-studios and control rooms. On 15 October 1944 this work was authorized by PWD, SHAEF from plans drawn by the local architect of the studio building. Owing to difficulties in obtaining labor and materials the work proceeded slowly. One studio and control room was placed in operation 10 February 1945, the second at the end of April 1945.

On 23 October 1944, Lt. Col. Samuel R. Rosenbaum was designated Commanding Officer, Radio Luxembourg Detachment of PWD, SHAEF and Fourth MRB Company (less certain Detachments, elsewhere attached) was designated to provide the required administrative and some of the technical personnel for the station. Personnel of Radio Luxembourg Detachment were attached to Fourth MRB Company, a self-contained administrative unit, for rations and quarters only. The Detachment was authorized to employ local civilian help for necessary services, to be paid out of funds available to PWD through civilian agencies. Shortly thereafter arrangements were completed under which all payments for local civilian services are made by the Luxembourg Government under revenue land-lease.

On 24 October 1944 a group of British civilians made available by BBC arrived at the station to assist in the preparation and production of SHAEF programs. This group consisted of Patrick C. Gordon Walker, to serve as General Editor, Alan I. Huet-Owen to serve as Central News Editor, Ralph Poston to serve as Features Editor, and Etienne Amyot to serve as Supervisor of Music, all under the general direction of William H. Hale, U. S. Civilian, as Chief of Broadcasting (originally designated Chief of Station). On the same date Wendell Adams of OWI and ABSIE arrived to serve as Program Director.

On 26 October 1944, the Commanding Officer assumed command.

On 28 October 1944 PWD was authorized to set up a separate prisoner of war house at Luxembourg to house approximately eight (8) German prisoners of war to participate in Psychological Warfare to Germany. Shortly thereafter this house was set up and was operated by Radio Luxembourg Detachment for the join use of Twelfth Army Group and SHAEF, until May 1945.

On 30 October 1944, Capt. Donald V. McGranahan of Intelligence Section, PWD, SHAEF arrived to organize and control the flow and use of intelligence material received from SHAEF and Army Groups and lower echelons. This material consisted of reports from PW interrogators and G-2 interrogators in the field, captured enemy documents, and military intelligence reports. These were available to Radio Luxembourg immediately on receipt, subject to declassification and release of such portions as were passed by the Intelligence Section for output, and subject to censorship stops for security. The use of field intelligence provided programs from Radio Luxembourg with a background of local color from the fronts and from inside the enemy lines which gave these programs the special character they possessed of front-line broadcasting as contrasted with news programs emanating from transmitters in London and New York.

On 5 November 1944, Robin Gordon Walker, British civilian on loan from PID, arrived to serve as General Editor of programs addressed to foreign workers in Germany. He was joined on 10 November 1944 by Lt. Jan Van Overloop, representative of the Belgian government, to produce programs in French and Flemish to workers in Germany.

On 7 November 1944 the Fourth MRB Company arrived in Luxembourg and took over the majority of the administrative duties. A number of enlisted men from the Fourth MRB Company were selected for training and service in the preparation and processing of news and intelligence for radio output in English, German and other languages.

On 10 November 1944 the first daily SHAEF program period of news and intelligence, a program of 15 minutes at 2130 hours was begun on the air. It was given a distinctive musical theme selected by Etienne Amyot, Supervisor of Music, chosen from the Nimrod Movement of Elgar's Enigma Variations. This theme was used on all the SHAEF news periods and became well known to millions of listeners in Germany as an identification.

Additional daily SHAEF program periods of news and intelligence were gradually added. On 1 December 1944 a second period was instituted at 1930 hours daily. On 11 December 1944 a third period was added at 1230 hours daily. On 3 February 1945 a fifth period was added at 2230 hours daily. Some of these programs were regularly devoted to special audiences such as young people in Germany, women in Germany, etc. On 18 March 1945, two half-hour programs were created consisting of recorded music interspersed with news from inside Germany based on intelligence material.

On 17 December 1944 word was received of the approach of German troops at the beginning of the Rundstedt counter-offensive. Close contact was maintained with operating forces of Twelfth Army Group, under whose direction broadcasting from the transmitter was suspended at 2100 hours on 19 December 1944 when the enemy was in force within a few kilometers of the transmitter. Certain essential parts were removed from the transmitter instrument and transported to Verdun for safety. At the same time under instructions of local military authorities all preparations were in readiness for evacuation of the studio building in Luxembourg City. However, owing to hardening of the military situation, the transmitter was reassembled and transmissions were resumed at 2300 hours on 23 December 1944. The special Christmas programs designed for 24 and 25 December were produced in full.

On 27 December 1944 the 7.5kw short-wave transmitter at Junglinster was placed in service after several months of preparations and repairs. It had been damaged by the Germans on evacuation. It was hoped to use this transmitter for relay of live programs to London for BBC and ABSIE. However, owing to inability to obtain satisfactory frequency allocations such relays have not proved possible. The short-wave transmitter was used for regular communication with New York, beginning in June 1945, to send programs to the stations at Munich, Stuttgart and Frankfurt, in the American zone of occupation, for relay.

During January 1945 Luxembourg City was under intermittent German fire from small rocket bombs. On several nights when this was intense a number of hits were registered in the neighborhood of the studio building but the studio building was not hit. All preparations were made to continue broadcasting in the event of damage to the building. The studio building was occasionally strafed from the air.

Until 15 November 1944 the long-wave transmitter was on the air for a total of 11½ hours per day, including seven (7) relays from New York, twenty-three (23) relays from BBC and four (4) relays from ABSIE.

On 15 November 1944 operating hours were changed to a total of 12 hours per day, with twelve (12) relays from New York and seventeen (17) relays from BBC.

Over this period the long-wave transmitter was off the air from 1345 hours to 1758 hours. During and after the Rundstedt counter offensive, it was observed that the enemy was operating a long-wave transmitter during these hours on approximately the same frequency as Radio Luxembourg, giving news and instructions to the populations in Luxembourg, Belgium. Holland and the Rhineland at variance with Allied instructions. Owing to the risk of overworking the large tubes at the transmitter it was not possible to increase operating hours until adequate provision for replacing the tubes could be effected. This took place on 18 February 1945 when hours of operations were increased to 15½ hours per day, including the afternoon hours, carrying thirteen (13) relays from New York and nine (9) from BBC.

On 18 March 1945 with hours of operation unchanged, the relay schedule was reduced to ten (10) relays from New York and eight (8) relays from BBC.

Each reduction in the number of relays carried from New York and London was balanced by increases in local programs originating at Radio Luxembourg.

Valuable service was rendered in return by Radio Luxembourg to OWI, New York and to BBC. As of April 1945, Radio Luxembourg was supplying by short-wave to OWI, New York a total of from 5,000 to 10,000 words per day of news, special events and intelligence. These consisted of 4-minute live inserts in the New York German Wehrmacht, Polish news, French news, and English news programs, in addition there were special feeds of intelligence material to New York for 45-minutes daily, including military commentary. During the month of March 1945, Luxembourg fed New York 277 special events spots.

For BBC an average of 30 minutes of material was prepared daily at Radio Luxembourg and recorded; the recordings were sent via courier to Paris where they are relayed by landline to BBC. This material was primarily for use by the German Station of the European Service of the BBC.

Several hours per day of operation of the short-wave transmitter were placed at the disposal of the Public Relations Division, Twelfth Army Group for transmitting news and talks to the American radio networks and press.

On 18 March 1945 the four (4) Twelfth Army Group 15-minute programs during the day were consolidated into one 60-minute program from 2000 to 2100 hours and shortly thereafter the SHAEF news room at Radio Luxembourg was reorganized to establish an early morning shift for producing news and intelligence for broadcasts beginning at 0630 hours daily.

After the advance of the American Forces into Germany beginning in February 1945 frequent field reporting and recording expeditions were sent out from Radio Luxembourg into German occupied territory; material so obtained was effectively used in improving the local color and timeliness of program output.

On 27 March 1945 the first special program of news and comment produced by 21st Army Group was prepared and presented by a group of British officers sent from 21st Army Group Headquarters under the direction of Lt. Col. Keith N. H. Thomson, British Army. These programs were presented three times a week emphasizing news from the 21st Army Group fronts, until the British unit left in May to operate Radio Hamburg.

At the end of April the 12th Army Group Radio Detachment left the station and moved into Germany, but for several weeks continued to furnish and produce its daily hourly program by recording it on tape which was sent to Luxembourg.

In May, after V-E day, the remaining British contingent was gradually withdrawn and returned to England, their places being filled with American personnel.

During June and July 1945 the stations at Munich, Stuttgart, and Frankfurt in the American zone of occupation commenced operations under American military control. Luxembourg furnished them with ten hours of program material daily sent by short-wave for relay.

Upon the dissolution of SHAEF, 18 July 1945, Radio Luxembourg Detachment was reconstituted as Radio Operating Detachment (Luxembourg) of Information Control Division of United States Forces European Theatre.

Upon the dissolution of ABSIE in London, 4 July 1945, a number of OWI employees from its German section were sent to Luxembourg as replacements and to assist in production of the German and musical output.

In August 1945 the United States Press Services Headquarters and personnel were moved from Inveresk House, London to Radio Luxembourg. Their monitoring service was thereupon consolidated with that of Radio Luxembourg to received the news files from OWI, New York, and other sources.

Beginning in August 1945 the turnover of personnel became rapid owing to redeployment and discharge of both military and civilian personnel from the services.

Plans were prepared in September 1945 to discontinue the originating of programs at Radio Luxembourg for the stations in the American Zone of occupation in Germany and to move origination of such programs into studios to be prepared in the Frankfurt district close to USFET headquarters.

Changes in BBC Sunday Programming

Comparative Listings from *Radio Times*

The comparisons are taken from *Radio Times* for the first Sunday in March in the years 1939, 1942 and 1946 respectively.

Sunday, 5 March 1939
National Programme

9.25:	*A Religious Service* from Lichfield Cathedral
10.15:	Interval
10.30:	*Weather Forecast for Farmers and Shipping*
10.45:	*Falkman and his Apache Band* [Light Orchestral music]
11.30:	*This Symphony Business* [Feature examining the working of a Symphony Orchestra]
12.00:	*Mario de Pietro* [Mandolin and Banjo Recital]
12.15:	*The London Palladium Orchestra* [Light Orchestral Music]
1.00:	*The Bernard Crook Quintet* [Chamber Music]
1.30:	*These You Have Loved* [Records, presented by Doris Arnold]
2.00:	*In Your Garden*, presented by C.H. Middleton and W.P. Matthew
2.20:	*Orchestral Hour* – The BBC Welsh Orchestra
3.20:	*The Willis Walker Octet* [Light Chamber music]
4.00:	*The Fourth Gospel* [Religious talk]
4.20:	*The BBC Military Band*
5.00:	*The Search for God* [Religious talk]
5.20:	*Recital, Violin and Piano* [Chamber Music]
6.10:	*Bookshelf* [Literary review]
6.30:	*The Last Crusade* [Dramatised feature about the Spanish Armada, produced by Stephen Potter]
7.30:	*Reginald Foort at the BBC Theatre Organ*
7.50:	Interval
7.55:	*A Religious Service* from St. Edmund's College Chapel, Ware.
8.45:	*The Week's Good Cause*
8.50:	*The News*
9.05:	*Les Miserables* [Episode 9 of serial production]
9.35:	*The BBC Theatre Orchestra* [Light orchestral]
10.30:	*Epilogue* [Religious readings]
11.00	*Shipping Forecast*, Close Down.[1112]

1112 *Radio Times*, 3 March, 1939, Vol. 62, No. 805, pp. 17–18.

Sunday, 7 March 1943

Home Service		Forces Programme	
6.00:	*Revielle – Cheerful Gramophone Records*		
7.00:	*News*	7.00:	*News, Programme Parade*
7.15:	*Midland Light Orchestra*	7.15:	As Home Service
8.00:	*Listen to the Band*	8.00:	*Rhythm on Records*
8.30:	*O.H. Peasgood* [Lt. Classical Organ]	8.30:	*Cairo Calling* [Messages from the Forces]
9.00:	*News and Programme Parade*	9.00:	As Home Service
9.30	*Morning Service*	9.30:	*Sunday Serenade – the Scottish Variety Orchestra*
10.15	*The Czech Army Choir*	10.15:	*For Isolated Units* [Religious Service]
10.30	*Music While You Work*	10.30:	*For the Indian Forces.* [Messages for Indian forces serving away from home]
11.00:	*Music Lovers' Diary*	11.00:	*BBC Military Band*
11.20:	*Religious Service in Welsh*	11.30:	*Workers' Playtime*
11.50:	*The London Gypsy Orchestra*	12.00:	*Billy Ternent and the Sweet Rhythm Orchestra*
12.15:	*NBC Symphony Orch/Toscanini*	12.35:	*The Bob Hope Programme*
12.50:	*Mainly for Women*		
1.00:	*News*	1.00:	As Home Service
1.15:	*Country Magazine*	1.15:	*Sunday Startime: Records*
1.45:	*Under Discussion: the Music of Cesar Franck*	1.45:	*John Blore and his Orchestra* [Light Orchestral]
2.15:	*In Your Garden*	2.20:	*Johnny Canuck's Review* [Variety show presented by the Canadian Army and the Royal Canadian Air Force]
3.30:	*The Talk of the Town* [Radio Adaptation of film, starring Cary Grant, Jean Arthur and Roland Coleman]	2.50:	*What I Believe* [Religious Talk]
4.45:	*Christian New Bulletin*	4.15:	*The Brains Trust*
5.05:	Welsh Language Programmes	5.00:	*Transatlantic Call – People to People*, US Broadcaster Bob Trout visits South London [Simultaneous Transmission with CBS, America]
5.20:	*Children's Hour* [Religious Songs & Stories]	5.30:	*Canadian Hockey*, relayed in association with CBC
6.00:	*News*	6.00:	As Home Service
6.30:	*News in Norwegian*	6.30:	*Good Hunting: Stephane Grappelly and his Orchestra*
6.45:	*A Cautionary Tale* [Talk]		
6.55:	*Field Fare*, Brian Vesey-Fitzgerald		
7.00:	*Liebestraum – BBC Theatre Orchestra and Soloists* [Light Orchestral]	7.00:	*American Sports Bulletin*
7.10:	*The Happidrome*		
8.00:	*Choral Evensong*	8.00:	*Intermission – the BBC Variety Orchestra with Joyce Grenfell*
8.30:	*Sunday Half Hour* [Community Hymn Singing]		
8.40:	*The Week's Good Cause*		
8.45:	*The Four Freedoms* – Talk by Louis MacNeice		
9.00:	*News*	9.00:	As Home Service
9.30:	*The Man Born to be King* by Dorothy L. Sayers	9.30:	*BBC Scottish Orchestra* Sayers, produced by Val Gielgud, part 2, *The King's Herald*
10.15:	*Piano Recital, Arthur Dulay & Sidney Davey*	10.00:	*Epilogue*
10.08:	*Weekly News Letter* [Review of the week's news]		
10.30:	*Epilogue*	10.20:	*The Week's Films*
10.38:	*Theme & Variations, Gramophone Records*	10.30:	*Music While You Work*
11.00:	Close Down		
11.10:	*V for Verse*, Sir Owen Seaman Reads from his Works		
11.15:	*Norfolk Hotel Orchestra* [Light Orchestral]		
11.45:	*The Gregori Tcherniak Balalaika Trio*		
12.00:	*News*		
12.20:	Close Down [1113]		

1113 *Radio Times*, 5 March 1943, Vol. 78, No. 1014, pp. 6–7.

Sunday, 3 March 1946
The Light Programme

9.00: *News*
9.10: *Morning Melodies; Al Bollington at the BBC Theatre Organ*
9.45: *Sid Phillips and his Band*
10.15: *Family Favourites* [Record requests from Forces overseas]
11.15: *As the Commentator Saw It: an edited version of one of yesterdays 6th Round F.A. Cup Ties*
11.30: *Rocky Mountain Rhythm: Big Bill Campbell and his Company*
12.00: *The People's Service*
12.30: *Merry-Go-Round* [Records]
1.30: *Three's Company: George Melachrino, his Orchestra and Soloists*
1.45: *Transatlantic Quiz. America v. Britain. A contest to find out who knows more about the other's country.*
2.15: *Music Parade: The Combined Stoll Theatres Orchestra*
3.00: *Serenade in Sepia: Sweet Music in the Negro Style*
3.30: *British Film Festival: Excerpts from notable British films produced during the six years of war*
5.00: *Musical Theatre of the Air: Jack Buchanan and Elsie Randolf in "Lady in Love"*
6.00: *Variety Bandbox: An entertainment for Forces overseas*
7.00: *News and Interlude*
7.15: *Anne Ziegler and Webster Booth: Music for Romance*
7.45: *Grand Hotel* [Light Orchestral Music]
8.30: *Tommy Handley in "ITMA"*
9.00: *Sunday Half Hour* [Community Hymn Singing]
9.30: *Cyril Fletcher in "Thanking Yew Tew"* [Comedy/variety]
10.00: *News*
10.10: *Talking With You: a talk by D.R. Davies*
10.15: *The Twilight Hour: Sandy Macpherson at the BBC Theatre Organ*
10.45: *In a Sentimental Mood: Reg Leopold and his Orchestra*
11.15: *Quiet Melody: Records*
11.50: *News*
12.00: *Big Ben*, Close Down[1114]

1114 *Radio Times*, 1 March 1946, Vol. 90, No. 1170, pp. 6–7.

Appendix H

Archival audio examples

Accompanying CD

Track 1:	*There's Something of Importance in the Air* (Radio For Sale)
Track 2:	Christopher Stone presenting a promotional programme for Vox Publicity Products, Circa Spring 1934 (Radio For Sale/Appendix B)
Track 3:	*The League of Ovaltineys* (Radio for Sale)
Track 4:	Blattnerphone recording, *Sweeney Todd* (Recording for Radio)
Track 5:	Disc Recording, *Radio Normandy Calling* (Recording for Radio)
Track 6:	Tape, Mozart *Symphony No. 39* (Recording for Radio)
Track 7:	Philips Miller, Mozart *Alleluja* (Recording for Radio)
Track 8:	Poste Parisien Gong, and commercial (Appendix A/Appendix G)
Track 9:	Radio Normandy Wavelength change (Appendix A)
Track 10:	Joe Murgatroyd and Poppet (Appendix A)
Track 11:	*IBC Goodnight Melody* (Appendix A)
Track 12:	Radio Luxembourg Theme, *Tune In* (Appendix A)
Track 13:	*Carrol Levis and His Discoveries* (Appendix A)
Track 14:	Radio Luxembourg close-down theme: *It's Time to Say Goodnight*

Please note: Many of these recordings are extremely rare, and are inevitably of poor technical quality due to their age. Every attempt has been made to enhance the audio wherever possible.

Index

Crossing the Ether